POLITICAL THOUGHT AND THE ORIGINS OF THE AMERICAN PRESIDENCY

The Alan B. and Charna Larkin Series on the American Presidency

UNIVERSITY PRESS OF FLORIDA

Florida A&M University, Tallahassee
Florida Atlantic University, Boca Raton
Florida Gulf Coast University, Ft. Myers
Florida International University, Miami
Florida State University, Tallahassee
New College of Florida, Sarasota
University of Central Florida, Orlando
University of Florida, Gainesville
University of North Florida, Jacksonville
University of South Florida, Tampa
University of West Florida, Pensacola

POLITICAL
THOUGHT
AND THE
ORIGINS
OF THE
AMERICAN
PRESIDENCY

EDITED BY
BEN LOWE

Foreword by David Armitage

University Press of Florida
Gainesville · Tallahassee · Tampa · Boca Raton
Pensacola · Orlando · Miami · Jacksonville · Ft. Myers · Sarasota

First cloth printing, 2021
First paperback printing, 2024

29 28 27 26 25 24   6 5 4 3 2 1

Library of Congress Cataloging-in-Publication Data
Names: Lowe, Ben, 1956– editor. | Armitage, David, 1965– author of
    foreword.
Title: Political thought and the origins of the American presidency /
    edited by Ben Lowe ; foreword by David Armitage.
Description: Gainesville : University Press of Florida, 2021. | Series: The
    Alan B. and Charna Larkin series on the American presidency | Includes
    bibliographical references and index.
Identifiers: LCCN 2020045519 (print) | LCCN 2020045520 (ebook) | ISBN
    9780813066813 (hardback) | ISBN 9780813057750 (pdf) | ISBN 9780813079271 (pbk.)
Subjects: LCSH: Presidents—United States—History. | Executive
    power—United States—History. | Electoral college—United
    States—History. | Constitutional history—United States. | United
    States—Politics and government. | Political science—United States.
Classification: LCC KF4910 .P65 2021 (print) | LCC KF4910 (ebook) | DDC
    342.73/062—dc23
LC record available at https://lccn.loc.gov/2020045519
LC ebook record available at https://lccn.loc.gov/2020045520

The University Press of Florida is the scholarly publishing agency for the State University System
of Florida, comprising Florida A&M University, Florida Atlantic University, Florida Gulf Coast
University, Florida International University, Florida State University, New College of Florida,
University of Central Florida, University of Florida, University of North Florida, University of
South Florida, and University of West Florida.

University Press of Florida
2046 NE Waldo Road
Suite 2100
Gainesville, FL 32609
http://upress.ufl.edu

In Memory of Alan B. Larkin (1922–2002)

CONTENTS

FIGURES

FOREWORD

Historians of the U.S. presidency have lately taken a monarchical turn. In their quest to understand the origins of the office and the genesis of its powers, students of the presidency now increasingly look to the contemporary species of unitary executive with which the framers were most familiar: the kings and princes of early modern and Enlightenment Europe. "We were educated in royalism," Thomas Jefferson reminded James Madison in 1789; "no wonder if some of us retain that idolatry still." And no wonder, then, that present-day historians have returned to royalism in search of one genealogy for the modern presidency.

For most of the twenty-first century, U.S. presidents, both Republican and Democratic, have sought to assert their authority and extend their prerogatives, often in contention with Congress and sometimes with the acquiescence of the judiciary. At the same time, and not coincidentally, scholars of the founding era such as Saikrishna Prakash, Eric Nelson, and Brendan McConville have reconstructed a history of the presidency that was "imperial from the beginning" because it was the product of a "Royalist revolution" that took place in "royal America." The outstanding essays in *Political Thought and the Origins of the American Presidency* expand on their important work by excavating the tangled roots of America's elective monarchy in the theory and practice of the founding era set in amply Atlantic context.

Among all the innovations of the U.S. Constitution, the presidency was paradoxically the most novel and the most traditional. Novel because there was no immediate precedent for a secularized, nonhereditary ruler endowed with such a wide panoply of powers, including command of the armed forces; the right to make war, peace, and treaties; and the ability to veto legislation. And yet traditional because those powers were vested in a single person and derived mostly from the suite of capacities Sir William Blackstone enumerated in his description of the British monarchy in the *Commentaries on the Laws of England* (1765–69). In fact, after all the wrangling that accompanied the framing and ratification of the Constitution, the U.S. presidency was innovative by virtue of being almost hyper-traditional. When George Washington became the first president of the United States in 1789, he possessed powers that George III could only envy or barely recall as appurtenances of his office—for example, the veto power or acting as commander-in-chief. Moreover, within two years of his inauguration, during the initial constitutional royalist phase of the French Revolution, the French Constitution of 1791 would deprive Louis XVI of competencies that Washington still retained, such as the right to make treaties.

If the U.S. presidency was originally a kind of monarchy, it was an enlightened executive built on conventional (even for its time somewhat conservative) foundations. The revival of monarchy in some form was of course what opponents of a strong unitary executive feared and what some enemies of the infant United States expected. Writing from New York in December 1782, the British commander-in-chief in North America, Guy Carleton, observed with palpable schadenfreude that postrevolutionary schisms there seemed so acute "that a Monarchy must of necessity take place; under this persuasion [*sic*] three ideas are formed, a Prince of the blood of England, one of France, and General Washington, to whom, 'tis added, the Monarchy has been offered, and by him refused." (The echo of the refusal in 1657 of the crown by Oliver Cromwell, another revolutionary general turned executive "single person," was surely not accidental.) In the debates on the Constitution, Edmund Randolph of Virginia warned against the presidency becoming "the foetus of monarchy," while his fellow Virginians Patrick Henry and Thomas Jefferson were worried that "it squints toward monarchy" or would be merely "a bad edition of a Polish king." Friends and critics alike of the new executive viewed their prospective ruler through monarchical spectacles.

Nonetheless, as the chapters in the first part of this volume persuasively argue, the existing monarchies best known to the founders were as dynamic as they were diverse. The institution was adaptable and adaptive across Europe in the face of increasingly confident representative assemblies, the pressures of fiscal-military states, and a rising generation of educated princes with enlightened aspirations in Madrid, Windsor, Potsdam, and St. Petersburg. Many Atlantic anglophones, their histories flecked with paeans to princes from Elizabeth I to Frederick the Great, viewed monarchs as models. They were also well acquainted with the constraints that curtailed monarchical overreach, such as bills of rights and potent party systems, as components of a kinetic system of checks and balances that had been engineered since the mid-seventeenth century. At the moment of the U.S. founding, monarchy, like the institution of slavery, was modern because it was modernizing. The president was a finite prince among mostly hereditary monarchs, time-limited when they ruled for life. Yet as an elected executive he still had something in common with the Polish king of whatever edition or even with the pope, the best-known (but not the only) elective monarch even in our own time.

Like contemporary monarchies, the U.S. presidency was not set in aspic; it began evolving from the moment of its creation. The second part of this volume displays some of the branches of this evolutionary tree as they were revealed in the constitutional debates around the executive and the union. Each of these chapters asks why some early ideas flourished while others perished—for example, the competing forms of nationalist constitutionalism that Hamilton, Gouverneur Morris, and James Wilson argued over—and why other problems that had long-term implications, most notably the admission of new states to the union, were sidestepped with sometimes minimal reflection. As these chapters suggest, colliding visions and unfinished business from the framing continue to inform present-day theories of the presidency and its functions and limitations.

Practice necessarily shaped the institution's evolution from the beginning. The third and final group of essays shows how the personalities and intellectual commitments of the first three presidents inflected the office. Washington, Adams, and Jefferson animated constitutional abstractions with their own experiences and preferences, from the former general's military brusqueness to the aggressive informality of his Virginia successor. They also learned on the job, as every president still must, but they came equipped for the task with mirrors for princes, conduct books for gentlemen, and compendia of the law of nations. Their adaptations bequeathed a repertoire of presidential roles that would define but not confine the options for their successors in generations to come.

The infant United States was a novel republic in a world of monarchies and a new state—or congeries of new *states*—in an age of empires. Political emulation ensured that the state would acquire imperial traits. The presidency would likewise bear the imprint of monarchy but with one crucial difference: gender. According to Samuel Johnson's *Dictionary* (1755), a president was "one placed with authority over others; one at the head of others," while his third meaning for "monarch" was simply "President." By coincidence, Johnson illustrated each usage with a quotation from Shake-speare's *Antony and Cleopatra*. "Come, thou *monarch* of the vine, / Plumpy Bacchus, with pink eyne" was his evidence for "monarch" meaning presi-dent; even more suggestive were Cleopatra's words, which Johnson quoted under the heading "President":

> A charge we bear i' the war,
> And, as the *president* of my kingdom, will I
> Appear there for a man. (*Antony and Cleopatra*, III.7)

By Johnson's lights, as for Shakespeare, not only was a monarch a presi-dent but a president was a monarch—and, in Cleopatra's case, a female one. Yet here was one idea that did not occur to the framers or their op-ponents, despite their knowledge of Queens Elizabeth and Anne in British history or Empresses Maria Theresa and Catherine the Great among the moderns. One anti-Federalist could complain that according to the draft Constitution, once qualifications of birth and age were met, "a Pagan, a Mahometan, a Bankrupt may occupy the highest seat," but no one imag-ined a woman as president. Even to those who originated the American presidency, some political thoughts remained unthinkable.

DAVID ARMITAGE
Lloyd C. Blankfein Professor of History
Harvard University

ACKNOWLEDGMENTS

The essays published here are revised versions of solicited papers originally presented in February 2019 at the Alan B. and Charna Larkin Symposium on the American Presidency. Hosted by the history department at Florida Atlantic University, the symposium and the series that shares its name are testaments to the vision and generosity of the Larkin family. Their gift to the university has been a gift to history itself and is a fitting tribute to the late Alan Larkin's personal fascination with America's past.

It was one of the great pleasures of my academic career to host at the 2019 symposium the collection of renowned scholars who appear in this volume. While my research and interests rest largely in sixteenth- and seventeenth-century European intellectual history, I have always been fascinated by how the political ideas of my era developed and emerged in particular ways at the time of the founding of the United States. Of course, much has been written on this period of the nation's history, but in my reading I found little scholarship that directly addressed the intellectual origins of the American presidency. I would therefore like to thank Steve Engle, the symposium director, for allowing me the opportunity to explore the topic in one of our triennial conferences.

Once the theme was settled on, I knew who I wanted to invite, while I also took a few suggestions from expert colleagues on how I might fill a gap or two in the program. To my surprise, almost everyone I asked to participate readily and enthusiastically agreed to do so, beginning with the very generous Caroline Winterer, who provided the first day's keynote address. I would like to thank her and Blair Worden, Max Skjönsberg, Eric Slauter, Jonathan Gienapp, Claire Rydell Arcenas, François Furstenberg, Lindsay Chervinsky, Daniel Hulsebosch, and Rosemarie Zagarri for taking time from their busy schedules and existing research projects, to join in this endeavor and come together to deliver an exhilarating conference.

While we all had the luxury of reveling in exciting ideas for two days, there was much that went on behind the scenes to make the event successful. In addition to Steve Engle, I would like to thank the department program assistant, Zella Linn, and our graduate students, Camila Giraldo, J. D. Reiner, Colton Babbitt, Michael Sackett, Rhiannon Callahan, Diana Ortiz, and Robert Mooney, for making it all run so smoothly. I also owe a debt of gratitude to my early Americanist colleagues, Adrian Finucane and Jason Sharples, for chairing panels and for their good advice throughout. Others who played a key part in the symposium's success include Polly Burks, Nicole Jacobsen, Carol Hixson, and the Conservatory of Music at Lynn University.

An accompanying exhibit of early imprints connected to the conference theme, taken from Florida Atlantic University's unique Marvin and Sybil Weiner Spirit of America Collection, was wonderfully curated by the university's S. E. Wimberly Library Special Collections staff. My deep appreciation goes out to Vicky Thur, Teresa Van Dyke, Stephen Krzeminski, and the Weiner family for the many hours they spent creating this brilliantly realized project.

The papers presented and the discussions that followed produced a natural coherence around the symposium theme that was honed by the participants as they wrote their essays for this volume. I would like to thank David Armitage, whose encouragement and avid interest in writing the foreword gave the project additional momentum. The resulting contributions here and elsewhere will certainly leave a lasting imprint on early U.S. intellectual history and provide prolegomena for future research.

The University Press of Florida has been a pleasure to work with and the staff there have been nothing but enthusiastic about publishing this volume. I am particularly grateful for the sustaining encouragement and sage shepherding of the manuscript to successful completion by Sian Hunter and Mary Puckett and to the marketing team of Rachel Doll and Victoria Reynolds, among others. Additional thanks go out to copy editor Kate Babbitt and project editor Valerie Melina for their attention to important details that resulted in a much more polished final product.

Finally, it is to Charna Larkin and her family that I extend my deepest heartfelt appreciation, since without their generous support this book would not have happened. Through their unwavering commitment to ongoing research and education about an important part of the American past, they have honored their beloved Alan's memory in a way that certainly does him proud.

1

Political Thought and the Intellectual Origins of the American Presidency

Royalism, Executive Power, and the History of Ideas

BEN LOWE

The smash hit musical *Hamilton* attempts to pack a lot of history into a show that runs just under three hours, mainly through fast-paced rap lyrics inspired by Ron Charnow's best-selling biography of the title character. Two songs sung by the actor playing George III bring levity to an otherwise intense and rollicking portrayal of the protagonist's life. At one point in the tongue-in-cheek "You'll Be Back," which playfully asserts a long-standing fondness between George and his American subjects, the king declares: "You'll remember that I served you well. Oceans rise, empires fall. We have seen each other through it all. . . . You say our love is draining and you can't go on. You'll be the one complaining when I am gone." While this is meant to be humorous, even ironic, it in fact may not be far from historical truth. Modern scholarship on the American Revolution has consistently played up the close relationship the patriots had with their monarch, and with British royalty in general, which left a profound imprint on the framers' conception of executive power in their new federal constitution.

To varying degrees, the essays in this volume reiterate that point, building on recent studies that have examined the charged, fluctuating nature of patriot ideology that emerged throughout the course of the War of Independence and for years afterward when a new national government was being constructed. All the authors here clearly recognize the pathbreaking work of their predecessors, who also wrestled with just how monarchical early Americans thought a republican executive should be. In fact, to enter the realm of eighteenth-century American intellectual history is in some ways to annotate and extend the work of its pioneers, Bernard Bailyn, Gordon Wood, and John Pocock.

Bailyn's *The Ideological Origins of the American Revolution* (1967) challenged Progressive historians who claimed the Revolution was largely about economics by taking seriously the impact of English oppositional thought that within a uniquely American context formed a "logic of rebellion." Bailyn found especially important the commonwealth literature encapsulated in *Cato's Letters* (1720–23), written by John Trenchard and Thomas Gordon, which represented a country party of landowners who were sympathetic to republicanism and concerned about early Georgian political corruption. For Bailyn, "more than any other single group of writers they shaped the mind of the American Revolutionary generation."[1]

More so than Bailyn, who found ideas to be more of a cultural product,[2] Wood coupled social conflict with ideology. Several essays contained in this volume echo his contention that after 1776, the nation shifted toward radical democracy and egalitarianism and away from classical republicanism, leading federalists to construct a newer, constitutional republicanism fixed on a balance of powers that included an "energetic president."[3] The obsession of patriot leaders with governmental tendencies toward corruption that Bailyn and Wood identified gets extended treatment in Pocock's groundbreaking *Machiavellian Moment: Florentine Political Thought and the Atlantic Republican Tradition* (1975), which grew out of a groundbreaking 1968 article.[4] Pocock's investigation into the various ways adherents of classical republicanism struggled with how to preserve liberty and civic virtue during periods of crisis in Renaissance Florence, Civil War England, and the American revolutionary age permeates much subsequent scholarship, most notably on the political debates waged during the period between independence and the writing of the Constitution.[5]

All of these works may only tangentially deal with how both the office of the presidency and executive power came to be defined during a time of political turmoil and national anxiety after independence had been won, but they set the scene with their concern for the questions patriot leaders asked themselves in their quest to configure the new republic. Was it to be essentially a democratic state that the people ruled through their elected representatives or did there need to be a check residing in some form of separated executive power to protect against potential legislative despotism? Bailyn and Wood both held that attitudes toward this problem shifted over time and that the swings were often swift, fervent, and tinged with paranoia and fears of "freedom" being eroded.

Many current historians and political scientists have decided that the existence of any such panic has probably been exaggerated due to a scholarly bias toward seeing the American experiment as founded on noble, uncompromising republican principles. For example, Eric Nelson has most recently argued that the colonists actually had an affinity for the king and that in the 1760s a strong royalist sentiment existed in America that did not end until the drafting of state constitutions in 1776. Patriot leaders such as James Wilson, Benjamin Rush, Alexander Hamilton, and Thomas Jefferson held that after abolishing the monarchy and passing the Navigation Acts of 1651, England's Rump Parliament began to assert greater—eventually tyrannical—control over the American colonies. The early Stuarts, by contrast, had granted colonial charters through an exercise of their royal prerogative, which limited Parliament's role in colonial policy. In addition, after the Stamp Act crisis, Benjamin Franklin and others insisted that the colonies were autonomous dominions subject only to the authority of the Crown, not to Parliament. It was only after the Continental Congress in 1775 called on George III to reclaim his prerogative powers and he refused, insisting that king and parliament formed a sovereign, unitary authority, that the colonists rescinded their loyalty and moved decisively toward independence.[6]

Thomas Paine's popular *Common Sense*, according to Nelson, so delegitimized monarchy that once the war had ended and fears of a disorderly, tyrannical legislative reemerged, the founders of the new nation reverted back to embracing the trappings of royalty and prerogative power but vested it now in a new chief executive, or president.[7] These "patriot royalists" ended up convincing skeptics that the presidential office would help unify a divided nation, and because it exercised a limited negative over Congress and its other powers could be checked, it would not simply reconstitute a newfangled form of monarchy (though some of them would have liked as much).[8]

Nelson is not the only scholar who has detected a royalist strain in the American political culture of the 1780s that helped shape the eventual conformation of the presidential office. The earlier imperial school historians and many of their followers argued that until the 1770s, the colonists sincerely wanted "to rebalance the English constitution in favor of the Crown."[9] In an important recent study, Saikrishna Bangalore Prakash invokes originalism as he seeks to understand the intended meaning of Article II and concludes that the presidency has been "imperial from the beginning." Unlike Arthur Schlesinger Jr.'s famous thesis that the framers gave only narrow powers to the president and that occupiers of the office have wrongly expanded them over the years, Prakash insists that the vesting clause in Article II was made broad deliberately, giving the chief executive unrestrained power except where it is specifically limited elsewhere in the Constitution. The actual language here is determinative, as the framers endowed Congress with "all legislative Powers herein granted" in Article I but then followed it with "the executive Power shall be vested in a President of the United States of America" without a comparable qualifier. The derivation of Prakash's originalism is both contextual and intertextual. In state practice and within the overall legal culture, "president" and "monarch" were essentially equivalent terms in eighteenth-century usage. In creating their new office, Americans were essentially aping a British convention with which they remained enamored.[10]

A number of scholars have taken issue with the way Prakash arrived at his notion of originalism and the meaning of Article II, but like most of his contemporaries, he is very attentive to method.[11] He and most of those who study the history of ideas today owe a great debt to the Cambridge School, which established the contours of modern practice in the 1970s and 1980s, beginning with Quentin Skinner's justly famous and influential 1969 essay in *History and Theory*.[12] Skinner recognized that intellectual history had fallen on hard times within the academy, largely because of the sloppy readings of canonical texts by scholars looking for how writers anticipated modern ideas such as humanitarianism, democracy, balance of power, separation of church and state, individualism, liberty, etc. The value of a text was often based on how close it came to prefiguring future ideas. There was no rigorous attempt to root ideas within particular historical contexts as the assumption was that these "classics" were simply engaging in a timeless dialogue across centuries and cultures. Skinner demonstrated that this kind of purely textual historical investigation was spurious as it enabled the investigator to manipulate texts to say things that the writer could not have possibly meant. The quest for authorial intention was therefore the necessary corrective to this careless approach, and some sense of the illocutionary force applied by the author. The context of the written "speech act" was thus critical in understanding the original meaning.

For those interested in eighteenth-century American history the search for the original meaning of those foundational yet protean concepts that served as underpinnings for the new republic and its constitution continues to the present day. It is no wonder then that Bailyn considers himself a Skinnerian with his attention to context and his focus on pamphlets that do not usually constitute part of the canon.[13] Eric Nelson dedicated his *Royalist Revolution* to Skinner, his "friend and teacher," while almost everyone in the field acknowledges the other major Cambridge School pioneer, John Pocock, as an inspiration and touchstone for their work.

As we have seen, Pocock's *Machiavellian Moment* proved highly influential in the study of early American political ideas, but he also made a major contribution to the practice of intellectual history as a whole. In one of his most impactful essays, he extended Skinner's appeal to authorial intention by calling on intellectual historians to consider the writer's linguistic context and the languages within which they expressed their ideas. These *langues* exist within a particular cultural realm, or *habitus* (to use Pierre Bourdieu's term), in which each has its own "vocabularies, rules, preconditions and implications, tone and style." As paradigms, they attempt to structure thought and speech in certain unique ways. "The language determines what can be said in it, but is capable of being modified by what is said in it; there is a history formed by interactions of *parole* and *langue*. . . . History can be viewed as the interaction of speech act and language." Languages—or discourses—are learned through frequent usage that breeds familiarity with them; some examples are common law, civil law, classical republicanism, medieval scholasticism, and Renaissance emblematic.[14] In the essays collected here, therefore, you will find that concepts such as checks and balances, bill of rights, social contract, and even nation all possess different, unfamiliar meanings as appropriated by interlocutors of particular historically constituted languages.

While much of the earlier work on early American political ideas has resulted in sweeping arguments made through studying works of political theory, legal treatises, pamphlet literature and letters, the authors in this volume tend to follow a Pocockian course by establishing a deep familiarity with contemporary words and languages while paying careful attention to and adopting the discourses in which positions were staked and commitments to action were taken up. Simultaneously, much as Joseph Levine describes it, they also conceive of language as an event, as "a process of thinking that results from having both outward circumstances and internal thought . . . put together by the historian who wishes to understand [an event's or text's] original historical meaning."[15] This is particularly important for understanding the early presidency, since many of the debates over its character—and its description in the final version of the Constitution—were formulated within particular historical settings and discursive environments that when studied carefully give us some sense of what the framers were thinking. In addition, engaging in such a practice reveals just how far removed we are today from the eighteenth century and original intentions.

This volume constitutes a collaborative effort to understand the presidency as a novel idea for a republic. The authors are engaged in stripping away accumulated meanings that have been layered onto the office since the time of George Washington. The essays are divided into three groups. The first set examines the intellectual antecedents of executive office in European thought and culture. As stated, many early Americans were familiar, even comfortable, with Britain's monarchical government. As Blair Worden shows us, that was at least in part because of the difficult if not disastrous experiment with republicanism during the Cromwellian period. The arbitrary actions of the Rump Parliament exposed the prospect of a tyrannical legislature and propelled new discussions about balanced government as the various political players began drafting the nation's first written constitution, the Instrument of Government. One writer in the middle of it all, the underappreciated Marchamont Nedham, and the lord protector himself posited a separation of executive power from the legislature as a necessary fixture of mixed constitutionalism while recasting the meaning of government "balance" to include a system of interlocking "checks" that deemphasized harmony in favor of setting interests against each other so no one power could become overly dominant. It is with this understanding that "the principle of checks and balances was a guiding premise in the drafting of the Constitution and in the definition of the presidency," as Blair Worden notes in chapter 2.

In chapter 3, Max Skjönsberg argues that checks and balances were central to the development of political parties. In fact, England's Whigs and Tories "represented the two pillars of the mixed constitution, parliament on the one hand and monarchy on the other," with "mutual checking and balancing" existing between them. David Hume believed that parties were at root about conflicting economic interests, and Bolingbroke held that there needed to be an organized opposition to whichever one was in power in order to help protect the government against corruption. In a similar vein, James Madison came to hold that freedom coupled with ambition necessitated political parties to manage competing interests and enable mutual restraint. Skjönsberg shows that Jeffersonian Republicans took up Bolingbroke's argument for a loyal opposition party in the 1790s, when they came to believe that George Washington's popularity had been co-opted by Federalists such as Alexander Hamilton ("another Walpole") and had so intimidated the Congress that the balanced constitution was at risk of being upset. In this way, organized political parties served as a necessary good for parliamentary governments, and as they were theorized in eighteenth-century Britain, they came to have a profound effect on early America and the president's role as party leader.

At the time of the ratifying conventions, Jefferson did not anticipate the need for parties to ensure a balanced government but instead promoted a constitutional guarantee of rights to prevent any branch from attempting to curtail essential personal liberties. As Eric Slauter points out in chapter 4, "bills of rights" were a contested "idea" or "genre" in postrevolutionary America since they had traditionally been extended only by monarchs under pressure as "an antimonarchical barrier against royal prerogative" and had never been associated with republics. To federalists such as Hamilton and James Wilson, rights were to be assumed in republics and need not be enumerated, for "the people might be said to gift rights and powers to their new chief executive, the president, not the other way around." But Madison, who originally opposed a bill of rights yet eventually sided with Jefferson, more fundamentally changed what the genre or idea meant when he reasoned that danger could come from legislatures as much as from kings, a position that detached bills of rights from their usual monarchical context. For Slauter and many of the other contributors to this volume, the combination of the persistence of royalist sentiment in early America and a new executive office that had few precedents to draw from created an institutional void that both European antecedents and novel, homegrown designs attempted to fill.

One influential model of executive power was not British but embodied the contemporary trend in enlightened absolutism that was prevalent in continental Europe. In chapter 5, through an assessment of the impact of King Frederick the Great's writings in America, Caroline Winterer shows us that the leaders of the new United States were not as radical as conventional scholarship would suppose. For many, Frederick represented the highly educated virtuous ruler, committed to reform, whose executive power and self-identification as the country's "first citizen" might unify a nation. Because monarchy was the executive prototype most were familiar with, it comes as no surprise that some early Americans saw the presidency as analogous to a constitutional monarchy. Frederick, who was held in high esteem for his strength and intelligence, famously wrote against Machiavelli, but unlike Rousseau and other Enlightenment political thinkers, he "interpreted the social contract in authoritarian terms." Following in the tradition of Jean Bodin and Thomas Hobbes, Frederick believed that the people had handed him an irrevocable, indivisible, and inalienable sovereign power that because it was tempered by natural law would eschew despotism. Frederick held that he could be restrained only by natural law and thus might grant freedoms and rights at his own pleasure. In the end, this tendency doomed his relevance for the founders, and by the time of the American ratification debates, the king had died along with much of his legacy. For a season, though, "Frederick had supplied revolutionary Americans with a compelling example of a king who wrestled, as they did, with the great question of how to imagine executive power in an age of Enlightenment and republicanism."

At first, however, patriot leaders were not even sure whether to create an executive office separate from the legislature, and if they did, they wondered if it should be filled by an individual or a "council of state." According to Jack Rakove, because the division of power under the Articles of Confederation between states and a national assembly spotlighted an ungovernable lack of restraint in the former as a result of their faulty constitutions, "the new Constitution was thus framed less in reaction to the Articles of Confederation than in response to a seasoned critique of politics and government at the level of the states."[16] Part II, therefore, looks closely at how received notions of executive power generated new iterations, based on the American experience, that were most fully developed and debated at the Constitutional Convention of 1787. In keeping with the overall sentiment at the time that excessive legislative power had the potential to threaten the new republic and the liberties it espoused, a strong presidential office emerged from the convention, but as Jonathan Gienapp convincingly argues in chapter 6, a controlling, even hegemonic national government also emerged. The inability of the Articles of Confederation and new state constitutions to govern effectively led a few influential framers, including James Wilson, Alexander Hamilton, and Gouverneur Morris, to posit a strong national interest as fundamental to the effective operation of the Constitution. Wilson defined the new union of states as a unitary force rather than a federated collection of individual entities. As Gienapp points out, while most are familiar with Hamilton's assertion of an energetic executive and with how his nemesis, Thomas Jefferson, worried about too much national power, few seem to recognize that they both agreed on limited, enumerated powers for the Congress. In a careful study of Morris's and Wilson's role in drafting the final version of the Constitution, Gienapp shows that these two made a robust and largely successful case for a strong national government that embraced all three branches equally, granting no privilege to the presidency. In 1787, however, no one yet knew that Hamilton's views would mainly prevail, and, as Gienapp notes, it is clearly a task of the intellectual historian "to probe the distinct variations of nationalist constitutionalism at the founding and begin charting, analyzing, and understanding why some endured while others disappeared."

Hamilton was certainly the main architect of the idea of an energetic executive as the framers came to understand it. In numbers 70 and 72 of *The Federalist Papers*, he argued that without a strong, vigorous president to handle with resolve the many pressures the country would face, the result would be a "feeble execution of the government," and he posited that such "a government ill executed, whatever it may be in theory, must be, in practice, a bad government." As Claire Rydell Arcenas lays out clearly in chapter 7, early Americans were deeply concerned with government designs by "closet philosophers" and "theoretic politicians" that could not succeed in the real world. Learning from experience was the key to effective leadership, which is why Hamilton and others advocated for the reeligibility of presidents. It may seem virtuous on paper for a politician to serve only a short term in office, but that deprives the people of a wiser, more seasoned leader who could bring the benefit of experience to the office and be more effective by serving a longer or additional term. Such a president would thus "be more responsible to the people." As with the other essays in this volume, Arcenas seeks to recover the lost intellectual contexts in which eighteenth-century political discourses took place and thus give us a more accurate and nuanced understanding of the ideas that emerged and set the new government in motion.

Another theme that arises in the essays here—if indirectly—concerns the adaptability of the U.S. Constitution. Modern jurists and legal professionals who seek to determine the framers' original intent too often fail to problematize that quest. Why should we assume that the conditions facing a new, fledgling republic in the late eighteenth century are comparable to the much more complex governmental needs of the early twenty-first century? The addition of amendments over the years, including the initial Bill of Rights, has been the focus for scholars who study the established means for "updating" the Constitution. However, this is not always as simple or direct as it seems, especially when amending involves protecting the perceived status quo and the amenders suddenly find themselves in the minority due to an unintended consequence of an underexplored idea. As François Furstenberg reveals in chapter 8, that seems to have been the case when it came to the constitutional language that set out how to admit new states to the union. After an extended debate at the convention over whether new states should be admitted on an equal footing with the original thirteen, the final document sent mixed messages by omitting such a condition while also allowing for admittance by a simple majority vote in Congress rather than the two-thirds majority required for important matters, such as impeaching the president, ratifying treaties, overriding vetoes, and amending the Constitution.

Furstenberg wonders if the delegates, cognizant of the Northwest Ordinance, assumed that no states would be formed west of the Mississippi River, which would limit the total number of new states and consequently maintain the dominance of the original thirteen, or fifteen. Although the unfairness of the Electoral College, a current hot-button political issue, proved to be far-reaching even by the early 1800s, Furstenberg asks "whether it is the primary structural cause of the country's current political impasse" or if the "real constitutional flaw" is in the all-too-simple statement found in Article IV, Section 3: "New States may be admitted by the Congress into this Union." The fact that delegates were unable to think beyond a provisional western policy to contemplate a large union of fifty states and so did not fathom an eventual loss of control by the original thirteen raises the question of whether a frame of government that could not anticipate something so elemental regarding its future makeup remains relevant today and whether originalism is a proper or worthwhile pursuit.

In Part III, the authors explore how the first presidents understood their roles and sought to take the skeletal outlines of their office, which were minimally delineated in the Constitution, and flesh out their full duties according to the everyday burdens and operations required in order to succeed. In chapter 9, Lindsay M. Chervinsky's examination of the relationship between the first three presidents and their cabinets reveals that each one brought their unique personality to the job along with a willingness to learn from experience and in so doing helped define the office. George Washington's leadership skills as commander of the Continental Army kept him from becoming involved in the rough-and-tumble of policy disagreement as "he preferred to consider all options. Once he selected a plan of action, he implemented it with firmness and alacrity." By his second term, he had developed a "deep conviction in the need for a strong, independent executive" that could exercise its authority when circumstances required quick, decisive action. In contrast, John Adams, by relying on Washington's secretaries, whose loyalty was questionable, often lost control of his bickering cabinet. The XYZ Affair exposed the weakness of Adams's personal style but also established the right of presidents to remove members of their cabinet at will. Finally, Thomas Jefferson was able to minimize conflict by developing relationships with officials outside of formal meetings and by using back channels to Congress to see his legislative priorities realized. Collectively, the main legacy of these three early presidents was to establish precedents that added to executive power and thus provided an amorphous office with a lasting modus operandi.

Daniel J. Hulsebosch would agree with Chervinsky's contention that "Washington wielded significant authority because of his reputation and unparalleled status." In fact, Washington carefully cultivated that reputation for integrity and self-mastery and through his careful reading of Emer de Vattel's legal treatise, *The Law of Nations* (1758), came to affect how the new nation presented itself to the international community. As Hulsebosch argues in chapter 10, the United States needed to be seen as a serious diplomatic player, and that meant establishing strong commercial relationships that would be to the young country's benefit. Washington saw this as a vital part of the executive office, and he and his government, in the absence of precedents, relied on legal treatises such as Vattel's more than other nations to give direction. By pursuing a policy of "engaged detachment" and maintaining neutrality that avoided permanent alliances and inconsistent behaviors, Washington made the president's credibility and capacity to conduct foreign policy a key feature of the emerging office and helped catapult it to a respected place on the world stage.

While Washington never received much formal education, he became interested in the law of nations through his voluminous reading of political works and was thus immersed in a "shared premise of Enlightenment-inflected republicanism." The value system associated with enlightened government in his day, with its repudiation of Machiavellian stratagems (which, as we have seen, was even the case with absolutists such as Frederick the Great), proved easier to champion verbally than to model exactingly. Many feared creeping tyranny should the ideals of that value system be abandoned and so insisted on holding the new American government's feet to the fire lest it falter in its republican experiment. One of the most dedicated to this task was patriot writer Mercy Otis Warren. Warren and Washington shared a devotion and commitment to the ideals of classical republicanism, including its promotion of civic virtue and dedication to the common good and the preservation of liberty. Rosemarie Zagarri shows that while both upheld classical republican values during the revolutionary war, once it was over Warren increasingly came to believe that Washington had betrayed those principles as he struggled to put them into practice. While the first president claimed that he had not wavered in his commitment, compromises based on the exigencies of office required some adjustments based on experience. Warren never had to implement her ideals and thus could not fathom fully the pressures Washington was under or how he tried his best to navigate his ship of state with a clear conscience.

The gap between theory and praxis is a theme that is raised across many of the essays here. It affected political debates about topics that ranged from calculating an energetic executive office to perpetuating civic virtue. The early presidents were constantly beleaguered as they tried to resolve the pressures republican theorists and purists imposed on them lest they stray too far and fail to ennoble the experiment in a constitutional separation of powers. Recent scholarship may tell us that most people were not too worried about presidential royalism or tyranny, as there were many other problems worth greater attention if the new nation were to survive, but today the political climate is much different. In living memory, Americans have witnessed three congressional impeachment proceedings over supposed presidential abuses of power when there had been only one prior to 1974. During an interview with David Frost in 1977, Richard Nixon boldly proclaimed that "when the president does it that means it's not illegal."[17] Forty-three years later, Donald Trump claimed during a speech to young supporters that "I have an Article II, where I have to the right to do whatever I want as president," in what turned out to be just one of several occasions when he seemed to assert that any action on his part was justifiable by virtue of his office, including even pardoning himself.[18] Fears of arbitrary and illegal uses of executive privilege bedevil constitutional purists who insist that today's presidency—with its assertion of a wide latitude of operation—is not what the framers intended. They wonder why these eminent, intelligent statesmen were unable to anticipate future abuses of power and put more and better safeguards into their new frame of government.[19] But as David Armitage has noted, "The context within which a concept emerges does not determine its future usage, though the history of its usage across time will reveal a great deal about the history of later contexts with which it was deployed. The origins of a concept, as of any other object of historical inquiry, are not necessarily connected to any later outcome, causally or otherwise; aetiology is not simply teleology in reverse. Conversely, present usage or practice offers no sure guide to the origins of a concept or activity."[20] Or to put it another way, although we might wish it were otherwise, the actions of the current president may not tell us much about the origins of the office or of original intentions regarding executive power; but the way both were realized over time reveals a lot about the historical moments in which certain meanings were generated. The essays here provide an essential starting roadmap for that journey of discovery.

Notes

1. Bernard Bailyn, *The Ideological Origins of the American Revolution* (Cambridge, MA: Harvard University Press, 1967), 34–48, quote on 35. Bailyn was drawing on the groundbreaking study of the commonwealth party, Caroline Robbins's *The Eighteenth-Century Commonwealthman: Studies in the Transmission, Development and Circumstance of English Liberal Thought from the Restoration of Charles II until the War with the Thirteen Colonies* (Cambridge, MA: Harvard University Press, 1959). Bailyn's highly influential work was reissued in new editions in 1992 and 2017. The fifty-year anniversary sparked numerous reflections, including "Anniversary Roundtable: The Ideological Origins of the American Revolution at Fifty," *Eighteenth-Century Studies* 50 (2017): 303–25, and a special edition of the *New England Quarterly* (91 [2018]: 3–208). Several authors in this volume contributed essays to these retrospectives.

2. Bernard Bailyn, "The Central Themes of the American Revolution," in *Essays on the American Revolution*, ed. Stephen G. Kurtz and James H. Hutson (Chapel Hill: University of North Carolina Press, 1973), 10–11. "Formal discourse becomes politically powerful when it becomes ideology; when it articulates, and fuses into effective formulations, opinions and attitudes that are otherwise too scattered and vague to be acted upon; when it mobilizes a general mood; . . . when it crystallizes otherwise inchoate social and political discontent and thereby shapes what is otherwise instinctive, and directs it to attainable goals; when it clarifies, symbolizes, and elevates to structured consciousness the mingled urges that stir within us."

3. See Gordon Wood, *The Creation of the American Republic, 1776–1787* (Chapel Hill: University of North Carolina Press, 1969); and his *The Radicalism of the American Revolution* (New York: Alfred A. Knopf, 1992). See also essays by Jonathan Gienapp, Claire Rydell Arcenas, Lindsay M. Chervinsky, and Daniel J. Hulsebosch in this volume.

4. J. G. A. Pocock, "Civic Humanism and Its Role in Anglo-American Thought," *Il Pensiero Politico* 1, no. 2 (1968), reprinted in J. G. A. Pocock, *Politics, Language, and Time: Essays on Political Thought and History* (Chicago: University of Chicago Press, 1989), 80–103.

5. J. G. A. Pocock, *The Machiavellian Moment: Florentine Political Thought and the Atlantic Republican Tradition* (Princeton, NJ: Princeton University Press, 1975). For a

more recent "appreciative" critique, see J. A. W. Gunn, "Republican Virtue Reconsidered, or a Sop to Cerberus," in *The Political Imagination in History: Essays concerning J. G. A. Pocock*, ed. D. N. DeLuna, Perry Anderson, and Glenn Burgess (Baltimore, MD: Owlworks, 2006), 101–28. See also the essay by Rosemarie Zagarri in this volume.

6. Eric Nelson, *The Royalist Revolution: Monarchy and the American Founding* (Cambridge, MA: Harvard University Press, 2014), 32–64. Brendan McConville believes the king's refusal to champion colonial interests over intrusive parliamentary interference ended the colonists' love affair with royal government. Brendan McConville, *The King's Three Faces: The Rise and Fall of Royal America, 1688–1776* (Chapel Hill: University of North Carolina Press, 2006).

7. Nelson, *The Royalist Revolution*, 108–45.

8. Nelson, *The Royalist Revolution*, 186–215. Patrick Collinson has traced the royal/republican dynamic of a "monarchical republic" that the architects of the Constitution debated all the way back to the reign of Elizabeth I. See John F. McDiarmid, ed., *The Monarchical Republic of Early Modern England: Essays in Response to Patrick Collinson* (London: Routledge, 2007).

9. Barry Alan Shain, "American Founding Narratives, Monarchy and Republicanism: The Largely Unsought and Incomplete Democratic Revolution," *Early American Literature* 53, no. 1 (2018): 193.

10. Saikrishna Bangalore Prakash, *Imperial from the Beginning: The Constitution of the Original Executive* (New Haven, CT: Yale University Press, 2015), 12–36, 63–83. See also Arthur M. Schlesinger Jr., *The Imperial Presidency* (Boston: Houghton Mifflin, 1973).

11. For example, see reviews of *Imperial from the Beginning* by Richard J. Ellis in *Presidential Studies Quarterly* 45 (2015): 821–23; by David J. Siemers in the *Journal of American History* 103 (2016): 459–60; and by Kimberley L. Fletcher in the *Tulsa Law Review* 52 (2017): 453–65.

12. Quentin Skinner, "Meaning and Understanding in the History of Ideas," *History and Theory* 8, no. 1 (1969): 3–53.

13. Bernard Bailyn, "Confessional Thoughts on Re-reading *The Ideological Origins*," *New England Quarterly* 91, no. 1 (2018): 16. Bailyn claimed in his preface to the enlarged edition of *The Ideological Origins* that he sought "to understand that world not as it anticipated the future but as it was experienced by those who lived it." Bernard Bailyn, *The Ideological Origins of the American Revolution*, enlarged edition (Cambridge, MA: Belknap Press of Harvard University Press, 1992), v. Gordon Wood also considers Bailyn "an out-and-out contextualist . . . who is determined to recover that different past as accurately as possible," while recognizing that some critics take this to be "a political stance itself, somehow justifying the rightness of the Revolution and America." Gordon Wood, "Reassessing Bernard Bailyn's *The Ideological Origins of the American Revolution* on the Occasion of Its Jubilee," *New England Quarterly* 91, no. 1 (2018): 107.

14. J. G. A. Pocock, "The Concept of a Language and the Métier d'Historien: Some Considerations on Practice," in *The Languages of Political Theory in Early-Modern Europe*, ed. Anthony Pagden (Cambridge: Cambridge University Press, 1987), 20–23. See also Pierre Bourdieu, *Outline of a Theory of Practice* (Cambridge: Cambridge University

Press, 1977). Conal Condren famously cautioned against asserting that political theorists make contributions or exercise influence over later writers due to the inherent telos of these terms and so prefers invoking relevance and usage instead. Conal Condren, *The Status and Appraisal of Classic Texts: An Essay on Political Theory, Its Inheritance, and the History of Ideas* (Princeton, NJ: Princeton University Press, 1985), 119–41. For critics of the Cambridge School, many of whom believe that Skinner tends to reduce intellectual history to an antiquarian exercise, see James Tully, ed., *Meaning and Context: Quentin Skinner and His Critics* (Princeton, NJ: Princeton University Press, 1988); especially Joseph V. Femia's "An Historicist Critique of 'Revisionist' Methods for Studying the History of Ideas," *History and Theory* 20, no. 2 (1981): 113–34; David Harlan, "Intellectual History and the Return of Literature," *American Historical Review* 94, no. 3 (1989): 581–609; and Anthony Grafton, "The History of Ideas: Precept and Practice, 1950–2000 and Beyond," *Journal of the History of Ideas* 67, no. 1 (2006): 1–32.

15. Joseph M. Levine, "Intellectual History as History," *Journal of the History of Ideas* 66, no. 2 (2005): 190–91. Levine faults Skinner and Pocock for seeking linguistic context apart from the "outside" meaning of a text: "Establishing the discourse must itself rest on a prior activity: recovering the meaning and intention of each of the many speech acts that constitute the discourse, by first placing each in its own situation—and by conceiving of ideas as the result of a process of thinking, not merely as a set of conclusions" (190). For example, just as a detective must infer a murderer's intention through a close examination of the crime scene, so would a historian want to know the process by which Francis Bacon wrote his *Advancement of Learning* (1605), including its alterations, by situating it within an intellectual "succession of events" (195).

16. Jack N. Rakove, *The Beginnings of National Politics: An Interpretive History of the Continental Congress* (New York: Alfred A. Knopf, 1979), 396.

17. "Transcript of Frost's Television Interview," *New York Times*, May 5, 1977, B10, https://www.nytimes.com/1977/05/05/archives/transcript-of-frosts-television-interview -with-nixon-about.html.

18. Michael Brice-Saddler, "While Bemoaning Mueller Probe, Trump Falsely Says the Constitution Gives Him 'The Right to Do Whatever I Want,'" *Washington Post*, July 23, 2019, https://www.washingtonpost.com/politics/2019/07/23/trump-falsely- tells-auditorium-full-teens-constitution-gives-him-right-do-whatever-i-want/; David A. Graham, "Trump: When the President Says It, That Means It's True," *The Atlantic*, March 23, 2017, https://www.theatlantic.com/politics/archive/2017/03/trump -time-interview-ex-post-facto/520551/.

19. Erin Peterson, "Presidential Power Surges," *Harvard Law Bulletin* (Summer 2019), https://today.law.harvard.edu/feature/presidential-power-surges/.

20. David Armitage, *The Ideological Origins of the British Empire* (Cambridge: Cambridge University Press, 2000), 5.

PART I

The European Origins of
the American Presidency

2

Checks and Balances

The Cromwellian Origins of the Presidency

BLAIR WORDEN

The principle of checks and balances was a guiding premise in the drafting of the Constitution and in the definition of the presidency. It is a frequent and sometimes controversial element of political or constitutional discussion in the modern world. Yet with the significant exception of a distinguished long essay by David Wootton (which this chapter aspires to complement)[1] its history has barely been written. Where did the concept come from? Its emergence is customarily placed in the eighteenth century, where Wootton's emphasis falls. Montesquieu, in his *L'Esprit des Lois* of 1748, mapped the notion of checks and balances with the virtues of the English constitution in his mind. Nearly forty years later the principle was employed in the design and defense of the American one. Interest in the principle and the use of its language intensified in the last two decades of the century on both sides of the Atlantic. Yet the birth of the concept lay not in the eighteenth century but in the mid-seventeenth, a time when the constitution that would be lauded in Hanoverian times had broken down. It was invented to vindicate Oliver Cromwell's occupation of the office of lord protector, which he held as ruler of England from 1653 to his death in 1658. I shall explore the emergence of the principle in his time and, in the concluding section of the chapter, trace its descent to the eighteenth century.

The delegates at Philadelphia were unaware of its Cromwellian antecedents and would have been troubled to learn of them. If Cromwell's government had a place in their minds, it was not as a model but as a warning. In America, as in England, the memory of his regime was associated with

brutal destruction, ruthless ambition, cloaked hypocrisy, military usurpation, and standing armies. In answering the supposition "that we had
nothing to fear from an abuse of the executive power," Pierce Butler asked
the Constitutional Convention "why might not a Cataline or Cromwell
arise in this country as well as in others"?[2] Yet if we turn from the hostile
images of Cromwell to the constitutional provisions the protector pledged
to observe, we find analogies of content and purpose to the decisions of
1787.

In both countries, the concept was linked to another one, to whose evolution historians have given much more attention: the separation of legislative from executive power. The connection was made by the leading
apologist of the Cromwellian protectorate, Marchamont Nedham. Like the
delegates at Philadelphia who designed the presidency and the authors of
The Federalist who defended it, he had a new office to define. To grasp the
nature and extent of his achievement and of his contribution to the principle of checks and balances, we need to place his initiative in its political
and intellectual context. When we do so we see, as so often in the history
of political thought, the interaction of ideas and events. The convention at
Philadelphia was indebted to what happened in England's civil wars, not
merely to what was written in them.

America's constitution is famously a written one; England's is famously un-
written. Yet England has had two written constitutions of its own, which
were the sanctions of Cromwell's rule. The first, which became known as
the Instrument of Government, will be our greater concern. It was proclaimed in December 1653 at the ceremony of Cromwell's installation. In
1657, the Instrument was replaced by a new constitution, a revised version
of its predecessor known as the Humble Petition and Advice. It enabled the
succession of Oliver's son Richard in 1658, but it collapsed on Richard's fall
in 1659.[3] Both constitutions were imposed not only on England but on the
countries that Oliver's army had recently conquered, Ireland and Scotland.

It may seem demeaning to place the U.S. Constitution, assembled as it
was by civilian politicians schooled in the comparative political science of
the Enlightenment, beside those transitory, pre-Enlightenment expedients,
the first of which was in effect a military decree and the second destroyed
by the same army. Yet their failure was no more predictable than the en-
durance of the formula of 1787. They were undone less by weaknesses of
design than by political circumstances and decisions. Failure is fatal to
the reputations of constitutions. David Hume mocked the Instrument of

Government as a "motley" document, "crude and undigested," the work of men radically deficient in "the spirit of legislation."[4] It was certainly completed in haste, which left loose ends.[5] Yet the great late-Victorian historian of the civil wars S. R. Gardiner, who gave closer attention to constitutional issues than most of his successors, was "struck with the ability of its framers."[6] Like the Constitution, the Instrument was exposed to close scrutiny and extensive argument after its promulgation. In September 1654, Cromwell submitted it to Parliament for ratification. The ensuing debates dominated the business of the House of Commons until the dissolution of the Parliament in January 1655. They seem to have occupied at least as much time as the sessions at Philadelphia, although they are far less well documented. Guibon Godard, the backbench MP who is our principal source for the debates, overcame his innate political skepticism in his account of one critical session, when "the arguments on both sides were very rationally urged" and the Commons "did proceed with a great deal of ingenuity, modesty, and candour; and this cannot be denied, but [is] fit to be remembered to all ages."[7] In 1654, as in 1787, a country's constitutional future lay open.

The parallels between the Instrument and the Constitution derived from a shared experience. In both cases, the removal of a tyrant—Charles I, George III—had been followed by a swing in an opposite direction that took the revolution on a course the creators of the document had not intended. In America, that outcome was called the "tyranny" or "usurpations" or "despotism" or "vortex" of bodies with legislative powers—the Confederation Congress and the ruling institutions of individual states—that replaced the monarchy and usurped its executive functions. The presidency was meant to end that error and prevent a recurrence. The protectorate justified itself on parallel grounds. Before England's civil wars, Parliament had been an occasional body, summoned and dissolved at the king's behest and having no share in the exercise of government. The institution was transformed by the exigencies of revolution. In 1642, the year civil war broke out, the Parliament that had met in November 1640—the Long Parliament, as it came to be known, for it lasted thirteen years—took over the government,[8] to which wartime administration and taxation had given unprecedented powers.[9] The transformation became more fundamental in the winter of 1648–49, when the Cromwellian army forcibly purged the Parliament and secured the trial and execution of the king. The compliant remnant of the Commons, the "Rump" as it came to be derisively termed, abolished the monarchy. It also abolished the House of

Lords and set itself up as a unicameral government.[10] The executive functions were handed to a newly created council of state, composed mainly of MPs and jealously controlled by the Commons.

The army wearied of every constitutional arrangement it set up. Cromwell expelled the Rump in April 1653 and replaced it in July with an assembly to which contemporaries gave another unflattering epithet, Barebone's Parliament. At this stage, he did not challenge Parliament's occupation of executive power. Barebone's Parliament also appointed a subordinate council of state, again mostly from its own members. Cromwell, to whom constitutional provisions were "as Paul says dross and dung in comparison of Christ,"[11] adopted and abandoned them as his pursuit of godly reformation demanded. The Rump had resisted reforms. Barebone's Parliament headily embarked on them and brought the nation to the brink of chaos. On December 12, it too succumbed to a military coup. There followed four days of hectic consultation and drafting before the Instrument of Government, and Cromwell's occupancy of the office of lord protector defined in it, were announced.

The architect of the Instrument was the army officer John Lambert, whose "cunning pencil" and "subtle and working brain" were acknowledged by opponents of his constitutional schemes.[12] In 1647, when the army had held negotiations with the king and expected his return to his throne, Lambert had participated in drawing up peace terms. Now he brought similar thinking to the appointment of a ruler in the king's place, in whose hands executive authority, separate from the legislature, would be restored. In the Instrument as in the Constitution—but in no intervening constitution—the first article allocates legislative power (in the Instrument, "the supreme legislative authority") and the second allocates executive power (in the Instrument, "the exercise of the chief magistracy and the administration of the government"). Both the Instrument and the Constitution then proceed to define the powers of the two branches and the relationship between them.

If Lambert was the designer, Marchamont Nedham was the explicator. A mercenary propagandist armed with an educated and lively intelligence and a nimble pen, he served competing and opposing parties in turn. Yet amid his abrupt and startling transfers of allegiance he had a mind of his own, a corner of which retained a defiant independence.[13] Alongside that quality, he had a gift for conceptual improvisation, a sense of intellectual smell that detected embryonic ideas in the controversies around him, a capacity to give them shape and direction, and an ability to spot their political usefulness and press them into political service. If political thought is judged by the incisiveness of its analytical perceptions, he has no exalted place in it. Yet his influence outlived his time, for his footprints are to be found in a range of long-term theoretical developments. One of his achievements was to pioneer in the 1640s the application to English politics of the argument that the key to the resolution of conflicts lies in the identification and management not of the professed principles of the contending parties but of their "interests."[14] Then, in the service of the Rump Parliament, he was an innovative figure in the development first of de facto vindications of power[15] and after that of English republicanism.[16] Then, in his subsequent service of Cromwell, he helped shape the language of "civil and religious liberty," a potent social and political force down to the earlier twentieth century. It turned religious freedom from a divine injunction that was independent of secular arguments into a human entitlement.[17] Nedham's relations with Cromwell, as with many people, oscillated violently. Under his previous allegiances he had savagely assailed him, on behalf of first the royalists and then the Rump. But after Cromwell had expelled the Rump, Nedham was an invaluable aid to him. From the outset of the protectorate, he was at the heart of the regime, for which, alongside his intimate friend John Milton, he worked in the office of Cromwell's secretary of state, John Thurloe. He was Cromwell's in-house political thinker.

The standard history of the doctrine of the separation of powers, M. J. C. Vile's *Constitutionalism and the Separation of Powers*, shows that although the principle had classical and medieval roots, "it was in seventeenth-century England that it emerged for the first time as a coherent theory of government, explicitly set out, and urged as the 'grand secret of liberty and good government.'" Vile's quotation is from the protectorate's apologia for the Instrument of Government, Nedham's *A True State of the Case of the Commonwealth*, a pamphlet of about 17,000 words published in February 1654.[18] Here too Nedham points ahead. The new constitution, as the passage from which Vile's quotation is taken explains, avoids the hazard to which the Long Parliament had succumbed. Nedham attacks the principle of combining "the supreme powers of making laws, and of putting them in execution . . . in the same hands," whether those of "a single person" or of "many." For "placing the legislative and executive powers in the same persons is a marvellous in-let of corruption and tyranny: whereas [in] the keeping these two apart, flowing in distinct channels, so that they may never meet . . . , there lies a grand secret of liberty and good government."[19] Were it not for Nedham's silence on the subject of judicial power, which was irrelevant to his purpose, we might virtually be reading *The Federalist*, where "the accumulation of all powers, legislative, executive, and judicial, in the same hands, whether of one, or a few, or many . . . may justly be pronounced the very definition of tyranny."[20]

The Rump Parliament's plans for the constitutional future, Nedham remembers, envisaged no division of powers and "no manner of balance or check" upon the legislature. Nedham was, as far as we can tell, the first person to join the words "check" and "balance" in a discussion of forms of government. The theme led him to a further conceptual breakthrough. He annexed the principle of separation to that of mixed constitutionalism and to the repudiation of simple forms of government. Nedham's tract of 1654 explains that whereas the Rump sought an undivided and "absolute authority" for parliaments, the Instrument of Government, wherein "the legislative and executive powers are separated," combines the virtues of the three classical forms of government: monarchy, aristocracy, and democracy.[21] The Rump, having eliminated the monarchical and aristocratic components of the constitution, was identified by its enemies with the simple form of democracy.

The discovery made in the civil wars, however, was not that democracies can be tyrannical, a trait familiar to the English from classical history, but that parliaments can be tyrannical. Charges Americans leveled at Congress and the state legislatures—disorder, division, factionalism, injustice, corruption, dilatoriness, delay, the multiplication of inept or inequitable legislation, the failure to pay public debts, and in the case of Congress the difficulties in raising a quorum—echoed ones that were leveled at the Rump, many of them by Nedham. If Americans were unaware of their debt to Cromwell's constitutions, they did know about the Long Parliament's usurpation of executive power in the early 1640s, which in the eighteenth century Rapin, Hume, and Blackstone highlighted and condemned.[22] Americans also knew of the further usurpation of it in 1649, which British historians had likewise excoriated.[23] It was heightened in American memory by the measures through which the Rump had subordinated the colonies' interests to those of England.[24]

The record of the Long Parliament, before and after 1649, informed the thinking of the most influential of the champions of executive independence at Philadelphia, James Wilson. Well before the Declaration of Independence, Wilson had maintained that "kings are not the only tyrants: the conduct of the Long Parliament will justify me in adding, that kings are not the severest tyrants."[25] Thereafter, he watched his countrymen learn their mistake of "dreading danger only on one side."[26] At Philadelphia, he indicated that the rule of the Rump, "a more pure and unmixed tyranny" than the king's, illustrated the common experience of the two countries, for in both of them the "association" of "king and tyrant" had yielded to that of "legislature and tyranny."[27] There was a further resemblance. The misrule of the Long Parliament had been ceaselessly linked, as it was by Nedham, to the assembly's instinct for self-"perpetuation" and to the constancy of its sitting. In America, analogous anxieties colored discussions of new or planned constitutional arrangements. In 1641, Parliament had persuaded the king to pass an act forbidding its dissolution without its own consent.[28] In John Adams's view, the measure "destroyed the liberty of the subject."[29] Wilson dwelt on the same consequence of the measure.[30]

The Constitution followed a war of independence that had evicted an external power. The Instrument of Government followed a civil war whose divisive legacy explains a number of clauses in the document to which Americans needed no equivalent and that need not concern us. Equally, the issue of federalism, so fundamental at Philadelphia, has no counterpart in the English story. There is a more pervasive contrast. Independence enabled and required Americans to plan afresh. Although the founders learned from past and present constitutions, they had no tie to them. In England, where Nedham commended the conformity of the Instrument to the wisdom of "our ancestors,"[31] there was the tug of inherited practice. The protector, wanting reconciliation as well as reform, sought to win over the mainstream and traditionalist parliamentarians who had sought a regulated or limited monarchy under Charles I and been appalled by the republic of 1649–53. He wanted to exert the allure of royal tradition without incurring the odium of tyranny or self-aggrandizement. He took over royal accoutrements, royal buildings, and royal administrative machinery, and yet he eschewed the title of king and accepted the protectorate as an elective rather than a hereditary office. On his behalf, Nedham explained that the Instrument of Government would preserve the virtues of monarchical authority while removing its scope for arbitrary power. It would thus satisfy "the original ground of our taking up arms."[32]

The office of the presidency has features that would have been too remote from English monarchical practice to occur to the Cromwellians: tenure for fixed terms rather than for life, the payment of a stipend, provision for removal from office, and a vice-presidency. Nevertheless, the analogies of circumstance produced ones of stipulation. On a succession of subjects, the two documents defined relations between executive and legislature in formulae that, while never identical, sprang from parallel considerations: the exercise of a qualified veto, the command of the army, the power to make war and peace,[33] the appointment of officers, and the granting of pardons.

In both countries, demands for a separate executive had to counter arguments for popular sovereignty. In removing the monarchy, the Rump had asserted the right of peoples, which the Declaration of Independence would affirm, to choose and change their governments.[34] The republic professed to rule as the representative of "the people," who were "the origin of all just power." Admittedly, the Rump ignored the notion, which the Levellers had advanced in the late 1640s and which would be echoed in mainstream American thinking, that Parliament is the mere servant of the people, who "reserve" rights on which their representatives may not impinge.[35] To the Rump, the people's will meant Parliament's will. The protectorate made the same equation. Even as it terminated parliamentary sovereignty, it too wanted to be seen as ruling by the consent of the people's representatives. Nedham explained that in the national emergency that brought Cromwell to power there had been no opportunity for national consultation but that the Instrument of Government ensured that consent would be established over time.[36] Crucial to his claim was the Instrument's most ingenious provision, which established a council by whose "advice" and "consent" the protector was to rule. There are some resemblances between its role and the Senate's relationship to the president in the Constitution.[37] The initial councilors, all Cromwellians, were named by the Instrument, but when a vacancy arose Parliament was to propose six candidates, of whom the council itself would choose two, from whom the protector would select one. Thus, the council's composition would in time be authorized by the people's representatives. So would the identity of Cromwell's successors. Because they were to be chosen by the council, their rule would "take its rise originally and virtually from the people." Thus, "all power both legislative and executive" would "flow from the community."[38]

Nedham summoned the principles of separation and checking and balancing to the cause of executive authority. They would serve an analogous goal at Philadelphia. Yet his arguments for protectoral power, like American ones for presidential power, hovered between the claims of authority and the competing ones of liberty. The two offices were commended as a necessary source of national unity and governmental energy and strength but also as alternatives to tyranny, whether exercised by a legislature or by an insufficiently restrained executive. In both countries, however, the prospect of independent executive power, whatever restrictions might be imposed on it, aroused fear and resentment. At Philadelphia, Roger Sherman "said he considered the executive magistracy as nothing more than an institution for carrying the will of the legislature into effect." It therefore "ought to be appointed by and accountable to the legislature only, which was the supreme will of the society."[39] In England, the thrust of parliamentarian opinion, which the Instrument of Government challenged, had said the same. All legitimate executive power, it affirmed, was derived from the legislature and was confined to the implementation of its will. On that front, at least, the defender of the ancient constitution William Prynne, who maintained in 1643 that "the parliament is the superior sovereign power, the king but the ministerial,"[40] was at one with the Leveller Richard Overton, who argued three years later that "the power of the king" was "only executive" and lay beneath "the sovereign or legislative power."[41] Although the constitutional settlements proposed in the years around the regicide posited a return to parliaments of brief duration, the principle of parliamentary sovereignty would survive in the intervals between them, for each successive parliament was to appoint a council to govern after its own expiry and to report to its successor and be accountable to it.

Only with the launching of the protectorate did the claims of the executive fight back. The undivided power Parliament had assumed since 1642 was now ended. As at Philadelphia, a long and strong tide was reversed. The framers of the Instrument of Government were initially nervous about extending autonomous powers to the protector. Until a late stage, the drafts of the Instrument envisaged the single ruler exercising some of his main functions only between parliaments and subject to retrospective parliamentary approval. The discarding of those provisions in the final version was a bold move. It presented the new regime with a challenge of explanation that advocates of a strong executive in America would also face. If executive power did not derive from the legislature, where did it come from? The American solution, a convention independent of existing legislatures and ratified independently of them, placed the origins of both branches in popular consent. A convention was beyond the thinking and the practical options of 1653–54. Cromwell looked for a document that would be "somewhat fundamental, somewhat like a Magna Charta, that should be standing and unalterable" and would thus be beyond challenge by either protector or Parliament.[42] Only by the endorsement of the legislature, however, could he hope to bring legality to a regime that, as Nedham had to admit, had reached power "in a way irregular and extraordinary."[43] The protector wanted the Parliament of 1654 to pass a motion at the outset to accept the Instrument of Government, but his hope was overborne by an assembly where Roger Sherman would have recognized kindred spirits. MPs warned each other not to "approve of any thing which takes not its root and foundation and rise from themselves."[44]

The heart of the parliamentary resistance to Cromwell came not from former members of the Rump, fierce as their opposition was, but from moderate parliamentarians who had been excluded from the Rump or had boycotted it. It was not that they wished Parliament to resume the executive powers it had held until 1653. They did not maintain that legislative and executive functions ought ordinarily to be combined. The Long Parliament's takeover of the executive had been justified not as a constitutional alteration but as a necessary response to an emergency: one that required Parliament to exercise duties that the king had abandoned or perverted. What the MPs of 1654 insisted on was the legislature's power to define and restrict the power of the executive. They were ready to authorize a separate executive authority and to grant Cromwell many of the executive powers which the Instrument had vested in him—but on an overriding condition: Cromwell must recognize Parliament's consent as the sole legitimate source of the executive power that it sanctioned. The requirement would have highlighted the illegality of the introduction of the Instrument of Government and of the subsequent nine months of Cromwellian rule. It would also have made the protectorate revocable. The only means of legalizing the regime acceptable to Parliament was the issuing of a statute, a route which could afford Cromwell no security, for statutes can always be reversed by subsequent parliaments and so cannot, "somewhat like a Magna Charta," be "standing and unalterable."[45]

The Parliament of 1654 produced a draft statute containing a revised version of the Instrument of Government. The document made plain the assembly's commitment to the subordination of executive to legislature. The powers of the executive are placed not, as in the Instrument and in the U.S. Constitution, alongside those of the legislature but well down the list of clauses.[46] During the debates the famous judge and legal thinker Mathew Hale, whom Blackstone would cite as an authority on the powers of Parliament, made a proposal which swayed the House and endured in public memory: "the government should be in the parliament and a single person, limited and restrained as the parliament should think fit."[47]

An angry Cromwell first forcibly purged the House and then, when the prospect of agreement faded, dissolved it, so that the whole question of the regime's constitutional basis was left in abeyance. Even so, the parliamentary failure of the Instrument may not have been foredoomed. As at Philadelphia, the pressures toward compromise, during what might be a unique opportunity for political settlement, were strong. A decisive vote, which seems to have outraged the protector, was passed by only twelve votes, 107–95.[48] When we remember the narrow margins by which some of the American states ratified the Constitution, we realize that an alternative history might have awaited both countries.

The principles of separation and checking and balancing were Nedham's and Cromwell's answer to the principle of parliamentary sovereignty. Behind their evolution, as behind other conceptual innovations of the civil war period, lay four developments that arose from the conflict and that the framework and language of traditional political thought were unable to accommodate. We have met the first development, the realization that a royal tyranny had been replaced by a parliamentary one. If king and Parliament could both break their bounds, arguments were needed that would confront the dangers of power itself, not merely the powers of one of its agencies. Second, until the wars, the components of the English constitution had been supposed to complement and support each other. Whatever the difficulties between Crown and Parliament, it was hard to conceive of them as rivals or enemies. Now they had become competing powers whose relations needed to be newly described. Third, the breaches of ancient practice and principle into which the contending parties were driven impaired the conventional claims of precedent and historical entitlement to determine the locations of political authority. Fourth, the breakdown of order and of the constitution, and the task of reconstruction, directed thinkers beyond the rights and wrongs of the wars—passionately debated as they were—to problems of constitutional architecture of the kind James Harrington's *Oceana* addressed in 1656. It became increasingly common to describe political authorities not in the terms of their historic identities, which their occupants regarded as permanent and inalienable, but in the abstract terms of transferable functions. Thus, the notion of an "executive" power that was detachable from the monarchy and attachable to other persons or bodies did not come into focus until the civil wars, when its application to current events grew with the years. The collective outcome of the four developments was a shift of emphasis, across a range of political argument, from the pursuit or preservation of rights or ideals to the management of reality.

The terms "check" and "balance" were not obvious allies. They had separate histories, and even in their eighteenth-century maturity would appear more often apart than together; "check" was always the more common.[49] In marrying them, Nedham cut through norms of language. "Balance" was an old constitutional concept that went back to Plutarch and Polybius,[50] whereas "check" was a new one. "Balance" had a pleasing sound, "check" an unpleasing one. "Balance" conventionally indicated harmony or accommodation, "check" conflict or competition. "Balance" was an ideal, "check" a reality. When Nedham portrayed the Instrument of Government as a mixture of the virtues of monarchical, aristocratic, and democratic rule, he was silently adopting and adapting a passage of Charles I's *Answer to the XIX Propositions* of 1642, that long-remembered document where the Crown, in a tactical deviation from its normal absolutist position, accused Parliament of upsetting a constitution that prospers "as long as the balance hangs even between" the three genres of government.[51] The *Answer* played on customary associations, which both sides frequently articulated in the early stages of the Long Parliament, between "balance" (or sometimes "beam") and the "equal" or "even" scales of justice.[52] The words also implied stability and tranquility. Tip a balance to one side or the other and tyranny or chaos will ensue.

The two sides entered the civil war with a shared ideal of kingship. Each blamed the other for undermining it. In its healthy form, kingship had the glory of majesty, which royalists and parliamentarians concurred in associating with the harmony of balance that the *Answer to the XIX Propositions* saluted. The leading parliamentarian theorist of the early 1640s, Henry Parker, rejoiced in the English constitution as he took it to be. Under it, he explained in 1640, "the beam hangs even between the king and the subject."[53] An MP of 1641 concurred: the king's "glory and splendour . . . can never be eclipsed, if the balance of justice go right."[54] "Check" was a different matter. In 1642, Parker told the king not that his power needed checking but that if he would only follow Parliament's advice, the "check" or "cloud" that occluded his glory would disappear.[55]

"Check" was not new to political discussion during the civil wars, but it did not enter into accounts of constitutional arrangements until the 1650s. In everyday usage, the word had old meanings, independent of politics (although they were applicable to them), which it retained during and after the civil wars even as new meanings arose. It could signify a reproof.[56] Or it meant a repulse (as in a battle) or a block (as on the chess board). Or, in the most common connotation in daily life, to "check" was to "curb," "bridle," "restrain," "limit," or, most frequently, "control." That definition supported a low view of human nature, which saw "checks" as means to withstand humanity's "sinfulness," "evil," "rage," "fury," "lusts," "insolence," "ambition," the "restlessness" of appetites, and such other "exorbitances." When that signification was applied to politics, "tyranny" was easily added to the list.

Nedham's view of human nature was also low, although his attitude was realistic rather than censorious. He maintained that "true policy ever sup- poseth that men in power may be unrighteous; and therefore (presuming the worst) points always, in all determinations, at the enormities and rem- edies of government."[57] It was "very evident, how prone men in power are to keep up themselves."[58] Here, as elsewhere, Nedham's outlook had a long future. "Checks," the widely influential early-Hanoverian publication *Cato's Letters* explained, are necessary because of "the unruly and partial appe- tites of men" and because "power" is "restless as long as any thing stands in its way."[59] Hume recognized an "established . . . maxim, that in . . . fixing the several checks and controls of the constitution, every man ought to be supposed a knave."[60] Nedham brought the same realism to his pioneering insistence on the identification and adjustment of "interests." Again, later commentators would mirror his perceptions. A late seventeenth-century writer who pleaded for the executive and the legislature to "check" each other deemed it "certain that every man will act for his own interest" and maintained that "all wise governments are founded upon that principle."[61] At Philadelphia, Gouvernour Morris argued in the Constitutional Conven- tion that in the Constitution's arrangements for "checking," "one interest must be opposed to another interest. Vices as they exist, must be turned against each other."[62]

In joining "balance" and "check," Nedham shed the idealistic aura of the first and the derogatory aura of the second. Instead, he gave to both words a neutral coloring that was appropriate to the political realism that the civil wars advanced and that was his own literary hallmark. His adjust- ment of "balance" was the easier, for in other walks of public life the word already had a realistic cast. The concepts of the international "balance" of "trade" and of "power," as aids to the peace and prosperity of nations, were already familiar by the mid-seventeenth century[63] (and were ubiquitous by its end). Indeed, it could be that Nedham, who had transposed to domestic politics the notion of the accommodation of the "interests" of separate nations, consciously did the same to the idea of the international balance of power, for a prominent exponent of the principle, the Huguenot writer Henri duc de Rohan, was also Nedham's model for his writing on "interest."[64] In any event, even as he borrowed from the tribute paid to "balance" in the *Answer to the XIX Propositions*, Nedham dispensed with its elevation of tone. In *A True State*, it was in complaining of the Rump Parliament's failure to provide any "manner of balance or check" that he alerted readers to the proneness of "men in power" to "keep up themselves." The skeptical resonance of "balance" that Nedham introduced to constitutional issues would be prevalent in the eighteenth century, when, as Wootton says, "ways of discussing checks and balances" turned on "the claim that self-interest is the sole principle on the basis of which governments must be constructed."[65] In the Hanoverian age, both a "balance of power" between branches of government and the "check" they can give each other were deemed essential because "in the nature of things . . . men's . . . interests will often vary and clash."[66] Nedham's writing did not extinguish the idealistic aura of "balance." Here too the old would survive with the new, sometimes blending with it, sometimes jostling with it. Yet in bringing "check" and "balance" together he had wrought a decisive change.

He did not effect it alone. He seized on an existing movement of thought and language that we can follow over the seven years before the publication of his tract of 1654. The movement began with the emergence of the new model army as a political force in 1647, the year after the end of the civil war. The army's political pretensions added a third dimension to the conflict between king and Parliament, whose followers were themselves divided with increasing bitterness into competing factions. The conjuncture of the words "check" and "balance" appears to have first occurred early in 1647, although it arose in a military rather than political context. That year, in a history of the new model's achievements, the army chaplain Joshua Sprigge described the "check or balance" that the deployment of its forces had placed on the king's forces in 1645, the year the army was created.[67] Here was the realistic connotation of "balance" that Nedham would apply to constitutional matters. Sprigge's wording signaled not a harmonious poise, as the *Answer to the XIX Propositions* had done, but a counterpoise that was needed in a world of conflict to correct an undesirable imbalance.

In the army's public statements of the summer of 1647, we find the words "check" and "balance" first brought together on a political subject, although not yet on a constitutional one. Nedham had recently taken up employment as a propagandist for the army, and he probably had a hand in the pertinent statements.[68] At this stage, however, the army was not seeking to vindicate a constitutional practice, as Nedham would do in 1654. It was aiming to justify an unconstitutional one. The soldiery of 1647 claimed that they needed to break "ordinary and common bounds of known law" in order to "check and balance" the treasonous activities of its opponents at Westminster—although as yet the army's target was only a party within the assembly, not the institution of Parliament itself, which it would soon assault.[69] The statements were thrown back at the army by a pamphleteer who rebuked its presumption in seeking "boldly to teach, check and balance the power of parliament, to force them to do and undo what you please."[70]

The new inflection of "balance" lay dormant between 1647 and Nedham's return to it in 1654. In the interim, the political range of "check" expanded. It was in 1648, as the trial of the king approached and the army developed a revolutionary intent, that the word acquired a constitutional signification. The army's language was a world away from the parliamentary complaints of 1642 about checks on the glory of majesty. Calling for Charles's punishment, the army and voices within it remembered his attempts to free himself of the "check" of parliaments. Now and in the future, constitutional "checks" were desired or opposed as political principle or need determined. Thus, the army defended Parliament's "check" on the king but also demanded an end to the "check" of his "negative voice,"[71] the veto on legislation that in subsequent generations would be the constitutional subject that the language of checks and balances most frequently addressed. Shortly before the regicide, the Rump Parliament likewise denounced the "check" of the royal veto.[72]

If "check" had been used only to challenge the claims of the Crown, the word would never have acquired a theoretical aspect. The term did not become an abstract principle until there were competing constitutional agencies to be restrained. The critical development was the army's direction of "check" not only at Charles I but at the Parliament that opposed him. The immediate cause was the army's resentment at the ever-expanding exercise of the Long Parliament's judicial powers, which were used to impose allegedly arbitrary punishments, especially on soldiers and their Leveller allies. Parliament's victims resented the "check" that the assembly exerted on "the regulated course of justice" and condemned the "gross mistake" of "confounding the legislative power with the power judicial."[73] The idea of judicial independence was as yet articulated only occasionally, perhaps because alongside the resentment there lay a contrasting sentiment that saw safeguards of liberty in Parliament's status as the highest court in the land and in the function of the House of Lords as a court of appeal.[74] Even so, the swelling of parliamentary power on that and other fronts made the legislature vulnerable to the language that was used against the king. It became all the more so when the monarchy was succeeded by the unfettered powers of the Rump Parliament and by its monopolist constitutional claims.

The Rump was an uneasy coalition, many of whose members had accepted the abolition of kingship only from necessity. They recognized that in any lasting settlement, the improvised arrangements of its rule would have to yield to fresh dispositions. In 1650–51, the future Quaker Isaac Penington published two pamphlets that were critical of the Rump Parliament even though he was a son of one of its members. The first, in February 1650, warned the Rump that, "having nothing to check it," it risked "arbitrary rule" and might become "the greatest oppression."[75] The second, in May 1651, raised the related subject of the separation of powers. It urged "a clear distinction between the administrative or executive power, and the legislative," "the one not intermixing or intermeddling with the other." Under the monarchy, "How prone was the administrative power to entrench upon the bounds of the legislative, and how afflictive did it become thereby! Is not the legislative power as prone to entrench upon the administrative? And in doing so, is it not likely to prove as afflictive?" In 1786, in the same spirit, a gazetteer in America remarked that "at the commencement of the Revolution, it was supposed that what was called the executive part of the government was the only dangerous part; but we see now that quite as much mischief, if not more, may be done, and as much arbitrary conduct acted, by a legislature."[76]

Constitutional checks were undesirable to supporters of the Rump's powers. Perhaps it was in response to Penington that the Rump's defender John Dury asserted in 1651 that "the legislative and executive power doth primarily belong to parliament" and commended the absence of "any controlment or check" on the Rump. Dury also provides an alternative perspective to Nedham's charge of 1654 that the Rump had lacked a "balance" to its power, for under its rule, Dury was glad to observe, "the scales" are "so fully cast on one side, that there is no power left on the other."[77] There is no sign that Penington's tracts aroused much public interest. But the second of them did attract one approving reader: Nedham. Four months after its publication, he took silently ideas and phrases from it in developing the notion of the separation of powers,[78] to which, in 1654, he would attach the language of checking and balancing in *A True State*. In October 1651, writing in the Rump's employment but standing in a murky and ambiguous relation to its conflicted counsels, he briefly broached the subject of separation in one of the weekly editorials of his newsbook, *Mercurius Politicus*. Characteristically drawing on a historical parallel, he approvingly noted that republican Rome had divided the "making of laws," which was "reserved to the grand assemblies," from "the managing of state-affairs," which had been allocated to the senate.[79]

At this stage, Nedham proposed separation as a maxim of prudence. Nine months later, in an editorial of July 1652, he made it a maxim of liberty: in all "kingdoms and states whatsoever, where they have had any thing of freedom among them, the legislative and executive powers have been managed in distinct hands." With tactical adjustments of wording, Nedham from the same editorial of 1652 took the passage of *A True State* that Vile cited as a significant moment in the evolution of the doctrine of separation. Yet by 1654, Nedham's position had moved on. In 1652, when he was in the Rump's employment, he suggested only a separation of personnel and function, not the division of sovereignty that he would vindicate in *A True State*. Whereas Penington had called for a large degree of executive independence, Nedham's 1652 editorial cautiously represented executive authority as the legislature's appointee and stated that the executive should be "liable to give an account of government to the supreme council of lawmakers," a sentiment that the Parliament of 1654 and Connecticut's Roger Sherman would both have endorsed.[80]

The editorials were reproduced in 1656 as *The Excellencie of a Free-State*, which was republished in 1767. A copy of the later edition was given to John Adams in 1787. He attacked the work in a long section (which he apparently completed by October of the same year) of his *Defence of the Constitutions . . . of the United States*. Although Adams respected Nedham's intelligence, he saw him as an English Turgot, committed, as he indeed is in most of *The Excellencie*, to the concentration of power in a single body. So Adams read with "astonishment" the deviant passage of the editorial of July 1652. The discovery of it did not assuage him. The executive that Nedham there envisaged failed to meet the future president's test for the separation of powers, for its authority was, in Adams's words, "derived from" the legislature. Had Adams known of Nedham's tract of 1654, he might have judged differently, for there, writing for the protectorate rather than for the Rump, Nedham proposed something much closer to the kind of separation Adams wanted.[81]

A *True State* became well known in Nedham's own time.[82] Yet the language of checks and balances could enter the mainstream of political argument only when it moved beyond the world of pamphlets into that of parliamentary debate. It happened when the Instrument of Government was submitted to Parliament in September 1654. "Check" now became a tactical keyword on the government's behalf.[83] We can date the moment. On September 9, five days after the opening of the Parliament, when the Instrument was encountering strong opposition there, a copy of *A True State* was handed to every MP as they entered the chamber.[84] The government had decided to base its argument on Nedham's. Guibon Godard reveals that in the Commons that day, "the court party" invited MPs to distinguish between "the legislative power and the executive power" and pointed to the need for "a check . . . upon a parliament."[85] Two days later, the courtiers urged that Cromwell should have a veto as "a check upon the parliament; something to control it."[86] The conceptual novelty of Nedham's application of "check" is indicated by Godard's unfamiliarity with—perhaps initial puzzlement at—"check" as a term of constitutional discussion. Twice Godard tells us of the courtiers' demand for the protector "to have a check, as they called it," upon Parliament.

Their call was unavailing. On September 12, Cromwell tried to stem the opposition to the Instrument of Government by a forcible purge of the Commons and by addressing the House. If Nedham, in February, had been the first person to apply the words check and balance jointly to constitutional matters, Cromwell now became the second. In the Instrument of Government, his speech claimed, the control of the "militia," which was a bone of sharp contention in the Parliament, is "well and equally placed," as it needed to be if there were to be "a balance at all." For if the protector were denied a share in the militia, what "check" would he have against the "perpetuating of parliaments"? Nedham's tract had warned of the same peril. Cromwell recalls *A True State* again in his claim that "without a check," Parliament would have "liberty to alter the frame of government to aristocracy, to democracy, to anarchy."[87]

Another report of the speech presents Cromwell's reasoning in a more adventurous light. It has him recognizing the need not merely for one power to check and balance another but for rival authorities to check and

balance each other. It was on the checking and balancing of rival powers that the future of the vocabulary would thrive. Cromwell is recorded
as saying that Parliament "ought to have a check upon the protector, to
prevent excesses in him; so on the other hand, the protector ought to have
a check upon the parliament in the business of the militia, to prevent excesses in them." In the Instrument of Government, "the militia being dis-
posed as it is, the one stands as a counter-poise to the other, and renders
the balance of government more even, and the government itself more
firm and stable."[88] If his words are accurately reported, Cromwell might
almost have been reading Montesquieu. The words, and the purge that accompanied them, had their effect. On the day before the purge, MPs had
responded to the courtiers' demand for a "check" on the Commons by asserting that if Parliament were to share its authority with the protector, the
result would be "two supremes, that would always check one the other,
and . . . would never be at peace."[89] Yet nine days after the purge, in an admittedly fleeting mood of compromise, MPs offered to allow the protector
to share "the legislative authority" with Parliament, "with some proviso of
putting checks upon both."[90]

Cromwell, who had no capacity for abstract conceptualization in politics, would not have produced his words of September 12 on his own. His
tutor is not hard to identify. In his speech dissolving the Parliament in
January 1655, the protector explicitly invoked A True State before defending the Instrument of Government as the "most likely" means "to avoid the
extremes of monarchy on the one hand, and democracy on the other" and
to put the government "upon a true and equal balance."[91]

In Cromwell's lifetime no one other than he and Nedham seems to have
brought "check" and "balance" together in any discussion of constitutional
matters. In 1657 Cromwell did so again, this time during his second Parliament, where the Humble Petition and Advice was being debated. Now
he applied the language to a different subject matter. At Philadelphia, the
powers of the president were only one of the subjects to which the concept of checks and balances was applied. Another, bicameralism, had also
arisen in the drafting of the Humble Petition. That new constitution, a further move back toward the prewar one, dropped the Instrument's opening distinction between legislative and executive authority. Even so, one
provision of the document enters our story. The House of Lords had been
abolished in 1649 not, or not primarily, because of principled opposition to
its existence but because most of its members were royalists, a feature that

until the later 1650s restrained even the most moderate parliamentarians from proposing the revival of the upper chamber. When in 1654 Nedham adapted the defense of mixed monarchy that Charles I had propounded twelve years earlier, he quietly substituted the protectoral council for the House of Lords as the aristocratic component of the Instrument of Government.[92] But in 1657, another adopter of the *Answer to the XIX Propositions*, Lord Say and Sele, who had broken with the Cromwellians at the regicide, defended the memory of the House of Lords as "the beam keeping both scales, king and people, in an even posture."[93]

The subject had arisen because the Humble Petition and Advice supplied a second chamber, not the House of Lords, as Say wanted, but an assembly that was merely termed the "Other House." Its members were to be named by the protector and confirmed by Parliament. Shortly before the introduction of the Humble Petition to Parliament, Cromwell had watched that unicameral assembly threatening his treasured principle of liberty of conscience by prosecuting the Quaker James Nayler. The episode, declared Cromwell, showed that the House of Commons "stand in need of a check or balancing power."[94] It was what Nedham had said of the Rump Parliament, which he had rebuked for providing "no manner of balance or check" on Parliament. Cromwell's return to Nedham's formula cloaked a wider motive, for more than the issue of bicameralism was at stake. The power of the executive was also at issue. Through the years of Puritan government, the minds of rulers were divided between the desire to win public consent and the craving for a process of reformation that was unlikely to secure it. Cromwell always knew that parliamentary consent was essential to the establishment of his authority, but he also knew that the electorate's outlook was not his own. His answer in 1657 was to balance an unelected chamber against an elected one. He welcomed the Other House not because of any commitment to bicameralism but as a means by which he could check the legislature from within.

The same approach was turned to a different end after the fall of the protectorate in 1659, when the Rump Parliament returned to power but when the conflict between the claims of consent and reformation persisted. Now that the neo-monarchy of the Cromwells had been removed, bicameralism replaced the question of single rule as the fundamental issue of constitutional debate among England's rulers, with fatal consequences for the Puritan cause. Proposals were made, though they were never implemented, for the creation of a "senate," consisting of "faithful friends" of the "good old cause," as a "balancing-house,"[95] a republican equivalent to Cromwell's

Other House. Perhaps it would also act as an "executive,"[96] perhaps not. In any event, it would "check" the people's representatives—although the rival impulse to subordinate the executive to the legislature endured and the language of checking was cast back at the schemes by supporters of the Rump's unicameral rule.[97] The political fragmentation of 1659–60, when the revolution collapsed, was a fertile period in the evolution of political vocabulary.[98] "Checking" and the combination of "checking" and "balancing" were among the practices of public language that widened.[99] It was also in 1659 that the political thought of James Harrington first aroused widespread interest. His proposals for bicameral assemblies rested on premises about political and economic "balance" that broadened the usage of the word, though advocates and opponents of a balancing senate refused his pleas for nonpartisan attention to the challenges of constitutional architecture even as they exploited his ideas.

Thus did a habit of vocabulary unknown at the start of the civil wars become common by their end. It survived after the Restoration of 1660, when the prewar constitution returned. Yet while the nouns or verbs "check" and "balance" are occasionally found together in constitutional discussion during the reign of Charles II,[100] much less was now heard about balancing than about checking. Especially in the years immediately following the Restoration[101] and during the anti-Whig reaction of the 1680s,[102] royalists and then Tories would recurrently oppose "checks" on the royal prerogative and demand "checks" on parliamentary presumption. After the humiliating reverse of 1660, parliamentarians were slower to demand "checks" on the Crown, but in the 1670s the counter-movement began.[103] However, the language of checking had, for now, little fresh work to do. With idiosyncratic exceptions,[104] it did little more than add a descriptive terminology to a struggle over the prerogative that was essentially a return to the conflict of 1640–42, which had managed without it. Under Cromwell, there had been a legislature as well as an executive to be simultaneously checked and a balance to be struck between them. The febrile polarization of the later Stuart reigns concentrated on one side of the problem: Should the executive be checked or should it not? Parliament now needed to be "checked" only in its own assertions on that subject, not as a rival for the exercise of power.

To attain its eighteenth-century prominence, the language had to be extended beyond its later Stuart usages. It was also extended beyond its Cromwellian ones, for the range of authorities to be balanced was wider in the Hanoverian age than in the 1650s. The principles expounded by Montesquieu and in America were applied to multiple agencies that checked or balanced one or some or all of the others: executive, judiciary, and more than one legislative body. The proper distribution of them came to be thought of as a system, even a machine or a science.[105]

The turning point came in the years around 1700.[106] It was achieved by the cooperation of three writers, John Toland (known for his deist as well as for his political tracts) and the politicians and political thinkers John Trenchard and Walter Moyle.[107] They called, as Nedham had done in comparable wording in A True State, for "a poise and balance between the two extreme contending powers of absolute monarchy and anarchy" and for "a check and curb" on agencies that threatened it.[108] Here was another route toward American thinking, for in calling for "balances and checks" in The Federalist, Hamilton remembered the chaos of republics that were kept "in a state of perpetual vibration between the extremes of tyranny and anarchy."[109] The trio of English writers extolled the native constitution—in its proper form, which they took to be under threat—in the language of mixed constitutionalism that Nedham had deployed in 1654. Yet Nedham had then been answering the claims only of a unicameral Parliament. His three successors, in pleading for "a mutual check and balance" or "an exact balance and proportion," wanted each of the three legislative estates to resist "encroachments" by the other.[110]

In broad terms, the new outlook can be ascribed to the Revolution of 1688, which gradually widened the confrontation of the executive and the legislature into the more elaborate conflicts of a mixed constitution. However, there was a more particular influence. The three authors can loosely be called radical or "country" Whigs. Regarding the gains of 1688 as incomplete and insecure, they were drawn together after the Peace of Ryswick with France in 1697, when the government made the intensely controversial decision to maintain a standing army in peacetime.[111] The resolution threatened what the writers called the "precious jewel liberty" that neighboring nations had lost and that England had hitherto "preserved" by "a due balance between king, the House of Lords, and the House of Commons."[112] The "country" program coupled hostility to standing armies with an antagonism that was more immediately pertinent to the theme of checks and balances: hostility to the swelling ranks of government office holders or "placemen" in the Commons. Their block votes were eroding the independence of that house and making it not a check on the executive but an arm of it, so that it became not the protector of liberty but a danger to it. The influence of placemen seemed to belong to a pattern of erosion of freedom. After 1688, the fear arose of "arbitrary power . . . not under a king alone, for that might receive some check from a parliament standing up stiffly for our laws, but (which is incomparably worse) under the monarchical, aristocratical, and democratical parts of our government; that is, by king, Lords and Commons conspiring to their ruin."[113]

Such complaints had a long life ahead of them on both sides of the Atlantic, for both countries could find it hard to tell whether the greater threat of eighteenth-century tyranny came from the executive or the legislature. What Toland, Trenchard, and Moyle did know was that liberty depended on the separation of the two branches, neither of which must be at the other's mercy. As good Whigs, they were eager to curb the executive. On that front, the straightforward demands that had flourished in the later part of Charles II's reign lived on.[114] Our writers were true to that tradition in stipulating that the nation must "keep the legislative and executive parts asunder" so that "the former may be a check upon the latter."[115] Yet they also returned to the theme of the 1650s that had been absent since then: the checking and balancing of the legislature and the protection of what were now called the executive's "proper channels" and of "those who are entrusted with the administration of the laws."[116] The writers blamed the threat principally on ministers who used their control of Parliament to subjugate the Crown to their interests. For "when the executive power is transferred to the legislature, there is no control, nor can there be a check upon them," the people being "oppressed by their own representatives."[117] So the royal veto was "absolutely necessary to preserve the executive," which must be accorded "all due honour."[118] Such arguments appealed, as they were meant to do, well beyond the country party. Over the eighteenth century, anxieties about monarchical power competed with fears of a "parliamentary yoke."[119]

Where did the three authors find the language of checking and balancing? Their writings dwelt repeatedly on the lessons of mid-seventeenth-century England. Toland in particular was an expert in the field. He studied pamphlets of the period, explored its chronology, and edited the works of Harrington, Sidney, and Milton and the *Memoirs* of the civil war regicide Edmund Ludlow.[120] Published in the radical Whig cause, the editions were designed to give it an ancestry. They appeared in 1698–1700, at the time when the writers were collaborating in the campaign against standing armies, to which they related the editions. Thanks to eighteenth-century republications, the editions were eagerly read in England and America alike.[121] There was, however, a striking omission from the authors Toland edited: Marchamont Nedham. Although his *The Excellencie of a Free-State* would be republished in 1767 by people who also revived Toland's editions, it was not reproduced by Toland himself, even though its rhetorical pleas for liberty were in keeping with the demands of the other texts he edited[122] and even though Nedham was associated in the public mind of the 1690s with other "antimonarchical" authors of the civil wars, including Harrington and Sidney.[123]

The omission is not to be explained by indifference. On the contrary, Toland and his collaborators knew Nedham's writing well and put it to their own uses. Yet their debt to him dared not speak its name and Toland dared not republish him. Nedham remained infamous for his mercenary and mutable allegiances and as a "scurrilous news-monger,"[124] characteristics incompatible with the image of stoic incorruptibility that Toland attached to the authors he edited. There was also a venturesome dimension of popular protest in Nedham's arguments that was at odds with the gentry-oriented country-party philosophy that Toland, as nimble a political and intellectual opportunist as Nedham, sought to foster. So whereas the three writers proclaimed their debts to Harrington and Sidney, they could appropriate Nedham's writings only silently. In 1697, the first of the group's attacks on standing armies appropriated two passages either from his *The Excellencie* or from the editorials of 1651–52 that it reprinted.[125] One of them, the shorter but the more closely related to our theme, supplied the statement of the need to "preserve" the "precious jewel liberty," an injunction that the tract of 1697 links to the necessity of "balance" among the three estates. Toland also used the longer passage, on the virtues of citizen militias, in his *The Militia Reform'd*, a contribution to the same controversy in 1698.[126] Walter Moyle's *Essay upon the Roman Government* likewise silently borrows from the editorials or *The Excellencie*.[127]

Although Toland's, Trenchard's, and Moyle's debt to *The Excellencie* or to the editorials it reproduced is clear, we cannot state firmly that they also knew *A True State of the Case of the Commonwealth*, where Nedham introduced the phrase "balance or check." While *A True State* was the kind of work that Toland picked up in his researches on the civil wars, other parallels of wording between it and works of Toland's circle are not strong enough to prove its influence on them. Yet language so distinctive as that of checking and balancing seems unlikely to have been independently reinvented, at least by writers whom we know to have appropriated other words of the first inventor. Conceivably Toland and the others discovered the combination of the two words in its occasional appearances over the last four decades of the century. Yet it was in the 1650s that the term had previously been conspicuous. Whatever the source of Toland's, Trenchard's, and Moyle's use of the language of checks and balances, it was Nedham and his master Cromwell who had put it into political currency. By extending the sophistication of the arguments Nedham and Cromwell introduced, Toland and his allies bridged them to the premises that would flourish in the eighteenth century and guide the delegates at Philadelphia.

Notes

1. David Wootton, "Liberty, Metaphor, and Mechanism: 'Checks and Balances,'" in *Liberty and American Experience in the Eighteenth Century*, ed. David Womersley (Indianapolis: Liberty Fund, 2006), 209–74. Material in his essay is freshly deployed in David Wootton, *Power, Pleasure and Profit: Insatiable Appetites from Machiavelli to Madison* (Cambridge, MA: Harvard University Press, 2018), 136–53. His and my approaches sometimes overlap. I am grateful to Professor Wootton for his encouragement and to the advice of Jonathan Gienapp and Ben Lowe as I prepared this chapter.

2. James Madison, *Notes of Debates in the Federal Convention of 1787 Reported by James Madison* (Athens: Ohio University Press, 1985), 63 (for comparable perceptions, see 464); James Madison, Alexander Hamilton, and John Jay, *The Federalist Papers*, ed. Isaac Kramnick (London: Penguin, 1987), 74; Philip B. Kurland and Ralph Lerner, eds., *The Founders' Constitution*, 5 vols. (Chicago: University of Chicago Press, 1987), 4:106; Joseph H. Ellis, *Passionate Sage: The Character and Legacy of John Adams* (New York: Norton, 1994), 170; Ron Chernow, *Washington: A Life* (London: Penguin, 2001), 710; Eric Nelson, *The Royalist Revolution: Monarchy and the American Founding* (Cambridge, MA: Harvard University Press, 2014), 136. Although the Cromwellian constitutional arrangements were reprinted in volumes known to American politicians—*The Parliamentary or Constitutional History of England* or "Old Parliamentary History" and the *Memorials* of Bulstrode Whitelocke—no one thought to cite them at Philadelphia. It is true that the writings of participants in the Cromwellian conflict—John Milton, Algernon Sidney, James Harrington, Henry Neville—were widely read in eighteenth-century America, but those men were eloquent critics of Cromwellian tyranny. See Blair Worden, "Harrington's *Oceana*: Origins and Aftermath, 1651–1660"; Blair Worden, "Republicanism and the Restoration, 1660–1683," both in *Republicanism, Liberty, and Commercial Society, 1649–1776*, ed. David Wootton (Stanford, CA: Stanford University Press, 1994), 111–38 and 139–96, respectively; and Blair Worden, *Literature and Politics in Cromwellian England: John Milton, Andrew Marvell, Marchamont Nedham* (Oxford: Oxford University Press, 2007), 105–115 and 289–358. In America, as in England, there was, it is true, occasional eighteenth-century admiration for or ambivalence toward Cromwell and his deeds.

3. The texts are reproduced in S. R. Gardiner, ed., *Constitutional Documents of the Puritan Revolution* (Oxford: Oxford University Press, 1889), 405–17, 457–64.

4. David Hume, *The History of England*, 6 vols. (Philadelphia: Robert Campbell, 1795–1796), 5:311–12.

5. On its composition, see Blair Worden, "Oliver Cromwell and the Instrument of Government," in *The Nature of the English Revolution Revisited*, ed. Stephen Taylor and Grant Tapsell (Woodridge, UK: Boydell and Brewer, 2013), chapter 6.

6. Gardiner, *Constitutional Documents*, lvi.

7. J. T. Rutt, ed., *Diary of Thomas Burton*, 4 vols. (London: Henry Colburn, 1828), 1:xxviii.

8. Donald Pennington, "The Making of the War, 1640–1642," in *Puritans and Revolutionaries*, ed. Donald Pennington and Keith Thomas (Oxford: Clarendon Press, 1978), 161–85; Michael Mendle, "The Great Council of Parliament and the First Ordinances: The Constitutional History of the Civil War," *Journal of British Studies* 31, no. 2 (1992): 133–62. See also Michael Mendle, *Henry Parker and the English Civil War* (Cambridge: Cambridge University Press, 1995).

9. John Morrill, *The Revolt of the Provinces* (London: Longman, 1976).

10. I describe its rule in Blair Worden, *The Rump Parliament: 1648–1653* (Cambridge: Cambridge University Press, 1977).

11. W. C. Abbott, *The Writings and Speeches of Oliver Cromwell*, 4 vols. (Cambridge, MA: Harvard University Press, 1937–1947), 1:540.

12. Rutt, *Diary of Thomas Burton*, 4:61; Bulstrode Whitelocke, *Memorials of the English Affairs* (London: Nathaniel Ponder, 1682), 257.

13. I have written about him in Blair Worden, "'Wit in a Roundhead': The Dilemma of Marchamont Nedham," in *Political Culture and Cultural Politics in Early Modern England*, ed. Susan D. Amussen and Mark Kishlansky (Manchester, UK: Manchester University Press, 1995), 301–37; Worden, *Literature and Politics in Cromwellian England*; and Marchamont Nedham, *The Excellencie of a Free-State: Or, the Right Constitution of a Commonwealth*, ed. Blair Worden, (Indianapolis: Liberty Fund, 2011).

14. J. A. W. Gunn, *Politics and the Public Interest in the Seventeenth Century* (London: Routledge, 1969), 33–35, 43–44, 52.

15. Marchamont Nedham, *The Case of the Commonwealth of England, Stated*, ed. Philip A. Knachel (Charlottesville: University Press of Virginia, 1969).

16. Worden, *Liberty, Republicanism, and Commercial Society*, 45–81.

17. Blair Worden, "Oliver Cromwell and the Cause of Civil and Religious Liberty," in *England's Wars of Religion, Revisited*, ed. Charles W.A. Prior and Glenn Burgess (Farnham, UK: Ashgate, 2011), 231–51; and Blair Worden, *God's Instruments: Political Conduct in the England of Oliver Cromwell* (New York: Oxford University Press, 2012), 313–54.

18. M. J. C. Vile, *Constitutionalism and the Separation of Powers*, 2nd ed. (Indianapolis: Liberty Fund, 1998), 3. Nedham's role in the formulation of the separation of powers is also recognized in F. D. Wormuth, *The Origins of Modern Constitutionalism* (New York: Harper, 1949); William B. Gwyn, *The Meaning of the Separation of Powers: An Analysis of the Doctrine from its Origin to the Adoption of the United States Constitution* (New Orleans, LA: Tulane University Press, 1965). See also J. H. Burns, "Regimen Medium: Executive Power in Early-Modern Political Thought," *History of Political Thought*, 29, no. 2 (2008), 213–29, at 224–25; and Wootton, "Liberty, Metaphor and Mechanism," 243–44.

19. Marchamont Nedham, *A True State of the Case of the Commonwealth* (London: Thomas Newcomb, 1654), 10.

20. James Madison, "General View of the Powers Conferred by the Constitution," no. 47 in Madison, Hamilton, and Jay, *Federalist Papers*, 303.

21. Nedham, *A True State of the Case of the Commonwealth*, 51. The separation and the mixture of powers may sound like opposing principles and they have sometimes been at odds in practice, as happened in America. See Gordon S. Wood, "The American Revolution," in *The Cambridge History of Eighteenth-Century Political Thought*, ed. Mark Goldie and Robert Wokler (Cambridge: Cambridge University Press, 2006), 601–25, at 623–24. As a rule, however, they are companions, for both have the concentration of power as their enemy. The principle of mixed constitutionalism was invoked against both royal absolutism and the Rump Parliament and was opposed by supporters of those concentrated authorities. Mixture, it is true, inherently qualifies separation. Yet without separation there is nothing to mix. The designers of the Instrument and the Constitution separated powers and then arranged their mixture.

22. Paul Rapin de Thoyras, *The History of England*, 15 vols. (London: James and John Knapton, 1726–31), 12:542; Hume, *The History of England*, 5:18, 46, 64, 93; Kurland and Lerner, *The Founders' Constitution*, 2:24 (for Blackstone).

23. Paul Rapin de Thoyras, *The History of Whig and Tory*, translated by Thomas Ozell (London: S. Baker, 1718), 27; Rapin de Thoyras, *The History of England*, 13:2; Henry Lord Bolingbroke, *A Dissertation upon Parties* (London: H. Haines, 1735), 20, 23. For American perceptions, see Madison, *Notes of Debates*, 251; Jonathan Elliot, ed., *The Debates in the Several State Conventions*, 4 vols. (Washington: Printed for the Editor, 1836–45), 2:319; John Adams, *A Defence of the Constitutions of Government of the United States of America*, 3 vols. (London: C. Dilly, 1787–88), 3:484; and Nelson, *The Royalist Revolution*, 146–49, 171.

24. Nelson, *The Royalist Revolution*, 3, 38, 45, 52, 61, 152, 157, 159–60, 190.

25. James Wilson, *Considerations on the Nature and Extent of the Legislative Authority of the British Parliament* (Philadelphia: W. and T. Bradford, 1774), 10.

26. Elliot, *Debates in the Several State Conventions*, 2:404.

27. Madison, *Notes of Debates*, 251, 464–65; cf. Gouverneur Morris's remark on p. 464.

28. The Leveller John Lilburne maintained in 1649 that the Rump Parliament was taking advantage of that "perpetual Act" to establish "an arbitrary power, without bounds, limits, check, or control." John Lilburne, *Strength Out of Weaknesse* (London, 1649), 11. Lilburne frequently called for "checks" on tyranny and opposed "checks" on liberty but did not use the word with constitutional formulas in mind.

29. Nelson, *The Royalist Revolution*, 171.

30. Wilson, *Considerations on the Nature and Extent of the Legislative Authority of the British Parliament*, 10.

31. Nedham, *A True State of the Case of the Commonwealth*, 10, 35.

32. Nedham, *A True State of the Case of the Commonwealth*, 4.

33. The topic occupied four days of discussion in the parliament of 1654, even in the first round of debates, which was held in "grand committee," a procedural device also adopted at Philadelphia. Rutt, *Diary of Thomas Burton*, 1:xliii, xlvi.

34. Worden, *God's Instruments*, 284.

35. See especially Gardiner, *Constitutional Documents*, 334. Although Americans spoke disparagingly of a "levelling spirit" in their country, sometimes even of "the Levellers," they are likely to have known little if anything of the seventeenth-century English Levellers; see Blair Worden, *Roundhead Reputations: The English Civil Wars and the Passions of Posterity* (London: Penguin, 2001), chapter 12.

36. The Instrument implemented the army's long-held wish to overhaul the electoral system (Worden, *The Rump Parliament*, chapter 8). The subject had provoked debates about the proper distribution of constituencies—for example, whether the level of population or the level of taxation should be the basis of apportionment—that have analogies at Philadelphia.

37. Another early apologia for the new regime explained that the council would be an effective "check" on protectoral power, see Johannes Cornubiensis, *The Grand Catastrophe* (London: R. I., 1654), 12.

38. Cornubiensis, *The Grand Catastrophe*, 28–29.

39. Madison, *Notes of Debates*, 46.

40. William Prynne, *The Soveraigne Power of Parliaments* (London: Michael Sparke, 1643), 39.

41. Richard Overton, *An Arrow against All Tyrants* (London: Martin Claw-Clergy, 1646), 11–12. Until 1649, the picture was complicated by the role of the king both as the executive authority and as one of the estates of the legislature. The framers of the Instrument showed their traditionalist instincts in investing "the supreme legislative authority" in "one person, and the people assembled in parliament." That phrasing contrasts with the allocation by the Constitution of "all legislative power" to Congress, though the divergence is not discernibly responsible for any practical difference between the proctectoral and the presidential powers. What the "supreme legislative authority" invested by the Instrument was supreme over was perhaps an intentionally moot point, for ambiguity was a hallmark of Cromwellian verbal formulas.

42. Abbott, *The Writings and Speeches of Oliver Cromwell*, 3:459.

43. Nedham, *A True State of the Case of the Commonwealth*, 11.

44. Rutt, *Diary of Thomas Burton*, 1:25.

45. *A Representation concerning the Late Parliament* (London, 1654), 21.

46. Gardiner, *Constitutional Documents*, lviii–lx, 427–37.

47. Rutt, *Diary of Thomas Burton*, 1:xxxii, 3:142; Alan Cromartie, *Sir Matthew Hale, 1609–1676: Law, Religion and Natural Philosophy* (Cambridge: Cambridge University Press, 1995), 79. The lawyer-MP Bulstrode Whitelocke, writing long after the event, stated that in a conversation of November 1652, Cromwell told him that kingship needed to be restored as a "check" on the "exorbitances" of the Rump. Whitelocke, *Memorials of the English Affairs*, 524. This is possible, but Whitelocke's account is characteristically colored by retrospect. It seems more likely that he was conflating the discussion he recorded with events of 1654, when he, like his fellow lawyer Hale, was a prominent figure in Parliament; see Worden, *God's Instruments*, 337n.

48. Rutt, *Diary of Thomas Burton*, 1:cvvvii (from the journal of the House of Commons, January 10, 1655); Abbott, *The Writings and Speeches of Oliver Cromwell*, 3:581.

49. Developments in phraseology—which in any case are an incomplete guide to developments in thought—can never be fully recovered. While I have confidence in the outline of the picture of evolution presented in this chapter, there may be much that I have missed, for even in an age when so many documents can be digitally searched (though also when so many cannot), the range of any reader will be limited. Breadth of textual acquaintance is not an interpreter's only challenge. Fluidity and variety of terminology can elude recovery. No abstract term will have quite the same resonance in one age as in another, and anyway we only have the evidence of the written word to go on, not of the spoken one (although, unless on a subject too dangerous for written commentary, which that of checks and balances should not ordinarily have been) we would expect concepts familiar in conversation to appear on the page also.

50. Wootton, "Liberty, Metaphor, and Mechanism," 243–47.

51. *His Majesties Answer to the XIX Propositions* (London: Leonard Lichfield, 1642), 9.

52. *Speeches and Passages of this Great and Happy Parliament* (London, 1641), 16; Thomas Fannant, *A True Relation of that Memorable Parliament* (London, 1641), 7; *The Humble Petition of the Wretched, and most Contemptible, the Poore Commons of England* (London: Printed for E. P. and E. B., 1642), 7; *Londons Desire and Direction* (London: Printed for T. I., 1642), 3; Sir Robert Cotton and Sir John Hayward, *The Histories of the Lives and Raignes of Henry the Third, and Henry the Fourth, Kings of England* (London: Printed for William Sheares, 1642), 41; George Eglisham, *The Fore-Runner of Revenge* (London, 1642), 5. See also Sir William Constantine, *The Interest of England* (London: E. Griffen, 1642), 29.

53. Henry Parker, *The Case of Shipmony* (1640), 7, quoted in Jonathan Gienapp, *The Second Creation: Fixing the American Constitution in the Founding Era* (Cambridge, MA: Harvard University Press, 2018), 25. For "beam," see "beam," n.1, entry 6a, *OED Online*, June 2020, Oxford University Press.

54. *Speeches and Passages of this Great and Happy Parliament*, 408. Under Elizabeth I, Sir Philip Sidney had castigated rulers who thought in perversely inharmonious terms: they "make themselves (as it were) another thing from the people; and so count it gain what they can get from them: and (as if it were two counter-balances, that their estate goes highest when the people goes lowest) by a fallacy of argument" think themselves "most kings, when the subject is most basely subjected." Sidney, *The Countesse of Pembrokes Arcadia* (London: John Windet, 1590), 128.

55. Henry Parker, *Observations upon Some of His Majesties Late Answers and Expresses* (London, 1642), 31.

56. For political examples, see John Rushworth, *Historical Collections* (London: Thomas Newcomb, 1659), 248, 260, 419, and appendix, p. 8; Marchamont Nedham, *A Check to the Checker of Britannicus* (London: Andrew Coe, 1644).

57. Nedham, *The Excellencie of a Free-State*, 109–10.

58. Nedham, *A True State of the Case of the Commonwealth*, 10.

59. John Trenchard and Thomas Gordon, *Cato's Letters*, 4 vols. (London: W. Wilkins, T. Woodward, J. Walthoe, and J. Peele, 1724), 1:268, 2:258.

60. Quoted in Wootton, *Power, Pleasure, and Profit*, 142.

61. David Womersley, ed., *Writings on Standing Armies* (Indianapolis: Liberty Fund, 2020), 259, 262.

62. Madison, *Notes of Debates*, 233, 272.

63. The balance of trade was an established principle by the 1620s, even though Thomas Mun's famous exposition *England's Treasure by Forraign Trade, or, The Balance of our Forraign Trade is the Rule of Our Treasure* appeared only posthumously, in 1664. See Thomas Mun, *A Discourse of Trade* (London: Nicholas Okes, 1621), 27; Edward Misselden, *The Circle of Commerce: Or, the Ballance of Trade in Defence of Free Trade* (London: John Dawson, 1623).

64. Henri duc de Rohan, *A Treatise of the Interest of the Princes and States of Christendom* (Paris: Thomas Broun, 1640), 14, 19.

65. Wootton, *Power, Pleasure, and Profit*, 145.

66. John Trenchard, *The Thoughts of a Member of the Lower House* (London: J. Roberts, 1719), 6–7.

67. Joshua Sprigge, *Anglia Rediviva* (London: R. W. for John Partridge, 1647), sig. B2. There is a comparable use of "balance" in the same year in Nathaniel Bacon, *An Historicall Discourse of the Uniformity of the Government of England* (London: Mathew Walbancke, 1647), 215–16. Bacon found balance a useful metaphor on a range of subjects.

68. Cf. Worden, *Literature and Politics in Cromwellian England*, 183.

69. *The Declaration of the Armie under His Excellency Sir Thomas Fairfax, as It Was Lately Presented at Saffron Walden* (London, 1647), 4; *A Declaration of His Excellency Sir Thomas Fairfax, and his Councell of Warre, on Behalfe of Themselves and the Whole Armie; Shewing the Grounds of Their Present Advance towards the City of London* (London: George Whittington, 1647), 5; *A Cleere and Full Vindication of the late Proceedings of the Armie under the Conduct of his Excellencie Sir Thomas Fairfax* (London: William Larnar, 1647), 10.

70. *A Word to Lieut. Gen. Cromwell* (London, 1647), 31.

71. *A Remonstrance of His Excellency Thomas Lord Fairfax, Lord Generall of the Parliaments forces, and of the Generall Councell of Officers Held at St Albans the 16. of November* (London: John Partridge and George Whittington, 1648), 16; *The Peoples Friends* (London: 1648), 4. See also John Geree, *Siniorragia the Sifters Sieve Broken* (London: Christopher Meredith, 1648), 115.

72. *A Declaration of the House of Commons Assembled in Parliament, Expressing Their Reasons for the Adnulling and Vacating of Those Ensuing Votes* (London: Edward Husband, 1649), 11.

73. *A Declaration, or Representation from His Excellency, Sir Thomas Fairfax, and the Army under his Command Humbly Tendred to the Parliament, Concerning the Iust and Fundamentall Rights and Liberties* (London: George Whittington, 1647), 11, 13.

74. By 1648, an MP had precociously identified a tripartite division between legislative, "governing," and judicial power; see Clement Walker, *The History of Independency* (London, 1648), 150–53; and Max Radin, "The Doctrine of the Separation of Powers in Seventeenth Century Controversies," *University of Pennsylvania Law Review* 86 (1937–38): 851–57. More commonly, judicial power was equated with "executive" power, for the executive's function was (and would long be) perceived as the implementation of

laws passed by the legislature. The difficulty, evident in America as in England, was that legislatures do more than pass laws and executives do more than execute them. The consequent problem, and perhaps the arbitrariness, of determining the frontiers between executive and legislative power may be seen from a comparison of the Constitution with Walker, *History of Independency*, 151. Powers that Walker accuses the legislature of having usurped are vested in it by the Constitution. Writers proposing constitutional arrangements, from the Levellers to Harrington to Madison, hesitated to define the functions and powers of the executive, which the unexpectedness of events places beyond the predictive science of constitutional design. Nedham, seeing that problem with "executive," sometimes used alternative phrasing; he referred to the government's responsibilities for "mysteries of state" (the old notion of *arcana imperii*; see Burns, "Regimen Medium," 224) and for "administration" (see Nedham, *The Excellencie of a Free-State*, 109; and Nedham, *A True State of the Case of the Commonwealth*, 11, 23). The second term, which he may have picked up from Isaac Penington, is used in clause 2 of the Instrument, perhaps at Nedham's suggestion. Another common formulation was "governing" (as in Walker) or "gubernative" (most influentially in Philip Hunton, *A Treatise of Monarchy* [London: John Bellamy and Ralph Smith, 1645], 5). Until a late stage in the composition of the Instrument, Cromwell was to have been called "governor," the term Hamilton proposed at Pennsylvania. Perhaps "protector" and "president" sounded less threatening. The application of "executive" or "administrative" (or "ministerial") to political structures appears to have been an extension of their ecclesiological usages (cf. Burns, "Regimen Medium," 213–14), which can be commonly found in the 1640s.

75. Isaac Penington, *A Word for the Common Weale* (London: Charles Sumptner, 1650), 10.

76. Quoted in Kramnick's introduction to Madison, Hamilton, and Jay, *Federalist Papers*, 27.

77. John Dury, *Conscience Eased* (London: T. H., 1651), 6; Dury, *The Reformed Spirituall Husbandman* (London: Richard Wodenothe, 1652), 23.

78. Phrases: compare Penington, *Fundamental Right*, 6 ("avoiding of that corruption which standing pools are subject to") with Nedham, *A True State of the Case of the Commonwealth*, 36 ("corrupt like standing pools"); and *Fundamental Right*, 9 ("Parliaments are great bodies, and consequently slow in motion") with *A True State*, 24 ("those great moliminous bodies of parliaments are but slow in motion").

79. Nedham, *The Excellencie of a Free-State*, 15, 135. Nedham was feeling his way toward the bicameralist principles that James Harrington would expound later in the decade.

80. Nedham, *The Excellencie of a Free-State*, 109–10.

81. For Adams's reading of Nedham's text see Nedham, *The Excellencie of a Free-State*, lxxxvi–xcv. Adams exaggerated the impact of Nedham's tract in America (xciii–xcvi), though it may have affected some readers (e.g., James Madison, xcv) through Adams's extensive quotations from it.

82. *Representation of the Late Parliament*, 19; Philolethus Philomystes, *A Petition Humbly presented to His Hignesse the Lord Protector* (London, 1654), 2; William Prynne, *The First and Second Part of a Seasonable . . . Vindication* (London, 1655), sig. I; Michael

Hawke, *Killing Is Murder* (London, 1657), 3; William Prynne, *Concordia Discors* (London: Edward Thomas, 1659), 12; sig. I; William Prynne, *A True and Perfect Narrative* (London: Edward Thomas, 1659), 14, 60; Roger L'Estrange, *Considerations and Proposals* (London: Printed by A. C., 1663), 14. In 1654, Nedham's imitator John Streater drew on the tract in *Observations Historical, Political, and Philosophical* (N.p.: n.p., June 27–July 4, 1654), 83, as did Nedham's close associate John Hall, in *Confusion Confounded* (London: Henry Hills, 1654), 20. See also *A Memento for the People: About Their Elections of Members for the Approaching Parliament* (London: Printed for Rich. Moone, 1654), 1.

83. Perhaps the prominent MP John Lambert, the architect of the Instrument and Cromwell's leading councilor, played a part. In subsequent parliaments, he made his own uses of the language of checking and of balancing. See Rutt, *Diary of Thomas Burton*, 1:281, 3:189.

84. *A Perfect Diurnall; or, Ocurrences* (N.p.: n.p., September 4–11, 1654), 152; *A Perfect Account of the Daily Intelligence* (N.p.: n.p., September 6–13, 1654), 1535.

85. Rutt, *Diary of Thomas Burton*, 1:xxvii–xxvii.

86. Rutt, *Diary of Thomas Burton*, 1:xxviii, xxxii.

87. Abbott, *The Writings and Speeches of Oliver Cromwell*, 3:459–60.

88. *A Declaration of the Proceedings of His Highness the Lord Protector; with His Reasons Touching the late Change and Revolution in Parliament* (London: R. Wood, 1654), 5; see also *The Declaration of the Free and Well-Affected People of England Now in Arms* (London, 1655), 1. It is an indication of the flexibility of the word that both common parlance and Cromwell himself described the purge of September 12 as a "check"; see Abbott, *The Writings and Speeches of Oliver Cromwell*, 3:580; *A Representation concerning the Late Parliament*, 7; *A Looking-Glasse for, or an Awakening Word to, the Superiour and Inferiour Officers* (London: 1656), 7.

89. Rutt, *Diary of Thomas Burton*, 1:xxix.

90. Rutt, *Diary of Thomas Burton*, 1:xl. For other uses of "check" recorded by Godard, see 1:lv, cvi.

91. Abbott, *The Writings and Speeches of Oliver Cromwell*, 3:587–88.

92. Nedham, *A True State of the Case of the Commonwealth*, 51.

93. C. H. Firth, ed., "A Letter from Lord Saye and Sele to Lord Wharton," *English Historical Review* 10, no. 37 (1895): 106–7.

94. Abbott, *The Writings and Speeches of Oliver Cromwell*, 4:417.

95. *A Negative Voyce: or, A Check for Your Check: Being a Message of Non-Concurrence for the Ballancing-House, or Co-ordinate Senate* (London, 1659).

96. Henry Stubbe, *A Letter to an Officer of the Army Concerning a Select Senate* (London: T. B., 1660), 75; cf. 8.

97. *The Humble Petition and Address of the Officers of the Army . . . May 12* (London: Henry Hills, 1659), 10–11; *The Armies Declaration Examined and Compared* (London, 1659), 24; *The Grand Concernments of England Ensured* (London, 1659), 22, 23, 65; cf. Sir Henry Vane, *A Healing Question Propounded* (London: Printed for T. Brewster, 1656), 18.

98. Worden, *God's Instruments*, 308, 343.

99. For the combination, see, e.g., Christopher Feake, *A Faithfull Searching Home Word* (London, 1659), 24; Stubbe, *A Letter to an Officer of the Army Concerning a Select Senate*, 73–77; *A Letter to His Excellency the Lord General Monck* (London, 1660), 1.

100. Abraham-Nicolas Amelot de La Houssaie, *The History of the Government of Venice* (London: H. C. for John Starkey, 1677), 170 (where the terms are introduced into an English translation of a French work where they are not paralleled: la Houssaie, *Histoire du Governement de Venise* [Amsterdam, 1695], 202–3); Bartholomew Lane, *The Prerogative of the Monarchs of Great Brittain Asserted* (London, William Bateman, 1684), 57. The words were occasionally linked outside politics too: e.g., *A Free Conference Touching the Present State of England* (London, E. T. for R. Royston, 1668); Slingsby Bethel, *The Present Interest of England* (London: Printed for D. B., 1671), 29.

101. James Howell, *Divers Historicall Discourses* (London: J. Grismond, 1661), 98; John Allington, *The Period of the Grand Conspiracy* (London: J. Grismond, 1663), 8; George Morley, *A Sermon Preached at the Magnificent Coronation* (London, R. Norton, 1661), 13; David Jones, *The Secret History of Whitehall* (London: R. Baldwin, 1697), 5.

102. Laurence Womock, *Suffragium Protestantium* (London: Robert Clavel, 1683), 193; George Mackenzie, *Jus Regium* (London: R. Chiswel, 1684), 42, 45, 108; Thomas Long, *The Original of War* (London, J. C. and F. Collins for Daniel Brown, 1684), 25; Nathaniel Johnston, *The Excellency of Monarchical Government* (London: T. B. for Robert Clavel, 1686), 140, 142, 305. Cf. Abednego Seller, *The History of Passive Obedience since the Reformation* (London: Theodore Johnson, 1689), 87, 108; and William Sherlock, *The Case of Resistance* (London: Fincham Gardiner, 1684), 162–63.

103. *A Letter from a Parliament Man to His Friend, Concerning the Proceedings of the House of Commons This Last Sessions* (London, 1675), 3; Andrew Marvell, *An Account of the Rise and Growth of Arbitrary Government* (Amsterdam, 1678), 144; William Penn, *England's Great Interest* (London, 1679), 1; Thomas Rymer, *A General Draught and Prospect* (London: Thomas Benskin, 1681), sig. A3 and pages 38, 45, 59. See also *The Nations Agrievance* (London, 1679), 3; and Algernon Sidney, *Discourses concerning Government* (London, 1698) (but written in the early 1680s), 354, 377, 459. But the Harringtonian Henry Neville, one of the minority among proponents of mixed constitutionalism who opposed the separation of powers, thought the use of constitutional machinery to "check" a king a "sullen device"; Henry Neville, *Plato Redivivus* (London: Printed for S. I., 1681), 261.

104. Sir John Pettus, *The Constitution of Parliaments* (London, Thomas Basset, 1680), 10; [Denzil Holles?], *The Case Stated of the Jurisdiction of the House of Lords* (London, 1676), 5, 98–101. See also Johnston, *Excellency of Monarchical Government*, 44, 52, 67.

105. Wootton, "Liberty, Metaphor, and Mechanism."

106. Wootton, "Liberty, Metaphor, and Mechanism," 216–19, 237–38.

107. Although they did not always speak with one voice, they so often agree and so often echo each other's words that the individual attribution of anonymous pamphlets from their pens can be impossible.

108. *The Danger of Mercenary Parliaments* (London, 1698), 1.

109. Alexander Hamilton, "The Union as a Safeguard Against Domestic Faction and Insurrection," no. 9 in Madison, Hamilton, and Jay, *Federalist Papers*, 118–19; cf. Max Farrand, ed., *The Records of the Federal Convention of 1787*, 3 vols. (New Haven, CT: Yale University Press, 1911), 2:432.

110. John Toland, *The Art of Governing by Parties* (London: B. Lintott, 1701), 31–33; John Toland, *Dunkirk or Dover* (London: A. Baldwin, 1713), 9. The danger of "encroach-

ments" by one power upon another had been a refrain of Nedham's *The Excellencie of a Free-State*.

111. Worden, *Roundhead Reputations*, chapter 3.

112. Womersley, *Writings on Standing Armies*, 11–12; cf. *Danger of Mercenary Parliaments*, 1.

113. *The Humble Petition of the Common People of England* (London, 1693), 8.

114. Francis Carswell, *England's Restoration* (London: Awnsham Churchill, 1689), 21; *A Collection of Speeches of the Right Honourable Henry late Earl of Warrington* (London: Printed for Richard Baldwin, 1694), 10; cf. *A Letter Out of the Country to a Member of This Present Parliament Occasioned by a Late Letter* (London, 1689), 4.

115. *Free Thoughts concerning Officers in the House of Commons* (London: 1698), 4; Womersley, *Writings on Standing Armies*, 262.

116. *Danger of Mercenary Parliaments*, 1; Womersley, *Writings on Standing Armies*, 263.

117. *The Whole Works of Walter Moyle* (London: J. Knapton, A. Bettesworth, E. Curll, J. Pemberton, and J. Batley, 1727), 56–57; see also *Considerations upon the Choice of a Speaker* (London, 1698), 5.

118. *Free Thoughts concerning Officers*, 4; *Danger of Mercenary Parliaments*, 1.

119. Mark Goldie, "The English System of Liberty," in *Cambridge History of Eighteenth-Century Political Thought*, ed. Mark Goldie and Robert Wokler (Cambridge: Cambridge University Press, 2006), 40–78, at 40–42, 64, 70.

120. Worden, *Roundhead Reputations*, chapter 2.

121. Nedham, *The Excellencie of a Free-State*, lxii–lxiv.

122. Nedham, *The Excellencie of a Free-State*, lxvii–lxxxiii.

123. Matthew Prior, *State-Poems* (London, 1697), 20; *Remarks upon the Most Eminent of Our Antimonarchical Authors* (London, 1699), 501, 522, 523, 552; cf. Thomas Beverley, *Evangelical Repentance* (London: R. Smith, 1693), 102.

124. William Nicolson, *The English Historical Library* (London: Timothy Childe, 1699), 124.

125. If Toland knew only the editorials, he might have seen an added difficulty in republishing Nedham, for their form would have presented practical difficulties to a publisher. (In my edition of *The Excellencie of a Free-State*, I assumed that Nedham was responsible for the reappearance of the editorials there and for the preface that precedes them, but I now think it possible that the work of 1656 was prepared for publication without his involvement, though if so he may still have connived at it.)

126. Nedham, *The Excellencie of a Free-State*, lviii–lix, 9, 10; Womersley, *Writings on Standing Armies*, 12, 16.

127. Compare Caroline Robbins, ed., *Two Republican Tracts* (London: Cambridge University Press, 1969), 240 ("tribunes, sacred and unalterable") with Nedham, *The Excellencie of a Free-State*, 13 ("tribunes . . . sacred and inviolable") and 88 ("sacred . . . tribunes"). The preceding pages of Moyle's tract contain a number of correspondences to Nedham's arguments and wording.

3

Party and Faction in Eighteenth-Century Political Thought from Montesquieu to Madison

MAX SKJÖNSBERG

In *On Revolution* (1963), Hannah Arendt wrote that James Madison's appreciation of the politics of party was a "flagrant contradiction to classical tradition, to which the Founding Fathers otherwise paid the closest attention."[1] In Federalist No. 10, Madison argued that "party and faction in government correspond to the many voices and differences in opinion which must continue 'as long as the reason of man continues fallible, and he is at liberty to exercise it.'"[2] In Federalist No. 50, Madison was even more unequivocal: an exclusion of parties in the state "ought to be neither presumed nor desired; because an extinction of parties necessarily implies either a universal alarm for the public safety, or an absolute extinction of liberty."[3] Arendt argued that the Founding Fathers did not invent anything new but rather sought to master and apply the best existing political theory available to them.[4] In this essay, I will situate some of the founders' takes on party against the backdrop of the eighteenth-century debate in Europe about internecine discord.[5] This context is as important as classical republicanism for understanding the party question in the early American republic. Machiavelli of the Florentine Renaissance continued to hold a position of prominence in the political imagination of the founders and early American presidents, particularly (and significantly) John Adams. Classical republicanism, however, was largely something they wanted to transcend rather than resurrect.[6]

Eighteenth-century political thinkers argued that free governments, or republics (that is to say, governments with a degree of citizen participation), were, notwithstanding their other blessings, most prone to factionalism. David Ramsay, one of the first native historians of the American Revolution, closed his 1789 two-volume work by saying that the fledgling republic needed to "avoid discord, faction, luxury and the other vices which have been the bane of commonwealths."[7] This essay will concentrate on the first two dangers Ramsay identified, but it will also briefly show how the third could be seen as related. Americans were interested in—and worried about—social conflict and not just conflict based on speculative religious and political principles. Arendt argued that the absence of a "social question" in the early American republic was one major reason why the American Revolution was more successful than the French. However, many prominent American writers and politicians in the late eighteenth century were concerned with social conflict and economic parties in much the same way as Machiavelli and Roman writers such as Livy were.

This essay will begin by considering the context of European power politics. Eighteenth-century Western and, to a large degree, world history was dominated by the rivalry between two very different monarchical empires, the French absolute monarchy and the mixed monarchy of Britain. Montesquieu—one of the most cited political writers of the period—believed that Britain was a republic disguised as a monarchy.[8] While Montesquieu viewed Britain as a political system dedicated to the principle of political liberty,[9] it was also generally considered to be unstable and prone to internal strife. Although Montesquieu is often seen as an Anglophile, he was far from upbeat about the prospects for Britain. Indeed, he believed that Britain was going to fail as a state when parliamentary corruption became too endemic, echoing Bolingbroke's *Craftsman*.[10] Montesquieu was far from being the only one who was pessimistic about Britain in the eighteenth century. Some of the major Scottish thinkers of the century, including David Hume and Adam Ferguson, were alarmed about factionalism in the British metropole in the 1760s and 1770s. Against this backdrop, many of the founders and politicians in the early American republic set themselves the task of not only creating a political system without a monarch and a hereditary aristocracy but also creating one that would be less fractured and prone to party spirit than Britain's system. This emphasis is different from Steve Pincus's recent contention that the founders were British "Patriots" who wanted to restore the pre-1760 political equilibrium.[11] As with classical republicanism, while British thought and institutions provided the starting point, British parliamentary government was something the founders wanted to transcend rather than copy.[12] There were of course "Anglophiles" among the founders, notably Alexander Hamilton and, with more qualifications, John Adams, but they may have been in the minority. Moreover, their more positive views about Britain became a stick with which Thomas Jefferson and his followers would beat the Federalists in the 1790s. Yet in their attempt to avoid British "corruption," Jefferson and his followers borrowed from British political thought. The essay will conclude by stressing the importance in 1790s America of the theory of constitutional, partisan opposition along Bolingbrokean lines.

The Unexpected Rise of a Turbulent State

The fastest-rising state among what have become known as the emerging great powers in the eighteenth century was Britain (even though Russia and Prussia also made enormous strides).[13] During the Glorious or Williamite Revolution of 1688–89, England and the Netherlands entered an agreement that locked England (or Britain after the Acts of Union of 1707) into continental warfare against the French. The postrevolution state was supported by a "financial revolution" that created a national debt to pay for a standing army to fight wars and protect the new regime. Helped by its financial strength and its continental allies, Britain held its own against the more populous and bigger France in the Nine Years' War (1688–97), the War of the Spanish Succession (1701–14), and the War of the Austrian Succession (1740–48). Against all odds, it even emerged as the clear victor after the Seven Years' War (1756–63). Few would have been surprised when France—still the more apparently powerful state—overturned some of Britain's victories in the American War of Independence.[14]

England, the senior partner in the British composite monarchy and imperial state, was a country known for turbulence. As Samuel Pufendorf had written in 1682: "[The English] Histories are sufficient evidences, that they have been always inclined to Rebellion and intestine Commotions. Wherefore their Kings can never be secure, except they keep a watchful Eye over the restless Spirit of the People."[15] According to Pufendorf, the English people were especially prone to religious enthusiasm and fanaticism. Indeed, he argued that "there is not any Nation 'under the Sun' [in Christendom], where more different and more absurd Opinions are to be met withall in Religion than in *England*."[16] Religious strife plagued the three kingdoms in the seventeenth century, a century during which one monarch was executed and another was driven from the throne. In the eighteenth century, Jacobitism—the movement to restore the exiled Stuarts after the Glorious Revolution—exacerbated divisions within the British polity in England, Ireland, Wales, and particularly in Scotland; both opportunists and genuine loyalists rallied periodically under the Jacobite banner and frequently schemed against the established regime.

Jacobitism was a crucial component of British party politics. The names of the Whig and Tory parties—which originated in older usages in Scotland and Ireland—had come to the fore during the Exclusion Crisis of 1678–81; the Whigs wanted to exclude the Duke of York and future James II/VII from succession to the throne on account of his Catholicism and the Tories defended the hereditary principle. James's short reign was an unhappy one for the Tories, however, as the Catholic monarch attempted to create an alliance with Protestant Dissenters in order to promote religious toleration and Catholicism in unison. In 1688, leading politicians invited his son-in-law and nephew, William of Orange, to negotiate with James; the end result was that William became joint sovereign together with his wife and James's daughter Mary. As a result of this "parliamentary settlement," the names Whig and Tory were revived and became a regular feature of British politics. Jacobitism became a political option for the disaffected under the new regime, which initially included both Tories and Whigs who were unhappy with William's hands-on ruling style.[17] After the Hanoverian Succession in 1714, however, the Tories became closely associated with Jacobitism because they were prohibited from holding political office under the Hanoverian regime.

Alongside Jacobitism, Britain continued to be divided along religious lines, despite many compromises and settlements. During the Restoration of the monarchy in 1660, Parliament passed a series of laws to strengthen the Church of England's position vis-à-vis Protestant Dissenters that were collectively known as the Clarendon Code. Although Dissenters were formally excluded from public offices, they could qualify through the practice of "occasional conformity." This and other practices split the Church into Latitudinarians, who were allied with the Whigs, and High Church Tories. The Restoration also reestablished the supremacy of episcopacy in Scotland, which was replaced by Presbyterianism thirty years later under William of Orange. The Scottish Episcopalian Church was entwined with Jacobitism and recognized the Stuarts as rightful monarchs until the death of Charles Edward Stuart in 1788. In Ireland, a Protestant minority ruled over a disenfranchised Catholic majority. The outcry following the

Jewish Naturalisation Act of 1753 and its repeal the following year demonstrates the continued importance of religious politics in Britain.[18] These
dynastic and religious questions not only informed party politics; they
also informed popular protest. Dissenters' property was often attacked by
"Church and King" and "Tory" mobs, many of whom also celebrated the
Pretender's birthday.[19] The anti-Catholic Gordon Riots of 1780 are also examples of religious protest.[20]

Economic policy was yet another source of conflict. The erection of a national bank and sovereign debt to fund Anglo-Dutch wars against France
in the 1690s formed what has become known as a "fiscal-military state"
and, at least in the political imagination, the creation of a new moneyed
interest.[21] Particularly during the Walpole era (1721–42), Tories and opposition Whigs protested against this moneyed interest of stockjobbers and
City speculators, many of whom were foreign (in particular Dutch). This
opposition argued that the new economic interest was separate from the
national interest, understood as the landed and commercial interests combined.[22] The most successful campaign against Walpole's financial system
was the opposition to his proposed extension of internal taxation to wine
and tobacco in 1733–34—an opposition led by an alliance between the Tory
Henry St John, Viscount Bolingbroke and the Whig William Pulteney.[23] In
the second half of the century, imperial affairs rose to prominence as West
and East Indian merchants lobbied the government for preferential treatment. Edmund Burke famously identified "Indianism," referring to such
partial and sometimes monopolistic interests, as a key threat to the British
polity.[24]

Many Enlightenment thinkers were as disconcerted about British, and
in particular English, proneness to turbulence in the second half of the
eighteenth century, as Pufendorf had been nearly a century earlier. The dis-
turbances in London over "Wilkes and Liberty" in the late 1760s and early
1770s made a deep impression, especially on many of Scotland's literati. At
that point, Hume's private letters took an increasingly anti-English tone.
His compatriot Adam Ferguson was as dismayed.[25] Considered in context,
Hume's view that "the English" enjoyed more liberty than was compatible
with political stability was neither as outrageous nor as unusual as it might
seem.[26] American writers such as David Ramsay shared Hume's worries
about the threat to stability excessive liberty posed.[27]

Historical and cultural ties made the British context the most important
one for early American political debate. It was also the key context for debates about party since Britain was regarded as the parliamentary system

par excellence in the eighteenth century. In the next section, I turn to these debates.

Theorizing Party Division

The most famous writer on party in the eighteenth century was Edmund Burke, but perhaps because of the specificity of his *Thoughts on the Cause of the Present Discontents* (1770), he appears to have been less significant for American party thought in the eighteenth century than might be supposed.[28] The most important writers for this debate were the English country Tory (and former Jacobite) Bolingbroke, the French aristocrat Montesquieu, and the Scottish philosopher and historian David Hume. Hume's approach of analyzing parties in terms of different categories and emphasizing parties that were animated by principle was indebted to the French Huguenot Paul de Rapin-Thoyras. Rapin was most famous for his *History of England* (1724–27). It was the standard history until it was replaced by Hume's own in the 1750s and 1760s and was the most important Whig interpretation of the English constitution in the eighteenth century. Both Jefferson and Adams preferred Rapin's *History* to Hume's.[29]

Before his *History*, Rapin had written a long pamphlet entitled *A Dissertation on the Whigs and the Tories* that was published in 1717. This is a momentous text, not only in terms of its historical insights, but also in the sphere of political theory, since it is the first text that offered a powerful argument in favor of political parties rather than the social forces and private factions in Machiavelli's writings. Rapin argued that the two parties in Britain, the Whigs and Tories, represented the two pillars of the mixed and balanced constitution, Parliament on the one hand and the monarchy on the other, and that both parties were necessary to maintain the equilibrium between these two parts of the constitution. Both parties were likewise necessary for balance in the religious sphere, which was as important as secular matters in public life at the time. One party favored the Church of England and the other favored tolerating Protestant Dissenters, and the only way to achieve a sustainable medium between the two extreme positions was competition and mutual checking and balancing, according to Rapin.[30] These parties would alternate in government and take turns holding their opposite number to account when out of power.

It is sometimes thought that Rapin's only intention was to narrate and idolize the mythical Anglo-Saxon constitution, but it would be more precise to say that his underlying and main aspiration was outlining how civil and religious peace could be achieved. This is very understandable, as he wrote about a country that had been torn asunder by civil and religious strife in the middle of the seventeenth century and had recently ousted its king in the Glorious Revolution for trying to push the nation toward Catholicism and absolutism. Rapin himself had been evicted from France after the revocation of the Edict of Nantes in 1685, and he had in fact been on the same ship as William of Orange when he landed in Torbay in 1688. In the 1690s, he fought for William against the Jacobite army in Ireland at the Battle of the Boyne and the Siege of Limerick. Rapin was thus clearly a man who knew what civil and religious strife looked like. For him, the whole point behind the rhetoric about the ancient constitution in state and church was that it was a formula for how each estate and each sect could be kept in its proper place without aspiring to the superiority that had proved to be a recipe for civil war. By espousing different political and religious principles, the political parties in Parliament could achieve a delicate stability of the kind the British Isles had not known since the Reformation, according to Rapin.

Hume wrote at length about party in general and in its British guise in a series of essays published as *Essays, Moral and Political* in instalments starting in 1741. Hume believed that parties—or factions, terms he used interchangeably—based on principles were particularly pernicious and "unaccountable." Religious principles had the potential to make people fanatical and ready to both proselytize and persecute dissidents. Because they were more transparent and less extreme, parties based on interests, by which he meant different economic interests, were more tolerable.[31] His early essays on party treated the phenomenon as inevitable since the British parliamentary system naturally gave birth to court and country parties, or parties of government and opposition. He did not try to disguise his own personal distaste for political parties at this point. In later writings, however, Hume was more prepared to acknowledge the potentially salutary aspects of party politics. In "Of a Coalition of Parties" (1758), Hume opened by arguing that it might be neither possible nor *desirable* to seek to extinguish parties. The essay was an apologia for his *History of England* (1754–61). In that earlier work, Hume had written that "while [the Court and Country parties] oft threaten the total dissolution of the government, [they] are the real causes of its permanent life and vigour."[32]

Hume's formulation was highly reminiscent of an earlier phrasing in Montesquieu's *Spirit of Laws* (1748), which Hume had read and studied in the year it was published. Montesquieu had written about the British constitution in two long chapters. After describing the British constitution (or the English constitution, as he called it) in book eleven of his *chef-d'œuvre*, in the final chapter of book nineteen Montesquieu argued that Britain was perpetually divided into two "parties," one inclining to the executive and the other to the legislature, the two visible powers in the state.[33] With the power of patronage, "all those who would obtain something from [the executive] would be inclined to move to that side, and it could be attacked by all those who could expect nothing from it."[34] The competition will generate "hatred, envy, jealousy, and the ardor for enriching and distinguishing oneself . . . to the full extent."[35] However, since liberty is the animating principle of the British constitution, "if this were otherwise, the state would be like a man who, laid low by disease, has no passions because he has no strength."[36] Besides, the hatred between the two parties would be "powerless," Montesquieu claimed: "As these parties are made up of free men, if one party gained too much, the effect of liberty would be to lower it while the citizens would come and raise the other party like hands rescuing the body."[37] As the citizens would be afraid to lose their free constitution, they "would believe themselves to be in danger even at the safest of moments."[38] Those in opposition to the executive would be unable to admit their self-interested motives and desire for office and would instead seek to fan the flames of public fears. This would have the good effect of making the people attentive in order to avoid "the real perils to which they might sometimes be exposed."[39] Finally, as the representatives of the legislative body were more enlightened than the people, they could calm down stormy sentiments and commotion.[40]

Montesquieu's analysis of the British constitution and its party competition relied on the opposition writings of Bolingbroke's *Craftsman*, which Montesquieu studied when he was in England for eighteen months in 1729–31. Bolingbroke and Montesquieu knew each other from the *Club de l'Entresol* in Paris during Bolingbroke's exile, which had ended in the middle of the 1720s.[41] During his stay in England, Montesquieu reconnected with Bolingbroke. Historians have usually interpreted Bolingbroke as the paradigmatic anti-party writer of the eighteenth century, as Richard Hofstadter did in his important study of party in early American politics.[42] I have argued elsewhere that it is better to regard Bolingbroke as a partisan political writer who made a case for a systematic opposition party and who never envisaged politics without parties.[43] Bolingbroke conceived of his "country party" as a constitutional party that contended that the government of the day (Walpole's Whigs) had betrayed the core principles of the constitution by corrupting politics and society.[44] To save the nation, he argued, they must be opposed, and opposition needed to be systematic and concerted.[45] In order to oppose them, Bolingbroke and his "party" had to describe themselves as the true patriots; two of Bolingbroke's most famous texts were titled *A Letter on the Spirit of Patriotism* and *The Idea of a Patriot King*. In eighteenth-century Britain, "patriot" became synonymous with opposition politician, which is probably at least part of the meaning Samuel Johnson had in mind when he told James Boswell that "patriotism is the last refuge of a scoundrel." Johnson, who had a Jacobite background, had himself been a writer for the Tory-Patriot opposition, but after the accession of George III he became a pensioner of the court and a pamphleteer for the government.[46]

In the next section, I shall argue that Bolingbroke's argument for a systematic opposition party became crucial when the Jeffersonian Republicans launched their opposition against the Federalists in the 1790s.

The American Reception

The party debate in Europe left an ambivalent legacy for early American political thinkers. Alexander Hamilton told the New York ratifying convention of 1788 that "we are attempting by this Constitution . . . to abolish factions, and to unite all parties for the general welfare."[47] The same Hamilton reserved a more positive space for conflict in Federalist No. 70. There he argued that whereas unity was necessary in the executive part of the constitution,[48] the legislative arm was a different matter: "The difference of opinion, and the jarrings of parties in that department of the government, though they may sometimes obstruct salutary plans, yet often promote deliberation and circumspection, and serve to check excess in the majority."[49] Hamilton is more famous, however, for having drafted George Washington's deeply anti-party farewell address of 1796.

In many ways, John Adams embodied the alarm about party in the early American republic.[50] For example, he wrote in his diary in 1765 that "the spirit of party . . . wrought an entire metamorphosis of the human character. It destroyed all sense and understanding, all equity and humanity, all memory and regard to truth, all virtue, honor, decorum, and veracity."[51] Later in life, he wrote that "there is nothing which I dread so much as a division of the republic into two great parties. . . . This, in my humble apprehension, is to be dreaded as the greatest political evil under our Constitution."[52] At the same time, Adams did not entertain any utopian views of eradicating disagreement. As he put it in his correspondence: "An opposition in parliament, in a house of assembly, in a council, in Congress, is highly useful and necessary to balance individuals, and bodies, and interests one against another, and bring the truth to light, and justice to prevail."[53] It is likely that Adams was thinking of individual disagreement, separation of powers, and constitutional checks and balances rather than partisan opposition, which he rather consistently opposed, but it remains clear that Adams accepted certain internal division as inevitable. When he wrote about the need to balance different elements in the state, he drew heavily on the writings of Montesquieu.[54]

Many writers in the early American republic agreed that political division was inevitable. John Taylor of Caroline, one of Adams's chief critics, evolved from criticizing parties to accepting them as unavoidable.[55] His *Definition of Parties* (1794) was a partisan attack on Hamiltonian finance.[56] Jefferson and Madison were both convinced that factionalism was "sown into the nature of man."[57] Whig and Tory belonged to natural rather than civil history, Jefferson claimed.[58] The question for many was not whether America should have factions but rather what kind of factions it would have. Interestingly, parties based on economic interest that represented different orders in the state rather than parties of principles were key worries. David Ramsay interpreted the 1780s as a period of crisis due to excessive democracy and increases in social mobility.[59] At the outset of the Revolution, the economic base in the thirteen colonies had been simpler and more agrarian than that of its mother country. That remained the case in the 1780s, but the country was developing and growing fast. Benjamin Lincoln and John Adams were both concerned with party struggle between patricians and plebeians, the rich and the poor, drawing on Machiavelli.[60] As far back as Aristotle, political philosophers had been committed to the idea that a division between rich and poor was inevitable in any society. For a while, Adams sought to investigate whether this source of conflict could be defused, but he was disappointed in his inquiries and came to hold the view that such a dichotomy was inescapable. America did not have an aristocracy in the European sense, but it certainly had a class of "gentlemen" with social significance. For Adams, this order required separate representation in the shape of the senate. Representation of social interest and mutual checking and balancing was thus a way of managing this form of political division, according to Adams, for whom constitutional balance was the solution to inevitable conflict.[61]

To be sure, some did not accept that division was inevitable. Crucially,

James Monroe disagreed with Madison and Jefferson that party was a feature of human nature. For Monroe, America's fifth president, only bad constitutions such as Britain's suffered from parties and they were certainly not necessary in free governments.[62] In this way, Monroe's views on party exemplify the anti-British attitude. "Discord does not belong to our system. . . . The American people . . . constitute one great family with a common interest," he said.[63] Similarly, the suspicion of party was fundamental for Gouverneur Morris's rejection of parliamentary government, in which competing party leaders were the *real* kings: "Some leader of party will always covet [the incumbent minister's] seat, will perplex his administration, will cabal with the Legislature, till he succeeds in supplanting him."[64]

The most famous discussion of "faction" in the early American republic occurs in Madison's Federalist No. 10. This canonical essay, probably the most cited among *The Federalist Papers*, is about party in the way it was understood in the eighteenth century and not just about religious sectarianism. Madison defined the "causes of faction," in a way that was highly reminiscent of Hume, as "a zeal for different opinions concerning religion, concerning Government and many other points, as well of speculation as of practice; an attachment to different leaders ambitiously contending for pre-eminence and power; or to persons of other descriptions whose fortunes have been interesting to the human passions."[65] Like Hume, Madison believed that such differences and "mutual animosities" could not be extinguished in free governments. He further agreed with Hume that parties of interest were generally more peaceful and governable than parties that were united and actuated by passion.[66] His solution to party violence was similar to that found in Hume's "Idea of a Perfect Commonwealth" (1752): the effects of faction could be better controlled in larger states and federations than in city-states. Thanks to the greater scale of a larger area, the impact of each faction would be mitigated. Borrowing this Humean argument, Madison could argue, against much eighteenth-century political thought, that republicanism was possible and maybe even preferable in large, federative states.[67] The key was to ensure that no faction would become overly dominant. Ambition needed to be counteracted by ambition, as Madison wrote in Federalist No. 51.[68]

In his seminal work on the reception of Hume in eighteenth-century America, Mark Spencer has demonstrated the importance of Hume's philosophical, political, and historical writings for Madison.[69] In doing so he has rehabilitated earlier pathbreaking research by Douglas Adair that had come under criticism.[70] In America, John Stevens Jr. had anticipated

Madison's Humean argument,[71] but Madison's appropriation of Hume's argument is more famous. In addition to Hume's influence, Spencer rightly points out that Federalist No. 10 shares common ground with the writings of Hume's friend Adam Smith. In *The Wealth of Nations*, Smith had argued that a proliferation of religious sects tended to make them more peaceful since they would balance each other out and moderate their behavior to attract followers. This stood in opposition to Hume's embrace of a state church (in order to supervise the nation's zealots) in *The History of England*.

A less philosophical but arguably as historically significant party argument surfaced in the 1790s. After Madison and Hamilton cooperated as Publius in *The Federalist*, they became ideological rivals when the early American republic split into Federalists and Republicans (or Democratic-Republicans).[72] Washington's Proclamation of Neutrality in 1793 led to a sharp disagreement between the two on the question of executive power in the constitutional order.[73] Madison allied with his old friend and fellow Virginian Jefferson—Hamilton's rival in Washington's first administration until he resigned in December 1793—to oppose Hamilton's centralizing ambitions.[74] After Jefferson resigned as secretary of state, his opposition became more formal, especially in the wake of the Washington administration's Jay Treaty (1794) with Britain, which Hamilton had designed. In this political environment, a party argument emerged that had more in common with Bolingbroke than with Hume: the idea of partisan opposition.[75] National unity was the ideal for Jefferson and other opponents of the Federalists such as John Taylor of Caroline. However, because of what they perceived as the corruption of Federalists such as Hamilton, they believed that an opposition party in the shape of the Republican Party was necessary in order to defeat the enemies within. Jefferson believed that the Hamiltonians and the Federalists were monarchists and he viewed the 1790s as an ideological battle between liberty and tyranny. In this struggle, partisanship became a necessary evil. Justifying opposition was also Madison's new preoccupation in his essays on party in the 1790s, notably in "A Candid State of Parties" (1792). As he wrote in this essay:

> The republican party, as it may be termed, conscious that the mass of people in every part of the union, in every state, and of every occupation must at bottom be with them, both in interest and sentiment, will naturally find their account in burying all antecedent questions, in banishing every other distinction than that between enemies and

friends to republican government, and in promoting a general harmony among the latter, wherever residing, or however employed.[76]

This phase was crucial for the development of "constitutional opposition,"
a phrase Alexander Addison used in 1800.[77]

The specific policies the Jeffersonian Republicans opposed bore strong
resemblances to what Bolingbroke's country platform had criticized. Just
as Bolingbroke and William Pulteney had censured Walpole's financial
system of debt financing and excise taxes,[78] Jefferson and his followers
attacked excise taxes and Hamilton's national bank, which was modeled
on the Bank of England. Indeed, the Republican press branded Hamilton "another Walpole."[79] Later in the 1790s, the Jeffersonians attacked the
Federalist Alien and Sedition Acts, just as opposition Whigs and Tories
in Bolingbroke's days had censured authoritarian legislation such as the
Riot Act and Walpole's repeated attempts to crack down on the press.[80]
Most important, they condemned similar policies for the same reasons.
The constitutional differences between Britain and America notwithstanding, both oppositions feared the growing power of the executive and its
influence over the legislative power that risked upsetting the constitutional
equilibrium.[81] These similarities are arguably not accidental but are related
to similar political outlooks. Jeffersonian Republicans were fundamentally
steeped in the country party tradition, which was called Whig in America
but had been both Tory and Whig in Britain and Tory during the years of
Whig oligarchy after the Hanoverian succession.[82] The fact that Jeffersonians accused Hamilton of being Tory illustrates this point,[83] even though
his financial system was modeled on British Whig politics.

Jefferson appears to have been a keen reader of Bolingbroke. He recommended him for his nephew's education in a letter in 1790, even though
he emphasized style rather than content at that time.[84] In 1821, when one
of Jefferson's grandsons asked him to compare Bolingbroke with Thomas
Paine, Jefferson commented again on Bolingbroke's style but also spoke
highly of his politics while cautioning about his controversial views on
religion.

> They [Bolingbroke and Paine] are alike in making bitter enemies of
> the priests and pharisees of their day. Both were honest men; both
> advocates for human liberty. Paine wrote for a country which per-
> mitted him to push his reasoning to whatever length it would go.
> Lord Bolingbroke in one restrained by a constitution, and by public
> opinion. He was called indeed a tory; but his writings prove him a

stronger advocate for liberty than any of his countrymen, the whigs of the present day. Irritated by his exile, he committed one act unworthy of him, in connecting himself momentarily with a prince rejected by his country [the Stuart Pretender]. But he redeemed that single act by his establishment of the principles which proved it to be wrong. . . . Lord Bolingbroke's, on the other hand, is a style of the highest order. The lofty, rhythmical, full-flowing eloquence of Cicero. Periods of just measure, their members proportioned, their close full and round. His conceptions, too, are bold and strong, his diction copious, polished and commanding as his subject. His writings are certainly the finest samples in the English language, of the eloquence proper for the Senate. His political tracts are safe reading for the most timid religionist, his philosophical, for those who are not afraid to trust their reason with discussions of right and wrong.[85]

While there clearly was a country tradition and an anti-executive language of opposition in both Britain and America in the eighteenth century, it is more questionable whether there could be said to have been a "court" tradition to which Hamilton belonged. Court politics in eighteenth-century Britain was the outcome of the negotiations between the monarch of the day and his or her ministers. Walpole's court party had of course been Whig in the strong sense that its raison d'être was defending the Glorious Revolution and the Protestant succession from Catholicism and Jacobitism. In the process, the Whigs increasingly promoted the politics of order and authority—for example, by prolonging the duration of parliaments from three to seven years in 1716.[86] However, they did so in order to protect political and religious liberty from what they viewed as the absolutist and intolerant politics of the Stuart dynasty and from French encroachments. The purpose of the financial system erected in the 1690s was to pay for wars in defense of the Protestant interest in Europe and against French ambitions to erect a "universal monarchy." In other words, the politics of authority and finance was intended to secure liberty as the Whigs understood it. In theoretical terms, Hume—who has often been called a court Whig even though he also shared much in common with the country opposition, especially fears about the size of Britain's national debt—spoke of the need for governments to achieve a balance between liberty and authority.[87] This argument was influential for Hamilton, who, like Madison, was a careful reader of Hume.

Hamilton sought to quench the Republican opposition as effectively as the Whigs had kept the Tories at bay in eighteenth-century Britain. In the event, however, it was the Federalists who were emasculated and eventually disappeared as a serious political force in the years after Jefferson was elected as president in 1800, an event the new president referred to as a "revolution."

Conclusion

American political thinkers in the late eighteenth century thought about the issue of division in expansive terms. As Madison told the Constitutional Convention, all "civilized societies" are "divided into different Sects, Factions, & interests, as they happened to consist of rich & poor, debtors & creditors, the landed the manufacturing the commercial interests, the inhabitants of this district or that district, the followers of this political leader or that political leader, the disciples of this religious Sect or that religious Sect."[88] It is evident that not all American political thinkers were writing about partisan conflict in the modern, parliamentary, or congressional sense. Importantly, Adams was primarily justifying separate representation of different orders in the state and checking and balancing between different parts of the constitutional makeup. He had little time for partisanship in any other sense. Others did, however, and besides Federalist No. 10, the most important contribution to the development of the idea of party in the early American Republic was the appreciation of an opposition party along Bolingbrokean lines.

Richard Hofstadter argued that an important shift took place between the generation of Jefferson, Madison, and Monroe and the following one of Andrew Jackson and especially Martin van Buren (president 1837–41). The first generation was much more influenced by the eighteenth-century party debate, philosophical questions about human nature, and ideological and constitutional considerations. Van Buren and the second generation of American politicians were more concerned with party organization.[89] Many Republicans at this time "began to see clearly and consistently what such predecessors as Madison and Jefferson had seen only dimly and fitfully—the merits of party organization as a positive principle, and of two-party competition as an asset to the public interest."[90] Hofstadter's point is important, despite its teleological bent. At the same time, Hofstadter may have underestimated the importance of earlier arguments about party and, perhaps most important, the Republicans' justification of organized opposition to the Federalist party in the 1790s. I have elsewhere demonstrated that Bolingbroke's theory of a systematic opposition party has been undervalued in the existing literature. The rise of organized popular politics is of course a nineteenth-century rather than an eighteenth-century phenomenon, even though there were more important precursors than has sometimes been recognized. In this chapter, I have highlighted that the argument for systematic opposition party politics—which paved the way for the notion of constitutional opposition that has become fundamental in democratic politics—is not a nineteenth-century argument but one that originates in the eighteenth century. Bolingbroke theorized it in Britain in the 1730s and Jeffersonian Republicans picked it up in the 1790s.[91]

Notes

1. Hannah Arendt, *On Revolution* (1963; repr., London: Penguin, 2006), 84.

2. Arendt, *On Revolution*, 84.

3. "The Federalist No. 50 [Madison]," in Alexander Hamilton, James Madison, and John Jay, *The Federalist Papers with the Letters of "Brutus,"* ed. Terence Ball (Cambridge: Cambridge University Press, 2003), 251.

4. Arendt wrote in a memorable sentence that John Adams collected constitutions like other people collect stamps; *On Revolution*, 112.

5. This chapter draws on the large body of literature that since the 1960s has emphasized the importance of British political thought for eighteenth-century America in various ways. The classics are J. G. A. Pocock, *The Machiavellian Moment: Florentine Political Thought and the Atlantic Republican Tradition* (Princeton, NJ: Princeton University Press, 1975); Gordon Wood, *The Creation of the American Republic, 1776–1787* (Chapel Hill: University of North Carolina Press, 1969); Bernard Bailyn, *The Ideological Origins of the American Revolution* (Cambridge, MA: Harvard University Press, 1967); and Caroline Robbins, *The Eighteenth-Century Commonwealthman: Studies in the Transmission, Development and Circumstance of English Liberal Thought from the Restoration of Charles II until the War with the Thirteen Colonies* (Cambridge, MA: Harvard University Press, 1959). See also John M. Murrin, *Rethinking America: From Empire to Republic* (New York: Oxford University Press, 2019); and Isaac Kramnick, *Republicanism and Bourgeois Radicalism: Political Ideology in Late Eighteenth Century England and America* (Ithaca, NY: Cornell University Press, 1990). More recent studies include Steve Pincus, *The Heart of the Declaration: The Founders' Case for an Activist Government* (New Haven, CT: Yale University Press, 2016); Mark G. Spencer, *David Hume and Eighteenth-Century America* (Rochester, NY: University of Rochester Press, 2005); J. C. D. Clark, *The Language of Liberty, 1660–1832: Political Discourse and Social Dynamics in the Anglo-American World* (Cambridge: Cambridge University Press, 1994); and Lance Banning, *The Jeffersonian Persuasion: Evolution of Party Ideology* (Ithaca, NY: Cornell University Press, 1978).

6. Jason Frank, *Publius and Political Imagination* (Lanham, MD: Rowman & Little-field, 2014), 10.

7. David Ramsay, *The History of the American Revolution*, 2 vols. (1789; repr. Indianapolis: Liberty Fund, 1990), 2:355.

8. Baron de Montesquieu, *The Spirit of the Laws* (1748; repr., Cambridge: Cambridge University Press, 1989), 70. The legacy of Montesquieu is complicated; see, e.g., Will Selinger, *Parliamentarism: Burke to Weber* (Cambridge: Cambridge University Press, 2019).

9. Montesquieu, *The Spirit of the Laws*, 156.

10. For Montesquieu's reliance on Bolingbroke, see Robert Shackleton, *Montesquieu: A Critical Biography* (Oxford: Oxford University Press, 1961); and Rachel Hammersley, *The English Republican Tradition and Eighteenth-Century France: Between the Ancients and the Moderns* (Manchester, UK: Manchester University Press, 2010).

11. Pincus, *The Heart of the Declaration*.

12. M. J. C. Vile, *Constitutionalism and the Separation of Powers* (Indianapolis: Liberty Fund, 1998), especially chapter 6.

13. Paul Kennedy, *The Rise and Fall of the Great Powers: Economic Change and Military Conflict from 1500 to 2000* (New York: Random House, 1987), especially chapter 3.

14. Richard Whatmore, "Luxury, Commerce, and the Rise of Political Economy," in *The Oxford Handbook of British Philosophy in the Eighteenth Century*, ed. James Harris (Oxford: Oxford University Press, 2013), 575–95.

15. Samuel Pufendorf, *An Introduction to the History of the Principal Kingdoms and States of Europe*, translated by Jodocus Crull, ed. Michael J. Seidler (1682; repr. Indianapolis: Liberty Fund, 2013), 181.

16. Pufendorf, *Introduction to the History of the Principal Kingdoms and States of Europe*, 181.

17. Mark Goldie and Clare Jackson, "Williamite Tyranny and the Whig Jacobites," in *Redefining William III: The Impact of the King-Stadtholder in International Context*, ed. Esther Mijers and David Onnekink (Aldershot: Routledge, 2007), 177–99.

18. Istvan Hont, "Irishmen, Scots, Jews, and the Interest of England's Commerce: The Politics of Minorities in a Modern Composite State," in *Il Roulo Economico delle Minoranze in Europa seccoli XIII–XVIII*, ed. Simonetta Cavaciocchi (Florence and Prato: Le Monnier, 2000), 81–112.

19. Nicholas Rogers, *Crowds, Culture, and Politics in Georgian Britain* (Oxford: Oxford University Press, 1998), 1–20.

20. Ian Haywood and John Seed, eds., *The Gordon Riots: Politics, Culture and Insurrection in Late Eighteenth-Century Britain* (Cambridge: Cambridge University Press, 2014).

21. P. G. M. Dickson, *The Financial Revolution in England: A Study in the Development of Public Credit, 1688–1756* (New York: St. Martin's Press, 1967); John Brewer, *The Sinews of Power: War, Money and the English State 1688–1783* (New York: Routledge, 1989).

22. Earlier, Marxian historians placed a misleading amount of emphasis on land rather than trade in their interpretation of the thought of Bolingbroke and his circle.

See Isaac Kramnick, *Bolingbroke and His Circle: The Politics of Nostalgia in the Age of Walpole* (Ithaca, NY: Cornell University Press, 1968).

23. Paul Langford, *The Excise Crisis: Society and Politics in the Age of Walpole* (Oxford: Oxford University Press, 1975).

24. Richard Bourke, *Empire and Revolution: The Political Life of Edmund Burke* (Princeton, NJ: Princeton University Press, 2015). See also Perry Gauci, *William Beckford: First Prime Minister of the London Empire* (New Haven, CT: Yale University Press, 2013).

25. Max Skjönsberg, "Adam Ferguson on Party Conflict, Partisanship and Popular Participation," *Modern Intellectual History* 16, no. 1 (2019): 1–28.

26. Hume's late pessimistic phase is best treated in J. G. A. Pocock, *Virtue, Commerce, and History: Essays on Political Thought and History, Chiefly in the Eighteenth Century* (Cambridge: Cambridge University Press, 1985), 125–42; and Moritz Baumstark, "The End of Empire and the Death of Religion: A Reconsideration of Hume's Later Political Thought," in *Philosophy and Religion in Enlightenment Britain: New Case Studies*, ed. Ruth Savage (Oxford: Oxford University Press, 2012).

27. Karen O'Brien, *Narratives of Enlightenment: Cosmopolitan History from Voltaire to Gibbon* (Oxford: Oxford University Press, 1997), 222.

28. Richard Hofstadter, *The Idea of a Party System: The Rise of Legitimate Opposition in the United States* (Berkeley: University of California Press, 1969), 34–35. In *Edmund Burke in America: The Contested Career of the Father of Modern Conservatism* (Ithaca, NY: Cornell University Press, 2013), Drew Maciag traces the earliest citation of *Present Discontents* to the *New England Magazine* in 1834; it avoided Burke's famous defense of party (74–75).

29. Spencer, *David Hume and Eighteenth-Century America*, 254–55, 258.

30. Paul Rapin de Thoyras, *Dissertation sur l'origine du gouvernement d'Angleterre, et sur la naissance, les progres, les vues, les forces, les interets, et les caractères des deux partis des Whigs et des Torys* (1716–17), in Bernard Cottret and Marie-Madeleine Martinet, *Partis et factions dans l'Angleterre du premier XVIIIe siècle* (Paris: Presses de l'Université Paris-Sorbonne, 1987). See also Hugh Trevor-Roper, *From Counter-Reformation to Glorious Revolution* (Chicago: University Press of Chicago, 1992), chapter 13.

31. David Hume, *Essays, Moral, Political and Literary* (Indianapolis: Liberty Fund, 1987), 58.

32. David Hume, *The History of England*, 6 vols. (1778; repr., Indianapolis: Liberty Fund, 1983), 5:556.

33. Montesquieu, *Spirit of the Laws*, 325.

34. Montesquieu, *Spirit of the Laws*, 325.

35. Montesquieu, *Spirit of the Laws*, 325.

36. Montesquieu, *Spirit of the Laws*, 325, 156.

37. Montesquieu, *Spirit of the Laws*, 325–26.

38. Montesquieu, *Spirit of the Laws*, 326.

39. Montesquieu, *Spirit of the Laws*, 326.

40. Montesquieu, *Spirit of the Laws*, 326.

41. Nick Childs, *A Political Academy in Paris, 1724–1731: The Entresol and Its Members* (Oxford: Voltaire Foundation, 2000).

42. Hofstadter, *The Idea of a Party System*, 19–23. See also Harvey Mansfield, *Statesmanship and Party Government: A Study of Burke and Bolingbroke* (Chicago: University of Chicago Press, 1965); and Nancy Rosenblum, *On the Side of the Angels: An Appreciation of Parties and Partisanship* (Princeton, NJ: Princeton University Press 2009).

43. Max Skjönsberg, "Lord Bolingbroke's Theory of Party and Opposition," *Historical Journal* 59, no. 4 (2016): 947–73.

44. This is the core argument in Bolingbroke's *Dissertation upon Parties*, serialized in the *Craftsman* in 1733–34.

45. This is the core argument in Bolingbroke's *Letter on the Spirit of Patriotism* (1736).

46. On Johnson, see J. C. D. Clark, *Samuel Johnson: Literature, Religion and English Cultural Politics from the Restoration to Romanticism* (Cambridge: Cambridge University Press, 1994).

47. Quoted in Hofstadter, *The Idea of a Party System*, 17.

48. This excluded the Roman and Spartan models, which had two consuls and two kings, respectively, and the executive councils that had prevailed in some of the early state constitutions.

49. "The Federalist No. 70 [Hamilton]," in Hamilton, Madison, and Jay, *The Federalist Papers*, 344.

50. See John R. Howe Jr., *The Changing Political Thought of John Adams* (Princeton, NJ: Princeton University Press, 1966), chapter 7.

51. John Adams, *The Works of John Adams*, 10 vols. (Boston: Little, Brown and Company, 1856), 2:152.

52. John Adams, *The Works of John Adams*, 9:511.

53. John Adams, *The Works of John Adams*, 9:485.

54. For Adams and Montesquieu, see Jacob T. Levy, *Rationalism, Pluralism, and Freedom* (Oxford: Oxford University Press, 2017), 205–8.

55. C. William Hill Jr., *The Political Theory of John Taylor of Caroline* (Cranbury, NJ: Associated University Presses, 1977), chapter 2.

56. John Taylor, *Definition of Parties, or, The Political Effects of the Paper System Considered* (Philadelphia, 1794).

57. "The Federalist No. 10 [Madison]," in Hamilton, Madison, and Jay, *The Federalist Papers*, 41. Taylor disagreed on this point; see Hill, *The Political Theory of John Taylor of Caroline*, 85.

58. See Rosenblum, *On the Side of the Angels*, 18.

59. O'Brien, *Narratives of Enlightenment*, 222.

60. Gordon Wood, *Friends Divided: John Adams and Thomas Jefferson* (New York: Penguin, 2017), chapter 6.

61. See C. Bradley Thompson, *John Adams and the Spirit of Liberty* (Lawrence: University Press of Kansas, 1998).

62. Hofstadter, *The Idea of a Party System*, 196.

63. Hofstadter, *The Idea of a Party System*, 197.

64. Cited in Vile, *Constitutionalism and the Separation of Powers*, 170–71.

65. "The Federalist No. 10 [Madison]," in Hamilton, Madison, and Jay, *The Federalist Papers*, 41–42.

66. Frank, *Publius and Political Imagination*, 87–96.

67. Montesquieu anticipated this conclusion, even though this fact is often ignored.

68. "The Federalist No. 51 [Madison]," in Hamilton, Madison, and Jay, *The Federalist Papers*, 252.

69. Spencer, *David Hume and Eighteenth-Century America*, chapter 6.

70. Douglas Adair, "The Tenth Federalist Revisited," *William and Mary Quarterly* 8, no. 1 (1951): 48–67; Douglas Adair, "'That Politics May Be Reduced to a Science': David Hume, James Madison and the Tenth Federalist," *Huntington Library Quarterly* 20, no. 4 (1957): 343–60. For criticisms, see Edmund S. Morgan, "Safety in Numbers: Madison, Hume, and the Tenth Federalist," *Huntington Library Quarterly* 49, no. 2 (1986): 95–112.

71. Spencer, *Hume and Eighteenth-Century America*, 240.

72. Noble E. Cunningham Jr., *The Jeffersonian Republicans: The Formation of Party Organization, 1789–1801* (Chapel Hill: University of North Carolina Press, 1957) remains a key study.

73. As George Thomas argues in *The Madisonian Constitution* (Baltimore, MD: The John Hopkins University Press, 2008), constitutional conflict has been a perennial feature of American politics.

74. See Colleen A. Sheehan, *James Madison and the Spirit of Republican Self-Government* (Cambridge: Cambridge University Press, 2010).

75. See Banning, *The Jeffersonian Persuasion*, chapters 5–6; and Hofstadter, *The Idea of a Party System*, chapters 3–4.

76. Gaillard Hunt, ed., *The Writings of James Madison*, 9 vols. (New York: G. P. Putnam's Sons, 1900–1910), 6:119.

77. Alexander Addison, *Reports of Cases in the County Courts of the Fifth Circuit and in the High Court of Errors & Appeals, of the state of Pennsylvania* (Washington, PA: Printed by John Colerick, 1800), 49, quoted in Spencer, *Hume and Eighteenth-Century America*, 282.

78. Skjönsberg, "Bolingbroke's Theory of Party and Opposition"; Langford, *The Excise Crisis*; Dickson, *The Financial Revolution in England*.

79. Cited in Banning, *The Jeffersonian Persuasion*, 237.

80. Max Skjönsberg, "Hume's 'Of the Liberty of the Press' (1741) in Its Original Contexts," in *Freedom of Speech, 1500–1850*, ed. Alex Barber, Robert Ingram, and Jason Peacey (Manchester, UK: Manchester University Press, 2020).

81. For a very different interpretation that emphasizes a Patriot tradition of interventionist government, see Pincus, *The Heart of the Declaration*.

82. This makes the usage of "British Whig" as a catchall term for the discourse that influenced Americans somewhat problematic. See, for instance, Richards, *The Founders and the Classics*, introduction; and J. G. A. Pocock, "The Varieties of Whiggism from Exclusion to Reform: A History of Ideology and Discourse," in Pocock, *Virtue, Commerce, and History*, 215–310.

83. See Banning, *Jeffersonian Persuasion*, 287.

84. Thomas Jefferson to John Garland Jefferson, June 11, 1790, in *The Works of Thomas Jefferson*, ed. Paul Leicester Ford, 12 vols. (New York: G. P. Putnam's Sons, 1904–1905), 6:72–73.

85. Jefferson to Francis Eppes, January 19, 1821, in Ford, *The Works of Thomas Jefferson*, 12:194–95.

86. Max Skjönsberg, "Ancient Constitutionalism, Fundamental Law, and Eighteenth-Century Toryism in the Septennial Act (1716) Debates," *History of Political Thought* 40, no. 2 (2019): 270–301.

87. Hume, "Of the Origin of Government," in Hume, *Essays*, 40–41.

88. Quoted in Spencer, *Hume and Eighteenth-Century America*, 175.

89. Donald B. Cole, *Martin van Buren and the American Political System* (Princeton, NJ: Princeton University Press, 1984), chapter 2.

90. Hofstadter, *The Idea of a Party System*, 212.

91. In addition to the Alan B. and Charna Larkin Symposium on the American Presidency at Florida Atlantic University, I presented a draft of this essay at the International Conference for the Study of Political Thought (ICSPT) at Yale University in May 2019. I would like to thank participants and attendees at both events for enlightening discussions, Ben Lowe for many helpful suggestions, and Turkuler Isiksel and Melissa Schwartzberg, who gave formal comments at the latter event.

4

Does the United States Need a Bill of Rights?

Monarchs, Presidents, and the Persistence of a Political Genre in the Age of the American Revolution

ERIC SLAUTER

What sense does a "bill of rights" make without a king? The question may seem odd, given the centrality of the Bill of Rights to American law since the adoption of the Fourteenth Amendment in 1868. But prominent framers such as James Wilson of Pennsylvania, Alexander Hamilton of New York, and James Madison of Virginia posed this question repeatedly in 1787 and 1788 as they tried to explain the omission of a bill of rights in the Constitution drafted in Philadelphia. Important advocates for the Constitution, including John Jay of New York and James Iredell of North Carolina, who would later join Wilson as justices on the new Supreme Court, asked the same question. These politicians and lawyers declared that bills of rights were a "modern" invention, a political genre with no analog in the democracies and republics of the ancient world. In modern politics, such documents had been exclusively a feature of monarchies, drafted by legislators and directed toward kings specifically as limitations on executive power. In English history, declarations of rights had served as an antimonarchical barrier against royal prerogative, an instrument that, in the absence of a written constitution, declared illegal and unconstitutional certain actions by the Crown, encroachments that would only ever be made by tyrants. What use then was a bill of rights for a republican people with a written constitution and a president instead of a king?

A bill of rights could not have the same meaning, James Wilson argued early in the ratification debates, as the grants or even "gifts" of liberty from a sovereign to his subjects represented in such famous English declarations of rights as the Magna Charta of 1215, the Petition of Right of 1628, and the Bill of Rights of 1689. If the rights of Englishmen enumerated in such documents did not ultimately originate with kings—some believed they did, while others described specific rights as natural and inalienable—then those rights nevertheless found force in being declared against and accepted by kings. But the proposed Constitution of the United States was a different kind of instrument for a different kind of government, a written document whose delegated powers were grants from the sovereign people themselves. Under such a system, the people might be said to gift rights and powers to their new chief executive, the president, not the other way around. To put it bluntly, as Federalists often did in the press and at state ratifying conventions, a bill of rights without a king was unnecessary, superfluous, and possibly even dangerous. As future lexicographer Noah Webster observed in late 1787, putting his finger on precisely the word so many supporters of the Constitution had used, a bill of rights in a republic was "absurd."[1]

To label bills of rights as a political anomaly in a republic, an absurd or even dangerous throwback to monarchy, was hardly the only Federalist explanation for omitting a formal enumeration and declaration of rights in the Constitution. But it was often the first defense in an arsenal of arguments that grew over the course of debates in the states as the absence of a bill of rights became the most unifying argument against the Constitution. Modern historians and legal scholars have often described the arguments of the Constitution's supporters against bills of rights as theoretically sophisticated and forward looking, part of a delicate balance Jack N. Rakove has dubbed "the dilemma of declaring rights."[2] As Gordon S. Wood noted on the occasion of the bicentennial of the ratification of the Bill of Rights in 1991, the absence of a bill of rights in 1787 proved fortunate for American political thought, since "much of the new and original contributions that Americans of 1787–1788 made to political theory came out of [the] need to explain the Constitution's lack of a bill of rights."[3] Few of the theoretical explanations satisfied opponents of the Constitution, who looked backward in part to British precedents and more recently to the bills of rights attached to five of the state constitutions written just before and after the Declaration of Independence. Nevertheless, taking this small aspect of the wider debates over ratification seriously offers a chance to recover what the *idea* and the *genre* of a "bill of rights" meant in the transition from monarchy to republic and in the renegotiations between legislative and executive power in the postrevolutionary United States.[4]

Declaring rights constituted a major political practice of the American Revolution, an activity that blended philosophical and historical thinking and energized different groups, including women and unfree people of African descent, to express their grievances in what seemed to many a powerful new language—or at the very least a language that had suddenly gained new power.[5] While British philosopher Jeremy Bentham lamented that appeals to natural rights were hopelessly nonsensical and backward, ideas that had not been philosophically au courant for at least a century, American revolutionaries made written declarations that blended both natural and civil rights into one of the central political genres of the period.[6] The study of early modern rights talk has become more expansive and exciting in the past few years, as cultural and intellectual historians have come to join political and legal historians in a debate about the relative significance of eighteenth-century rights declarations as a possible background for the rise of "human rights" in the twentieth century.[7] The scholarship is more technically and more textually savvy than ever before; scholars have mined large databases of printed matter for clues about what Dan Edelstein terms "rights regimes" in Europe and British North America in an attempt to tie the historical rise of natural rights to the modern concept of human rights in the late twentieth century or to sever the two ideas.[8]

It has become easier for scholars to draw lines of legal and linguistic influence *backward* to older English models and traditions such as the English Bill of Rights of 1689 or *forward* to documents such as the French Declaration of the Rights of Man and Citizen of 1789 or the Universal Declaration of Human Rights of 1948 than to recover the shifting political and cultural meanings of the idea and the genre in the revolutionary period itself. As important as continuity in form and practice can be, we should now turn our attention away from questions about the origins and trajectories of certain rights in order to ask what, exactly, revolutionaries meant by a "bill of rights," shifting from an investigation of origin and influence to a focus on understanding and meaning. Instead of seeing these documents as inevitable links in a generic chain, we should attend to basic changes in what a "bill of rights" was, who it addressed, and what it was designed to circumscribe. To begin to do so, this chapter revisits the debate over whether the United States needs a Bill of Rights, exploring the persistence of a central political genre in light of new historical, political, cultural, and legal studies that posit a persistence of monarchism in the age of the American Revolution.

A Monarchical Synthesis?

How do we explain the persistence of bills of rights, documents with deep roots in English political thought and practice, in the age of the American Revolution? To ask the question is to enter in part into a recent scholarly debate about the nature and character of the American Revolution that may surprise some readers. In contrast to the common claim that the Revolution represented the crumbling of monarchy and the rise of republicanism or even democracy, some of the most arresting recent work across the wide field of early American studies challenges the view that the American Revolution represented a radical break with a monarchical past. This revisionary body of scholarship, spread across disciplines as diverse as literary studies, history, political science, and law, does not yet form a coherent or connected school of thought. But if its faint outlines were to be filled in, it would present a significant challenge to our understanding of the American Revolution and a fitting point from which to begin to appreciate the problem bills of rights posed for political thought and practice in the American Revolution.

Did the Revolution truly sweep away as much monarchism as we imagine? This simple question animates Paul Downes's prizewinning book *Democracy, Revolution, and Monarchism in Early American Literature* (2002). Downes is a literary critic, a practitioner of deconstruction, who believes that most modern commentators on the American Revolution have fallen too easily under "the spell of democracy" to the point where they cannot recognize real continuities across the change of regimes. Modern historians can perhaps be forgiven for this oversight, Downes concedes, since in a real sense they are simply listening, but not closely enough, to the words of their subjects, the eighteenth-century revolutionaries themselves. His book attempts "to deconstruct the revolutionary opposition between democracy and monarchism by considering some of the ways in which the democratic state and the democratic subject inherit the *arcana imperii* of the absolute monarch."[9]

In a series of readings of familiar revolutionary-era texts such as Benjamin Franklin's *Autobiography*, the Declaration of Independence, and J. Hector St. John de Crèvecœur's *Letters from an American Farmer*, Downes argues that the authors of the United States' founding texts and documents, even when they espoused what he terms "democratic monarchophobia," never wholly abandoned or completely displaced what they claimed to oppose and that consequently they "borrowed and adapted central features of Monarchical rule." These authors' commitment to the opposition between monarchy and democracy ultimately, in Downes's view, had real consequences: "it undermined some of the revolution's most valuable political innovations," including the expansion of political participation and opportunity. It also created some absurdities. "As a series of laws against laws ('Congress shall make no law')," he observes in a footnote about the Bill of Rights, "the amendments are irreducibly at odds with themselves." In Downes's telling, the new, modernizing "democratic" order (Downes largely avoids debates over "republicanism" or "liberalism" of the period) did not so much erode older, premodern vestiges of monarchy (the claim of Gordon S. Wood, the most-cited historian in Downes's study) as it repackaged them. Scholarly attempts to find hints of democratization before the Revolution and to "reject democracy's inheritance from monarchy" after it, Downes contends, force us "to participate in the discourse of the Revolution, not to analyze it." His answer? Scholars must abandon deeply held forms of democratic "monarchophobia" if they ever hope to understand an event like the American Revolution.[10]

Historian Brendan McConville delivers a similar message, inviting his readers to take a leap of faith and to "forget the American Revolution" happened in order to see the contours of prerevolutionary British America through that period's "own political culture rather than through the future's political demands." As he argues in his 2006 study *The King's Three Faces: The Rise and Fall of Royal America, 1688–1776*, scholars should abandon the assessment Bernard Bailyn made half a century ago in *The Origin of American Politics* that the period between the Glorious Revolution and the American Revolution was a "latently revolutionary" age, a period populated with (in McConville's characterization of Gordon S. Wood's work) "protorepublicans, readers of Country pamphlets, rising assemblies, plain-folk Protestants, budding contract theorists, protocapitalists, protoproletariat, protoliberals, modernizers—in short, future Americans." Building on two prominent strands of recent scholarship, the new imperial school, and studies of provincial Anglicization, McConville describes the period between the English Revolution and the American Revolution as a time when monarchism was *increasing* rather than declining. McConville even wagers that eighteenth-century Americans were more committed to monarchy than Britain itself was. At the very least, he finds significant colonial "conceptual divergences from metropolitan norms," and for McConville these divergences made the difference. As politics and society changed after 1740, "institutionally unconditioned royalism" became "latently subversive to the provincial order and ultimately to the entire empire."[11]

McConville's study blends an account of political culture with the new history of emotions, tracing the strong emotional attachment and consequent emotional break members of colonial society felt toward Britain's monarchs. The central focus of prerevolutionary political culture was "a physically distant but emotionally available Protestant British monarch who had the provincial population's impassioned loyalty," McConville observes, and consequently "affection for and faith in imagined kings and constitutions, coupled to unique understandings of British history, informed the colonists' actions in the imperial crisis as much as Country thought or natural rights ideology did." In McConville's account, even the famous English Bill of Rights of 1689 fed into rather than contested a providential "neoabsolutism" in the colonies following the Glorious Revolution, a rebirth of ideas of divine right such that as late as 1774 a *New England Primer* published in Boston would illustrate the letter *K* with a picture of a crowned sovereign and the rhyme: "Our King the Good / No Man of Blood." (For the letter *O*, at least through 1750, the *Primer* pointed to a famous tree that Charles II hid in after his defeat by Cromwell: "The noble Oak it was the Tree, / That sav'd his royal Majesty.") Reading forward from 1688 rather than backward from 1776 and focusing instead on royal "rites" (a word he uses three times as often as "rights"), McConville sees the American Revolution as a drama in which deferential practices lost their force and the "unseen fabric of assumptions and emotional attachments to practices and visual signs of imperial authority decayed and then disintegrated." Ultimately, McConville's colonists' prerevolutionary participation in an "empire of love" yielded to what Thomas Jefferson in 1780 described as a nascent "empire of liberty."[12]

Recasting the American Revolution as a revolt against Parliament rather than against the Crown—"a revolution against a legislature, not against a king"—political scientist Eric Nelson begins where McConville ends and reaches a startling conclusion of his own: the American Revolution was "a rebellion in favor of royal power." Looking closely at key thinkers in the 1760s and 1770s, writers such as John Adams, James Wilson, Alexander Hamilton, and Benjamin Rush, Nelson's *Royalist Revolution: Monarchy and the American Founding* (2014) contends that American patriots made their arguments against Parliament by appealing to the kind of king who no longer existed in Britain after the Glorious Revolution. These thinkers, "patriot Royalists," far from being forward looking, wanted "to turn back the clock on the English constitution by over a hundred years—to separate the king from his Parliament and his British minister and to restore ancient prerogative of the Crown that had been extinguished by the whig ascendancy." Nelson's Patriot Royalists "wanted more monarchy, not less," and they thus "gravitated toward the political and constitutional theory of those who had waged the last great campaign against the 'usurpations' and 'encroachments' of Parliament: the reviled Stuart monarchs of the seventeenth century."

Nelson's thesis follows in the wake of McConville's but upends it. While McConville sees a breakdown in "royalism" in the 1760s and a subsequent turn to "radical whiggery," Nelson finds instead that eighteenth-century colonial political thought was "essentially whig, that the imperial crisis provoked an unprecedented turn toward the 'prerogativism' of the Stuarts, and that the revolutionary period marked the beginning, not the end, of this ideology's American journey." At issue, Nelson explains in a footnote, is the difference between McConville's "royalism" (which Nelson calls "monarchism") and Nelson's "Royalism," by which he means "the political and constitutional theory of those who defended Charles I."[13] In Nelson's account, thinkers such as Adams, Wilson, and Hamilton never changed their minds: their turn to "prerogativism" in the 1770s continued to fuel their sense "that sweeping prerogatives in a single chief magistrate were not only compatible with the liberties of citizens and subjects, but in fact were necessary for the preservation of free states." Indeed, Nelson goes so far as to argue that "the turn to the royal prerogative was *the* formative moment in the history of what would emerge as American constitutionalism."[14] These men sought to consolidate older forms of executive power in the office of a "president," a modest term suggesting simply a person who presides at a meeting but one that allowed the framers to cloak the return of much older forms of authority. Though the Constitution would "exclude the office of king" it would nevertheless "assign its rechristened chief magistrate far more power than any English monarch had wielded since William of Orange landed at Torbay in 1688."[15] Declarations of rights, whether in England in 1689 or in revolutionary America, play an unusual role in Nelson's narrative: his patriot Royalists seem to long for the moment before such documents abridged executive prerogatives.

Published only a few months after Nelson's book, legal scholar Saikrishna Bangalore Prakash's *Imperial from the Beginning: The Constitution of the Original Executive* (2015) reaches some similarly provocative conclusions about the character of the American presidency. Prakash, a practicing constitutional originalist, pushes common narratives about the differences between regal and republican constitutions to the side, reminding readers that the term *monarch* merely means a single ruler. Exploring the variety of monarchies that the Constitution's framers would have known alongside the voiced dissatisfaction of key framers with the "frail executives" many state constitutions created, Prakash recounts "how a robust executive both attracted and repulsed the Framers" in 1787 and how (in his telling) they produced "what one European ruler [William V, prince of Orange in 1788] called 'a king, under the title of President.'"[16] For Prakash, our commitments to seeing a sharp break between monarchy and democracy mean that we can barely see the original conception of the American presidency for the veiled form of monarchy that some at the time saw. As he puts it, "The picture that emerges from the founding era is of an elective monarch, constitutionally limited in a number of significant ways." Prakash finds that "while nothing like an absolute sovereign, the Constitution's original presidency rivaled, and in some cases exceeded, several European monarchies in the scope of its powers."[17] For Prakash, the presidency is both "imperial" in origin and "imperiled" in its current state. Prakash's citations of the English Declaration of Rights of 1689 all confirm for him that Parliament had gained great power against the Crown and, like Nelson, Prakash argues that the framers in 1787 hoped to return some of that power to the new chief executive.[18]

Where collectively does this recent scholarship leave us? These four works paint an unusual picture of the American Revolution and of the constitutionalism that grew out of it: would-be democratic "monarchophobes" who cannot help but borrow and mimic political and cultural features of the monarchy they claim to hate, a prerevolutionary America that was possibly more "overtly monarchical than England itself," framers who returned to the political thought of the seventeenth century not for its republicanism but for its royalism, and the original president conceived of as an elected king with more power than many European monarchs. Such seeming heresies have certainly not persuaded all reviewers, but the convergence of thought by serious scholars working from the vantage point of four different academic disciplines—literature, history, politics, and law—suggests that we should not simply brush these interpretations to the side.

Indeed, we may now need some kind of program statement to help organize this work akin to the one Robert Shalhope offered nearly fifty years ago in his much-cited essay "Toward a Republican Synthesis: The Emergence of an Understanding of Republicanism in American Historiography." This provocative vein of scholarship pushes past older debates about liberalism and republicanism and makes a case for the persistence of all kinds of forms, ideas, feelings and practices across what otherwise looks like a great revolutionary divide. A "monarchical synthesis" would reveal more fully what is at stake in all of the new work on royalism and monarchy and how it fits with other emerging viewpoints of the Revolution that have emerged in the past twenty-five years. Such a synthesis is beyond the scope of this essay, but this new scholarly context, as contested as it may be, may nevertheless help shed light on the meanings eighteenth-century Americans attached to the idea and genre of a "bill of rights."[19]

In the 1760s and early 1770s, Americans pointed to the English Bill of Rights of 1689 to support arguments against the Crown. They also created a political iconography rich with images of Magna Charta, incorporating graphic references to the thirteenth-century agreement between King John and the English barons on everything from silver punch bowls to paper currency to crude almanac portraits of "Pennsylvania Farmer" John Dickinson—all of which Paul Revere fashioned, designed, and engraved in Massachusetts in the period 1768 to 1775, although similar imagery survives from the middle and southern colonies.[20] On at least two occasions, in New York in 1765 and again in Philadelphia in 1774, colonial American politicians came together and produced documents that a few contemporaries referred to as an "American Bill of Rights." John Dickinson, looking back from 1768, retrospectively dubbed the resolutions of the Stamp Act Congress as "an American 'bill of rights,'" although he noted that it had failed to get a hearing in Britain.[21] Arthur Lee of Virginia, on learning that British politicians could not find any mentions of Americans in the English Bill of Rights, declared that American legislators should study the "great men" who had produced the Petition of Right in 1628 and the Bill of Rights in 1689 and "draw up a petition of rights, and never desist from the solicitation till it be confirmed into a bill of rights."[22] By 1774, a number of provincial legislatures from Massachusetts to South Carolina had read aloud and approved the Declaration and Resolves produced that October in Philadelphia.[23] In the words of a New York almanac maker, the document "may truly be called The American BILL of RIGHTS."[24] The provincial legislature in Massachusetts held that the "American Bill of Rights appears to be formed with the greatest ability and judgment" and was "essential to liberty." And a loyalist from Pennsylvania sneered that the "famous American bill of rights, this pillar of American liberties" was hardly worth the effort.[25] Such documents sought recognition and protection from the Crown. Two years later, in June 1776, Thomas Jefferson fashioned the text of the Declaration of Independence by looking to both the form and language of the nearly 90-year-old English Declaration of Rights and to the Virginia Declaration of Rights drafted just weeks earlier. In 1789, Congress lifted language for the earliest amendments to the Constitution, a document many refer to as the Bill of Rights, directly from these documents, creating the semblance of continuity over different centuries and across different political forms.

From Federalist No. 86 to a "Continental Bill of Rights"

On January 13, 1789, a few weeks before the Electoral College selected George Washington as the first president, James Madison wrote a letter designed to defend himself against the charge that he was "a strenuous advocate for the perfection of the Constitution as it stands, and an inflexible opponent to the change of a single letter." While the Constitution remained unratified, as Madison explained in a short note to his fellow Virginian Thomas Mann Randolph, he had opposed the idea of conditional amendments or a second convention to revise the proposed text. During the debates in the Virginia ratifying convention in the summer of 1788, he had kept to arguments that fellow supporters of ratification had espoused: the idea that a bill of rights in a federal constitution was at best unnecessary, a historical holdover more appropriate to a monarchy than a republic. At worst, Madison had insisted, enumerations of the rights of the people in a constitution that emanated from them were dangerous, for it risked augmenting governmental power in all areas where explicit reservations were not made. But, after the Constitution was ratified, Madison wrote that it was his opinion "that the clearest, and strongest provision ought to be made, for all those essential rights, which have been thought most in danger, such as the rights of conscience, the freedom of the press, trials by jury, exemption from general warrants, &c." This was work that should be taken up by the new Congress, and Madison hoped to be part of it. His letter was part of a calculated public about-face, an attempt to persuade voters that he would be the right kind of representative for a state that had so reluctantly ratified the Constitution.[26]

At the time, Madison faced a tough campaign for a seat in the new House of Representatives against his friend (and fellow future president) James Monroe. Just before the Virginia Convention of 1788, Monroe himself had caused a pamphlet to be printed (and then quickly suppressed) in which he claimed that "the rights of men [are] too loosely guarded" by the proposed Constitution. At the Virginia Convention itself, Monroe had declared, drawing in part from his uncirculated pamphlet, that "it may be attributed to the prejudice of my education, but I am a decided and warm friend to a *Bill of Rights*—the polar star, and great support of American liberty." Monroe ultimately voted against the Constitution, one of seventy-nine delegates (or 47 percent) to oppose ratification. In the new Congress, Monroe would presumably be a reliable voice for the many amendments that opponents of the Constitution in Virginia had recommended upon ratification. Those proposals from the Virginia Convention included forty articles, a separate "Declaration or Bill of Rights asserting and securing from encroachment the essential and unalienable Rights of the People" that consisted of twenty statements largely drawn from the Virginia Declaration of Rights of 1776 and another twenty changes to the body of the Constitution.[27]

Although Madison's letter to Randolph was addressed to an associate, it was meant for the newspapers, an open letter of appeal from a would-be congressman to his potential constituents. By the time he wrote the letter, Madison had already failed in what he surely saw as a hopeless bid to have the state legislature of Virginia name him a senator. The legislature was controlled by Patrick Henry, Madison's great opponent at the Virginia ratifying convention, and it resolved on William Grayson (who voted against ratification) and Richard Henry Lee (one of the strongest voices against the Constitution) as the state's first senators. It was Henry himself who promoted the idea that Madison believed no words should be changed in the text of the Constitution. It was clear Madison would need to mount a public campaign for a seat in the House during which he defended his position during ratification and showed his flexibility. In the letter to Randolph, candidate Madison showed a public political change of heart, although perhaps it is significant that in pledging himself to amendments Madison carefully chose not to use the phrase "bill of rights," a phrase Monroe had used and that appeared in Virginia's ratification instrument.

Madison's letter appeared in the *Virginia Independent Chronicle* of Richmond on January 28, 1789, five days before the House election.[28]

The open letter, a public about-face, clearly played a role in Madison's subsequent victory, and it was worth preserving. Although the physical letter Madison addressed to Randolph does not seem to have survived, a clipping of the printed version of the letter, cut from the columns of the Richmond newspaper, is among the Madison Papers at the Library of Congress.[29] In addition, we know that Richard Henry Lee made a handwritten transcript of parts of Madison's letter to Randolph and docketed it among his papers, now held by the Virginia Historical Society. Lee had lobbied against the Constitution from the beginning; he refused to be named a delegate to the Federal Convention in Philadelphia and then proposed that the Continental Congress make significant alterations to the product of that meeting before sending it to the states for ratification. On September 27, 1787, Lee remarked that it was "necessary to protect the just rights and liberty of mankind from the silent, powerful, and ever active conspiracy of those who govern" and that "such precautions are proper to restrain and regulate the exercise of the great powers necessarily given to Rulers." He therefore recommended that the proposed Constitution "be bottomed upon a declaration, or Bill of Rights, clearly and precisely stating the principles upon which this Social Compact is founded." And he went further: he suggested a structural change to Article II's creation of the executive branch. In place of the vice president, Lee wished to see an eleven-member "Council of State or Privy Council" be appointed by the president "to advise and assist in the arduous business assigned to the Executive power." Lee's remarks, attached to his name, formed the postscript to an open letter to Virginia governor Edmund Randolph (dated October 16, 1787) that became one of the most circulated public statements against the ratification of the Constitution.[30] The fact that Madison had finally come around to support amendments, even if only as a matter of political expedience, must have struck Lee as significant enough to warrant keeping a record of it.

Perhaps more intriguing, a clipping of Madison's letter from its first appearance in the Richmond newspaper also found its way into a copy of *The Federalist* that Thomas Jefferson once owned and the Newberry Library now holds. In the blank front pages of the book, someone—probably Jefferson, though possibly Madison himself—pasted Madison's campaign pledge, cutting the letter into three roughly equal sections and then centering them on three pages of the front endpapers, effectively creating a new preface from "Publius," a Federalist No. 86 to reverse the claims in Federalist No. 84 that a bill of rights of the kind that opponents and some supporters had wanted, including Jefferson, was unnecessary and dangerous.[31] Jefferson knew that Madison was not the author of the only Federalist paper to deal directly with the absence of a bill of rights, for just above the first clipping (and likely subsequent to its placement) he made a manuscript note identifying the papers Jay, Madison, and Hamilton had each written. "Col. Hamilton" was responsible for Federalist No. 84.

Hamilton had tactically waited an extraordinarily long time, until the very close of the series of essays, to comment on the absence of a bill of rights. Federalist No. 84 appeared first in book form on May 28, 1788, in time to reach delegates attending the ratifying conventions in Virginia and New York in June; it was not published in a newspaper (where it was numbered 83) until July 16, after Virginia had ratified but while New York continued to debate. The delayed paper, which perhaps gave Hamilton a chance to summarize the best arguments, was little more than a catalog of the various points that others had made, especially James Wilson in his remarks at the Pennsylvania ratifying convention in November 1787. There Wilson had confessed a "certain pride" when he contrasted the proposed Constitution with the British constitution, for while the "Magna Charta of England is an instrument of high value to the people of that country" it was nothing but "the gift or grant of the king." While "petitions and bills of rights" might make sense under a monarchy, they had no real place in a country where the "fee simple" of freedom rests in the people themselves. As Wilson had put it earlier in his statehouse speech of October, a bill of rights for this Constitution was "superfluous and absurd."[32] Hamilton agreed, while Jefferson found such thinking to be gratuitous and contrary to other clear reservations in the 1787 text.[33]

In Federalist No. 84 Hamilton made the common point that bills of rights found their origin and meaning in monarchy. "It has been several times truly remarked that bills of rights are, in their origin, stipulations between kings and their subjects, abridgements of prerogative in favor of privilege, reservations of rights not surrendered to the prince," he observed, citing the Magna Charta, the Petition of Right, and the Bill of Rights of 1689. In their "primitive signification," such documents "have no application to constitutions professedly founded upon the power of the people, and executed by their immediate representatives and servants." "Publius" reminded his readers of the significance of the preamble, although he abbreviated it in order to bring the agent and the action closer together: "WE, THE PEOPLE of the United States, to secure the blessings of liberty to ourselves and our posterity, do ORDAIN and ESTABLISH this Constitution for the United States of America." Here, Publius claimed, "is a better recognition of popular rights, than volumes of those aphorisms which make the principal figure in several of our State bills of rights, and which would sound much better in a treatise of ethics than in a constitution of government."[34] Hamilton's was one of the most common dismissals Federalists made of bills of rights.

John Jay, yet another "Publius," had made a similar point in April, likely before Hamilton drafted Federalist No. 84, in a pamphlet entitled *An Address to the People of the State of New-York on the Subject of the Constitution*. After observing that New York's constitution lacked a bill of rights, Jay observed that in "days and countries, where Monarchs and their subjects were frequently disputing about prerogative and privileges, the latter often found it necessary, as it were to run out the line between them, and oblige the former to admit by solemn acts, called bills of rights, that certain enumerated rights belonged to the people, and were not comprehended in the royal prerogative." "But thank God," Jay exclaimed, "we have no such disputes—we have no Monarchs to contend with, or demand admission from—the proposed Government is to be the government of the people—all its officers are to be their officers, and to exercise no rights but such as the people commit to them."[35]

At the failed North Carolina ratifying convention in July 1788, James Iredell made a similar point, directly linking the fact that the Constitution was a written document with the idea that a bill of rights was therefore unnecessary:

With regard to a bill of rights, this is a notion originating in England, where no written constitution is to be found, and the authority of their government is derived from the most remote antiquity. Magna Charta itself is no constitution, but a solemn instrument ascertaining certain rights of individuals, by the legislature for the time being; and every article of which the legislature may at any time alter. This, and a bill of rights also, the invention of later times, were occasioned by great usurpations of the crown, contrary, as was conceived, to the principles of their government, about which there was a variety of opinions. But neither that instrument, nor any other instrument, ever attempted to abridge the authority of Parliament, which is supposed to be without any limitation whatever. Had their constitution been fixed and certain, a bill of rights would have been useless, for the constitution would have shown plainly the extent of that authority which they were disputing about. Of what use, therefore, can a bill of rights be in this Constitution, where the people expressly declare how much power they do give, and consequently retain all they do not?[36]

This was a common Federalist line on the absence of a bill of rights, and while Madison hewed close to it in his public pronouncements, he reached a slightly different conclusion in his private correspondence.

By the time Madison's public letter to Randolph came to rest in Jefferson's copy of *The Federalist*, the two future presidents had already carried on a lengthy exchange about bills of rights in a series of private letters in the years 1787 to 1789 that is celebrated as one of the greatest political conversations in American history. Madison's position evolved and clarified over those two years. By late 1788, he had come to support a bill of rights and said he always had. That claim is hard to square with the record, but his private correspondence reveals that he landed very close to the positions Wilson, Jay, Hamilton, and Iredell outlined during the ratification debates. Madison's letter to Jefferson from New York on October 24, 1787, outlined Madison's cherished plan for a federal veto on the laws of the states, a plan that had found little support in Philadelphia but that Madison felt would defend minority rights against legislative majorities better than any declaration on paper.[37]

Jefferson's response from Paris of December 20, 1787, celebrated the framers' work, but it also enumerated aspects he did not like, the first being "the omission of a bill of rights providing clearly & without the aid of sophisms for freedom of religion, freedom of the press, protection against standing armies, restriction against monopolies, the eternal & unremitting force of the habeas corpus laws, and trials by jury in all matters of fact triable by the laws of the land & not by the law of Nations." Jefferson waved away Wilson's remarks of October 6 on the dangers of declaring rights (he was two months behind, but he seemed to echo the sentiments of the Pennsylvania minority, which he probably had not seen), adding that "a bill of rights is what the people are entitled to against every government on earth, general or particular, & what no just government should refuse or rest on inference." On July 31, 1788, after hearing that nine states had ratified (he did not know that by then eleven had approved, including Virginia in late June and New York in late July), he described the Constitution as "a good canvas, on which some strokes only want retouching." Most significant, he believed that Madison should listen to "the general voice from North to South, which calls for a bill of rights."[38]

Madison replied on October 17, 1788, enclosing a pamphlet that combined the various proposed amendments from the state ratifying conventions. The letter is the best attempt to explain his thinking we have. He began by explaining that his "own opinion has always been in favor of a bill of rights," although he had "not viewed it in an important light." He then proceeded to outline the arguments against a bill of rights: that it was unnecessary, given that the rights in question are reserved "though not in the extent argued by Mr. Wilson"; that "there is great reason to fear that a positive declaration of some of the most essential rights could not be obtained in the requisite latitude," in particular the rights of conscience, a subject dear to both Jefferson and Madison; that the limited power of the federal government and the jealousy of the states "afford a security" that does not exist within the states themselves; and, most significant to Madison, "because experience proves the inefficacy of a bill of rights on those occasions when its control is most needed." "Overbearing majorities in every State" had violated bills of rights, which Madison referred to as mere "parchment barriers." Here was Madison's central political issue, and crucially his thinking turned on the different functions of a bill of rights in monarchies and republics.[39]

Madison stressed to Jefferson that in republics such as the ones in the United States, the real danger did not come "from acts of Government contrary to the sense of its constituents, but from acts in which the Government is the mere instrument of the major number of the constituents." This was a fact that had impressed Madison, perhaps because he came to political maturity under republicanism while Jefferson's mind was habituated to thinking of abuses of power "issuing from a very different quarter." Jefferson had, after all, penned an address directed to the king (his *Summary View of the Rights of British America* of 1774) and was the primary draftsperson for the Declaration of Independence. Bills of rights belonged to monarchies for a reason, Madison explained, although in a way that was far more complex than the remarks Wilson, Jay, Hamilton, and Iredell would allow themselves to make in public:

> Wherever there is an interest and power to do wrong, wrong will generally be done, and not less readily by a powerful & interested party than by a powerful and interested prince. The difference, so far

as it relates to the superiority of republics over monarchies, lies in the less degree of probability that interest may prompt abuses of power in the former than in the latter; and in the security in the former agst. oppression of more than the smaller part of the society, whereas in the former it may be extended in a manner to the whole. The difference so far as it relates to the point in question—the efficacy of a bill of rights in controuling abuses of power—lies in this, that in a monarchy the latent force of the nation is superior to that of the sovereign, and a solemn charter of popular rights must have a great effect, as a standard for trying the validity of public acts, and a signal for rousing & uniting the superior force of the community; whereas in a popular Government, the political and physical power may be considered as vested in the same hands, that is in a majority of the people, and consequently the tyrannical will of the sovereign is not [to] be controuled by the dread of an appeal to any other force within the community.

"What use then it may be asked can a bill of rights serve in popular Governments?" Madison could point to only two, while he continued to argue that such declarations were "less essential than in other Governments," meaning monarchies. First, there was the point that Hamilton ridiculed in Federalist No. 84, where he said that most of the maxims and aphorisms in the various state bills of rights belonged more to a treatise on ethics: "The political truths declared in that solemn manner acquire by degrees the character of fundamental maxims of free Government, and as they become incorporated with the national sentiment, counteract the impulses of interest and passion." And second, although the true "danger of oppression lies in the interested majorities of the people rather than in usurped acts of the Government, yet there may be occasions on which the evil may spring from the latter sources; and on such, a bill of rights will be a good ground for an appeal to the sense of the community." Such a situation was unlikely, according to Madison, but it might happen.[40]

Jefferson replied from Paris five months later, on March 15, 1789, pointing out that he himself had once drafted a new constitution for Virginia in 1783 in which he "endavoured to reach all the great objects of public liberty, and did not mean to add a declaration of rights." To Madison's two points in favor of a bill of rights, Jefferson added one more: "the legal check which it puts in the hands of the judiciary." (Jack N. Rakove has observed that in fact, this has been the main forum in which the Bill of Rights found meaning and force, although not until after the Civil War.[41]) Jefferson couldn't resist answering Madison's points in order, often in a language of maxims that make him sound a bit like Benjamin Franklin's Poor Richard: "Half a loaf is better than no bread," he said of the difficulty of declaring rights. "A brace the more will often keep up the building which would have fallen with that brace the less," he replied about the inefficacy of the bills of rights in the states. Such colloquial aphorisms spoke to Madison's sense that a bill of rights might find its first use as memorable maxims of the kind Hamilton, writing as "Publius," had scoffed at.[42]

Finally, Jefferson came to Madison's central point, the notion that Jefferson's sense of political abuse was directed at the wrong quarter:

> The executive in our governments is not the sole, it is scarcely the principal object of my jealousy. The tyranny of the legislatures is the most formidable dread at present, and will be for long years. That of the executive will come in its turn, but it will be at a remote period. I know there are some among us who would now establish a monarchy. But they are inconsiderable in number and weight of character. The rising race are all republicans. We were educated in royalism: no wonder if some of us retain that idolatry still. Our young people are educated in republicanism. An apostacy from that to royalism is unprecedented and impossible.

In Jefferson's view, then, a bill of rights might at some future point serve as precisely the kind of hedge against encroaching executive prerogatives that the genre had been known for in England.[43]

When Madison first raised the topic of revisions to colleagues in the House of Representatives in June 1789, shortly after the election of George Washington, he noted that the British constitution did not protect two of the main protections many opponents of the Constitution had contended for, including the "freedom of the press, and the rights of conscience, those choicest flowers of the prerogative of the people." Although he believed that "We the People" had not expressly provided the government with specific powers to infringe upon those rights, nevertheless a "bill of rights" would help "quiet the minds of the people upon these points" and remove a lingering opposition. If nothing else, he tried to convince colleagues, there was "expediency" in such a declaration. But as he looked at the bills of rights that had been "annexed" to the constitutions of certain states, Madison observed that "the great object of these was, to limit and qualify the powers of Government—to guard against the encroachments of the

Executive." But in the federal government, "the Executive is weakest—the great danger lies not in the Executive, but in the great body of the people—in the disposition which the majority always discovers, to bear down, and depress the minority."[44] Here, as elsewhere in his most significant political thought of the period (his "Vices" memo, his speeches in Philadelphia, his letters to Jefferson, and Federalist No. 10), Madison seemed to worry more about the activities in the state legislatures than in the federal government.

The amendments Madison proposed to his colleagues on June 8, 1789, reflected his sense of where the threat to rights lay in the postrevolutionary (and postmonarchical) United States. Tellingly, these express declarations were intended to be addressed to the legislative and judicial powers as well as (in one crucial case) to the states themselves and not to the executive powers of the new president. Madison favored internal amendments to the text of the Constitution—that is, he preferred that changes be incorporated directly within the text at the point where modifications were to be made rather than as supplements to it. The parts of the original Constitution he wished to modify included the Preamble, Article I, and Article III; he also wished to add an additional article to the end of the text.

The new Preamble he proposed would contain a series of philosophical statements that echoed the language of many state declarations of rights and the Declaration of Independence about the source of power in the people, about the ends for which government was designed, including "the enjoyment of life and liberty, with the right of acquiring and using property, and generally pursuing and obtaining safety and happiness," concluding with a statement of the right of the people to reform or change their government when it is found to be adverse to or inadequate for those ends. Inside Article I, section 9, the section limiting the powers of Congress, Madison would have inserted the substance of what became (after subsequent debate) the First, Second, Third, Fourth, Fifth, Sixth, Eighth, and Ninth Amendments—nearly all of what, rightly or wrongly, we call the Bill of Rights. To Article I, section 10, the section limiting the powers of states, Madison would have added a limitation on state encroachments into the three areas anti-Federalists identified as most under threat: "No state shall violate the equal rights of conscience, or the freedom of the press, or the trial by jury in criminal cases." (As with his proposed federal legislative veto on state laws, this was a scheme that failed to win sufficient support from his colleagues.) In Article III, section 2, he would have placed what became in essence the Seventh Amendment. At the end of the Constitution, he proposed a final article with a new statement on the separation of powers, closing with the statement that "the powers not delegated by this constitution, nor prohibited by it to the states, are reserved to the states respectively," which, with slightly more expansive language, became the Tenth Amendment. This is what it meant to Madison to base or (as Richard Henry Lee would have it) to "bottom" a constitution on a bill of rights.[45] But it is unlikely that Lee would have seen the bill of rights he had called for as early as September 1787 in Madison's proposal.

Most significant, Madison's original amendment scheme left Article II and the executive power entirely untouched, a move that distinguished his plan from the many structural proposals from Virginia and elsewhere that would have amended how executive power was conceived and expressed through the Constitution. And although Madison lost the fight for internal revisions—and his cherished federal declaration against state violations of rights—the document he helped move through Congress in 1789 would not be, as the English Bill of Rights had been, a document addressed by legislators to encroaching executives. It was primarily directed against the legislators themselves. "Congress shall make no law," the U.S. Bill of Rights would instead begin. In its First Amendment, it covered two areas that the English Bill of Rights of 1689 did not mention: the "free exercise of religion" and the "freedom . . . of the press." And while some of the language in 1789 derived from that of 1689, the basic purpose of this new Bill of Rights was very different. The Eighth Amendment to the Constitution of the United States, with its prohibition on "cruel and unusual punishments" was very close in phrasing to a declaration in the 1689 English Bill of Rights and to the twelfth article in the 1776 Virginia Declaration of Rights that subsequently appeared in a few other state constitutions. Whereas the English in 1689 and the Virginians in 1776 had declared that "Excessive Bail ought not to be required, nor Excessive Fines imposed, nor cruel and unusual Punishments inflicted," the U.S. Bill of Rights stipulated that such things "shall not" rather than "ought not" happen. The central difference was not the change of a verb from a cautionary to a prohibitory mode, but the shift from a limitation on the executors of laws to the authors of them.[46]

Modern constitutional scholars and historians are not being overly precise when they point out that few contemporaries referred to the first ten amendments as a bill of rights. In several respects, the "Bill of Rights" we recognize today was not created in the late eighteenth century but was a product of the nineteenth and twentieth centuries.[47] It was perhaps impossible for revolutionary Americans to understand or to communicate the idea of the rights of Englishmen they imagined themselves struggling for without recourse to such touchstones as Magna Charta and the English Bill of Rights, documents in which kings had confirmed or conveyed rights. It would surely have been difficult for many to understand the language of rights that took hold of political imaginations across the Atlantic world in the seventeenth and eighteenth centuries—from London to Philadelphia to Paris—outside of the context of a sovereign to whom and against whom such rights were declared. But without a king, what purpose did a bill of rights serve? By moving away from a vision of a bill of rights as essentially antimonarchical, Madison's generation had altered both the idea and the genre of a bill of rights.

Notes

1. James Wilson at the Pennsylvania ratifying convention, November 28, 1787, in *The Documentary History of the Ratification of the Constitution*, ed. Merrill Jensen, John Kaminski, Gaspare Saladino et al., 27 vols. to date (Madison: Wisconsin Historical Society Press, 1976–), 2:389; "Giles Hickory," *American Magazine* (New York), December 1787, in Jensen et al., *Documentary History of the Ratification of the Constitution*, 20:553–54. For descriptions of a bill of rights as an absurdity in a republic in the earliest public debates of 1787, see Benjamin Rush at the Pennsylvania ratifying convention, November 30, 1787, in Jensen et al., *Documentary History of the Ratification of the Constitution*, 2:430.

2. Jack N. Rakove, "The Dilemma of Declaring Rights," in *The Nature of Rights at the American Founding and Beyond*, ed. Barry Alan Shain (Charlottesville: University of Virginia Press, 2007), 81–197.

3. Gordon S. Wood, "The Origins of the Bill of Rights," *Proceedings of the American Antiquarian Society* 101 (1991): 267.

4. On declarations of rights as an idea, see Keith Michael Baker, "The Idea of a Declaration of Rights," in *The French Idea of Freedom: The Old Regime and the Declaration of Rights in 1789*, ed. Dale Van Kley (Stanford, CA: Stanford University Press, 1994), 154–96; and on the genre of a declaration of rights, see David Armitage, *The Declaration of Independence: A Global History* (Cambridge, MA: Harvard University Press, 2007), 14–15.

5. For a summary of trends in the study of rights during the American Revolution, see Eric Slauter, "Rights," in *The Oxford Handbook to the American Revolution*, ed. Ed Gray and Jane Kamensky (New York: Oxford University Press, 2013), 447–64.

6. See Jeremy Waldron, ed., *"Nonsense upon Stilts": Bentham, Burke, and Marx on the Rights of Man* (London: Methuen, 1987), 53; and Armitage, *The Declaration of Independence*, 79–81, 174–76.

7. The basic positions in the debate over the question of whether human rights has an eighteenth-century history are set out in Lynn Hunt, *Inventing Human Rights: A History* (New York: Norton, 2007); and Samuel Moyn, *The Last Utopia: Human Rights in History* (Cambridge, MA: Harvard University Press, 2010).

8. Dan Edelstein, *On the Spirit of Rights* (Chicago: University of Chicago Press, 2019),

1–2. For another instance of quantitative work on the language of rights, see Peter de Bolla, *The Architecture of Concepts: The Historical Formation of Human Rights* (New York: Fordham University Press, 2013). Both de Bolla and Edelstein devote chapters to prerevolutionary America.

9. Paul Downes, *Democracy, Revolution, and Monarchism in Early American Literature* (Cambridge: Cambridge University Press, 2002), ix.

10. Downes, *Democracy, Revolution, and Monarchism*, ix, 3, 9, 196n11. The phrase about borrowing and adapting central features of monarchy appears in the promotional copy on the paperback edition of 2009. Downes cites Gordon S. Wood on pages 16, 24, 25, 29, 33, 66, 119–21, and 123–24. See Wood, *The Radicalism of the American Revolution* (New York: Knopf, 1992). The promotional subtitle for the hardcover edition of Wood's book was "How A Revolution Transformed A Monarchical Society into a Democratic One Unlike Any That Had Ever Existed."

11. Brendan McConville, *The King's Three Faces: The Rise and Fall of Royal America, 1688–1776* (Chapel Hill: University of North Carolina Press, 2006), 4, 9, and 11.

12. McConville, *The King's Three Faces*, 2, 3, 4, 9, 11, 70 plate 4, 105n1, 194 plate 8, 209–10, and 291. And see McConville, Review of *Democracy, Revolution, and Monarchy in Early American Literature* by Paul Downes, *William and Mary Quarterly* 60, no. 4 (2003): 917–20. For "empire of liberty," see Thomas Jefferson to George Rogers Clark, December 25, 1780, in *Papers of Thomas Jefferson*, ed. Julian P. Boyd et al. (Princeton, NJ: Princeton University Press, 1950–), 4:233–38.

13. Eric Nelson, *The Royalist Revolution: Monarchy and the American Founding* (Cambridge, MA: Harvard University Press, 2014), 2, 3, 5.

14. Nelson, *The Royalist Revolution*, 7, Nelson's italics.

15. Nelson, *The Royalist Revolution*, 239n29.

16. Saikrishna Bangalore Prakash, *Imperial from the Beginning: The Constitution of the Original Executive* (New Haven, CT: Yale University Press, 2015), 13.

17. Prakash, *Imperial from the Beginning*, 7, 20.

18. Prakash, *Imperial from the Beginning*, 10–11. Prakash's book is dense with citations to primary sources and articles in law reviews, but in nearly 2,000 footnotes, perhaps no more than a dozen refer to the work of contemporary historians. He cites Gordon S. Wood six times but does not mention Downes, McConville, or Nelson.

19. Robert E. Shalhope, "Toward a Republican Synthesis: The Emergence of an Understanding of Republicanism in American Historiography," *William and Mary Quarterly* 29, no. 1 (1972): 49–80.

20. On the shifting meanings of Magna Charta and its presence in the American Revolution, see Joyce Lee Malcolm, "Magna Charta in America: Entrenched," in *Magna Charta: The Foundation of Freedom, 1215–2015*, 2nd ed., ed. Nicholas Vincent (London: Third Millennium Publishing, 2015), 130; and Harry T. Dickinson, "Magna Charta in the American Revolution," in *Magna Charta: History, Context, and Influence*, ed. Lawrence Goldman (London: School of Advanced Study, University of London Institute of Historical Research, 2018), 79–100.

21. [John Dickinson], "Letter from a Farmer in Pennsylvania," no. 3, *Boston Gazette*, January 4, 1768.

22. [John Dickinson and Arthur Lee], *The Farmer's and Monitor's Letters, to the Inhabitants of the British Colonies* (Williamsburg, VA: William Rind, 1769), 62, 71.

23. *Pennsylvania Evening Post*, April 1, 1775.

24. "Extract from the Proceedings of the Continental Congress Assembled at Philadelphia the 5th of Sept. 1774, which . . . May Be Truly Called The American BILL of RIGHTS," *Gaine's Universal Register, or, American and British Kalendar, for the Year 1775* (New York: Hugh Gaine, [1774]), 149–51.

25. [Joseph Galloway?], *A Candid Examination of the Mutual Claims of Great-Britain, and the Colonies* (New York: James Rivington, 1775), 30.

26. James Madison to Thomas Mann Randolph, January 13, 1789, in *Papers of James Madison*, vol. 11, *7 March 1788–1 March 1789*, ed. William Hutchinson et al. (Charlottesville: University Press of Virginia, 1977), 415.

27. James Monroe, "Some Observations on the Constitution, ca. May 25, 1788," in Jensen et al., *Documentary History of the Ratification of the Constitution*, 9: 875; James Monroe at the Virginia ratifying convention, June 10, 1788, in Jensen et al., *Documentary History of the Ratification of the Constitution*, 9:1112; and "Amendments Proposed by the Virginia Convention, June 27, 1788, reprinted in Helen Veit, Kenneth R. Bowling, and Charlene Bangs Bickford, eds., *Creating the Bill of Rights: The Documentary Record from the First Federal Congress* (Baltimore: Johns Hopkins University Press, 1991), 17–21.

28. *Virginia Independent Chronicle* (Richmond), January 28, 1789. The letter also appeared subsequently in at least one newspaper in the North; see the *New Jersey Journal* (Elizabethtown), February 18, 1789.

29. "James Madison to Thomas Mann Randolph, January 13, 1789. Clipping from Virginia Independent Chronicle, January 28, 1789," Library of Congress, https://www.loc.gov/item/mjm023434/. Lee's manuscript transcript of parts of this letter survives at the Virginia Historical Society; see Hutchinson et al., *Papers of James Madison*, 11:417.

30. Richard Henry Lee, "Amendments Proposed to Congress, September 27, 1787," in *Declaring Rights: A Brief History with Documents*, ed. Jack N. Rakove (Boston: Bedford Books, 1997), 117–19; and "Copy of a Letter from the Honorable Richard Henry Lee, Esquire, to his Excellency the Governor, New York, Oct. 16, 1787," in *Various Extracts on the Foederal Government, Proposed by the Convention Held at Philadelphia* (Richmond, VA: August Davis, [1788?]), 55.

31. See Jefferson's note and the newspaper clipping in *The Federalist* (New York: McLean, 1788), catalogued as Ruggles 116, Newberry Library, Chicago.

32. James Wilson at the Pennsylvania ratifying convention, November 28, 1787, as reported by Thomas Lloyd and Alexander Dallas, in Jensen et al., *Documentary History of the Ratification of the Constitution*, 2:382; James Wilson, Statehouse Speech, October 6, 1787, in Rakove, *Declaring Rights*, 122.

33. Jefferson to Madison, December 20, 1787, in Rakove, *Declaring Rights*, 156.

34. [Alexander Hamilton], "The Federalist No. 84," [May 28, 1788], in *The Federalist*, ed. Jacob E. Cooke (Middletown, CT: Wesleyan University Press, 1961), 578–79.

35. [John Jay as "A Citizen of New York"], "An Address to the People of the State of New York," April 15, 1788, in Jensen et al., *Documentary History of the Ratification of the Constitution*, 20:933.

36. James Iredell at the North Carolina ratifying convention, July 28, 1788, in *Debates in the Several State Conventions on the Adoption of the Federal Constitution*, ed. Jonathan Elliot (Washington, DC: Elliot, 1836), 4:148.

37. James Madison to Thomas Jefferson, October 24, 1787, in Rakove, *Declaring Rights*, 150–52.

38. Jefferson to Madison, December 20, 1787, in Rakove, *Declaring Rights*, 156; Jefferson to Madison, July 31, 1788, in Rakove, *Declaring Rights*, 157.

39. Madison to Jefferson, October 17, 1788, in Rakove, *Declaring Rights*, 161–62; Jefferson to Madison, March 15, 1789, in Rakove, *Declaring Rights*, 165–66.

40. Madison to Jefferson, October 17, 1788, in Rakove, *Declaring Rights*, 161–62.

41. Jack N. Rakove, *Original Meanings: Politics and Ideas in the Making of the Constitution* (New York: Knopf, 1996), 288–90.

42. Jefferson to Madison, March 15, 1789, in Rakove, *Declaring Rights*, 165.

43. Jefferson to Madison, March 15, 1789, 166.

44. James Madison, June 8, 1789, as reported in the *Gazette of the United States* (New York), reprinted in *Creating the Bill of Rights: The Documentary Record from the First Federal Congress*, ed. Helen E. Veit, Kenneth R. Bowling, and Charlene Bangs Bickford (Baltimore, MD: Johns Hopkins University Press, 1991), 66–67.

45. Madison Resolution, June 8, 1789, in Veit, Bowling, and Bickford, *Creating the Bill of Rights*, 11–14.

46. The terms are Hamilton's, in "The Federalist No. 26," in Cooke, *The Federalist*, 167.

47. A number of scholars have made the case that the "Bill of Rights" was not born in 1789 or 1791. In *The Bill of Rights: Creation and Reconstruction* (New Haven, CT: Yale University Press, 1998), Akhil Reed Amar looked to the Reconstruction period and the framing of the Fourteenth Amendment in 1868 for the true birth of an understanding of the first ten amendments as the "Bill of Rights." In *Ratification: The People Debate the Constitution* (New York: Simon and Schuster, 2010), Pauline Maier builds on Amar's insight and finds that from September 1789 to early 1792, "nobody seems to have referred to either the twelve amendments proposed by Congress in September 1789 or the ten that were ratified by the end of 1791 as a 'bill of rights'" (459–60). More recently, Gerald N. Magliocca has placed emphasis on the rise of the phrase and its use to augment federal power in the early twentieth century; see *The Heart of the Constitution: How the Bill of Rights became the Bill of Rights* (New York: Oxford University Press, 2018). Madison did, in fact, introduce his proposed amendments on June 8, 1789, by describing some of them as "a bill of rights"; see the reports in the *Gazette of the United States*, June 10, 1789, and in the Congressional Register for June 8, 1789, in Veit, Bowling, and Bickford, *Creating the Bill of Rights*, 66–67, 80–81.

5

Enlightened Despotism
and the American Revolution

The Political Thought of Frederick the Great of Prussia

CAROLINE WINTERER

"All mankind, Sir, agree that you are as illustrious a personage as the King of Prusia ever was," one of George Washington's many admirers informed him in 1795.[1] This was high praise for the president of the young republic, for King Frederick II of Prussia (1712–86) was renowned in Europe and America as a military genius, a philosopher, and a patron of the arts. Even if not quite all humankind admired King Frederick, many people did, including George Washington himself. As a young man, Washington had ordered a small bust of Frederick II to adorn Mount Vernon.[2]

Why such admiration for this powerful king in an infant republic that had just thrown off monarchy? To answer this question, this essay charts revolutionary Americans' reception of the ideas of King Frederick II of Prussia. During his long reign, which extended from 1740 until his death in 1786, Frederick became a relentless public advocate for enlightened reform engineered through powerful monarchical rule. Americans listened and observed as they pondered how to build a republic for the age of enlightenment.[3] Having shrugged off not just their specific king but monarchy in general in 1776, they cast about for models for a new species of executive that was fit for a republic. The question of the republican executive would become especially urgent during the framing of the new office of the presidency that was eventually enshrined in Article II of the U.S. Constitution.[4]

For revolutionary Americans, Frederick filled an empty niche: the warrior-scholar. Unlike the Hanoverian kings of Britain, who by the middle of the eighteenth century had stopped leading troops into battle and were never renowned for their love of abstract topics, Frederick was both a brilliant tactician and an intellectually curious man. He reminded Americans of Julius Caesar and Marcus Aurelius, who had "immortalized themselves and their Actions by their own Pens."[5] No other chief executive in the eighteenth century offered a plausible alternative. Even the war hero George Washington "was not a Scholar," complained John Trumbull.[6]

Small wonder that revolutionary Americans read Frederick's prolific publications to see how a powerful executive and military commander confronted the pressing political and intellectual questions of the age. What most attracted Americans—especially in the late 1780s, as they set about imagining the American presidency—was the living example of executive power that was seemingly tempered by personal virtue and deployed in the interests of the people. Although some Americans were cynical about King Frederick's absolutist motives, the revolutionary-era interest in Frederick is a reminder of the dearth of models for executive power framers of the new federal Constitution confronted. Put simply, in this age of monarchies, a republican executive had to be modeled largely on monarchs.[7]

Frederick the Great's popularity suggests the urgent need to revise our current understanding of monarchical thought in revolutionary America. So far, the focus has been almost exclusively on British monarchy. Several recent studies have reminded us of Americans' deep-seated attachment to their Hanoverian king even at the very doorstep of revolution in 1775.[8] But Britain's Stuarts and Hanoverians hardly exhausted the range of monarchical models; Europe and most of the Americas were then governed by kings, queens, and emperors. There is no doubt that the memory of the hated absolutist Stuarts of seventeenth-century Britain haunted Americans on the eve of independence. But by then the long-dead Stuarts were paper tigers. The last Stuart monarch, Queen Anne, had died in 1714 without surviving heirs. Although colonial pamphleteers periodically unleashed them as reminders of the lurking threat of despotism, the Stuarts had slipped from the living memory of all but the oldest Americans by the time the first colonial protests against British taxation erupted in the 1760s. What is more, the personal animus patriotic Americans felt toward King George III still left room for surprisingly generous appraisals of other living European monarchs, such as France's Louis XVI, and for ancient despots such as Cyrus the Great of Persia, who was known to college-bound revolutionary Americans through required readings of Xenophon's *Cyropaedia*.[9] Finally, Americans had to remain up to date on the actions of European monarchs. For decades after the American Revolution, monarchy remained the hard reality of the international stage, where weak, kingless republics might go like lambs to slaughter. Napoleon recognized this when he crowned himself emperor of the French in 1804, in part to earn the respect of conservative European monarchs.[10]

Compounding this British-centric focus has been the general reluctance of American historians to take monarchy seriously as a modern or enlightened intellectual concern. "Especially in the United States," the editors of a recent volume assert, "there is almost no recognition that anyone ever saw any redeeming value in monarchy or monarchism. . . . Many take it for granted that a real monarchy must be socially backward, politically repressive, intellectually unjustifiable, the last gasp of feudalism, and fit only for the dustbin of history."[11] During the Cold War, historians such as Peter Gay, Henry May, and Henry Steele Commager constructed a mythical eighteenth-century "American Enlightenment" by identifying the American Revolution as the origin of the twentieth-century democratic ideals that would shield the United States from Soviet totalitarianism. Their new concept of the "American Enlightenment," which was popularized in the period 1945 to 1970, could not take monarchical thought seriously as a preoccupation of enlightened thinkers in North America, since the story of kings seemed to lead only backward into the mists of antiquity that Thomas Paine mocked in his best-selling *Common Sense* (1776). One result has been that Frederick II's many publications, which were well known in eighteenth-century America, have largely disappeared from view, erased even in the most influential analyses of the libraries of "enlightened" eighteenth-century Americans.[12]

And yet enlightened despots of Europe were major actors in their era. This means that American views about monarchy were shaped not just by British examples but also by living continental monarchs. King Frederick was just one of a clutch of "enlightened despots" who together reigned over large expanses of eighteenth-century Europe: Catherine of Russia (1729–96), Carlos III of Spain (1716–88), Gustav III of Sweden (1746–92), the Holy Roman Empress Maria-Theresa (1717–80), and her son and heir Joseph II (1741–90). Emerging from seventeenth-century divine-right monarchy, these rulers adjusted their mandate to the intellectual climate of their era. They claimed—by their actions, their publications, and their policies—that it was possible to mix formidable executive power with reforms aligned with the new ideal of enlightenment, whose core principle was that human reason could understand, change, and improve the world.[13] To greater and lesser degrees, they reformed law codes, criminal justice, and education; encouraged greater religious toleration; and promoted culture and the arts. To Americans watching from across the Atlantic, these monarchs provided widely known, dynamic, modern examples of how to mix monarchical rule with the new goal of enlightenment. Unlike the absolutist monarchs of the previous century, who could swat away kingless republican rule as a momentary infatuation, the enlightened despots of the eighteenth century were living in the new reality of popular opinion and (with the successful conclusion of the American Revolution) republican government. Furthermore, a number of revolutionary Americans believed that not all societies had evolved to the point where they were ready for republican government. Thomas Jefferson maintained that Tsar Alexander, who acceded to the Russian throne in 1801, embodied the ideal enlightened monarch, who could secure freedom and happiness for his people as they prepared for a future era of self-government.[14]

Nowhere was Americans' serious interest in enlightened despotism clearer than in their interest in the king of Prussia, the war hero, political philosopher, and enlightened reformer. Unlike the cardboard British tyrants of revolutionary American pamphleteers, Frederick II changed and adapted before American eyes. From the young prince who brashly invaded Silesia emerged the weathered statesman confronting a violent new age of revolution that no one could have foreseen half a century before.

Frederick II is a reminder that thinking about monarchy was never simply a pro or anti conversation. It was instead a kaleidoscopic dialogue across Europe and America that reached far into the nineteenth century as monarchical regimes rose and fell in the Old and New Worlds. Monarchy was never the ossified relic of a vanished ancien régime but rather an evolving, modern species of executive power whose perils and prospects continued to test modern minds. A century after the American Revolution, political scientist Theodore Dwight Woolsey complained that monarchy was difficult to define because it was always changing. "It may sometimes be a matter of doubt by what name a government in actual existence ought to be called," he wrote in 1877, "for the reason that it has changed since its history began by the rise of new interests and ideas."[15] Revolutionary American interest in Frederick's political and philosophical works was part of a larger question: what form of government—republican or monarchical—would yield the greatest enlightenment?

Frederick the Great, Philosopher King

Frederick II first became known to Americans for his military achieve-ments. A battle-tested soldier and skilled tactician who more or less dou-bled the size of Prussia's army and territory, Frederick was the eighteenth century's version of Louis XIV, who had steadily and relentlessly expanded France's borders during the previous century. And like the Sun King, Fred-erick's talents blossomed early; by age 30 he was already being called "the Great."[16] In contrast to France and Britain, Prussia was not a maritime power and never built an American empire. Still, during the Seven Years' War (1756–63), the conflict that defined Frederick's reputation as a skilled military commander, he allied with Britain against the common enemy of France. American newspapers of that era tracked the military achieve-ments of "the Brave King of Prussia."[17] Royal inbreeding also helped gen-erate a warm, familial glow of approval around Frederick. King George I of Britain was Frederick's grandfather, George II his uncle. One Boston stonecutter sold busts of both kings George III and Frederick II.[18]

More glory awaited King Frederick during the American Revolution. After Britain deserted Prussia to make a treaty with France in 1761, Fred-erick renounced his former ally.[19] He began publicly mocking Britain's Hanoverian kings as dogs wagged by the tail of their liberty-idolizing electorate.[20] Not inclined to support revolutionary Americans on the phil-osophical grounds of rule by the people, Frederick strove for a neutrality that would maximize Prussia's commercial prospects while not antagoniz-ing Britain. That was enough for the Americans, whose army desperately needed seasoned commanders. In Frederick, thought American general Nathanael Greene, they had "the greatest General of the age."[21] Freder-ick's former Prussian army officer, Baron Friedrich Wilhelm von Steuben, helped George Washington whip the undisciplined Continental Army into shape. Generals and soldiers alike consulted Frederick's various treatises on the art of war, such as the 1762 English translation of his *Military In-structions*.[22] Newspapers changed their mastheads to quote the King of Prussia. "The Entire Prosperity of Every State Depends upon the Disci-pline of Its Armies," announced the banner of Boston's *Continental Journal and Weekly Advertiser*.[23] Finally, in 1785 the two nations signed a Treaty of Amity and Commerce.

Yet there was much more to Frederick than war, commerce, and diplo-macy. Compared to Britain's mostly uncurious Georgian kings, Frederick had a lively, probing intellect. Where George II might be found occasionally glancing at peerages and hunting manuals, Frederick read Newton, Montesquieu, Rousseau, Christian Wolff, and Voltaire—by his own reckoning an "infinity" of books.[24] He published early, often, learnedly, and influentially. He saw himself as a beacon of what he called enlightenment—or, in the French terminology he preferred, of both *lumière* (the metaphor of light generally) and *lumières* (enlightenment as opposed to superstition).[25] And although he mangled the French language to the ongoing amusement of the philosophes, Frederick always preferred it to his native German (although critics during his lifetime and after were harsh, calling the king a "heavy German Muse . . . dreary with an unutterable dreariness").[26]

His mind brimming with the ideas of the philosophes, Frederick issued a stream of political and philosophical works beginning in his late twenties: the *Antimachiavel* (1740); *History of My Own Times* (1746); *Art of War* (1751); *Memoirs of the House of Brandenburg* (1751); *Political Testament* (1752); another *Political Testament* (1768), *Critical Examination of the Essay on Prejudice* (1770); *Essay on Self-Love Considered as an Ethical Principle* (1770); *Discourse on the Usefulness of the Sciences and the Arts within a State* (1772); *Essay on the Forms of Government and the Duties of Sovereigns* (1777); and *Concerning German Literature* (1780).[27] Even death did not silence him. Compilations and translations of his works continued to appear after his death in 1786.

An accomplished flautist and composer, Frederick also patronized poets, painters, and musicians. He liked to collect them at his rococo palace-cum-refuge at Sanssouci near Berlin, what a visiting John Quincy Adams called "the philosophical retreat of Frederic." In its complex architecture he assembled some of the most celebrated minds of the era: La Mettrie, d'Alembert, Maupertuis, Algarotti, Voltaire, and others. These he alternately befriended and alienated.[28]

Philosophy too found a home in Frederick's Prussia, even though the king personally found German philosophy abstruse. Frederick's father had banished the German philosopher Christian Wolff, whose philosophy of determinism struck his critics as being tantamount to atheism. Immediately upon ascending the throne, Frederick II reversed the royal decree and invited Wolff back to Prussia. According to the admiring John Quincy Adams, Wolff was "reinstated at Halle, with a handsome salary, the title of privy councellor, & the liberty of lecturing as he should think proper, without limitation."[29] From the city of Königsberg in Prussia's newly conquered eastern fringe, the philosopher Immanuel Kant reflected in published essays (ambivalently during the king's lifetime, more negatively after

Frederick's death) on his monarch's efforts at enlightened rule.[30] Frederick's hundreds of letters to and from these philosophers formed yet another channel for the circulation of his ideas. Many were published in several languages and widely disseminated during his lifetime and after. The printing press Frederick installed at Sanssouci became a factory for the dissemination of his epics, poems, and odes, beginning with the illustrated *Works of the Philosopher of Sans Souci* (1749–50).[31] Portraits of the king capture him in this middle world between Mars and Minerva. He stands smartly in his military garb even as his watery, round eyes seem to invite us to probe a complex inner ecology.

Frederick's political philosophy can be whittled down to some major themes. His starting point was the supremacy of the monarch, although along different lines than the absolutist monarchs of the previous century. Unlike Louis XIV of France, who had celebrated kingship by divine grace in a single person, Frederick thought monarchs should subordinate themselves to the love for and promotion of the state. He cast himself as the state's servant, a person just like other subjects except for an accident of birth that made him first among equals. Because the king represented the will of the people, he should align his own desire for glory with the well-being of his subjects. "The prince must often remind himself that he is a man like the least of his subjects," Frederick explained in his *Essay on the Forms of Government and Duties of Sovereigns* (1777). "If he is the first judge, first general, first financier, first minister of society, it is not so that he can represent it but so that he can fulfill his duties. He is merely the first servant of the State, obliged to act honestly, wisely, and with total disinterestedness so that his administration can be held to account by his citizens."[32] In eighteenth-century theory, there were no real institutional checks on the authority of this enlightened despot once he or she had accepted the limits and responsibility of natural law. It is thus no wonder that modern historians have debated the degree to which enlightened despotism was merely divine right kingship dressed up in enlightenment garb, or "Louis XIV without a wig," as one historian has put it.[33]

Frederick also followed new efforts to create a rigorous, empirical science of society. He was especially interested in Montesquieu's *The Spirit of Laws* (1748), which presented a taxonomy of regimes that included monarchies, despotisms, and republics. According to Montesquieu, each had a distinguishing principle that must animate that form of government if it were to function properly. In republics, for example, virtue was the spring of politics. Citizens were inspired to selfless action by the thought of the larger good; private ambition endangered the republic. The opposite was true in monarchies, which were driven by aristocratic ambition. The nobility's lust for honor set all the parts of the body politic in motion, each individual advancing the public good by promoting his or her own self-interest. Frederick believed that Montesquieu's notion of honor could be found in Prussia's nobility, which was transforming from a self-serving elite into a national class whose bond with the monarch helped Prussia's armies conquer Europe. Not only did the nobility have esprit de corps, thought Frederick, it also had esprit de nation.[34]

Finally, like others at this time, Frederick posited a social contract. By now, the social contract had become a term of art in political discussions, like "natural law" and "state of nature." It was generally thought to imply that legitimate political rule should be based on the consent of the ruled rather than on a divine or natural title to rule. In Jean-Jacques Rousseau's version, which appeared in his *Of the Social Contract* (1762), each individual in a political society gave up certain capacities to the "general will," which by representing the pooled rights and capacities of each person became a politically legitimate entity. Because popular sovereignty defined political legitimacy for Rousseau, he argued that only republican or popular rule was legitimate. Tyranny and despotism would always be illegitimate.[35]

By contrast Frederick interpreted the social contract in authoritarian terms. He believed that the inhabitants of a state of nature delegated enough authority to a sovereign to maintain security and order. Subjects had no right of resistance, having granted the sovereign power irrevocably and unconditionally. That said, in Frederick's view, the ruler should serve the interests of the whole. Unlike truly despotic regimes such as Russia and the Ottoman Empire, in Prussia the power of the monarch would be limited by the social contract. The king's duty was to uphold the rule of law and to dole out prosperity, security, and everything else that could ensure the welfare of the community. Frederick granted some freedom of the press, but this too reflected an absolutist view of the state, since the prince would grant those freedoms or not, depending on his personal preferences. Rousseau was horrified; his engraving of Frederick had these words underneath: "*Il pense en philosophe et se conduit en roi*" (He thinks like a philosopher and behaves like a king).[36]

We can glimpse Frederick's ideal of authoritarian virtue by looking closely at his first publication, the *Anti-Machiavel* (1740), which he conceived and wrote in the late 1730s, before he had ascended to the throne.[37]

As the title suggests, the book was a vigorous refutation of Niccolò Machiavelli's *The Prince* (1542). In that work, Machiavelli had broken with the ancient mirror-for-princes genre, which had schooled monarchs to reign with an eye to personal virtue at a time when political office and the private individual had not fully separated. Instead, Machiavelli offered a pragmatic treatise on acquiring and preserving power, which heretically for its time turns to the authority of history rather than the moral authority of God to ground its principles.[38]

Frederick utterly disagreed with Machiavelli's principles. A crown prince still in his 20s—and still untested by the gritty realities of actual rule—Frederick instead idealized a version of monarchy he thought better suited to the age of enlightenment. Adopting the new historical perspective characteristic of the eighteenth century, which imagined history progressing upward from a savage past to a civilized present, Frederick dismissed Machiavelli's era as a time of tooth-and-claw barbarity wholly inferior to his own age of "modern politicks."[39] The business of princes in the age of enlightenment, wrote Frederick, was to govern nations and administer justice to their subjects; their highest duty was to be moral, magnanimous, merciful, and good.[40]

Frederick's *Anti-Machiavel* bore the strong imprint of one of the great innovators of enlightenment-era history writing: Voltaire, who had been exiled from France for declaring Georgian Britain to be the nursery of political liberty. The prince and the philosopher had struck up a correspondence in 1736 that was to last until Voltaire's death forty years later. Frederick poured out his contempt for Machiavelli in long letters to Voltaire. Machiavelli was "*un malhonêtte homme*" and "*coquin méprisable*" (a dishonest man and contemptible rascal).[41] "I am working on the notes on his *Prince*," the young prince informed Voltaire in 1739, "and I have already begun a work which will entirely refute his maxims, by the opposition which is between them and virtue, as well as with the true interests of the princes."[42] In the late months of 1739, Frederick sent his *Anti-Machiavel*, chapter by chapter, for Voltaire's comments. Voltaire murmured flattering replies, praising Frederick for doing serious combat with Machiavelli for the good of mankind.[43] Finally, late in 1740, Voltaire had it published—against Frederick's wishes—by the publisher Van Duren in The Hague.[44]

Immediately Frederick found fault with it and pushed for a new edition under his direction ("*sous mes yeux*") in Berlin.[45] By 1749, he had confessed embarrassment at the *Anti-Machiavel*, especially after the deposed Polish king Stanisław Leszczyński (who had just had his own reformist pamphlet published) called it a schoolboy production. Could he do it again, Frederick vowed, it would be wiser and briefer.[46] Though the *Anti-Machiavel* established his reputation as a monarch fit for the age of enlightenment, the withering criticism was a hard lesson for Frederick on the realities of publishing in an age of growing public opinion—and the inevitable public criticism of established authority.[47]

Revolutionary Americans and Frederick's Political Thought

Although King Frederick's political philosophy was known to a few educated Americans by the 1760s, the outbreak of the American Revolution suddenly raised the king's ideas into high relief. What is more, the German states more generally—including Prussia—now became far more relevant to Americans' political concerns. (Two other significant ones for Americans were Hesse-Kassel and Hesse-Hanau, which Great Britain used as a source of mercenary soldiers in the American Revolution.) All America was now watching the "great philosopher and warrior," noted the *Pennsylvania Packet* in 1779.[48]

The German states, a confusing patchwork of powers nestled between Russia and France, struck some Americans as a monarchical version of their own thirteen republican states, each of a different size, population, and economy. Owing to Frederick's nearly ceaseless military campaigns since his invasion of Silesia in 1740, Prussia had emerged as the dominant German state by the era of the revolution, surpassing even the Holy Roman Empire under Maria Theresa and her son and successor, Joseph II. Here was a monarch for the age of enlightenment, dabbling in ideas as his armies conquered Europe. Frederick's growing fame led to his political works being translated into English and published in London, the chief source for Americans' books. The most commonly read version of Machiavelli's *Prince* in eighteenth-century America, for example, was Frederick's refutation in his *Anti-Machiavel*, which Ellis Farneworth published in an English translation in 1762. This work consisted of the original text by Machiavelli and Frederick's rebuttals in the footnotes and in an introduction that Frederick and Voltaire had written.[49]

American diplomatic activities in Europe during the 1780s brought the king himself into view. The marquis de Lafayette—the highest-ranking foreign officer in the Continental Army during the revolution—visited the king in 1785 and told George Washington that Frederick had asked him questions about "the Resources, the Union, and the future existence of America."[50] Lafayette believed that English newspapers were spreading throughout Europe "reports very much to the prejudice of the American character & politicks."[51] The old king, he told Washington, was very ill but "Has Been Most peculiarly Kind to me."[52] Lafayette called Frederick one of the "great Sovereigns and distinguished Characters" whom he hoped to see, despite his own "Republican Heart."[53]

John Adams also warmed to the Prussian king. Although he did not meet Frederick, he personally encountered several other reigning monarchs, including Louis XVI, Marie-Antoinette, George III, and Queen Charlotte. These episodes changed his mind about monarchs as people, if not monarchy itself as an institution. In 1776, as a provincial with no experience of living monarchs, Adams had scorned Frederick's "absolute Monarchy," arguing that republics were more militarily powerful than monarchies, which conquered only by "Corruption and Division."[54] Only a few years later, after actual experience in European courts, Adams changed his tune. Though he still confessed himself a republican, he "did not despise monarchy merely for the sake of despising it," he told Lafayette in 1782, while singling out the kings of France, Germany, and Prussia as living examples of "Humanity Wisdom and Beneficence."[55] Frederick in particular was "that Great Prince who does so much Honour to his age."[56]

Even the king-despising Thomas Jefferson found room for a grudging admiration of Frederick II. In 1785, from Paris, Jefferson sent to James Monroe a copy of Voltaire's scandalous *La vie privée du roi de Prusse* (The Private Life of the King of Prussia, 1784).[57] Voltaire had painted Frederick in lurid colors, alluding openly to the king's homosexuality and irreligion: "*Il n'entrait jamais dans le Palais n'y femmes n'y Prêtres: en un mot Frédéric vivait sans Cour, sans Conseil, & sans Culte*" (Neither women nor priests entered the palace; in a word, Frederick lived without court, without council, and without worship).[58] Jefferson contrasted the king's virtue with Voltaire's sarcasm. "I send you Voltaire's legacy to the K. of Prussia, a libel which will do much more injury to Voltaire than to the king. Many of the traits in the character of the latter to which the former gives a turn satyrical and malicious, are real virtues."[59] The next year Jefferson paid to see a wax statue of Frederick the Great in his dark blue Prussian uniform at the *cabinet de cire* at the Palais-Royal.[60]

Americans also observed Frederick's handling of the growing public sphere. In both Europe and America, newspapers, magazines, books, and literacy blossomed in the eighteenth century, creating a new "public" that both examined and at times criticized existing state power. The challenge for rulers who hoped for enlightenment was to balance public criticism with political stability. Frederick's response had been to allow the press a great deal of leeway to say what it would, as long as he remained in power. John Quincy Adams observed the result when he visited Berlin in 1781. He told his father that Frederick was tearing down old houses and erecting elegant new ones in their place. "But notwithstanding this, he is not beloved in Berlin, and every body says publicly what he pleases against the king; but as long as they do not go any farther than words, he don't take any notice of it but says that as long as they give him all he asks, they may say what they will. But they have a great reason to complain of him, for he certainly treats them like Slaves."[61]

As the weakness of the Articles of Confederation became manifest by the early 1780s, the political structure of the German states also became relevant as models and anti-models of confederated governments. The Articles of Confederation, drafted in 1777 and ratified in 1781, reflected the revolutionaries' fears of executive power. Affirming the sovereignty of each state, the founders envisioned the articles as "a firm league of friendship." Each state was to be represented by one vote in a national body whose inability to enforce taxation (especially during wartime), among other deficiencies, quickly led to weakness and chaos. It was the failings of the articles that led to the convention of 1787 that ultimately produced the U.S. Constitution.

One solution to the absence of a single-person executive under the articles came from Prussia in the person of Frederick's brother, Prince Henry. There is evidence that Nathaniel Gorham, president of the Confederation Congress, made overtures to Prince Henry, "desiring him to come to the United States to *be their King*."[62] From Prussia, probably in early 1787, Prince Henry replied to a letter from von Steuben that appears to have suggested that the prince come to the United States to become a constitutional monarch along British lines.[63] The prince's letter rolled out a Montesquieu-like admiration for the British constitution, which he considered *"la plus parfaite"* (the most perfect) for best balancing the rights of monarch and subjects.[64] Postponing further discussion until a cipher could be found to turn his letter into secret code, Prince Henry suggested that Americans were unlikely to dispense with the republican principles they had so vigorously fought for and that the cooperation of their French allies would be necessary for any sort of monarchical restoration.

Meanwhile, James Madison was reading about the "Germanic Confederacy" (the Imperial Diet) at his Montpelier plantation in 1786 to prepare for the revision of the Articles of Confederation. By that point, Madison's extensive reading in history had convinced him that confederacies were by definition fragile creations, prone to weakness and dissolution. He feared that this would be the fate of the new United States under the articles. Especially problematic in Madison's view was the absence of a central, controlling authority.[65] Here the German confederacy supplied a notable contrast. In his "Notes on Ancient and Modern Confederacies," written in 1786, Madison strove to understand the highly complex scheme of representation of the Imperial Diet, where the so-called imperial estates (made of numerous hereditary secular powers, ecclesiastical bodies, and cities) convened and exercised considerable privileges. The key point of interest for Madison was that the only authority above the imperial estates was the Holy Roman emperor himself (who at that time was Joseph II, another enlightened despot in the vein of Frederick the Great). Madison took extensive notes on the twenty-four powers specific to the emperor, which he called the "prerogative." These included a veto on the Diet's resolutions and the appointing of ambassadors. In fact, what glued the whole Germanic confederacy together, according to Madison, was "Jealousy of the Imperial authority."[66]

After the drafting of the new federal constitution in the fall of 1787, Americans debated the wisdom of confederations more generally. Some held up the "German confederation" as a model for the new federal government, in which the independence of the states remained great despite the centralization of authority. In the Pennsylvania ratification debates in the late fall of 1787, a proponent of the constitution pointed out that in the German states, a number of deputies met in the Diet to make laws that applied to the whole of the German states. "But has this general head subverted the independence and liberties of its constituent members? No: for, on the reverse," this member stated, "we find the House of Austria, a single branch, has become superior to the whole, except the King of Prussia."[67]

Others argued that the Germanic states revealed the inherent weaknesses of confederacies. Essay 19 of *The Federalist* (likely authored by Madison) offered a short history of the Germanic states. In that narrative, the emperor and numerous princes constantly vied for power in their Diet (which Americans now likened to their Congress), rendering them weak and vulnerable to foreign attack. Publius declared the Holy Roman Empire (despite its emperor) to be a "a nerveless body; incapable of regulating its own members; insecure against external dangers; and agitated with unceasing fermentations in its own bowels."[68] At the New York ratifying convention in June 1788, John Lansing concurred, speaking powerfully against the Germanic confederacy. "The Germanic Confederacy consists of a heterogeneous mass of powerful Princes, petty despots, and republics, differently organized, divided by religious jealousies, and existing only in its forms by the pressure of the great controlling power of the Emperor," he observed.[69] Alexander Hamilton also weighed in. "The German confederacy has also been a perpetual source of wars: They have a diet, like our Congress, who have authority to call for supplies: These calls are never obeyed; and in time of war, the Imperial army never takes the field, till the enemy are returning from it. The Emperor's Austrian dominions, in which he is an absolute prince, alone enable him to make head against the common foe. The members of this confederacy are ever divided and opposed to each other. The king of Prussia is a member; yet he has been constantly in opposition to the Emperor. Is this a desirable government?"[70]

Others argued that it was less a confederation of little monarchies than monarchy itself that posed a danger to the new nation. Antifederalists were especially vocal. Fearful of the consolidation of central power the proposed federal constitution represented, they warned of the dangers of a "military king" who would be elected by the people but would be a king "to all intents and purposes."[71] Predicting that this military king would simply gather a standing army behind him, one anti-Federalist accused the proposed president as having powers that would exceed those of the most despotic monarchy of modern times. Another called Frederick "that grand Prince of despots, the late King of Prussia."[72]

The dangers of powerful European monarchy frightened others. The ratification debates in Virginia showed the continuing fear that European monarchies such as Prussia would seek to influence either the American president or the members of the electoral college. The only solution was regular election of the president to make sure he "returned to a private station" and did not become an "elective Monarchy."[73]

Frederick's example also served as a model for the new judicial system in the United States. Committed to authoritarian enlightenment, Frederick had substantially reformed the legal system in Prussia, abolishing the use of torture, codifying and centralizing many aspects of the judicial system, and working to ensure that peasants and nobles were treated equally in the eyes of the law.[74] Although the reform efforts ended with the king's death in 1786, they continued to attract attention in the United States as the nation launched its judicial system based on ostensibly enlightened, republican principles in 1789. "Laws should be founded on justice, reason and utility, without regarding the precedents of any other nation," wrote an anonymous correspondent to President George Washington. "They ought to be simplified and reduced to as small a compass as possible, as the late king of prussia did for his subjects."[75]

For the American jurist James Wilson, Frederick became a symbol of the need for Americans to start afresh with their judiciary, distinguishing their republican principles from the monarchical basis of British law. In the colonial period, Americans had looked to the British jurist William Blackstone's influential *Commentaries on the Laws of England* (1765–69) as a guide to British common law. Blackstone's England was one of "rank and distinction"—of commoners, nobility, and Crown and all law ultimately flowing downward from the monarch.[76]

Wilson believed that the Revolution had delegitimized this innate hierarchy. He interpreted Blackstone to mean that law was nothing but the "rule of action prescribed by some superior, and which the inferior is bound to obey."[77] Wilson's *Lectures on Law* (1790–91), delivered in Philadelphia, argued instead that law rested on "consent of those whose obedience the law requires" rather than "the will of a superior."[78] To Wilson, Frederick's hierarchical conception of law was as unacceptable as Blackstone's. He quoted Frederick at length to make his point. Frederick had written that although princes were mere "men, as well as the least of their subjects," they stood above the people and society. They were "the first judges, the first generals, the first financiers, the first ministers of society."[79] Wilson countered that the king's doctrine of royal superiority was no longer necessary. Divine right of kings had emerged to counter the "tyranny of priests." But since that danger had passed, divine right of all superiors could be shelved in favor of consent only by "the people."[80] The American executive could safely rest on that principle, Wilson explained in a later lecture on the structure of government. Elected and nonhereditary, the American executive would rest entirely on "the publick choice." From the power of popular sovereignty, Wilson continued, "there is no appeal: to their errour there is no superior principle of correction."[81] For Wilson, Frederick's example showed that the errors of popular sovereignty were preferable to the illegitimate claims of princes.

Beyond Politics: The American Reception of Frederick's Philosophy

A military model in the revolutionary war and a political model in the constitution-making period, Frederick also became a controversial exemplum of extreme enlightenment philosophy for a few Americans in the 1790s and early 1800s. This new role was due in large part to the posthumous appearance of a French-language collection of his works, the *Oeuvres posthumes de Frederic II, roi de Prusse* (1788), published in Berlin in fourteen volumes.[82] The next year a thirteen-volume English translation by Thomas Holcroft appeared in London.[83] These multivolume works captured the sheer diversity of Frederick's interests, from metaphysics to religion to science to history. They also included some of his letters with philosophers such as Voltaire. Americans began citing the *Oeuvres posthumes* immediately after its publication. From Paris in 1789, Jefferson recommended to James Madison three books "of great merit," one of which was Frederick's posthumous works.[84] Madison responded enthusiastically to the prospect.[85]

One essay was especially popular: "L'Histoire de Mon Temps" (The History of My Own Times), which had originally appeared in 1746 and was reprinted in these French- and English-language editions. No other reigning monarch could deliver such a sweeping survey of complicated eighteenth-century politics accompanied by a lengthy disquisition on the last hundred years of revolutions in science and philosophy. Frederick also threw in some insults for good measure, calling the other monarchies of Europe "thrones on which imbecillity is seated."[86] John Adams turned to Frederick's "L'Histoire de Mon Temps" to console himself after his contemporaries failed to sufficiently appreciate his own work in effectuating the American Revolution. Writing from Europe in 1790, Adams quoted Frederick to John Trumbull, to the effect that he (Adams) should be remembered as a martyr to the American cause: "*Votre nom Sera placé dans le martyrologe où Se trouve le nom des enthousiastes qui Se Sont perdus pour le Service*" (Your name will be placed in the martyrologie where we find the names of those who lost themselves to service).[87] Two days later Adams quoted the same text to Benjamin Rush about the unfairness of historical memory, the fact that nations could adore only one hero at a time. But, Adams concluded, "'*La Raison n'a jamais fait grande chose.*' As the K. of Prussia says in his Histoire de mon tems."[88]

As the French Revolution unfolded, Frederick's association with Voltaire and Rousseau became cause for alarm. The king's vaunted religious toleration now seemed suspect in light of the wholesale dechristianization of France during the French Revolution. It was widely known that Prussia under Frederick II tolerated numerous Catholics, Protestant sects, and even Jews (as long as the last were limited in number). Frederick considered persecution unenlightened because it disrespected the private conscience of each individual; as a prince, he also thought it was bad state policy. In his *Memoirs of the House of Brandenburg*, he had pointed out that Louis XIV's revocation of the Edict of Nantes in 1685 had sent the most entrepreneurial and wealthy Protestants to competing realms of Great Britain and Holland.[89] By contrast, in Prussia, "All these sects live here in peace, and contribute to the prosperity of the state."[90] He himself was deeply hostile toward religion, partly a result of his upbringing by his rigidly pious and brutish father and partly as a matter of personal conviction. His views were no secret; he expressed his religious skepticism repeatedly and brazenly in his publications.

John Adams owned the complete works of Frederick the Great, so he was well acquainted with Frederick's hostility toward religion and his admiration for the *encyclopédistes* that Adams had dismissed as "Busy bodies" in the margins of his copy of Frederick's letters to Voltaire.[91] Just as bad was Frederick's *Anti-Machiavel*. Instead of convincing Adams that Frederick was a virtuous ruler, the *Anti-Machiavel*—because it was written in league with Voltaire—only heightened Adams's suspicions about Frederick's irreligion. He was unsure whether Frederick and Voltaire were any more "Sincere" than Machiavelli.[92]

The presence of Machiavelli's *Prince* in Frederick's edition may help explain the difficulty historians have in determining the precise influence Machiavelli's *Prince* had in revolutionary America. Was Machiavelli helping to resurrect a lost classical republican tradition, or was he the progenitor of modern natural rights theorists?[93] Frederick's edition of *The Prince* suggests a third option, that revolutionary Americans read Machiavelli through the prism of the ancient mirror-for-princes genre, now resurrected by the king of Prussia for the purposes of justifying eighteenth-century enlightened despotism. This would mean that for revolutionary Americans, Machiavelli's *Prince* was not necessarily about resuscitating a past classical tradition or anticipating a future natural rights tradition. Instead, Americans used it to think through the urgent problems of the present, when enlightened despotism was a live, relevant topic in Europe and America.

The Decline of Frederick the Great

Frederick's influence in the United States waned rapidly in the early nineteenth century. The immediate reason is not difficult to find. John Adams summed it up in one word, "Bonaparte," which he scrawled in the margins of his personal copy of the posthumous works of Frederick II.[94] The rise of Napoleon Bonaparte, an even more militaristic, despotic, and imperialistic monarch than Frederick the Great, fundamentally reshaped geopolitics in Europe and the Americas in the early nineteenth century.

The sheer scale of Napoleon's ambition and destructiveness could only make Frederick seem small-scale and increasingly irrelevant in an era of mass armies. Napoleon's army routed Prussia at the Battle of Jena in 1806, subjugating the once-mighty nation to the French empire. Napoleon's victory confirmed Americans' fear that (as Jefferson put it) "Bonaparte aims at universal Dominion."[95] Perhaps Napoleon would try to conquer the United States, which would be the "last devoured" territory after "the Destroyer of mankind" had swallowed the Near East, India, Peru, and Brazil.[96] In 1813, Adams reflected on how a few decades had changed the face of Europe. "35 Years ago, the very Word Prussia commanded respect in all Europe," Adams wrote to his friend Richard Rush. "Not only Ambassadors and Ministers of State; not only Generals and Armies, but Kings Emperors and Republicks trembled at the Sound. . . . But what are Prussian Armies now? mere Cockade and Uniform."[97]

Even in death, Napoleon continued to inspire future military leaders such as Simon Bolívar in a way that Frederick did not. Wrapping himself in the iconography of Roman emperors, Napoleon had grasped the importance of spectacle for modern propaganda in a new age of mass political mobilization. Frederick could only pale in comparison. From Paris in 1789, Gouverneur Morris summed up Frederick's historical fate after watching a play about the king. "Frederick appears like himself, Great without the Exterior of Greatness, and he not only comes on the Stage and goes off it precisely when he ought but while there he says exactly what he ought and no more."[98] No one, apparently, could share the stage with Napoleon.

Beyond Napoleon, enlightened despotism itself faded as an ideal of executive power. Liberal individualism and rising popular sovereignty undermined its presuppositions about political legitimacy. In the nineteenth century, American presidents modeled themselves on a variety of archetypes, from John Quincy Adams's aristocrat to Abraham Lincoln's self-made man. But none turned to the warrior-scholar model generally or to the specific persona of the now-irrelevant Frederick the Great. Today he is unknown to most Americans, except perhaps those who live near the King of Prussia mall in Pennsylvania, one of the largest shopping malls in the United States. Yet in his own era, Frederick supplied revolutionary

Americans with a compelling example of a king who wrestled, as they did, with the great question of how to imagine executive power and militarism in an age of enlightenment and republicanism.

Acknowledgments

This essay began as the keynote lecture for the 2019 Alan B. and Charna Larkin Symposium on the American Presidency at Florida Atlantic University. I am grateful to Professor Stephen Engle for assembling us for this stimulating conference and to Professor Benno Lowe for shepherding the resulting book to publication. I also thank the two anonymous referees for the University Press of Florida and the other faculty participants in the symposium for astute suggestions on revising the original essay. Some of the letters quoted here are from the early access versions of documents that have not yet been published in their respective series. Readers should consult these digital editions for status updates.

Notes

1. William Cooke to George Washington, October 29, 1795, in *The Papers of George Washington Digital Edition*, http://rotunda.upress.virginia.edu/founders/GEWN-05-19-02-0066, published in *The Papers of George Washington*, Presidential Series, vol. 19, *1 October 1795–31 March 1796*, ed. David R. Hoth (Charlottesville: University of Virginia Press, 2016). The incorrect spelling of "Prussia" is in the original.

2. Invoice to Robert Cary & Company from George Washington, September 20, 1759, Founders Online, National Archives, https://founders.archives.gov/documents/Washington/02-06-02-0189-0002, published in W. W. Abbot, ed., *The Papers of George Washington*, Colonial Series, vol. 6, *4 September 1758–26 December 1760* (Charlottesville: University Press of Virginia, 1988), 352–58.

3. I use lowercase for the term "enlightenment" so as to be true to eighteenth-century actors, who saw enlightenment as a never-completed process rather than an era or fait accompli. For a fuller discussion, see Caroline Winterer, *American Enlightenments: Pursuing Happiness in the Age of Reason* (New Haven, CT: Yale University Press, 2016).

4. The scholarship on the origins of the American presidency is vast. See, for example, Saikrishna Bangalore Prakash, *Imperial from the Beginning: The Constitution of the Original Executive* (New Haven, CT: Yale University Press, 2015); Forrest McDonald, *The American Presidency: An Intellectual History* (Lawrence: University Press of Kansas, 1994); Thomas E. Cronin, *Inventing the American Presidency* (Lawrence: University Press of Kansas, 1989); and Harvey Mansfield, *Taming the Prince: The Ambivalence of Modern Executive Power* (New York: The Free Press, 1989). On the deeper history of

thinking about executive power in America, see Timothy Breen, *The Character of the Good Ruler: Puritan Political Ideas in New England, 1630–1730* (New York: Norton, 1970).

5. Theodore Foster to Thomas Jefferson, July 25, 1801, in *The Papers of Thomas Jefferson Digital Edition*, vol. 34, *1 May to 31 July 1891*, ed. Barbara B. Oberg (Princeton, NJ: Princeton University Press, 2018), 632.

6. John Trumbull to John Adams, October 19, 1805, Founders Online, National Archives, https://founders.archives.gov/documents/Adams/99-02-02-5106, early access document.

7. On this point, see Jack Rakove, *Original Meanings: Politics and Ideas in the Making of the Constitution* (New York: Knopf, 1996), chapter 9.

8. Eric Nelson, *The Royalist Revolution: Monarchy and the American Founding* (Cambridge, MA: Harvard University Press, 2014); Frank Prochaska, *The Eagle and the Crown: Americans and the British Monarchy* (New Haven, CT: Yale University Press, 2008); Brendan McConville, *The King's Three Faces: The Rise and Fall of Royal America, 1688–1776* (Chapel Hill: University of North Carolina Press for the Omohundro Institute of Early American History and Culture, 2006). The postrevolutionary interest in the British monarchy is covered in Elisa Tamarkin, *Anglophilia: Deference, Devotion, and Antebellum America* (Chicago: University of Chicago Press, 2007). For other interpretations of monarchism in revolutionary America, see Caroline Winterer, *American Enlightenments* (New Haven, CT: Yale University Press, 2016), 223–51; Richard Alan Ryerson, "John Adams, Republican Monarchist: An Inquiry into the Origins of His Constitutional Thought," in *Empire and Nation: The American Revolution in the Atlantic World*, ed. Eliga H. Gould and Peter S. Onuf (Baltimore, MD: Johns Hopkins University Press, 2005), 72–92. See also Paul Downes's insightful *Democracy, Revolution, and Monarchism in Early American Literature* (Cambridge: Cambridge University Press, 2002); and Louise B. Dunbar, *A Study of "Monarchical" Tendencies in the United States from 1776 to 1801* (Urbana: University of Illinois Press, 1922).

9. Caroline Winterer, "The U.S. Founders and Cyrus the Great of Persia," Cyrus' Paradise: The World's First Online Collaborative Commentary to an Ancient Text, https://www.sunoikisis.org/cyropaedia/2013/06/01/the-u-s-founders-and-cyrus-the-great-of-persia/.

10. David A. Bell, *Napoleon: A Concise Biography* (New York: Oxford University Press, 2015), 60.

11. Hans Blom, John Christian Laursen, and Luisa Simonutti, "Introduction," in *Monarchisms in the Age of Enlightenment: Liberty, Patriotism, and the Common Good*, ed. Hans Blom, John Christian Laursen, and Luisa Simonutti (Toronto: University of Toronto Press, 2007), 3; John Adamson, "Introduction: The Making of the Ancien-Regime Court 1500–1700," in *The Princely Courts of Europe, 1500–1750: Ritual, Politics and Culture under the Ancien Régime*, ed. John Adamson (London: Weidenfeld and Nicolson, 1999), 7–41.

12. For the Cold War construction of an "American Enlightenment," see Caroline Winterer, "What Was the American Enlightenment?" in *The Worlds of American Intellectual History*, ed. Joel Isaac, James Kloppenberg, Michael O'Brien, and Jennifer Ratner-

Rosenhagen (Oxford: Oxford University Press, 2016), 19–36. Among a large literature on eighteenth-century American libraries, see David Lundberg and Henry F. May, "The Enlightened Reader in America," *American Quarterly* 28, no. 2 (1976): 262–93. Cold War historians of the American Enlightenment include Peter Gay, *The Enlightenment: The Science of Freedom* (New York: Knopf, 1969); Henry May, *The Enlightenment in America* (New York: Oxford University Press, 1976); and Henry Steele Commager, *The Empire of Reason: How Europe Imagined and America Realized the Enlightenment* (Garden City, NY: Anchor, 1977). Interest in Frederick II surged again in the United States in the late nineteenth and early twentieth centuries in conjunction with anxieties about German imperialism.

13. On enlightened absolutism, see Derek Beales, *Enlightenment and Reform in Eighteenth-Century Europe* (London: I. B. Tauris, 2005); and Hamish M. Scott, ed., *Enlightened Absolutism: Reform and Reformers in Later Eighteenth-Century Europe* (Basingstoke, UK: Macmillan, 1990).

14. Francis Cogliano, *Emperor of Liberty: Thomas Jefferson's Foreign Policy* (New Haven, CT: Yale University Press, 2014), 2–3.

15. Theodore Dwight Woolsey, *Political Science: Or, the State Theoretically and Practically Considered* (New York: Charles Scribner's Sons, 1877), 520.

16. Tim Blanning, *Frederick the Great: King of Prussia* (UK: Allen Lane, 2015), 117.

17. Beverley Robinson to George Washington, March 1, 1758, Founders Online, National Archives, https://founders.archives.gov/?q=Volume%3AWashington-02-05&s=1511311112&r=76, published in *The Papers of George Washington*, Colonial Series, vol. 4, *October 1757–September 1758*, ed. W. W. Abbott (Charlottesville: University of Virginia Press, Rotunda, 1983), 98–99.

18. Advertisement for Henry Christin Geyer, Stone-Cutter, Near Liberty-Tree, South-End, Boston, *Massachusetts Gazette, and the Boston Post-Boy and Advertiser*, February 26, 1770, 4.

19. Paul Leland Haworth, "Frederick the Great and the American Revolution," *American Historical Review* 9, no. 3 (1904): 460.

20. Frederic II, *Posthumous Works of Frederic II, King of Prussia*, translated by Thomas Holcroft (London: G. G. J. and J. Robinson, 1789), 21; Blanning, *Frederick the Great*, 124.

21. Nathanael Greene to George Washington, December 3, 1777, Founders Online, National Archives, https://founders.archives.gov/?q=Volume%3AWashington-03-12&s=1511311112&r=486, published in *The Papers of George Washington*, Revolutionary War Series, vol. 12, *October–December 1777*, ed. Frank E. Grizzard Jr. and David R. Hoth (Charlottesville: University Press of Virginia, 2002), 516–22.

22. Henry Knox to George Washington, December 1, 1777, Founders Online, National Archives, https://founders.archives.gov/?q=Volume%3AWashington-03-12&s=1511311112&r=448, published in *The Papers of George Washington*, Revolutionary War Series, vol. 12, 465–66.

23. *Continental Journal and Weekly Advertiser*, February 20, 1777.

24. Frederick II to Voltaire, June 26, 1739, in Voltaire, *Correspondence and Related Documents*, vol. 90, ed. Theodore Besterman (Geneva: Institut et musée Voltaire,

1969–), D2036. On the reading habits of George II, see Jeremy Black, *George II: Puppet of the Politicians?* (Exeter, UK: University of Exeter Press, 2007), 127; and Clarissa Campbell Orr, "Lost Royal Libraries and Hanoverian Court Culture," in *Lost Libraries: The Destruction of Great Book Collections since Antiquity*, ed. James Raven (New York: Palgrave Macmillan, 2004), 163–80.

25. Blanning, *Frederick the Great*, 367.

26. Lytton Strachey, *Books and Characters, French and English* (1905; repr., New York: Harcourt, Brace, 1922), 178.

27. These works were largely in French. I have given English translations of the titles here to facilitate understanding. Because of the confusing conditions under which some of his works were made public, dates of publication are at times difficult to discern precisely, so I have given my best estimate here.

28. John Quincy Adams to Abigail Adams, October 8, 1798, Founders Online, National Archives, https://founders.archives.gov/documents/Adams/04-13-02-0112, published in *The Adams Papers*, Adams Family Correspondence, vol. 13, *May 1798–September 1799*, ed. Sara Martin, Hobson Woodward, Christopher F. Minty, Amanda A. Mathews, Neal E. Millikan, Emily Ross, Sara B. Sikes, and Sara Georgini (Cambridge, MA: Harvard University Press, 2017).

29. John Quincy Adams to Thomas Boylston Adams, March 17, 1801, Founders Online, National Archives, https://founders.archives.gov/documents/Adams/99-03-02 -0918, early access document.

30. Immanuel Kant, "Beantwortung der Frage: Was ist Aufklärung?" *Berlinische Monatsschrift* (December 1784): 481–94; Georg Cavallar, "Kant's Judgment on Frederick's Enlightened Absolutism," *History of Political Thought* 14, no. 1 (1993): 103–32.

31. Frederick the Great, *Oeuvres du philosophe de sans-souci* (N.p.: Au donjon du chateau, 1750).

32. Frederick II, *Essai sur Les Formes de Gouvernement et sur Les Devoirs Des Souverains*, in *The Foundations of Germany: A Documentary Account Revealing the Causes of Her Strength, Wealth and Efficiency*, translated by J. Ellis Barker (New York: E. P. Dutton, 1916), 263.

33. François Bluche, *Le Despotisme Éclairé* (Paris: Fayard, 1968), 354. For a historiographical review of the concept of enlightened despotism, see Charles Ingrao, "The Problem of 'Enlightened Absolutism' and the German States," in "Politics and Society in the Holy Roman Empire, 1500–1806," supplement, *Journal of Modern History* 58 (December 1986): 161–80.

34. Charles de Secondat, baron de Montesquieu, *De L'Esprit Des Loix* (Geneva: Chez Barrillot & Fils, 1748), 39. For Frederick's reading of Montesquieu, see Blanning, *Frederick the Great*, 406.

35. Victor Gourevitch, ed., *Rousseau: The Social Contract and Other Later Political Writings* (1997; repr., Cambridge: Cambridge University Press, 2010), xvii.

36. Jean-Jacques Rousseau, *The Collected Writings of Rousseau*, vol. 5, *The Confessions and Correspondence, Including the Letters to Malesherbes*, ed. Christopher Kelly, Roger D. Masters, and Peter D. Stillman, translated by Christopher Kelley (Hanover, NH: University Press of New England, 1995), 496. For more on the relationship between

Frederick II and Rousseau, see Avi Lifschitz, "Adrastus versus Diogenes: Frederick the Great and Jean-Jacques Rousseau on Self-Love," in *Engaging with Rousseau: Reaction and Interpretation from the Eighteenth Century to the Present*, ed. Avi Lifschitz (Cambridge: Cambridge University Press, 2016), 17–32.

37. The complicated publication history of the *Antimachiavel* is documented in Charles Fleischauer, ed., *L'Anti-Machiavel* (Geneva: Institut et Musée Voltaire, 1958).

38. Jacob Soll, *Publishing the Prince: History, Reading, and the Birth of Political Criticism* (Ann Arbor: University of Michigan Press, 2008), 22–40; Allan H. Gilbert, *Machiavelli's Prince and Its Forerunners: The Prince as a Typical Book de Regimine Principum* (Durham, NC: Duke University Press, 1938).

39. Frederick II, *Anti-Machiavel: Or, An Examination of Machiavel's Prince, with Notes Historical and Political*, 2 vols. (London: T. Woodward, 1741), 1:11. On new practices of history writing in the eighteenth century, see Caroline Winterer, "History: Narratives of Progress," in *A Cultural History of Ideas in the Age of Enlightenment*, ed. Jack Censer (London: Bloomsbury Academic Press, 2020), forthcoming.

40. Frederick II, *Anti-Machiavel*, 1:vii.

41. Frederick II to Voltaire, March 31, 1738, https://doi-org.stanford.idm.oclc.org/10.13051/ee:doc/voltfrVF0890076a1c.

42. Frederick II to Voltaire, May 16, 1739, http://www.e-enlightenment.com.stanford.idm.oclc.org/item/voltfrVF0900381a1c/.

43. Voltaire to Frederick II, August 12, 1739, https://doi-org.stanford.idm.oclc.org/10.13051/ee:doc/voltfrVF0900451a1c.

44. Frederick of Prussia, *The Refutation of Machiavelli's Prince or Anti-Machiavel*, introduction, translation, and notes by Paul Sonnino (Athens: Ohio University Press, 1981), 14.

45. Frederick II to Voltaire, November 7, 1740, https://doi-org.stanford.idm.oclc.org/10.13051/ee:doc/voltfrVF0910354a1c.

46. Frederick II to Voltaire, September 16, 1749, https://doi-org.stanford.idm.oclc.org/10.13051/ee:doc/voltfrVF0950162b1c.

47. On the rise of the public sphere in revolutionary America, see, for example, Michael Warner, *Letters of the Republic: Publication and the Public Sphere in Eighteenth-Century America* (Cambridge, MA: Harvard University Press, 1990).

48. "To the Printer of the Pennsylvania Packet," *Pennsylvania Packet*, March 6, 1779, 1.

49. Ellis Farneworth, *The Works of Nicholas Machiavel*, 2 vols. (London: T. Davies, 1762). John Adams explained that "My English Machiavel contains his Florence, Art of War, Discourses on Livy, Prince, and Fredericks and Voltaires Examon du Prince, and his Marriage of Belphegor." John Adams to François Adriaan Van der Kemp, August 9, 1813, Founders Online, National Archives, https://founders.archives.gov/documents/Adams/99-02-02-6125, early access document.

50. Lafayette to Thomas Jefferson, September 4, 1785, Founders Online, National Archives, https://founders.archives.gov/?q=Volume%3AJefferson-01-08&s=1511311112&r=371, published in *The Papers of Thomas Jefferson*, Original Series, vol. 8, *25 February*

to 31 October 1785, ed. Julian P. Boyd (Princeton, NJ: Princeton University Press, 1953), 478–79.

51. David Humphreys to George Washington, November 1, 1785, Founders Online, National Archives, https://founders.archives.gov/documents/Washington/04-03-02 -0298, published in *The Papers of George Washington*, Confederation Series, vol. 3, *19 May 1785–31 March 1786*, ed. W. W. Abbot (Charlottesville: University Press of Virginia, 1994), 333–35.

52. Marquis de Lafayette to Washington, February 6, 1786, Founders Online, National Archives, https://founders.archives.gov/documents/Washington/04-03-02-0461, published in *The Papers of George Washington*, Confederation Series, vol. 3, 538–47.

53. Marquis de Lafayette to John Adams, July 13, 1785, Founders Online, National Archives, https://founders.archives.gov/documents/Adams/06-17-02-0133, published in *The Papers of John Adams*, Papers of John Adams, vol. 17, *April–November 1785*, ed. Gregg L. Lint, C. James Taylor, Sara Georgini, Hobson Woodward, Sara B. Sikes, Amanda A. Mathews, and Sara Martin (Cambridge, MA: Harvard University Press, 2014), 243–45.

54. Adams to John Trumbull, February 13, 1776, Founders Online, National Archives, https://founders.archives.gov/documents/Adams/06-04-02-0003, published in *The Adams Papers*, Papers of John Adams, vol. 4, *February–August 1776*, ed. Robert J. Taylor (Cambridge, MA: Harvard University Press, 1979), 21–22.

55. John Adams to Marquis de Lafayette, May 21, 1782, Founders Online, National Archives, https://founders.archives.gov/documents/Adams/06-13-02-0030, published in *Papers of John Adams*, vol. 13, *May–October 1782*, ed. Gregg L. Lint, C. James Taylor, Margaret A. Hogan, Jessie May Rodrique, Mary T. Claffey, and Hobson Woodward (Cambridge, MA: Harvard University Press, 2006), 65–68.

56. Adams to Jean Henry David Uhl, July 9, 1782, Founders Online, National Archives, https://founders.archives.gov/?q=Uhl&s=1111311111&r=3&sr=, published in *The Adams Papers*, Papers of John Adams, vol. 13, 169–71.

57. Voltaire, *La vie privée du roi de Prusse, ou Mémoires pour servir à la vie de M. de Voltaire, écrits par lui-même* (Amsterdam: Chez Les Héritiers de MM. Rey, 1784).

58. Voltaire, *La vie privée du roi de Prusse*, 80.

59. Thomas Jefferson to James Monroe, April 15, 1785, Founders Online, National Archives, https://founders.archives.gov/documents/Jefferson/01-08-02-0054, published in *The Papers of Thomas Jefferson*, Original Series, vol. 8, *25 February to 31 October 1785*, ed. Julian P. Boyd (Princeton, NJ: Princeton University Press, 1953), 88–89.

60. Jefferson saw a "figure of King of Prussia" on December 23, 1786; Thomas Jefferson, Memorandum Books, 1786, Founders Online, National Archives, https://founders. archives.gov/documents/Jefferson/02-01-02-0020#d1e16432a1048964-ptr, published in *The Papers of Thomas Jefferson*, Second Series, *Jefferson's Memorandum Books*, vol. 1, ed. James A. Bear Jr. and Lucia C. Stanton (Princeton, NJ: Princeton University Press, 1997), 605–49. An image of Frederick's wax likeness appears in Julius von Schlosser, "History of Portraiture in Wax," in *Ephemeral Bodies: Wax Sculpture and the Human Figure*, ed. Roberta Panzanelli (Los Angeles: Getty Research Institute, 2008), 266.

61. John Quincy Adams to John Adams, September 1, 1781, Founders Online, National Archives, https://founders.archives.gov/documents/Adams/04-04-02-0139, pub-

lished in *The Papers of John Adams*, Adams Family Correspondence, vol. 4, *October 1780–September 1782*, ed. L. H. Butterfield and Marc Friedlaender (Cambridge, MA: Harvard University Press, 1973), 206–7.

62. Dunbar, *A Study of "Monarchical" Tendencies*, 61.

63. Richard Krauel, "Prince Henry of Prussia and the Regency of the United States, 1786," *American Historical Review* 17 (1911): 44–51.

64. Krauel, "Prince Henry," 47.

65. James Madison, "Notes on Ancient and Modern Confederacies. Editorial Note," Founders Online, National Archives, https://founders.archives.gov/documents/Madison /01-09-02-0001, published in *The Papers of James Madison*, Congressional Series, vol. 9, *9 April 1786–24 May 1787 and Supplement 1781–1784*, ed. Robert A. Rutland and William M. E. Rachal (Chicago: University of Chicago Press, 1975), 3–23.

66. James Madison, "Notes on Ancient and Modern Confederacies."

67. Pennsylvania Convention: Friday, November 30, 1787, in *Pennsylvania and the Federal Constitution, 1787–1788*, ed. John Bach McMaster and Frederick D. Stone (Philadelphia: Historical Society of Pennsylvania, 1888), 293–94.

68. Publius, *The Federalist: A Collection of Essays, Written in Favour of the New Constitution, as Agreed upon by the Federal Convention, September 17, 1787*, 2 vols. (New York: J. and A. McLean, 1788), 1:116.

69. John Lansing, remarks at the New York ratifying convention, June 20, 1788, in *The Debates and Proceedings of the Constitutional Convention of the State of New York: Assembled at Poughkeepsie on the 17th June, 1788* (New York: Francis Childs, 1788; facsimile Poughkeepsie, NY: Vassar Brothers Institute, 1905), 13.

70. "New York Ratifying Convention. Remarks (Francis Child's Version), 20 June 1788," Founders Online, National Archives, https://founders.archives.gov/?q=Volume%3 AHamilton-01-05&s=1511311112&r=16#ARHN-01-05-02-0012-0005-fn-0003-ptr, published in *The Papers of Alexander Hamilton*, vol. 5, *June 1788–November 1789*, ed. Harold C. Syrett (New York: Columbia University Press, 1962), 16–26.

71. "Philadelphiensis No. IX," in *The Complete Anti-Federalist*, vol. 3, ed. Herbert J. Storing (Chicago: University of Chicago Press, 1981), 127–30.

72. "A Farmer II," *Baltimore Maryland Gazette*, February 29, 1788, in *The Documentary History of the Ratification of the Constitution*, vol. 11, *Ratification of the Constitution by the States: Maryland (1)*, ed. John P. Kaminski, Gaspare J. Saladino, Timothy D. Moore, Johanna E. Lannér-Cusin, Charles H. Schoenleber, Jonathan M. Reid, Margaret R. Flamingo, and David P. Fields, (Madison: Wisconsin Historical Society Press, 2015), 334, http://digicoll.library.wisc.edu/cgi-bin/History/History-idx?type=goto&id =History.DHRCv11&isize=M&submit=Go+to+page&page=334.

73. R. A. Brock, ed., *The History of the Virginia Convention, 1788*, vol. 1 (Richmond: Richmond Historical Society, 1890), 267.

74. Blanning, *Frederick the Great*, 387–400.

75. Anonymous to George Washington, September 9, 1794, Founders Online, National Archives, https://founders.archives.gov/documents/Washington/05-16-02-0453, published in *The Papers of George Washington*, Presidential Series, vol. 16, *1 May–30 Sep-*

tember 1794, ed. David R. Hoth and Carol S. Ebel (Charlottesville: University of Virginia Press, 2011), 656–62.

76. William Blackstone, *Commentaries on the Laws of England: Book the First* (Oxford: Clarendon, 1765), 13.

77. Robert Green McCloskey, 2 vols., "Introduction," in *The Works of James Wilson*, ed. Robert Green McCloskey (Cambridge, MA: Harvard University Press, 1967), 39.

78. McCloskey, *Works of James Wilson*, 1:121.

79. McCloskey, *Works of James Wilson*, 1:120.

80. McCloskey, *Works of James Wilson*, 1:120–21.

81. McCloskey, *Works of James Wilson*, 1:296.

82. Frederick II, *Oeuvres posthumes de Frédéric II, roi de Prusse*, 14 vols. (Berlin: Voss et Fils et Decker et Fils, 1788). John Adams owned all fourteen volumes and wrote extensive marginalia in volumes 6–9, which consisted largely of letters, including Frederick's correspondence with Voltaire. John Adams Library at the Boston Public Library.

83. Frederick II, *Posthumous Works of Frederic II, King of Prussia*, 13 vols. (London: G. G. J. and J. Robinson, 1789).

84. Jefferson to Madison, from Paris, January 12, 1789, Founders Online, National Archives, https://founders.archives.gov/documents/Jefferson/01-14-02-0208, published in *The Papers of Thomas Jefferson*, Original Series, vol. 14, *8 October 1788–26 March 1789*, ed. Julian P. Boyd (Princeton, NJ: Princeton University Press, 1958), 436–38. The other two books were Jean Jacques Barthélemy, *Voyage du jeune Anacharsis en Grèce*, 7 vols., 2nd ed. (Paris, 1789); and Condorcet, *Essai sur la constitution et les fonctions des assemblées provinciales*, 2 vols. (Paris, 1788).

85. Madison to Jefferson, May 9, 1789, Founders Online, National Archives, https://founders.archives.gov/?q=Volume%3AJefferson-01-15&s=1511311112&r=113, published in *Papers of Thomas Jefferson*, Original Series, vol. 15, *27 March to 30 November 1789*, ed. Julian P. Boyd (Princeton, NJ: Princeton University Press, 1959), 114–15.

86. Frederic II, *Posthumous Works of Frederic II, King of Prussia*, 1:59.

87. John Adams to John Trumbull, April 2, 1790, Founders Online, https://founders.archives.gov/documents/Adams/99-02-02-0898, early access document.

88. John Adams to [Benjamin?] Rush, April 4, 1790, Founders Online, https://founders.archives.gov/?q=La%20Raison%20n%E2%80%99a%20jamais%20fait%20grande%20chose&s=1111311111&sa=&r=4&sr=, early access document. The French phrase means "reason never accomplished much."

89. Blanning, *Frederick the Great*, 370–87.

90. Frederick II, King of Prussia, *Memoirs of the House of Brandenburg: From the Earliest Accounts to the Death of Frederick I* (Edinburgh: E. and J. Robertson, 1759), 213. John Adams owned this volume; John Adams Library at the Boston Public Library.

91. Adams marginalia in Frederick II, *Oeuvres posthumes de Frédéric II, roi de Prusse* (Berlin: Voss et Fils et Decker et Fils, 1788), 9:185, in John Adams Library at the Boston Public Library.

92. Adams to Van der Kemp, August 9, 1813.

93. C. Bradley Thompson, "John Adams's Machiavellian Moment," *Review of Politics* 57, no. 3 (1995): 389–417.

94. Frederick II, *Oeuvres posthumes de Frédéric II, roi de Prusse* 9:10.

95. James Wilkinson to Thomas Jefferson, March 12, 1807, Founders Online, National Archives, https://founders.archives.gov/documents/Jefferson/99-01-02-5260, early access document.

96. Joseph Shulim, "Thomas Jefferson Views Napoleon," *Virginia Magazine of History and Biography* 60, no. 2 (1952): 298–99.

97. John Adams to Richard Rush, July 15, 1813, Founders Online, National Archives, https://founders.archives.gov/documents/Adams/99-02-02-6104, early access document.

98. Diary entry for March 20, 1789, in *The Diaries of Gouverneur Morris, Supplement: A Diary of the French Revolution*, vol. 1, *March 1789–24 September 1790*, ed. Melanie Randolph Miller (1939; repr., Charlottesville: University of Virginia Press, Rotunda, 2015), 16.

PART II

---◆---

The Politics
of Constitution Making

The Executive and the Federal Union

6

National Power and the Presidency

Rival Forms of Federalist Constitutionalism at the Founding

JONATHAN GIENAPP

Two separate questions are often asked of the original Constitution. How powerful was the national government designed to be? and How powerful was the American presidency supposed to be? Given the contemporary significance of the answers, which need only be measured by landmark Supreme Court cases, both questions have spawned a massive and ever-expanding scholarly literature, neither of which show signs of abating any time soon. Despite such outsized attention, the relationship between the two questions remains uncertain. This is all the more striking, since as the literatures have swelled, the relationship has grown markedly complex. In contemporary legal debates, it is increasingly common for scholars and jurists to claim in one breath that under the Constitution, national power is neatly circumscribed while in another insisting that presidential power is vast and expansive. Perhaps this is because the questions are largely distinct—one a problem of federalism, the other a problem of separation of powers—and thus can be treated separately. Yet at a higher level of constitutionalism, the two are intimately intertwined. Each fundamentally concerns how the Constitution delegates and delimits power. Does it license only the powers explicitly expressed in its text or does it recognize unexpressed implied powers? Does it somehow delegate and delimit power differently in the context of executive authority than it does in the context of national power? If so, how?

These questions have furnished ground for important modern legal debates. But one especially illuminating way to explore the relationship between national and executive power is historical. If we put aside

contemporary interpretive concerns and instead try to decipher how leading founding-era framers made sense of the matter, we gain new insights
into the diverse and all-too-often obscured constitutional visions that accompanied the making of the Constitution. This is especially true if we
take a close look at the three Constitutional Convention delegates who
were arguably the most committed to increasing the powers of the national
government and almost certainly the most committed to constructing a
powerful national executive: James Wilson, Gouverneur Morris, and Alexander Hamilton.[1] Given their shared commitments, these three framers are
often—and with considerable justification—portrayed as staunch intellectual and political allies, as the driving force of the nationalist movement at
the Convention and beyond. Yet these three crucial framers made sense of
the complex constitutional relationship between national and presidential
power in conflicting ways that more generally reveal how their constitutional visions were subtly in competition. When we reconstruct how their
thinking on this front diverged, we are encouraged to see not a uniform
nationalist constitutional ideology at the founding but in fact several and
to begin the difficult yet vital work of sorting out how and why some vari-
ants of Federalist constitutionalism endured while others faded quietly
into the night.

The Modern Jeffersonian-Hamiltonian Synthesis

To illuminate these aspects of eighteenth-century constitutionalism, we
begin with the modern constitutional debates over national and executive power. They provide an effective entry point. This is especially true if
we focus on one strikingly prevalent position taken in these disputes, one
whose advocates—who consist of a significant cross-section of modern
constitutional scholars and jurists—purport to be guided by the thinking
of influential framers.[2]

In broad strokes, these constitutionalists tend to be Jeffersonian on
questions of national power but Hamiltonian on matters of executive
power. Like Thomas Jefferson, they think that in the context of federalism, the powers of the national government are relatively few and limited
while they also believe, like Alexander Hamilton, that in the context of
federal separation of powers, the president's powers are broad and expansive.[3] Given Jefferson's and Hamilton's bitter constitutional struggles
at the founding, these dual commitments might seem curious if not altogether paradoxical. After all, famously, Jefferson and Hamilton were the

arch-antagonists of the early American republic—Jefferson a champion of a weak national government based on a strict reading of the Constitution, Hamilton a vigorous advocate of a strong national government based on a more expansive reading of the nation's fundamental law—who drove so much of the period's explosive partisanship and intractable constitutional debate.[4] It might seem especially difficult to reconcile Jefferson's general opposition to national power (and his concurrent defense of the state governments) with Hamilton's staunch dedication to a powerful presidency.

But those today who espouse these dual commitments believe that, strange constitutional bedfellows aside, these twin readings logically follow from a faithful interpretation of the original Constitution. And to their eyes, Hamilton himself, in perhaps his most famous defense of presidential power, helped explain how. In 1793, while serving as secretary of the treasury and as one of President George Washington's closest advisers, Hamilton took to the press under the pseudonym "Pacificus" to defend the president's recently issued Proclamation of Neutrality, which sought to keep the United States out of the French Revolutionary wars.[5] Hamilton's primary goal was to vindicate the constitutionality of the proclamation—to justify why the president could take this action independent of Congress's input—but his broader objective was to defend an expansive vision of executive power. Hamilton contended that the power Washington had exercised was executive in nature, like all core areas of foreign affairs, including diplomacy, treaty making, and the prosecution of war. Moreover, properly read, the Constitution gave the president—and the president alone—control over almost all executive matters.

Hamilton ultimately built his case on the vesting clause of Article II, which read: "The executive power shall be vested in a President of the United States of America."[6] Given how this clause was written, he argued, it was mistaken to read the enumeration of executive powers that followed as uniquely limiting the broad grant of executive power vested in the president. "The enumeration ought rather," he contended, to be understood "to specify and regulate the principal articles implied in the definition of Executive Power; leaving the rest to flow from the general grant of that power." The enumerated executive powers, in other words, were neither exclusive nor comprehensive. They did not define the parameters of presidential power; rather, they either were illustrative of the kinds of powers that were executive in nature or specified "express restrictions" on or "qualifications" of the broader grant of executive power. Because executive power was by its nature capacious, it was improbable that "a specification of certain particulars" was designed as a substitute for the "general terms" found in the vesting clause.[7] Surely the Constitution was not meant to be read that way. The president thus had the right to issue a neutrality proclamation, Hamilton reasoned, because that power was executive in nature and the Constitution gave the president general executive authority without subsequently restricting or qualifying the exercise of that particular power.

Hamilton was not the first to read the Article II vesting clause in this way (various members of Congress had made much the same argument during the 1789 debate over the removal of executive officers[8]), but he took the argument further and broke novel ground. Fatefully, to clinch his case, he compared the vesting clause of Article II with the vesting clause in Article I that conferred legislative power on Congress: "All legislative powers herein granted shall be vested in a Congress of the United States."[9] Noting that this clause failed to vest "legislative power" generally in Congress but merely assigned the powers "herein granted," Hamilton asserted that "the different mode of expression employed in the constitution in regard to the two powers the Legislative and Executive serves to confirm th[e] inference" that the Constitution's grant of executive power was general and the president's constitutional authority transcended the narrow enumeration found in Article II.[10] Thus, Hamilton not only defended an expansive reading of executive power, he resoundingly limited legislative authority in the process.[11] By placing special comparative emphasis on Article I's vesting clause, he argued that congressional authority was neatly confined to the legislative powers enumerated, whereas presidential authority far exceeded the enumerated executive powers. Even though reading the Article II vesting clause broadly did not require a curtailment of congressional power, Hamilton was willing—at least rhetorically—to sacrifice broad legislative power on the altar of a powerful presidency.

Drawing on Hamilton's reasoning in "Pacificus No. I," a host of modern constitutionalists subscribe to the ever-more-influential (and controversial) unitary executive theory.[12] Weaker forms of the theory concentrate on the *exercise* of executive power: the president alone is vested with executive power and thus has a controlling influence over the entire executive branch.[13] Stronger forms of the theory also emphasize the *scope* of executive power: the president is vested with inherent executive power and thus has unique authority in distinctively executive areas of conduct—such as foreign affairs—not otherwise assigned by the Constitution.[14] Strong or weak, though, champions of the unitary executive are confident that their theory is most consistent with the original Constitution and founding-era evidence.[15]

To build their distinctively Jeffersonian conception of national power, many of these modern constitutionalists follow Hamilton's logic in the opposite direction. Not only does comparison of the Article I and II vesting clauses suggest that the president enjoys a general grant of executive power, it also suggests the inverse: Congress is merely assigned the few and defined legislative powers "herein granted" by Article I.[16] These modern lawyers and jurists—constitutional originalists most of all—generalize from the limited and enumerated nature of congressional authority to the limited and enumerated nature of national authority itself.[17] The Tenth Amendment, which states that all powers not delegated to the federal government are reserved to the states and the people at large, is often regarded as the Constitution's clearest indication of the limited scope of federal power.[18] But the circumscribed character of congressional power—and the fact that it is evidently confined to a positive enumeration in Article I, section 8—is commonly emphasized to give practical meaning to the Tenth Amendment's charge.[19] Since the scope of federal power has often been drawn in the context of adjudicating Congress's contested right to enact far-reaching laws, it has been easy to allow federal lawmaking to stand in for federal power.[20] Thus, when modern constitutionalists rehearse the orthodox incantation that the Constitution erects a system of limited and enumerated powers, they usually have congressional power foremost in mind.[21]

During the early republic, Jeffersonian Republicans often made similar observations. They repeatedly emphasized that national power was limited and defined. As Jefferson wrote in the Kentucky Resolutions, "the General Government" has been "delegated . . . certain definite powers, reserving each state to itself, the residuary mass of right to their own self Government."[22] To support this argument, Republicans often invoked the Tenth Amendment as the sine qua non of the constitutional system.[23] But just as often they stressed the enumeration of congressional powers. In fact, it was James Madison who, in opposing Hamilton's controversial proposal that Congress charter a national bank in 1791, argued that the national government's "essential characteristic" was that it was "composed of limited and enumerated powers."[24] While Hamilton and his nationalist allies certainly challenged their Jeffersonian opponents on all of these fronts, on many occasions they conceded the general premise on which the thinking was built. Hamilton's allowance in "Pacificus No. I" that congressional authority was confined to those enumerated powers "herein granted" was part of this story. John Marshall added to it in the landmark 1819 Supreme Court case *McCulloch v. Maryland* when, in a thoroughly Hamiltonian opinion, the chief justice declared that "this government is acknowledged by all, to be one of enumerated powers," its "powers . . . are limited."[25] Marshall, like Hamilton, endorsed a broad, nationalist reading of the Constitution, yet even he (whatever his motivations) was willing to concede that the national government was one of limited and enumerated powers.[26]

This is how a great many modern constitutionalists can be Hamiltonian and Jeffersonian at once. Following Hamilton's lead, they fixate on the differences between the vesting clauses of Article I and II to reach the decidedly Hamiltonian conclusion that the president enjoys a general grant of executive authority while also reaching the decidedly Jeffersonian conclusion that the powers of Congress (like those of the national government) are defined and limited. Even though Jefferson and Madison challenged Hamilton's account of executive power (Madison explicitly when he responded to "Pacificus" under the pseudonym "Helvidius"[27]) and Hamilton championed a strong national government throughout this life, these modern constitutionalists take comfort in the fact that their Hamiltonian-Jeffersonian synthesis is predicated on Hamilton's logic in "Pacificus No. I."

And, from a purely historical perspective, there is something to this. While Hamilton surely was no Jeffersonian when it came to national power, he did underscore the reading of Article I's vesting clause that was essential to it. He did so, moreover, to promote what was arguably his preeminent interest: a broad vision of presidential power. At the height of his power as treasury secretary—when he was acting as much like a prime minister as an executive officer—he was willing to defend his fervent commitment to expansive presidential power at the potential cost of limiting Congress's legislative powers. Even though the former did not necessitate the latter, he nonetheless willingly chose this argument. Hamilton was quite possibly engaging in opportunistic advocacy and had no intention whatsoever of accepting a substantive tradeoff that might curtail national power. But here it is critical to distinguish motive from speech act. Whatever his intention, in so unmistakably conceding that legislative power was limited by enumeration, Hamilton lent valuable credence to the idea that the powers of the national government were distinctly limited and enumerated. He was willing to grant a vital premise to his intellectual opponents at a time when, given the deep uncertainty surrounding American constitutionalism, legitimating constitutional premises carried far-reaching consequences.[28]

This is our entry point. Whatever one makes of certain modern constitutionalists' eagerness to braid an expansive conception of executive power with a limited vision of national power—much less their fervent belief that this combination comports with the original Constitution—this constitutional position raises a set of interesting historical questions. Given how conspicuous and significant Hamilton's choice seems to have been, did those founding-era leaders who were most clearly aligned with his constitutional views subscribe to the logic of "Pacificus No. I"? Did those who shared Hamilton's commitment to broad executive authority share his willingness to circumscribe legislative power, and potentially national power, in the process? Did they agree with his readings of the vesting clauses in Articles I and II? As we shall see, on these various fronts they departed from Hamilton. And seeing how helps reveal hidden features of eighteenth-century constitutional thought.

Three Champions of Executive Power

But it takes some work to get there, because at first glance, Hamilton's closest allies were, like him, fiercely committed to a broad and controversial conception of national executive power and wary of legislative intrusion upon it. At the Constitutional Convention, the two delegates who most vigorously championed the creation of a powerful national executive were James Wilson and Gouverneur Morris. There were others, Hamilton most of all, who endorsed their views, but none of them spoke as frequently on the issue as Wilson and Morris.

A great deal connected Wilson, Morris, and Hamilton. They were all relatively young and hailed from the same geographical region—Hamilton was from New York, Wilson was from Pennsylvania, and at different points in his political career Morris represented each. Morris and Hamilton developed a close personal relationship and all three collaborated regularly, most notably in their concerted efforts to persuade Congress to adopt Robert Morris's financial program during the final throes of the Revolutionary War.[29] They were all experienced lawyers who had played prominent roles in prior constitutional and legal debates.[30] And each was brilliant, erudite, and precocious with self-assuredness that verged on arrogance. William Pierce colorfully testified to their talents in his character sketches of Constitutional Convention delegates: Wilson "ranks among the foremost in legal and political knowledge" and nobody was "more clear, copious, and comprehensive"; Morris "is one of those Genius's in whom every species of talents combine to render him conspicuous and flourishing in public debate"; while Hamilton was "deservedly celebrated for his talents" as "there is no skimming over the surface of a subject with him, he must sink to the bottom to see what foundation it rests on."[31] Thanks to their talent and initiative, they became leading national politicians and, thanks to their common background and experiences, they forged an ideological alliance.

Throughout the 1780s, they represented the leading edge of constitutional nationalism. Well before most of their peers were willing, they critiqued the central flaws in the Articles of Confederation, the United States' inaugural system of federal government.[32] While it took most statesmen until 1787—when the full, bleak picture of collapsing public finances, economic turmoil and disorder in the states, and the national government's incapacity to meaningfully act on any of it had unmistakably come into view—to conclude that the articles were beyond salvation,[33] Wilson, Morris, and Hamilton had grown convinced years earlier of the need for dramatic change. Like other political leaders—such as James Madison, the Virginian who played such a crucial role in remaking the American constitutional order—these three favored comprehensive reform. Merely augmenting the national government's stock of existing powers would prove insufficient; the government itself needed an overhaul. At minimum, this meant replacing its existing structure (a unicameral legislative body) with a complete and independent government that consisted of separate legislative, executive, and judicial branches. This new national government also needed the power to act in its own right and to coerce the states to enforce its lawful commands.[34] Not all constitutional reformers agreed on the extent and character of this reform, however. In the eyes of more aggressive nationalists, nobody more so than Hamilton, the central government needed the essential powers of a traditional fiscal-military state, ones that would enable it to efficiently mobilize the nation's resources to project economic and political power abroad.[35] Partly with this ambitious aim in mind, Wilson, Morris, and Hamilton championed a dramatic set of ideas for the new executive branch that few other reformers could fully endorse.

At the Constitutional Convention, it quickly became clear how singular Wilson, Morris, and Hamilton's views on executive power were. Some fellow nationalists were simply less preoccupied by the subject. This was especially true of Madison, who is usually regarded as the convention's pivotal actor because he did so much to set the agenda, drove so much of the debate, and recorded the deliberations for later consideration.[36] Shortly before leaving for Philadelphia, he wrote to George Washington that "a national Executive must also be provided," but he confessed that "I have scarcely ventured as yet to form my own opinion either of the manner in which it ought to be constituted or of the authorities with which it ought to be cloathed."[37] Convinced that the key to constitutional reform lay in the structure of the legislature, he only sporadically contributed to convention debates over the national executive, which he later described as "tedious and reiterated."[38]

In other instances, delegates who otherwise agreed that the national government needed strengthening were skeptical about establishing a potent national executive. Based on the perceived lessons of experience and history, many American statesmen remained wary of executive power. Life under British rule, in particular the bitter struggles with crown-appointed royal governors and their minions that flared up throughout the eighteenth century and reached a boiling point prior to the Revolution, cultivated a deep bias against executive authority among Americans that only reinforced cautionary tales about power-hungry monarchs, none more ominous than the tyrannical English Stuarts of the seventeenth century.[39] This animosity only intensified on the eve of independence, when colonists furiously turned against King George III (and monarchy more generally) for failing to defend their interests against a corrupt Parliament.[40] Convinced that executive power was inherently prone to tyranny, in 1776 state constitution writers stripped governors of their independence and virtually all prerogative powers.[41] While the intensity of this initial enthusiasm eventually subsided, by the time of the Constitutional Convention the fear remained strong, especially as delegates began pondering the creation not of local executives (with which Americans had considerable knowledge) but of an unprecedented kind of figure: a non-monarchical national executive.[42]

Accordingly, various delegates balked at the prospect of creating a strong national executive, worried that it was incompatible with republicanism and would pave the way for a revival of monarchy. What else could a powerful national chief magistrate become if not a king? Some objected merely to the idea of a single magistrate. Edmund Randolph ominously "regarded it as the foetus of monarchy,"[43] while Hugh Williamson matter-of-factly thought that "a single Magistrate . . . will be an elective King."[44] To these delegates, a plural executive was more appropriate. At other times, delegates were especially wary of entrusting an executive with significant prerogative powers. John Dickinson claimed that "a vig[orous] executive"—even one "with checks"—could "not be republican" but instead was "peculiar to monarchy."[45] With this concern in mind, Roger Sherman held that "the Executive magistracy" was "nothing more than an institution for carrying the will of the Legislature into effect"—a mere executive devoid of any discretionary authority.[46] Dividing or neutering executive authority were considered to be effective ways to curb the monarchical threat. Suffocating the executive's independence was still another method; it motivated skeptics of executive power—nobody more so than George Mason—to propose establishing an executive council, similar to those set up in the states, to guide and constrain the national executive's decision making.[47] In manifold ways, an energetic national executive inspired controversy.

Wilson, Morris, and Hamilton were neither indifferent to nor wary of executive power. Quite the contrary, they fervently believed that vigorous executive power was essential. Even before independence, at a time when most American leaders were haunted by England's history of abusive royal power, Wilson and Hamilton had called on King George III to revive his dormant prerogative powers to shield the colonies from Parliament's legislation.[48] After 1776, as they grew increasingly skeptical of the legislative supremacy the early state constitutions had established, they supported (and in the case of Morris actively engineered) the restoration of executive power in the later state constitutions.[49] But their attitudes were most deeply shaped by their experience with Congress. An anomalous body, it was built and functioned like a legislature yet had assumed the executive powers that had previously belonged to the British Crown. In 1781, possessing neither the energy nor the efficiency to competently fulfill its administrative responsibilities—particularly during wartime—Congress finally authorized the creation of separate executive departments. The most important of these was the department of finance, initially headed by Robert Morris, the wealthy Pennsylvania merchant. Gouverneur Morris worked as his loyal deputy while, from their positions in Congress, Wilson and Hamilton campaigned the reluctant body to adopt Morris's ambitious financial program. All of them were struck by the transformation Robert Morris was able to effect and the broader lessons it carried. A once-foundering war effort, plagued by inefficient administration and unhealthy finances, had been resurrected under his skillful leadership.[50] While Morris's allies overstated the success of his program, they believed that his tenure as superintendent of finance, especially when contrasted with Congress's previous imbecility, confirmed the value of vigorous executive administration.[51]

James Wilson, Gouverneur Morris, and Alexander Hamilton thus arrived in Philadelphia convinced that the nation needed the sort of executive power that so many of the state constitutions and the Articles of Confederation had strangled. As Hamilton asked rhetorically, capturing their common attitude, "Can there be a good Govt. without a good Executive"?[52] No two delegates to the convention did more to defend the creation of a powerful national executive than Wilson and Morris, and later, during ratification, in the pages of *The Federalist*, no Federalist defended its virtues as actively as Hamilton.

These three valued a president (as the executive came to be called) who was free to act, empowered to act, and capable of defending the executive branch against potential encroachments—an executive who possessed, in a word, energy. If there was a single characteristic that defined properly constituted executive power, this was it. "A feeble executive implies a feeble execution of the government," Hamilton declared in Federalist No. 70. "A feeble executive is but another phrase for a bad execution: And a government ill executed . . . must be . . . a bad government." Quite simply, "Energy in the executive is a leading character in the definition of good government."[53] The frequent complaint that "a vigorous executive is inconsistent with the genius of republican government" was thus deeply mistaken; an energetic executive was not only compatible with republicanism but critical to its salvation.[54] Wilson, Morris, and Hamilton's investment in executive energy led them repeatedly to endorse a set of interlocking characteristics: unity, power, and independence. By giving the new national executive these qualities, it could be ensured the energy that was so crucial to good government.

Unity was essential. Most of the vital attributes of a sound executive derived from it. Wilson was the first at the convention to move that "the Executive consist of a single person," because, as he explained, "a single magistrate" gave the "most energy dispatch and responsibility to the office."[55] Proponents of a plural executive claimed that these conditions were as easily met in their favored scheme, but Wilson, Morris, and Hamilton were sure they were wrong. And in repeatedly noting why, they stressed the two distinct yet conjoined ways (their best gloss of "energy dispatch and responsibility") that unity was superior: strength and security.

Only a unitary executive could boast the requisite strength the new government required. A plural executive, Wilson insisted, would invite "nothing but uncontrouled, continued, & violent animosities" that would "interrupt the public administration" and sap the executive branch of its vigor.[56] "Decision, activity, secrecy, dispatch," Hamilton remarked, "will generally characterise the proceedings of one man, in a much more eminent degree, than the proceedings of any greater number."[57] A plural executive would struggle to bind the extensive and heterogeneous American union. To Morris, a primary reason republican government was not easily "adapted to a large extent of Country"—that familiar orthodoxy of political theory—was "because the energy of the Executive Magistracy can not reach the extreme parts of it." Because "Our Country is an extensive one," he reasoned, "We must either then renounce the blessings of the Union, or provide an Executive with sufficient vigor to pervade every part of it."[58] This was one of the primary reasons why proponents of executive authority resisted the addition of an executive council similar to those every state constitution had established. Skeptics of executive power had proposed such a council to ensure that the national executive could not act before securing its consent.[59] Constrained by a council, Hamilton complained, the president would merely be an "ostensible executive"—one in name only. Allowing for such a "diversity of views and opinions" would "enervate the whole system of administration" and "tincture the exercise of executive authority with a spirit of habitual feebleness and delatoriness."[60]

Not only was a unitary executive stronger, but, contrary to what its detractors claimed, it was also safer. For starters, even though it productively channeled the energy found in monarchy, it only superficially resembled that institution. "All know," Wilson stressed, "that a single magistrate is not a King."[61] Rather than "being the fetus of Monarchy," a unitary executive would in fact "be the best safeguard against tyranny." This was because unity promoted responsibility. "In order to control the Executive," Wilson argued, "you must unite it. One man will be more responsible than three." Indeed, "if divided the responsibility of the Executive is destroyed."[62] As Hamilton elaborated, "a plurality in the executive . . . tends to conceal faults, and destroy responsibility" by making it difficult to discover "with facility and clearness the misconduct" of those in power.[63] This was another reason to disfavor an executive council. It "oftener serves to cover" rather "than prevent malpractices," Wilson noted.[64] A single, responsible executive was less dangerous because, in the event of maladministration, it would be perfectly clear who was to blame.

To ensure adequate energy it was just as crucial that the president enjoy sufficient power. This certainly included a general power to execute the law, thus enabling the executive to enforce national laws without relying on the states, as previously had been the case.[65] Wilson, for one, singled out law execution as one of the few purely executive powers.[66] However, the president needed more than the mere capacity to carry the legislative will into effect. He needed a will of his own; his own prerogative powers. While it was inappropriate to assign to the executive all of the powers of the royal prerogative,[67] those the British monarchy had traditionally enjoyed, it was essential that he be given some of the vital powers that state executives had been stripped of in the early wave of state constitution making.[68]

On this score, no prerogatives were more important than the power to veto legislation and appoint government officers. Most delegates were willing to entrust the national executive with some kind of veto, but few thought it should be unqualified and thus not subject to congressional override. Wilson, Morris, and Hamilton, in contrast, favored assigning the executive an absolute veto. Wilson (unsuccessfully) introduced a motion (which Hamilton seconded) to vest this power.[69] "There was no danger," they thought, "of such a power being too much exercised."[70] "The Executive," Wilson stated bluntly, "ought to have an absolute negative."[71] The appointment power was no different. Where most delegates assumed the president would play some role in this process, Wilson, Morris, and Hamilton called for a broad, even exclusive executive role in making appointments. The power to appoint was among the other few powers that Wilson "conceived strictly Executive."[72] "Experience shewed the impropriety of . . . appointmts. by numerous bodies," he claimed. "A principal reason for unity in the Executive was that officers might be appointed by a single, responsible person," an unambiguously accountable president.[73] Wilson criticized the final version of the Constitution for allocating the appointment power to the president and the Senate in combination, complaining that "the President will not be the man of the people as he ought to be, but the Minion of the Senate."[74]

Vesting these prerogatives in the national executive helped ensure the final vital characteristic of energetic executive authority: independence. Wilson, Morris, and Hamilton's commitment to executive independence took many forms on a bewildering variety of issues raised during the convention's debates. But underlying all these arguments was a single concern that essentially drove their thinking on all fronts: encroachments on the executive by rival political bodies, none of which posed a greater threat than the legislature. It was an "indispensable necessity," as Morris put it, to "mak[e] the Executive independent of the Legislature."[75] If experience under republican politics had taught Wilson, Morris, and Hamilton anything, it was that legislatures, not the executive, posed the greatest threat to liberty and stability. This was among the clearest lessons they drew from the nation's experience under the early state constitutions. Since most Revolutionary Americans had been convinced that popular legislative assemblies best represented the people and thus most safely exercised authority, most of those constitutions had vested all meaningful powers in those bodies. Yet as these unchecked legislatures enacted a raft of popular legislation that, in the eyes of some elites, threatened property rights and damaged the economy, these skeptics became convinced that legislatures were in fact most threatening in republican regimes.[76] Wilson, accordingly, was principally worried about "the legislature swallowing up all the other powers,"[77] while Morris "concurred" that "the public liberty [was] in greater danger from Legislative usurpations than from any other source."[78] In the face of the convention's refusal to equip the president with an absolute veto, Wilson lamented that "we had not guarded agst. the danger" of legislative encroachment.[79] "Without such a Self-defence," he worried, "the Legislature can at any moment sink [the executive branch] into nonexistence."[80] Wilson feared that his fellow delegates harbored misplaced "prejudices agst the Executive" based on an unjustified association of executive authority with tyranny when, in fact, legislatures were no less prone to despotism.[81] There was a reason, Wilson reminded his peers, that during the Revolution "the people of Amer[ica] did not oppose the British King but the parliament—the opposition was not agt. an Unity but a corrupt multitude."[82] Unless the national executive was properly fortified, the legislature was liable to invade it and upset the delicate balance upon which all regimes depended.

In fact, concern about legislative encroachment was so strong that despite their parallel support for an absolute executive veto, Wilson and Morris strongly advocated establishing a council of revision in which federal judges would join with the executive to review congressional legislation.[83] Unless the executive and judiciary had "a joint and full negative," Wilson worried, "they cannot otherwise preserve their importance against the legislature."[84] Morris elaborated on this point, specifying why the executive would especially benefit from this partnership. "The interest of our Executive is so inconsiderable & so transitory, and his means of defending it so feeble," he explained, "there is the justest ground to fear his want of firmness in resisting incroachments." As "some check" was "necessary on the Legislature," the executive could use all possible help.[85]

Given the intensity of this preoccupation, in debating the interrelated issues of presidential selection, reeligibility, term length, and removal, Wilson, Morris, and Hamilton consistently favored whatever option kept the executive sufficiently insulated from the legislature's influence and thus able to enjoy the independence that they believed was so necessary to energetic governance.[86] The surest way the president would become dependent on the legislature was if that body selected him. "If the Executive be chosen by the Natl. Legislature," Morris warned, "he will not be independent [from] it; and if not independent, usurpation & tyranny on the part of the Legislature will be the consequence."[87] Accordingly, Wilson, often with Morris's support, repeatedly called for the people at large to help elect the executive—either directly or through a system of electors.[88] This would also allow the executive to be eligible for reelection, something that might promote the right kind of accountability but was out of the question if Congress controlled the selection of the president.[89] A similar logic dictated concerns about the impeachment power, which all delegates found necessary but Morris worried "will render the Executive dependent on those who are to impeach."[90] Another way to ensure the executive's independence was to give him a longer term, if not, as Hamilton famously proposed, allowing him to serve on good behavior.[91] Whenever any of these interconnected issues were raised, Wilson, Morris, and Hamilton championed whatever they felt would preserve executive independence and guarantee efficient and stable governance.

Wilson and Morris were thus every bit as devoted to muscular executive authority as Hamilton. Their shared commitment to a unitary, powerful, independent president exceeded that of all other framers. Moreover, in defending executive power, they also betrayed a common distrust of legislative power. While they did not achieve all of their goals and while Jack Rakove has perceptively noted that "the growth of the presidency owed more to doubts about the Senate than to the enthusiasm with which Hamilton, Morris, and Wilson endorsed the virtues of an energetic administration,"[92] in the end, the presidency strongly resembled these three delegates' desires and in no small measure because of their labors.[93]

From this perspective, Wilson and Morris were seemingly anticipating the kind of unitary executive, built on the same sort of interpretive arguments, that Hamilton would so urgently defend half a decade later as

"Pacificus." Add to this the fact that it was Morris, from his position as de facto final draftsman on the Committee of Style, who revised both the executive and legislative vesting clauses into their final forms—expanding the former while seemingly narrowing the latter through the introduction of the "herein granted" language that Hamilton so aggressively pressed into service—and it would appear that Hamilton was just carrying Morris's work to its logical conclusion. In 1787, Wilson, Morris, and Hamilton were the strongest defenders of executive power. Was Hamilton not speaking for his allies in 1793 when he claimed that, pursuant to the Constitution, executive power was expansive in all of the ways legislative power was not?

Expanding National Power

Yet here Wilson and Morris parted ways with Hamilton. That they endorsed a similarly broad conception of executive power does not mean that they were willing to shackle national legislative power in the process—and certainly not to the degree Hamilton proved willing.

Importantly, Wilson and Morris diverged from Hamilton over the nature and scope of executive power itself, particularly its relationship to foreign affairs. A century earlier, John Locke had famously distinguished between "executive" and "federative" powers—the former the execution of domestic law, the latter the management of relations with foreign nations. While Locke detected an underlying resemblance between the two powers, their relationship was far from settled by the late eighteenth century.[94] As "Pacificus," Hamilton ran the two powers together, claiming that "the management of the affairs of this country with foreign nations" was executive in character, thus justifying President Washington's right to issue a neutrality proclamation without congressional input.[95] Wilson, though, was not willing to collapse federative power into executive power. At the Constitutional Convention, he contended that "the Prerogatives of the British Monarch" were not "a proper guide in defining the Executive powers" because "some of these prerogatives were of a Legislative nature" while others, namely "that of war & peace &c." (the last part referring to the remaining federative powers), were neither strictly legislative nor executive in character.[96] While Wilson, like most of the framers, assumed that the president would often initiate foreign relations, he did not envision him as the sole or even the principal agent in this domain.[97] "The Senate," he stated at one point, "will probably be the depositary of the powers concerning" foreign affairs.[98] Then, as a member of the committee charged with producing an initial draft of the Constitution, Wilson helped make this proclamation a reality by giving most of the federative powers to the Senate, not the president.[99] Later, in debating the power to make treaties, not only did Wilson support the inclusion of the Senate in this process, he also proposed adding the House of Representatives.[100] Morris seemed more willing to afford the president a controlling role over foreign affairs—at one point calling him "the general Guardian of the National interests"—but, like Wilson, he called for more, not less, of a legislative role in treaty making.[101] Hamilton later admitted in Federalist No. 75 that treaty making "belong[ed] properly neither to the legislative nor to the executive."[102] Even if this concession was genuine (and it was surely born of the rhetorical needs of ratification), it fell short of Wilson's classification of foreign affairs powers. And in Federalist No. 72, Hamilton had declared that the president would administer "the actual conduct of foreign negotiations."[103] Whatever Hamilton's initial attitudes might have been, by the time he wrote as "Pacificus," he thought the authority to regulate foreign affairs was singularly executive in character.[104]

Meaningful as this divergence was, there were more fundamental reasons why Wilson and Morris deviated from Hamilton's "Pacificus" logic. Their overriding concern was expanding *national*, not executive, power. Expanding executive power, vital though it was, merely served this broader end. True, they were wary of *unbridled* legislative authority and did not share their peers' qualms about strong executive checks on it. But assuming that these safeguards were in place, the legislature needed its own power to act—and to act broadly. The crisis of the 1780s was, to their eyes, born of a weak national government, and unless the new Congress had the capacity to legislate to meet the challenges of nationhood, these problems would persist. Executive administration, no matter how energetic, could not remedy all that ailed the union. Ensuring that the national government *as a whole* had the power it required meant empowering the legislature and the executive.

Wilson and Morris's views on executive power must be placed in the broader context of their nationalist constitutionalism. It can be glimpsed through their formal statements but just as clearly through their immense influence on the drafting of the Constitution. Not only were they active participants in the floor debate—in fact, contributing more than any other delegates[105]—but in a sense they co-wrote the Constitution.[106] The document was first drafted in the Committee of Detail (which met roughly halfway through the convention) and then, at the end of the proceedings, finalized in the Committee of Style. Each committee consisted of five members, but Wilson arguably did the most to shape the Committee of Detail draft,[107] while Morris almost single-handedly molded the Committee of Style draft.[108] Whatever success Wilson and Morris had in incorporating their preferred constitutional text (and evidence suggests they had tremendous success), unpacking their committee contributions vividly illustrates the defining outlines of their broad nationalist thinking.

That said, the differences between Hamilton are more evident in Wilson's thinking than Morris's. Given the nature of the evidence—and Morris's retreat from constitutional life following the convention—we can only infer his attitudes on several important issues. But while he was closer than Wilson to Hamilton's thinking, he was ultimately closest to Wilson.

Wilson's nationalist constitutionalism was the most clearly developed. At bottom, it rejected the prospect of strictly apportioning national power (be it legislative or executive) through express enumeration. He first articulated this theory in defense of the Bank of North America, the United States' first national bank, which Congress had chartered in 1781 as part of Robert Morris's financial program. Complaints mounted that the bank was unconstitutional, both because the Articles of Confederation enumerated no power to charter such an institution and because Article II specified that the states retained all powers not "expressly delegated" to the national government. In 1785, to combat these criticisms, Wilson published a formal defense.[109]

To Wilson, the critics' reasoning misunderstood the nature of the union and the kind of powers that followed from it. It was wrong to begin with the Articles of Confederation, he claimed, because pinpointing the powers of the national government required first comprehending the Declaration of Independence. By Wilson's reading, separation from Britain had established not thirteen independent sovereign states but a single union of states—a nation.[110] The political entity that governed over that union was thus created not by the states but by the sovereign people of the United States, making it a *national* government. This meant, fatefully, that the nation's government derived its power from two distinct sources. Many of Congress's powers were indeed formally delegated by the states through the articles. But many others were not. As Wilson explained, by virtue of being brought into being by the Declaration, the United States government "have *general* rights, *general* powers, and *general* obligations, not derived from *any* particular States . . . but *resulting from the union of the whole*."[111]

Those inherent government powers that no individual state could competently exercise were automatically vested in the national government. The states could neither delegate nor retain these powers because they never had claim to them in the first place. They were the by-product of constituting the union. In advancing this ingenious argument, Wilson was articulating an expansive theory of national constitutionalism predicated on the dramatic idea that nationhood itself was a source of constitutional power.[112]

Wilson's understanding of delegated national authority dictated his arguments and key committee work at the Constitutional Convention, particularly when it came to the matter of enumerated legislative power. The initial proposal for a new constitution, the Virginia Plan, did not enumerate these powers. Instead, Resolution VI in the plan vested the national legislature with the authority "to legislate in all cases to which the separate States are incompetent, or in which the harmony of the United States may be interrupted."[113] This provision paralleled what Wilson had argued in defense of the bank and it is all but certain that he wrote it.[114] When Resolution VI was presented, some delegates criticized its vagueness and called for an enumeration of legislative powers to take its place. Wilson was uncompromising in his response, claiming that "it would be impossible to enumerate the powers which the federal Legislature ought to have."[115] He was clearly wary of restricting the national government's capacity to legislate. Whether other delegates agreed with his assessment, Resolution VI effectively remained in place two months later when the convention appointed the Committee of Detail.[116]

Wilson's work on that committee was highly creative and best illustrates his commitment to expansive national legislative power. Since, fatefully, the committee replaced Resolution VI with an enumeration of legislative powers, it might seem that it took significant steps to confine legislative authority. Because most of the committee's work and all of their debates have been lost, it is impossible to know why exactly it made this change. Even though the broad language of Resolution VI had been removed, it seems clear that Wilson did not think that it had been expunged. To the contrary, he surely thought it had been incorporated into the enumeration, thanks in no small measure to his own efforts.

Wilson's thinking can be inferred from his drafting work, which is possible to re-create from the surviving manuscripts and the careful work of William Ewald.[117] The first draft, which Edmund Randolph wrote, enumerated legislative powers. To ensure that the national legislature would have all necessary means at its disposal to carry out these powers, John Rutledge (who seemed to serve as chief editor throughout the drafting process) inserted an incidental powers clause vesting in Congress the "right to make all Laws necessary to carry the foregoing Powers into Execu[tion]."[118] When Wilson took over drafting responsibilities from there, he focused on Rutledge's late addition rather than on the enumeration of powers. Perhaps he thought challenging Randolph and Rutledge on a small committee was simply futile or (at least as likely) he regarded a legislative enumeration innocuous as long it was properly framed and understood. Surely with this latter aim in mind, as John Mikhail has shown, Wilson subtly expanded Rutledge's incidental powers clause, dramatically transforming it in the process.[119] Thanks to Wilson's concerted efforts, the final version of the clause stipulated that Congress had the power "to make all laws that shall be necessary and proper for carrying into execution the foregoing powers, and all other powers vested, by this Constitution, in the government of the United States, or in any department or officer thereof."[120] The so-called (and soon to be controversial) necessary and proper clause would become part of the final Constitution effectively as Wilson wrote it.

Read in light of his theory of national constitutionalism, Wilson's version of this clause clearly signaled that the enumeration of legislative power was not comprehensive. In reality, it was three separate clauses.[121] There was a "foregoing powers" clause, which, mirroring Rutledge's initial insertion, merely gave Congress all powers necessary to carry out its enumerated powers. But there were two additional "all other powers" clauses, which gave Congress the necessary means to carry out, first, all other powers vested in the various departments and officers of the national government and, more significantly, all other powers vested in the government of the United States as a whole. Wilson had built into this clause a firm reminder that independent of what any enumeration might include, there were certain powers automatically vested in the national government by "this Constitution." In other words, much as he had argued in his earlier pamphlet, the act of constituting (what "this Constitution" referred to) a specifically national government (Wilson made sure to refer to it as the "government of the United States") immediately conferred certain general powers on that government. The text of the "necessary and proper" clause did not delegate the "other powers" vested in the national government. Instead, that part of the clause merely announced what was already true, that the national government enjoyed distinct national powers, best defined as those needed to address distinctly national concerns over which the individual states were incompetent. In other words, to Wilson it did not matter that Resolution VI had been replaced by an enumeration. The United States government would have the general legislative powers identified in that resolution no matter what, and thanks to Wilson, the "necessary and proper" clause offered clear evidence of that fact.

For Wilson, Congress's legislative powers could not be confined to the strict enumeration in Article I and certainly not because the legislative vesting clause used the phrase "herein granted." There would always be "other powers" that the national legislature could fairly exercise beyond and outside of the enumeration—an idea that Hamilton proved unwilling to pursue, even when he defended Congress's constitutional right to charter a national bank (his definitive defense of the national government's expansive power).[122] Significantly, Wilson never hinted that these broad powers equated to plenary power.[123] Unlike the state governments, the national legislature was not vested with general governmental authority. But even so, because of how the national government came into being, it immediately laid claim to a significant class of general powers. This was the essence of Wilson's theory of national constitutionalism, and his efforts at the convention revealed how committed he was to making it part of the constitutional order.

But what about Gouverneur Morris, the man responsible for introducing the "herein granted" language to Article I's vesting clause? Wilson undoubtedly was committed to a brand of national constitutionalism that was incompatible with Hamilton's dual vesting clause argument in "Pacificus No. I." But whereas Wilson's efforts at the convention all pointed toward protecting and legitimizing implied national powers, Morris's contributions are less clear. After all, he was responsible for the asymmetry in Article I and II's vesting clauses. The legislative vesting clause in the Committee of Detail draft (which Wilson most likely engineered), paralleled the one that ended up in Article II: "The legislative power shall be vested in a Congress."[124] Yet Morris consciously revised this clause into its ultimate form. Was he more willing to circumscribe congressional power than Wilson? Possibly. But even if so, on balance Morris's drafting work reinforced Wilson's aims. Moreover, Morris's commitments, articulated throughout the convention, cast serious doubt on the idea that he was after anything other than broad, expansive, almost unchecked national authority.

Morris left his mark on the Constitution while serving on the Committee of Style and Arrangement, which in the waning days of the Convention compiled a final draft of the document.[125] There are no surviving records from the committee, but delegate testimony confirms what Morris told Timothy Pickering about the Constitution in 1814: "That instrument was written by the fingers, which write this letter."[126] Fellow committee member James Madison echoed Morris's claim in 1831, "The *finish* given to the style and arrangement of the Constitution fairly belongs to the pen of Mr. Morris; the task having, probably, been handed over to him by the chairman of the Committee."[127] For all intents and purposes, the five-man Committee of Style was a committee of one.[128]

Morris, in control of the committee, largely reinforced Wilson's earlier Committee of Detail work. Nowhere was this clearer than how Morris overhauled the preamble. The draft referred to the Committee of Style read:

> We the people of the States of New Hampshire, Massachusetts, Rhode-Island and Providence Plantations, Connecticut, New-York, New-Jersey, Pennsylvania, Delaware, Maryland, Virginia, North-Carolina, South-Carolina, and Georgia, do ordain, declare, and establish the following Constitution for the Government of Ourselves and our Posterity.[129]

But once Morris was finished, it read:

> We, the People of the United States, in order to form a more perfect union, to establish justice, insure domestic tranquility, provide for the common defence, promote the general welfare, and secure the blessings of liberty to ourselves and our posterity, do ordain and establish this Constitution for the United States of America.[130]

The revisions were profound and firmly bolstered Wilson's national constitutionalism. For one, Morris dramatically changed the Constitution's author—from the separate states to a single national people—echoing the Declaration of Independence that Wilson had called attention to and thus underscoring the nature of the union over which the newly constituted government would preside. Even more important, Morris added a set of purposes for which the Constitution was established. These provided a concrete reference point for Wilson's "all other powers" in the "government of the United States." Here, in Morris's list, were the general, national objects for which general, national powers were necessarily delegated.[131] Wilson had earlier latched onto the language in Article V of the Articles of

Confederation—that Congress was established for the "convenient management of the general interests of the United States"—to support his account of general powers.[132] Then, during the Constitutional Convention, he had stressed the need to prevent states "from obstructing the *general* welfare"—the exact phrase now designated, thanks to Morris, as an end of national governance.[133] To Wilson and Morris's eyes, the preamble was far more than rhetorical flourish. In identifying what kind of union was being constituted and for what purposes, it reinforced national power.[134]

It was much less clear how, or even if, Morris's changes to the Article I and II vesting clauses aided Wilson. But before concluding that Morris was simply anticipating Hamilton's later argument in "Pacificus No. I,"[135] his choices need to be placed in broader context.

Morris was eager to protect and enlarge executive power, and many of the changes he made on the Committee of Style might have been directed toward this end. For one, he seemed to expand the executive vesting clause. Whereas the Committee of Detail draft vested "the Executive Power of the United States" in the president, Morris dropped that qualification.[136] At the same time, of course, Morris rewrote the legislative vesting clause to include the language "herein granted." These changes were quite possibly born of Morris's abiding concern with legislative encroachments, which he had vividly articulated earlier in the convention: "The Legislature will continually seek to aggrandize & perpetuate themselves." Given this vital threat, "the Executive . . . ought to be so constituted as to be the great protector of the Mass of the people" against "Legislative tyranny."[137]

While Morris might have been promoting executive power at the expense of legislative power, the best way to interpret his motivation is that he was primarily interested in *elevating* executive power to the level of legislative power rather than lowering legislative power below it.[138] Consider another of Morris's revisions. Even more fundamental than his changes to the vesting clauses, he dramatically condensed the Committee of Detail draft. He reduced twenty-three unwieldy articles to a tidy seven, in the process introducing the familiar Article I-Article II-Article III structure outlining legislative, executive, and judicial power. In the Committee of Detail draft, the national legislature and its concomitant powers were spread across six articles, while the executive and judicial branches were each confined to one article each.[139] It was highly unconventional to organize constitutional powers as Morris did (none of the state constitutions parceled them in this manner). In allotting a single article to each branch,

Morris helped lift executive and judicial power to the same plane as legislative power.[140] At a time when it was widely assumed (based on elite opinion, history, and Americans' experience with self-government) that legislative power predominated in republican regimes—that, as Madison put it at the convention, "experience had proved a tendency . . . to throw all power into the Legislative vortex"—it was no small task to fortify the other branches.[141] Therefore, what to us, living in a much different context, can seem like inherent limitations on legislative authority, more likely were an attempt to afford the other branches necessary power and autonomy.[142]

Most striking of all, though, Morris was never shy about the importance of expanding national power. It is thus hard to believe that he had any interest in circumscribing national legislative power. Near the beginning of the convention, after the Virginia Plan had been unveiled, he called on the delegates to replace a "*federal*" government with a "*national, supreme*" one. The former was merely a "compact resting on the good faith of the parties," whereas "the latter ha[d] a compleat and *compulsive* operation."[143] A genuine national government, he explained, had "compelling capacities" in their "legislative, judicial or Executive qualities."[144] Later in the convention, he strongly opposed Roger Sherman's efforts to amend Resolution VI to prevent the national government from interfering with the internal police of the states. "The internal police" of the states, Morris bristled, "ought to be infringed in many cases."[145] (He later proposed instituting a "Secretary of Domestic Affairs" whose "duty" would be "to attend to matters of general police.")[146] Meanwhile, when discussing James Madison's cherished (and ultimately rejected) national negative on state laws, Morris registered his opposition to the proposal, not because he failed to share Madison's interest in reining in the state governments but because he deemed it "not necessary, if sufficient Legislative authority should be given to the Genl. Government."[147] Finally, in the letter Morris wrote to accompany the finished Constitution when it was transmitted to the Confederation Congress, he described the result of the convention's work as a "consolidation of our union."[148] These were anything but incidental expressions. Interfering with the "internal police" of the states and "consolidating" the separate states into a restructured union all betrayed fervent, nationalist commitments. Many years later Morris would remark, without a hint of concern, that "the influence of the General Government has so thoroughly pervaded every State that all the little wheels are obliged to turn according to the great one."[149] Given his robust nationalism, it seems inconceivable that he was trying to deflate national legislative power at the convention.[150]

Viewed in this light, arguably the most striking aspect of Morris's revised legislative vesting clause was actually how it bolstered Wilson's main objective. When it came to the clause's opening words, "All legislative Powers herein granted," Hamilton would come to fixate on "herein granted," but Wilson probably focused on "All." It meant all the difference in the world that Morris had used this word rather than "only," a choice that left open the possibility that the enumeration of legislative power was not exhaustive.

Competing Nationalisms

On many fronts, James Wilson, Gouverneur Morris, and Alexander Hamilton were ideological, political, and constitutional allies. Among statesmen at the founding, none championed strong, centralized authority and presidential power as fervently. Yet in crucial respects, their relative commitments to national power and executive power drove them apart. In 1793, having already done so much as treasury secretary to expand the reach of the new executive branch, Hamilton claimed ever more power for the presidency, this time by explicitly claiming that the Constitution's language limited the legislative power of Congress. Whatever his intentions were, today, Hamilton's logic undergirds one of the most prevalent modes of interpreting the Constitution. But neither Morris (most likely) nor Wilson (most assuredly) would have backed Hamilton's argument. No matter how much they valued national executive power, they would not have been willing to sacrifice robust national legislative power simply to strengthen the executive.

The same year that Hamilton unveiled his "Pacificus" argument, Wilson reiterated the essence of his national constitutionalism from the bench of the Supreme Court. To begin his opinion in *Chisholm v. Georgia*—the landmark case that probed whether a state government could be sued by a citizen of a different state—Wilson contended that the matter ultimately turned on a question "no less radical than this: 'do the people of the United States form a Nation?'" After a lengthy and sophisticated analysis, he concluded that "the general texture of the Constitution" revealed, clearly, that "the people of the United States intended to form themselves into a nation for national purposes. They instituted for such purposes a national government, complete in all its parts, with powers legislative, executive and judicial, and in all those powers extending over the whole nation."[151] That the people of the United States enacted a national Constitution explained why Chisholm could sue the state of Georgia. But it also explained why the national government as a whole was equipped with all necessary powers to tackle genuinely national problems.

Focusing on modern legal disputes over the Constitution's vesting clauses thus helps reveal something important, and largely neglected, about founding-era history. During this formative period, there was not one single nationalist constitutional ideology but several. On matters of profound importance, crucial framers such as Wilson, Morris, and Hamilton were moving in competing directions. Rather than continuing to lump all of them into a monolith and pitting their Federalist Constitution against the Jeffersonian Republican one that quickly emerged to combat it, we would do well to probe the distinct variations of nationalist constitutionalism at the founding and begin charting, analyzing, and understanding why some endured while others disappeared. We certainly seem to live in a present made more from Hamilton's ideas than Wilson's. From the perspective of 1787, there would have been no predicting that. To better understand the founding as well as our present, we must begin the hard work of explaining how and why this happened.

Notes

1. On Wilson, Morris, and Hamilton's nationalism, see Forrest McDonald, *Novus Ordo Seclorum: The Intellectual Origins of the Constitution* (Lawrence: University Press of Kansas, 1985), 186–87. On their commitment to executive power, see Jack N. Rakove, *Original Meanings: Politics and Ideas in the Making of the Constitution* (New York: Knopf, 1996), 255.

2. Most advocates of this position subscribe to the theory of constitutional originalism. For an overview, see Jonathan Gienapp, "Constitutional Originalism and History," Process: A Blog for American History, March 20, 2017, http://www.processhistory.org/originalism-history/.

3. For example, compare Steven G. Calabresi, "'A Government of Limited and Enumerated Powers': In Defense of *United States v. Lopez*," *Michigan Law Review* 94 (December 1995): 752–831; with Steven G. Calabresi and Saikrishna B. Prakash, "The President's Power to Execute the Laws," *Yale Law Journal* 104 (December 1994): 541–665.

4. For leading overviews of the early republic that are largely built around this conventional framing, see Stanley Elkins and Eric McKitrick, *Age of Federalism: The Early American Republic, 1788–1800* (New York: Oxford University Press, 1993); Gordon S. Wood, *Empire of Liberty: A History of the Early Republic, 1789–1815* (New York: Oxford University Press, 2009); and James Roger Sharp, *American Politics in the Early Republic: The New Nation in Crisis* (New Haven, CT: Yale University Press, 1993). On the Jefferso-

nian-Hamiltonian divide, see Andrew Shankman, *Original Intents: Hamilton, Jefferson, Madison, and the American Founding* (New York: Oxford University Press, 2017).

5. For this historical background, see Elkins and McKitrick, *Age of Federalism*, 303–73.

6. U.S. Constitution, art. II, America's Founding Documents, National Archives, https://www.archives.gov/founding-docs/constitution-transcript.

7. [Alexander Hamilton], "Pacificus No. I, [29 June 1793]," Founders Online, National Archives, https://founders.archives.gov/documents/Hamilton/01-15-02-0038, published in *The Papers of Alexander Hamilton*, vol. 15, *June 1793–January 1794*, ed. Harold C. Syrett (New York: Columbia University Press, 1969), 39.

8. For these arguments, see Jonathan Gienapp, *The Second Creation: Fixing the American Constitution in the Founding Era* (Cambridge, MA: Harvard University Press, 2018), 152–53; on the removal debate as a whole, see 125–63.

9. U.S. Constitution, art. I, America's Founding Documents, National Archives, https://www.archives.gov/founding-docs/constitution-transcript.

10. [Hamilton], "Pacificus No. I," 39.

11. In addition to defending executive control over core areas of foreign relations, Hamilton was trying to free executive power from legislative challenge. See [Hamilton], "Pacificus No. I," 39–43.

12. For leading defenses of the theory, see Saikrishna Bangalore Prakash, *Imperial from the Beginning: The Constitution of the Original Executive* (New Haven, CT: Yale University Press, 2015); Steven G. Calabresi and Christopher S. Yoo, *The Unitary Executive: Presidential Power from Washington to Bush* (New Haven, CT: Yale University Press, 2008); Saikrishna B. Prakash and Michael D. Ramsey, "The Executive Power over Foreign Affairs," *Yale Law Journal* 111 (November 2001): 231–356; and Calabresi and Prakash, "The President's Power to Execute the Laws." For important defenses of the theory by Supreme Court justices, see *Myers v. United States*, 272 U.S. 52, 136–39 (1926); *Morrison v. Olson*, 87 U.S. 654, 732 (1988) (Scalia, J., dissenting); *Zivitoksky v. Kerry*, 135 U.S. 2076, 2101 (2015) (Thomas, J., dissenting). For a deeper discussion of the theory— also labeled the "vesting clause" thesis—with full citations to the massive literature and case law, see Julian Davis Mortenson, "Article II Vests Executive Power, Not the Royal Prerogative," *Columbia Law Review* 119 (June 2019): 1181–88.

13. John Harrison, "The Unitary Executive and the Scope of Executive Power," *Yale Law Journal Forum* 126 (January 2017): 374–75.

14. See especially Prakash and Ramsey, "The Executive Power over Foreign Affairs"; and Saikrishna B. Prakash and Michael D. Ramsey, "Foreign Affairs and the Jeffersonian Executive: A Defense," *Minnesota Law Review* 89 (June 2005): 1591–1687.

15. This claim certainly has not gone unchallenged. See especially Martin S. Flaherty, "The Most Dangerous Branch," *Yale Law Journal* 105 (May 1996): 1755–1810; Curtis A. Bradley and Martin S. Flaherty, "Executive Power Essentialism and Foreign Affairs," *Michigan Law Review* 102 (February 2004): 545–688; Jack N. Rakove, "Taking the Prerogative out of the Presidency: An Originalist Perspective," *Presidential Studies Quarterly* 37 (March 2007): 89–99; Robert J. Reinstein, "The Limits of Executive Power," *American University Law Review* 59 (December 2009): 263–65, 307–9; Matthew Steilen,

"How to Think Constitutionally about Prerogative: A Study of Early American Usage," *Buffalo Law Review* 66 (May 2018): 557–68, 641–68; and, most recently, Mortenson, "Article II Vests Executive Power, Not the Royal Prerogative," especially 1177–80, which includes citations to other dissenters.

16. See, e.g., Randy E. Barnett, *Restoring the Lost Constitution: The Presumption of Liberty*, rev. ed. (Princeton, NJ: Princeton University Press, 2014), 277–80; and Prakash, *Imperial from the Beginning*, 68–73, 81. For further examples, see John Mikhail, "The Constitution and the Philosophy of Language: Entailment, Implicature, and Implied Powers," *Virginia Law Review* 101 (June 2015): 1080.

17. For leading examples, see Kurt T. Lash, "The Sum of All Delegated Power: A Response to Richard Primus, The Limits of Enumeration," *Yale Law Journal Forum* 180 (December 2014): 180–207; Barnett, *Restoring the Lost Constitution*, 277–80; Calabresi, "'A Government of Limited and Enumerated Powers'"; Richard A. Epstein, "The Proper Scope of the Commerce Power," *Virginia Law Review* 73 (November 1987): 1388–99; and Gary Lawson and Guy Seidman, *"A Great Power of Attorney": Understanding the Fiduciary Constitution* (Lawrence: University Press of Kansas, 2017), 95.

18. Lash, "The Sum of All Delegated Power," 198–202; Calabresi and Prakash, "The President's Power to Execute the Laws," 561–62.

19. David S. Schwartz, "A Question Perpetually Arising: Implied Powers, Capable Federalism, and the Limits of Enumerationism," *Arizona Law Review* 59 (2017): 581; Calvin H. Johnson, "The Dubious Enumerated Power Doctrine," *Constitutional Commentary* 22 (Spring 2005): 26–27; D. A. Jeremy Telman, "A Truism that Isn't True? The Tenth Amendment and Executive War Power," *Catholic University Law Review* 51 (Fall 2001): 135–36, 150.

20. See, e.g., *United States v. Darby Lumber Co.*, 312 U.S. 100 (1941); *Wickard v. Filburn*, 317 U.S. 111 (1942); and *United States v. Lopez*, 514 U.S. 549 (1995).

21. On the prevalence of this conflation, see Richard Primus, "The Limits of Enumeration," *Yale Law Journal* 124 (December 2014): 578. For a good illustration of it, see Richard Primus, "'The Essential Characteristic': Enumerated Powers and the Bank of the United States," *Michigan Law Review* 117 (December 2018): 418–19.

22. [Thomas Jefferson], "Resolutions Adopted by the Kentucky General Assembly," November 10, 1798, in *The Papers of Thomas Jefferson*, ed. Julian P. Boys, Charles T. Cullen, John Catanzariti, Barbara Oberg, and James P. McClure (Princeton, NJ: Princeton University Press, 2003), 30:550.

23. See Saul Cornell, *The Other Founders: Anti-Federalism and the Dissenting Tradition in America, 1788–1828* (Chapel Hill: University of North Carolina Press, 1999), 244–45, 260, 271–72; and Gienapp, *The Second Creation*, 228–29.

24. James Madison, February 2, 1791, in *Documentary History of the First Federal Congress of the United States of America, 4 March 1789–3 March 1791*, vol. 14, ed. William Charles DiGiacomantonio, Kenneth R. Bowling, Charlene Bangs Bickford, and Helen E. Veit, 22 vols. (Baltimore, MD: Johns Hopkins University Press, 1995), 371.

25. *McCulloch v. Maryland*, 17 U.S. (4 Wheat.) 316, 405, 421 (1819).

26. It is important to stress the complex and ambiguous relationship between Marshall's nationalist jurisprudence and the concept of enumerated powers, as the chief jus-

tice often left room for broader arguments even though he stressed the limitations of enumeration. See David S. Schwartz, *The Spirit of the Constitution: John Marshall and the 200-Year Odyssey of* McCulloch v. Maryland (New York: Oxford University Press, 2019), introduction and chapters 1–4. On Marshall's nationalism generally, see Charles F. Hobson, *The Great Justice: John Marshall and the Rule of Law* (Lawrence: University Press of Kansas, 1996), chapter 5.

27. On the "Pacificus"-"Helvidius" debate, see David M. Golove and Daniel J. Hulsebosch, "A Civilized Nation: The Early American Constitution, the Law of Nations, and the Pursuit of International Recognition," *New York University Law Review* 85 (October 2010): 1021–22, 1035–39, esp. 1022n348. Unitary executive theorists, however, have argued that Madison and Jefferson nonetheless believed (as did most at the time) that "executive power" generally vested power over foreign affairs. See Prakash and Ramsey, "The Executive Power over Foreign Affairs," 334–39; and Prakash and Ramsey, "Foreign Affairs and the Jeffersonian Executive," 1662–72. But for a more sensitive reading of what Madison was doing in these essays, see Jack N. Rakove, *A Politician Thinking: The Creative Mind of James Madison* (Norman: University of Oklahoma Press, 2017), 164–68.

28. On this theme, see Gienapp, *The Second Creation*, esp. 4–12. On distinguishing motives from speech acts, see 15–18.

29. William Michael Treanor, "Framer's Intent: Gouverneur Morris, the Committee of Style, and the Creation of the Federalist Constitution," 14–15, unpublished paper, https://papers.ssrn.com/sol3/papers.cfm?abstract_id=3383183.

30. Wilson and Hamilton authored two of the most important defenses of colonial rights during the imperial crisis with Britain. Morris was influential in the construction of New York's 1777 constitution. And Wilson and Morris collaborated to defend the legality of the Bank of North America before the Pennsylvania legislature.

31. "William Pierce: Character Sketches of Delegates to the Federal Convention," in *The Records of the Federal Convention of 1787*, vol. 3, ed. Max Farrand (New Haven, CT: Yale University Press, 1911), 91, 92, 89. After the first full citation, all three volumes of Farrand will be cited as Farrand, *Records*, followed by volume and page number(s).

32. Jack N. Rakove, *The Beginnings of National Politics: An Interpretive History of the Continental Congress* (New York: Knopf, 1979), 183–84, 293–94, 307, 319–26.

33. For an overview of the convergence of these factors, see Michael J. Klarman, *The Framers' Coup: The Making of the United States Constitution* (New York: Oxford University Press, 2016), chapters 1 and 2.

34. On these features of comprehensive reform and how Madison in particular arrived at them, see Rakove, *Original Meanings*, chapter 3.

35. Max M. Edling, *A Revolution in Favor of Government: Origins of the U.S. Constitution and the Making of the American State* (New York: Oxford University Press, 2003).

36. See Rakove, *Original Meanings*, especially 3–5, 36, 60–62. On how Madison's notes came to encourage this view of him, see Mary Sarah Bilder, *Madison's Hand: Revising the Constitutional Convention* (Cambridge, MA: Harvard University Press, 2015). On how Madison was an idiosyncratic Federalist, see Edling, *Revolution in Favor of Government*, 3–8.

37. Madison to George Washington, April 16, 1787, in *The Papers of James Madison*,

vol. 9, *9 April 1786–24 May 1787*, ed. Robert A. Rutland and William M. E. Rachal (Chicago: University of Chicago Press, 1975), 385. Also see Madison to Caleb Wallace, August 23, 1785, in *The Papers of James Madison*, vol. 8, *10 March 1784–28 March 1786*, ed. Robert A. Rutland, William M. E. Rachal, Barbara D. Ripel, and Fredrika J. Teute (Chicago: University of Chicago Press, 1973), 352; Madison to Edmund Randolph, April 8, 1787, in Rutland and Rachal, *The Papers of James Madison*, 9:370.

38. Madison to Thomas Jefferson, October 24, 1787, in *The Papers of James Madison*, vol. 10, *27 May 1787–3 March 1788*, ed. Robert A. Rutland, Charles F. Hobson, William M. E. Rachal, and Frederika J. Teute (Chicago: University of Chicago Press, 1977), 208; Eric Nelson, *The Royalist Revolution: Monarchy and the American Founding* (Cambridge, MA: Harvard University Press, 2014), 199–203; Rakove, *Original Meanings*, 60–61. Also see Madison to Wallace, August 23, 1785, in *The Papers of James Madison*, 8:350–52. On how Madison, confronted by political developments he had not initially anticipated, did not come to grasp the importance of executive power in republican politics until much later, see Rakove, *A Politician Thinking*, 153–59, 168–70, 178–84.

39. Bernard Bailyn, *The Origins of American Politics* (New York: Knopf, 1968), 66–80, 88–91, 136–39; Jack P. Greene, *Peripheries and Center: Constitutional Development in the Extended Polities of the British Empire and United States, 1607–1788* (Athens: University of Georgia Press, 1986), 28–42; Forrest McDonald, *The American Presidency: An Intellectual History* (Lawrence: University Press of Kansas, 1994), 89–92, 98–124.

40. Brendan McConville, *The King's Three Faces: The Rise and Fall of Royal America, 1688–1776* (Chapel Hill: University of North Carolina Press, 2006), 300–311; Nelson, *The Royalist Revolution*, 108–111. On the turn against monarchy in American writing leading up to 1776, see Pauline Maier, *From Resistance to Revolution: Colonial Radicals and the Development of American Opposition, 1765–1776* (New York: Knopf, 1972), 287–95.

41. Gordon S. Wood, *The Creation of the American Republic, 1776–1787*, rev. ed. (Chapel Hill: University of North Carolina Press, 1998), 132–50; Rakove, *Original Meanings*, 250–53.

42. Arguably, the convention faced no greater novelty than the creation of the presidency; see Rakove, *Original Meanings*, 245; and McDonald, *The American Presidency*, 9.

43. Randolph, June 1, 1787, in *The Records of the Federal Convention of 1787*, ed. Max Farrand, vol. 1 (New Haven, CT: Yale University Press, 1911), 66.

44. Hugh Williamson, July 24, 1787, in *The Records of the Federal Convention of 1787*, vol. 2, ed. Max Farrand (New Haven, CT: Yale University Press, 1911), 101. Also see George Mason, June 4, 1787, in Farrand, *Records*, 1:101–2.

45. John Dickinson, June 2, 1787, in Farrand, *Records*, 1:90. Also see Charles Pinckney, June 1, 1787, in Farrand, *Records*, 1:64–65.

46. Roger Sherman, June 1, 1787, in Farrand, *Records*, 1:65.

47. Mason, September 15, 1787, in Farrand, *Records*, 2:638–39; Rakove, *Original Meanings*, 268–70. Elbridge Gerry and Benjamin Franklin also advocated an executive council; see Gerry, June 1, 1787, in Farrand, *Records*, 1:66; and Franklin, September 7, 1787, in Farrand, *Records*, 2:542. The executive councils that the early state constitutions set up were designed to thwart executive independence. Governors were expected to heed their advice and, having been stripped of the traditional power to appoint their mem-

bers, they held little sway over them. See Wood, *The Creation of the American Republic*, 138–39.

48. Nelson, *The Royalist Revolution*, 35–37, 53–56, 102–3, 154–56.

49. Rakove, *Original Meanings*, 252–53; Nelson, *The Royalist Revolution*, 164–70, 178–79.

50. Rakove, *The Beginnings of National Politics*, 193–205, 281–82, 319, 324. For a more succinct discussion, see Rakove, *Original Meanings*, 253–55.

51. Rakove argues that Morris's success was more limited; see Rakove, *The Beginnings of National Politics*, 307–24. In contrast, E. James Ferguson contends that it was transformative; see Ferguson, *The Power of the Purse: A History of American Public Finance, 1776–1790* (Chapel Hill: University of North Carolina Press, 1961), chapters 6–8.

52. Hamilton, June 18, 1787, in Farrand, *Records*, 1:289.

53. Hamilton, "The Executive Department Further Considered" [Federalist No. 70], *New York Packet*, March 15, 1788, in *The Documentary History of the Ratification of the Constitution* (hereafter *DHRC*), vol. 16, ed. John P. Kaminski and Gaspare J. Saladino (Madison: State Historical Society of Wisconsin, 1986), 396. Also see Hamilton, "The Same Subject Continued, and Re-Eligibility of the Executive Considered" [Federalist No. 72], *New York Packet*, March 21, 1788, *DHRC*, 16:422.

54. Hamilton, "The Executive Department Further Considered" [Federalist No. 70], *DHRC*, 16:396. For a suggestive take on how the authors of *The Federalist* attempted to make this case, see Harvey C. Mansfield Jr., *Taming the Prince: The Ambivalence of Modern Executive Power* (New York: The Free Press, 1989), chapter 10.

55. Wilson, June 1, 1787, in Farrand, *Records*, 1:65.

56. Wilson, June 4, 1787, in Farrand, *Records*, 1:96.

57. Hamilton, "The Executive Department Further Considered" [Federalist No. 70], *DHRC*, 16:397.

58. Morris, July 19, 1787, in Farrand, *Records*, 2:52. Also see Wilson, June 1, 1787, in Farrand, *Records*, 1:71; and Treanor, "Framer's Intent," 62–63.

59. Klarman, *The Framers' Coup*, 217.

60. Hamilton, "The Executive Department Further Considered" [Federalist No. 70], *DHRC*, 16:399.

61. Wilson, June 1 and 4, 1787, in Farrand, *Records*, 1:71, 96. Also see Hamilton, "The Real Character of the Executive" [Federalist No. 69], *New York Packet*, March 14, 1788, *DHRC*, 16:387–88, 392.

62. Wilson, June 1 and 16, 1787, in Farrand, *Records*, 1:66, 254, 119, 266–67; also see Wilson, June 5, 1787, in Farrand, *Records*, 1:119.

63. Hamilton, "The Executive Department Further Considered" [Federalist No. 70], *DHRC*, 16:399–400.

64. Wilson, June 4, 1787, in Farrand, *Records*, 1:97. Also see Morris, September 7, 1787, in Farrand, *Records*, 2:542; and Hamilton, "The Executive Department Further Considered" [Federalist No. 70], *DHRC*, 16:400.

65. Michael W. McConnell, "James Wilson's Contributions to the Construction of Article II," *Georgetown Journal of Law & Public Policy* 17 (Winter 2019): 27–28. Resolution VII of the Virginia Plan provided for "a general authority to execute the laws,"

but the Committee of Detail transformed this provision into a duty, establishing that the president "shall take care that the laws of the United States be duly and faithfully executed"; see Virginia Plan, May 29, 1787, in Farrand, *Records*, 1:21; "Committee of Detail," August 6, 1787, in Farrand, *Records*, 2:185. This change was surely made to ensure that the president would not enjoy the most troublesome of executive prerogatives: the suspending power (the power to suspend laws) and the dispensing power (the power to free individuals from certain laws). The Stuart monarchs who had ruled over seventeenth-century England were known to have abused these powers, and the English Bill of Rights of 1689 (drafted in the wake of the Glorious Revolution of 1688) sought to eliminate them from future use. See Reinstein, "The Limits of Executive Power," 278–80.

66. Wilson, June 1, 1787, in Farrand, *Records*, 1:66.

67. While the royal prerogative had shrunk over the course of English history, thanks especially to the Glorious Revolution of 1688, it still encompassed a vast array of powers in the eighteenth century. For the most influential contemporary compilation, see William Blackstone, *Commentaries on the Laws of England*, 4 vols. (Oxford: Clarendon Press, 1765–1769), 1:230–70. Most observers recognized that some of these powers appeared to exist only in theory and had not been exercised by the monarch for some time (such as the veto and some foreign affairs powers), but they disagreed as to why. Some commentators believed that thanks to the rise of parliamentary supremacy and ministerial government, the monarch had been so weakened as to lose the practical authority to exercise these powers. Others thought that thanks to the growth of an extensive royal patronage system that had been fueled by the prerogative powers to create offices, appoint officials to them and remove officials from them, and dispense pensions and titles, the monarch in fact dominated Parliament and by extension the royal ministers and thus had no need to wield the particular powers that had fallen into abeyance. See Nelson, *The Royalist Revolution*, 16–23, 196–99, 218–20, 225–27; David Lindsay Keir, *The Constitutional History of Modern Britain*, 5th ed. rev. (London: Adam and Charles Black, 1957), 276–88, 293–98, 316–17, 330–35; and Goldwin Smith, *A Constitutional and Legal History of England* (New York: Scribner, 1955), 381–402. However, many of these prerogative powers were merely theoretical, they were understood to constitute the royal prerogative. Even resolute champions of executive power at the convention were not eager to vest all of them in the president. Wilson, for instance, did not think they were a "proper guide" for defining executive powers; Wilson, June 1, 1787, in Farrand, *Records*, 1:65. Accordingly, he helped ensure that many of these prerogative powers were vested in Congress, not the president; see McConnell, "James Wilson's Contributions to the Construction of Article II," 29–36, 40–41, 45–46. The final Constitution followed this general pattern: most of the royal prerogatives were ultimately given to Congress or prohibited to the president. For a comprehensive comparison of the royal prerogatives with the president's powers, see Reinstein, "The Limits of Executive Power," 271–307. A more complicated question is whether Wilson (or his allies) thought that vesting the president with the "executive power" gave him the unassigned royal prerogative powers. Many scholars have argued that it did, claiming that at the time of the founding, this phrase referred to the royal prerogative; see, e.g., Prakash, *Imperial from the Beginning*, 8, 31, and chapters 4 and 6; and Prakash and Ramsey, "The Executive Power over Foreign Af-

fairs," 234, 252–56. In a related vein, some have claimed that the phrase was understood to connote discretionary power to act beyond the law. See Edward S. Corwin, *The President: Office and Powers, 1787–1984*, 5th ed. (New York: New York University Press, 1984), 3–16; McDonald, *The American Presidency*, 181. For a challenge to this interpretation, see Robert Scigliano, "The President's 'Prerogative Power,'" in *Inventing the American Presidency*, ed. Thomas E. Cronin (Lawrence: University Press of Kansas, 1989), 236–56. Harvey Mansfield has claimed, on this front, that in the innovative hands of influential early modern political theorists and later leading American framers, executive power came to be defined by the fundamental ambivalence between these opposing conceptions of it: weak formality (in which an executive is conceived as a subordinate who merely carries out the will of another) and informal strength (in which an executive is positioned to respond independently and energetically to necessities created by emergencies or legal gaps and indeterminacies). Instead of choosing, theorists deliberately united these rival versions, allowing an executive to be a strong ruler who could always hide behind the weakness of a formal definition; see Mansfield, *Taming the Prince*, xv–20. But other scholars have countered that the eighteenth-century meaning of "executive power" was deeply contested and uncertain; see, e.g., Bradley and Flaherty, "Executive Power Essentialism and Foreign Affairs," 551–52; Rakove, "Taking the Prerogative out of the Presidency," 95–99; and, especially in the United States in light of the development of its distinctive constitutionalism, Flaherty, "Most Dangerous Branch," 1788–92. Still others have insisted not that the phrase was uncertain but that it decisively meant nothing more than the power to execute the law; see Mortenson, "Article II Vests the Executive Power, Not the Royal Prerogative," 1173–74, 1187–88; and Steilen, "How to Think Constitutionally about Prerogative," 641–52. Even Prakash has acknowledged that the power to execute was the "essential" feature of executive power; see Prakash, *Imperial from the Beginning*, chapter 5. Finally, Robert Reinstein has argued that the unassigned prerogatives point to implied presidential powers (particularly in the areas of law enforcement and foreign affairs) derived from and thus limited by the enumerated powers in Article II; see Reinstein, "The Limits of Executive Power," 312–15. Whatever the case may be, what is clear is that Wilson and other champions of executive power did not think the president should be vested with the full royal prerogative.

68. For more, see Nelson, *The Royalist Revolution*, 185–95.

69. June 4, 1787, in Farrand, *Records*, 1:98. George Read of Delaware later proposed this again, this time seconded by Morris; Morris, August 7, 1787, in Farrand, *Records*, 2:200.

70. Wilson and Hamilton, June 4, 1787, in Farrand, *Records*, 1:98. Hamilton also proposed vesting the executive with an absolute veto in his own plan, which he presented after his only extensive speech; Hamilton, June 18, 1787, in Farrand, *Records*, 1:292.

71. Wilson, June 4, 1787, in Farrand, *Records*, 1:98. Also see Morris, August 15, 1787, in Farrand, *Records*, 2:299.

72. Wilson, June 1, 1787, in Farrand, *Records*, 1:66. Also see Morris, July 19, 1787, in Farrand, *Records*, 2:52.

73. Wilson, August 15, 1787, in Farrand, *Records*, 2:300–301. Also see Morris, August 23, 1787, in Farrand, *Records*, 2:389; Wilson, August 23 and September 7, 1787, in Farrand,

Records, 2:389, 538; Hamilton, "The Provision for the Support of the Executive, and the Veto Power" [Federalist No. 73], *New York Packet*, March 21, 1788, *DHRC*, 16:448.

74. Wilson, September 6, 1787, in Farrand, *Records*, 2:523.

75. Morris, September 4, 1787, in Farrand, *Records*, 2:500.

76. See Wood, *The Creation of the American Republic*, chapters 8–11.

77. Wilson, June 4, 1787, in Farrand, *Records*, 1:105.

78. Morris, July 21, 1787, in Farrand, *Records*, 2:76.

79. Wilson, August 15, 1787, in Farrand, *Records*, 2:300–301.

80. Wilson, June 4, 1787, in Farrand, *Records*, 1:98.

81. Wilson, August 15, 1787, in Farrand, *Records*, 2:300–301. Also see Morris, August 15, 1787, in Farrand, *Records*, 2:299; Hamilton, "The Provision for the Support of the Executive, and the Veto Power" [Federalist No. 73], *DHRC*, 16:448.

82. Wilson, June 1, 1787, in Farrand, *Records*, 1:71.

83. Klarman, *The Framers' Coup*, 219–20. On why Wilson and his allies, especially Madison, thought including judges in the process of reviewing legislation would actually enhance executive power, see Rakove, *A Politician Thinking*, 80–81.

84. Wilson, June 4, 1787, in Farrand, *Records*, 1:105.

85. Morris, July 21, 1787, in Farrand, *Records*, 2:76.

86. Rakove, *Original Meanings*, 258–61. For a full discussion of these debates, see Klarman, *The Framers' Coup*, 226–38.

87. Morris, July 17, 1787, in Farrand, *Records*, 2:31, 29; also see Morris, July 24, 1787, in Farrand, *Records*, 2:103.

88. Wilson, June 1 and 2, 1787, in Farrand, *Records*, 1:68, 80; Wilson, July 17, 19 and 24, in Farrand, *Records*, 2:29–30, 56, and 103; and Wilson, September 4 and 6, 1787, in Farrand, *Records*, 2:501, 523; Morris, July 17, 19, 24, and 25, in Farrand, *Records*, 2: 29, 31, 54, 105, and 113; and Wilson, September 4, 1787, in Farrand, *Records*, 2:500.

89. Klarman, *The Framers' Coup*, 226–27; Morris, July 19 and 24, 1787, in Farrand, *Records*, 2:53, 104–5; Wilson, July 19 and September 4, 1787, in Farrand, *Records*, 2:56 and 2:501–2.

90. Morris, July 20, 1787, in Farrand, *Records*, 2:65; also see July 19, 1787, in Farrand, *Records*, 2:53.

91. For proposals that the executive serve on good behavior, see Hamilton, June 18, 1787, in Farrand, *Records*, 1:289; and Morris, July 17, in Farrand, *Records*, 2:33. For those who advocated a longer term, see Wilson, July 24, 1787, in Farrand, *Records*, 2:102; and Morris, July 24, 1787, in Farrand, *Records*, 2:105.

92. Rakove, *Original Meanings*, 267.

93. This is most true of Wilson, who not only skillfully navigated the floor debates but also exploited his role on the Committee of Detail to enhance the power of the presidency; see McConnell, "James Wilson's Contributions to the Construction of Article II," 23–50. Late in the convention, he also seemed to have an influence on the Committee on Postponed Parts, whose members (Morris among them) further molded the presidency into a Wilsonian form, not least by replacing legislative selection of the president with a system of presidential electors, a mechanism Wilson had originally introduced; see Wilson, June 2, 1787, in Farrand, *Records*, 1:80. Moreover, after the committee reported,

Wilson successfully introduced revisions that brought Article II more in line with his preferences; see William Ewald, "James Wilson and the Drafting of the Constitution," *University of Pennsylvania Journal of Constitutional Law* 10 (June 2008): 1000–1004. For the argument that Wilson generated the ideas but that Morris was the movement's floor leader, see Charles C. Thach Jr., *The Creation of the Presidency, 1775–1789: A Study in Constitutional History* (Baltimore, MD: Johns Hopkins University Press, 1922), 85–91, 99–101, 176–77. On how a surprising number of Hamilton's proposals became part of the Constitution, see William E. Scheuerman, "American Kingship? Monarchical Origins of Modern Presidentialism," *Polity* 37 (January 2005): 38–39.

94. John Locke, *Second Treatise on Government*, ed. C. B. Macpherson (Indianapolis: Hackett, 1980), 76–77. Also see Rakove, *Original Meanings*, 247–48.

95. [Hamilton], "Pacificus No. I," 36.

96. Wilson, June 1, 1787, in Farrand, *Records*, 1:65–66. Wilson would come to argue (rather fancifully) that in the distant Anglo-Saxon past, the power of making war and peace had in fact properly been lodged in a representative assembly rather than with the monarch; see *The Collected Works of James Wilson*, ed. Kermit L. Hall and Mark David Hall, 2 vols. (Indianapolis: Liberty Fund, 2007), 2:871; and Eric Nelson, "James Wilson and the Ancient Constitution," *Georgetown Journal of Law & Public Policy* 17 (Winter 2019): 189–90.

97. This ambivalence helps explain the ambiguous distribution of foreign affairs powers in the Constitution; see Rakove, *Original Meanings*, 263–67.

98. Wilson, June 26, 1787, in Farrand, *Records*, 1:426.

99. The Committee of Detail vested the Senate with the powers to make treaties and appoint ambassadors and Congress with the powers to make war and establish the armed forces, giving the president only the power to receive ambassadors and serve as "commander in chief." Eventually, due primarily to growing distrust of the Senate, the convention vested the president with the powers to make treaties and appoint ambassadors, subject to approval of the Senate. See McConnell, "James Wilson's Contributions to the Construction of Article II," 44–45, 49.

100. Wilson, September 7, 1787, in Farrand, *Records*, 2:538.

101. Morris, September 7 and August 23, 1787, in Farrand, *Records*, 2:541, 392.

102. Hamilton, "The Treaty Making Power of the Executive" [Federalist No. 75], *New York Independent Journal*, March 26, 1788, DHRC, 16:482.

103. Hamilton, "The Same Subject Continued, and Re-Eligibility of the Executive Considered" [Federalist No. 72], DHRC, 16:422.

104. On how Hamilton, writing as "Pacificus," deviated from earlier assumptions about the relationship between executive and federative power, see Rakove, "Taking the Prerogative out of the Presidency," 89–99.

105. In fact, of all the delegates, Morris gave the most speeches and Wilson the second most. Madison ranked third. See Clinton Rossiter, *1787: The Grand Convention* (New York: Macmillan, 1966), 252.

106. Mikhail, "The Constitution and the Philosophy of Language," 1102–3.

107. William Ewald, "The Committee of Detail," *Constitutional Commentary* 28 (Fall

2012): 213–14, 259, 276–78, 280–83. However, Ewald appropriately cautions against over-stating Wilson's influence, see especially 242–46.

108. Treanor, "Framer's Intent."

109. Robert Green McCloskey, "Introduction," in *The Works of James Wilson*, ed. Robert Green McCloskey, 2 vols. (Cambridge, MA: Harvard University Press, 1967), 1:21–23.

110. James Wilson, *Considerations on the Bank of North-America* (Philadelphia: Hall & Sellers, 1785), 10–11. On Wilson's use of the Declaration, see Danielle Allen and Emily Sneff, "Golden Letters: James Wilson, the Declaration of Independence, and the Sussex Declaration," *Georgetown Journal of Law & Public Policy* 17 (Winter 2019): 211–13; and John Mikhail, "A Tale of Two Sweeping Clauses," *Harvard Journal of Law & Public Policy* 42 (Winter 2019): 35–39.

111. Wilson, *Considerations on the Bank of North-America*, 10, Wilson's italics.

112. For more on Wilson's argument, see John Mikhail, "The Necessary and Proper Clauses," *Georgetown Law Journal* 102 (April 2014): 1074–78.

113. Virginia Plan, May 29, 1787, in Farrand, *Records*, 1:21.

114. Mikhail, "The Necessary and Proper Clauses," 1071–86.

115. Wilson, May 31, 1787, in Farrand, *Records*, 1:60; also see 1:53, 59–60.

116. The committee members were Wilson, John Rutledge, Edmund Randolph, Oliver Ellsworth, and Nathaniel Gorham.

117. On the work of the Committee of Detail, see Ewald, "Committee of Detail."

118. "Committee of Detail," in Farrand, *Records*, 2:144; Mikhail, "The Necessary and Proper Clauses," 1086–96.

119. Mikhail, "The Necessary and Proper Clauses," 1096–1106.

120. "Committee of Detail," in Farrand, *Records*, 2:168; "Committee of Detail," August 6, 1787, in Farrand, *Records*, 2:182.

121. Mikhail, "The Necessary and Proper Clauses," 1096–1106.

122. Discussion of this issue lies beyond the scope of this analysis, but for now it will suffice to note that Hamilton's opinion on the constitutionality of a national bank strikingly eschewed Wilsonian argument, focusing instead primarily on Congress's enumerated powers. See Jonathan Gienapp, "The Myth of the Constitutional Given: Enumeration and National Power at the Founding," *American University Law Review Forum* 69 (2020): 190–94, 207–9.

123. Thus, Wilson stressed the limited nature of federal authority during the ratification debates and then in his famed "Lectures on Law" (first delivered in 1790), in which he stressed the differences between the Pennsylvania Constitution and the United States Constitution; see Hall and Hall, *Collected Works of James Wilson*, 2:870. But nothing about these concessions necessarily contradicted his previous arguments about the delegation of implied national powers.

124. "Committee of Detail," August 6, 1787, in Farrand, *Records*, 2:177.

125. For the most detailed discussion of Morris's Committee of Style revisions, see Treanor, "Framer's Intent."

126. Morris to Timothy Pickering, December 22, 1814, in Farrand, *Records*, 3:420.

127. Madison to Jared Sparks, April 8, 1831, in Farrand, *Records*, 3:499.

128. The other committee members were William Samuel Johnson (chair), James Madison, Rufus King, and Alexander Hamilton.

129. "Committee of Detail," August 6, 1787, in Farrand, *Records*, 2:177.

130. "Committee of Style," in Farrand, *Records*, 2:590. The comma Morris added in "We, the People" was removed in the final version; see "The Constitution of the United States," in Farrand, *Records*, 2:651.

131. In his "Lectures on Law," Wilson built his discussion of national legislative power around the "great ends" of the national government as laid out in the preamble; see Hall and Hall, *Collected Works of James Wilson*, 2:870–72.

132. Wilson, *Considerations on the Bank of North-America*, 10.

133. Wilson, September 14, 1787, in Farrand, *Records*, 2:615.

134. For an incisive discussion of the importance of this change, see Treanor, "Framer's Intent," 78–87.

135. Thach, *The Creation of the Presidency*, 138–39.

136. "Committee of Detail," August 6, 1787, in Farrand, *Records*, 2:185; "Committee of Style," in Farrand, *Records*, 2:597.

137. Morris, July 19, 1787, in Farrand, *Records*, 2:52. Morris had earlier betrayed his frustration with state legislatures; see "Address to the Assembly of Pennsylvania on the Abolition of the Bank of North America" (1785), in *To Secure the Blessings of Liberty: Selected Writings of Gouverneur Morris*, ed. J. Jackson Barlow (Indianapolis: Liberty Fund, 2012), 184.

138. Putting the point somewhat differently, that Morris was reworking the vesting clauses to underscore that executive power was inherently capacious, see Treanor, "Framer's Intent," 90.

139. "Compare Committee of Detail," August 6, 1787, in Farrand, *Records*, 2:177–87; with "Committee of Style," in Farrand, *Records*, 2:590–601.

140. Treanor, "Framer's Intent," 88–89.

141. Madison, July 17, 1787, in Farrand, *Records*, 2:35. The prevalence of this assumption at the founding deeply complicates any attempt to understand what eighteenth-century Americans thought about the separation of powers. For more on this vital point, see Rakove, *A Politician Thinking*, 82–83, 86–95, 145–46. On the too rarely appreciated ambiguities that defined the doctrine of separation of powers in the eighteenth century, in particular the complex ways that it grew out of and remained entangled with the idea of mixed constitutionalism and government, see M. J. C. Vile, *Constitutionalism and the Separation of Powers*, 2nd ed. (Indianapolis: Liberty Fund, 1998), chapters 1–6; W. B. Gwyn, *The Meaning of the Separation of Powers: An Analysis of the Doctrine from its Origin to the Adoption of the United States Constitution* (New Orleans, LA: Tulane University, 1965); and Wood, *The Creation of the American Republic*, 150–61, 446–63, 545–53.

142. Precisely because defenders of executive power such as Morris assumed that the legislature would predominate in a republican government, it was important to take additional steps to fortify the other branches, not so each would have *equal* power but so each would have *sufficient* power and independence to exercise and safeguard its core functions. On these important distinctions, see David J. Siemers, *The Myth of Coequal*

Branches: Restoring the Constitution's Separation of Functions (Columbia: University of Missouri Press, 2018), introduction and chapter 2.

143. Morris, May 30, 1787, in Farrand, *Records*, 1:34.

144. Morris, May 30, 1787, in Farrand, *Records*, 1:43.

145. Morris, July 17, 1787, in Farrand, *Records*, 2:26.

146. Morris, August 20, 1787, in Farrand, *Records*, 2:343.

147. Morris, July 17, 1787, in Farrand, *Records*, 2:27.

148. "The President of the Convention to the President of Congress," September 17, 1787, in *Documentary History of the Ratification of the Constitution*, vol. 1, ed. Merrill Jensen (Madison: Historical Society of Wisconsin, 1976), 306.

149. Morris to Robert Walsh, February 5, 1811, in *The Diary and Letters of Gouverneur Morris*, ed. Anne Cary Morris, 2 vols. (New York: Charles Scribner's Sons, 1888), 2:529.

150. See Treanor, "Framer's Intent," 57–61, 90.

151. *Chisholm v. Georgia*, 2 U.S. 419, 453, 465 (1793) (Wilson, J., opinion).

7

Defending an Energetic Executive

Theory and Practice in *The Federalist*

CLAIRE RYDELL ARCENAS

A feeble executive implies a feeble execution of the government. A feeble execution is but another phrase for a bad execution; and a government ill executed, whatever it may be in theory, must be, in practice, a bad government.

Alexander Hamilton, *The Federalist*, No. 70

In September 1787, the Constitutional Convention adjourned and the American people were, as Alexander Hamilton explained, "called upon to deliberate on a new Constitution for the United States of America."[1] As the proposed Constitution made its way from Philadelphia to the thirteen states for ratification, its supporters put pen to paper and took to the newspapers in defense of the newly proposed plan of government.[2] The most famous of these constitutional defenses is *The Federalist*, a collection of eighty-five essays published in New York newspapers in late 1787 and early 1788.[3] Its authors—known collectively by their pseudonym Publius—were Alexander Hamilton, James Madison, and John Jay. There are many things that made—and continue to make—*The Federalist* stand out.[4] This chapter focuses on Publius's defense of the executive branch of the new federal government, which Hamilton, in particular, saw as an integral part of their overall defense of the Constitution.[5] Hamilton also understood that it was highly contentious. In Federalist No. 67, Hamilton wrote of the executive that "there is hardly any part of the system which could have been attended with greater difficulty in the arrangement of it than this; and there is, perhaps, none which has been inveighed against with less candor or criticized with less judgement."[6]

As *The Federalist*'s authors knew well, and as Jonathan Gienapp shows in the preceding chapter of this volume, the executive posed particular challenges—and opportunities—for the framers during the convention.[7] In the first place, the "layers of historical experience" that informed ideas about executive power, however diverse, did not provide an attractive model for the office, role, and authority of the president.[8] Indeed, the models Americans had the most immediate experience with—which ranged from the hereditary monarchy of King George III (for the period before 1776) to an array of decidedly and purposefully weak state governors who were usually limited to one term (for the period after 1776)—were invariably negative.[9] In the second place, while the writings of theorists such as Charles Secondat, Baron de Montesquieu and Sir William Blackstone provided guidance on topics related to the separation of powers and executive prerogative, they envisioned no president of the kind ultimately contained in Article II of the Constitution.[10] The uncertainties born of deficits in experience and theory required the framers to engage in what historians generally regard as their "most creative act": the creation of a unified, single president who would serve for four years but was eligible for reelection.[11]

For the framers, the issue of executive "energy" in particular was as thorny as it was important. In the eyes of its supporters, an energetic executive would be an effective, vigorous leader who would also be responsible (and feel responsibility) for the results of his government and administration, both domestically and internationally.[12] For its opponents, the prospect of an energetic executive evoked not-so-distant memories of monarchy or even tyranny. Edmund Randolph of Virginia, for example, argued that "a unity in the Executive magistracy"—that is, a single executive—was nothing short of being "the foetus of monarchy."[13] Prompted by these disagreements, Madison confided in Thomas Jefferson after the convention that the matter of ensuring "a proper energy in the Executive" had been "peculiarly embarrassing." In Philadelphia, he explained, there had been "tedious and reiterated discussions" on the subject.[14]

The fact that executive energy provoked such tedious discussions should not surprise us. What, after all, did it mean for the executive to be energetic? Why was an energetic executive an important and even necessary component of a good government? Answers to these questions were not self-evident. Given that executive energy was part and parcel of the government the framers envisioned, however, such questions were critical and needed to be addressed.[15]

In Federalist No. 70, the fourth of eleven essays on the executive branch, Hamilton directly addressed the matter of executive energy. He defended the proposition that "energy in the executive is a leading character in the definition of good government."[16] The efficacy of an energetic executive was not a new priority for Hamilton. Nearly a decade earlier, he had observed regarding the Articles of Confederation that a "defect in our system is want of . . . energy in the administration," which was a consequence, to "a great degree," of "the want of a proper executive."[17]

In Hamilton's eyes, lessons of the past of England—immediate and distant—and of the states under the Articles of Confederation provided ample evidence of the dangers of a weak executive. He wanted to ensure that the president—the executive branch—would be able to resist encroachments from the other branches of government, particularly the legislature, and carry out his duties on behalf of the republic. In fact, as evidenced by his early contributions at the Constitutional Convention, Hamilton desired an even more powerful executive than Article II envisioned. In Philadelphia, for example, he had declared support for a president who served a life term, at least "during good behaviour"; supported giving the president unqualified veto power; and proposed allowing the president to make certain appointments—to head the "departments of Finance, War and Foreign Affairs"—without requiring the consent of the Senate.[18] With the choice between ratification or rejection at stake, however, Hamilton, writing as Publius, deployed all his argumentative talent to defend the executive conceived by the Constitution.[19]

To counter arguments "that a vigorous executive is inconsistent with the genius of republican government," Hamilton began Federalist No. 70 by listing several benefits of having an energetic executive. An energetic executive, he argued, provided protections related to both internal and external security—the proper "administration of the laws" and "the protection of the community against foreign attacks." An energetic executive would ensure the well-being of the country's people and its good standing in the world of international relations governed by the law of nations.[20]

Hamilton then reminded readers of ancient Rome's history. He prompted them to recall with what regularity Romans had resorted to rule by an (extreme) energetic executive in the form of a dictator. Rome, Hamilton explained, had frequently been "obliged to take refuge in the absolute power of a single man" to protect it from a host of threats, which ranged widely, from overly "ambitious individuals" to "whole classes of the community whose conduct threatened the existence of all government" to dangerous "external enemies" keen to destroy it. It was not difficult to imagine that the United States might face the same menaces. Hamilton's point was that governments—and a people—could be vulnerable without a sufficiently energetic executive.

After presenting the historical example of Rome, Hamilton concluded his defense of executive energy as follows:

> There can be no need, however, to multiply arguments or examples on this head. *A feeble executive implies a feeble execution of the government. A feeble execution is but another phrase for a bad execution; and a government ill executed, whatever it may be in theory, must be, in practice, a bad government.*
> Taking it for granted, therefore, that all men of sense will agree in the necessity of an energetic executive, it will only remain to inquire, what are the ingredients which constitute this energy?[21]

The first and last sentences of the above passage—"There can be no need" and "Taking it for granted"—suggest that Hamilton considered his case for an energetic executive to be ironclad, strong enough that he could move on to explain which elements would "constitute this energy."

At first glance, Hamilton's confidence seems difficult to account for. The first two propositions of his argument—the sentences that begin with "A feeble executive" and "A feeble execution"—exhibit clear logical flaws. A feeble executive does not necessarily imply feeble execution. As the framers were well aware, a robust legislative branch—such as the British Parliament—could execute government quite energetically. Nor was feeble execution necessarily a synonym for bad execution. Indeed, many readers of Federalist No. 70 knew that points made in favor of a weak national government on the grounds that it would better allow individual states to exercise important powers were central to arguments against the proposed Constitution. The third proposition, meanwhile, is incongruous. While initially it appears to be a rather conventional opposition between theory and practice, it is, in fact, only a simple syllogism ("a government ill executed . . . must be . . . a bad government") onto which Hamilton has grafted the reference to theory and practice. Furthermore, its underlying premise that a government that is ill executed could be construed as anything other than bad government seems peculiar. Finally, the implication that those who argued against an energetic executive were doing so on the grounds that a feeble government was good in theory does not find support in the evidentiary record and it is difficult to imagine Hamilton having any such arguments in mind.

In the context of the 1780s, however, Hamilton's arguments carried more weight than we might initially suppose. The key to understanding Hamilton's defense of executive energy as he presented it to readers of *The Federalist* is grasping the power (rhetorical and otherwise) of the comparison he makes between how something appears in theory and what it is in practice, a distinction he used to counter opponents and would-be opponents of executive energy.[22] This chapter proceeds in four parts. First, it first surveys how Americans thought about the relationship between theory and practice at the time Hamilton was writing and identifies three broad strains of thought (section I). It then focuses on the strain that Hamilton exemplified in Federalist No. 70 (section II) and examines how Americans other than Publius understood the particular contrast between theory and practice that Hamilton employed (section III). Finally, it situates Hamilton's defense of executive power in *The Federalist* against the intellectual backdrop the preceding sections have sketched to show how it encapsulated key elements of what Hamilton's contemporaries were coming to see as the new science of politics in their country (section IV).

I.

For Publius and other supporters of the Constitution, theory and practice did not have just one relationship. Rather, there were multiple ways theory could relate to practice.[23] Three ways—two of which contrast with the configuration of Hamilton's argument in Federalist No. 70—bear mention here.

The first variation, what we can call the harmony variation, emphasized a perceived (or at least desired) agreement between theory and practice.[24] The harmony variation appeared both during the Constitutional Convention and in *The Federalist*. Often, it portrayed experience as justifying an idea. For example, when Madison recorded the ways James Wilson, a delegate from Pennsylvania and one of the key members of the drafting committee, grappled with the best mode of electing the president at the convention in June 1787, he noted the following: Wilson "would say . . . at least that in theory he was for an election [of the president] by the people" because "experience, particularly in N. York & Massts, shewed that an election of the first magistrate by the people at large, was both a convenient & successful mode."[25] By Madison's account, at least, Wilson supported his idea that selection of the president might best happen by popular election by referring to experience that supported the idea. Writing in defense of the executive in Federalist No. 76, Hamilton, too, argued that "experience justifies the theory" in his discussion of the nominating powers of the president as they related to the powers of the Senate.[26] The harmony variation of the sort Wilson and Hamilton used has been the primary focus of historical and philosophical work on the relationship between theory and practice around the time of the Constitutional Convention.

We can call a second mode of invoking theory and practice, or the experience of practice, contrast positive. Like the harmony variation, the contrast-positive variation involved portraying theory as a positive. Unlike the harmony variation, however, it involved distinguishing between what was achievable in practice (or what had transpired in the experience of practice) and what was achievable in theory. The contrast-positive variation is nicely illustrated in several writings by Henry Knox of Massachusetts, who later became the nation's first secretary of war.

In the autumn of 1787, before the Massachusetts ratifying convention met, Knox weighed how best to describe the Constitutional Convention's accomplishments. Observing from the outside what had transpired in Philadelphia that summer, Knox first wrote that "the proposed Constitution has been the result of the most laborious" before crossing out "most laborious" to settle on "the result of the deepest investgn and deliberations on government."[27] For Knox, it was important to convey that the labors of the framers had been sound philosophically (that is, scientifically, in eighteenth-century terms), not just that the Constitution was the product of hard work. Notably, Knox's attention to the process of investigation and deliberation undergirding the convention was echoed in Hamilton's contrast, in Federalist No. 1, between "good government from reflection and choice" and the "political constitutions" that emerge from "accident and force."[28]

Knox's assessment of the kind of work that had gone into creating the Constitution does a lot to explain his confidence that the Constitution would result in good government in practice, even if it did not provide for a perfect one in theory. From his vantage point in New York in the autumn of 1787, Knox put it this way: if the Constitution "should not perfectly correspond with the theory of the [closet?] [that is, with abstract philosophical reasoning] in every minutiae, it ought to be considered as the only constitution which could be obtained in a peaceable manner."[29] And to his colleague Jean-Baptiste Gouvion, a French military officer, Knox reckoned that the Constitution "might probably have been formed with greater consistency in the closet of a Philosophic—but a better could not be obtained by a free compromise."[30] For Knox, it was important to convey that the Constitution was the result of compromise and deliberation, not philosophical speculation—however perfect that speculation might be. That meant drawing a distinction between the practical good—what the convention had produced—and a theoretical ideal—what could be achieved in the philosopher's closet, a trope to which I shall return shortly. But it did not mean construing the ideal—the theory—in negative terms.

A third variation—what we can call contrast negative—did just that. This configuration of the relationship between theory and practice was what undergirded Hamilton's argument in Federalist No. 70, where he contrasted "whatever it may be in theory" with bad practice, relying on his audience's recognition that what was good in theory could (and often did) fail in practice. Like the contrast-positive arguments of Knox, this variation involved making a distinction between theory (understood as being what emerges from the closet of a philosopher or "theoretic" politician) and practice. In stark contrast, however, it emphasized showing that what may seem theoretically good could, in fact, result in bad practical outcomes. The following section explores this variation of the theory-in-relation-to-practice argument in more detail.

II.

In February 1787, the *Pennsylvania Packet* published "Remarks on Manners, Government, Law and the Domestic Debt of America—Addressed to the Citizens of the United States." Reflecting on the country's present state of affairs under the Articles of Confederation, its author observed that "perhaps it is impossible to frame a constitution of government, in the closet, which will suit the people, for it is frequent to find one, the most perfect in theory, the most objectionable in practice."[31] Throughout the founding era and the period of the early republic, distinctions such as these between political institutions being perfect in theory but bad in practice were ubiquitous. Often anxieties about such distinctions were conveyed through the figure of the closeted framer of government—usually construed as a closet philosopher or "theoretic" politician.

To make sense of Hamilton's argument in Federalist No. 70 and the central role the contrast-negative comparison played in Publius's overall defense of the Constitution, it will be useful to clarify what Publius and others meant by the concept of a closet philosopher. At the time, "closet" denoted privacy and seclusion, as Samuel Johnson's 1755 *Dictionary of the English Language* explained.[32] A closet was a private space of reflection like a study and so, for its eighteenth-century users, implied a separation from the public, from real-world knowledge, and from practice or experience. Importantly, closet could also refer to "the private apartment of a monarch or other person of high status," as in a royal closet, again suggesting separation from the mundane.[33] Along similar lines, "theoretic" denoted a separation from practice. According to Johnson's *Dictionary*, as a noun, "theorick" meant "a speculatist; one who knows only speculation, not practice." As an adjective "theoretical" meant "speculative; depending on theory or speculation; terminating in theory or speculation; not practical."[34]

It seems likely that late eighteenth-century Americans derived their understanding of the term closet philosopher from the writings of Scottish historian and philosopher David Hume. In "Of the Study of History," an essay first published in the 1740s, Hume popularized the trope of the philosopher in his closet who considered matters in only an abstract way. "When a philosopher contemplates characters and manners in his closet," Hume explained, "the general abstract view of the objects leaves the mind so cold and unmoved, that the sentiments of nature have no room to play, and he scarce feels the difference between vice and virtue."[35] In later work, particularly the essay "Whether the British Government Inclines More to Absolute Monarchy, or to a Republic," Hume again invoked a distinction between a "fine imaginary republic, of which a man may form a plan in his closet" and republics of, and existing in, the real world.[36] As historians have long recognized, Americans at this time—Publius included—were avid readers of Hume, although they did not always agree with him.[37]

Following the adjournment of the Constitutional Convention in September 1787, as discussions and debates over ratification ensued, distinctions of the sort Hume had in mind between imaginary republics planned in the closet of a philosopher and republics built on experience and made to stand the test of time were very much in the air. Publius confronted head on questions about the extent to which theoretical perfection in plans for governing was desirable. In short, while closet philosophers strove for theoretic perfection, the convention, according to Publius, did not. In Federalist No. 65, for example, Hamilton argued that "if mankind were to resolve to agree in no institution of government, until every part of it had been adjusted to the most exact standard of perfection, society would soon become a general scene of anarchy, and the world a desert."[38]

Indeed, through his distinction between closet philosophy and his own plans for a successful government, Publius's concerns about the contrast between theory and practice become clear. In his defense of the Constitution, Publius repeatedly employed references to "theoretic politicians" (Federalist No. 10) or the "skilful individual in his closet" (Federalist No. 56) to emphasize what the convention had *not* been—the work of some speculative philosopher in his study—and what the Constitution *would* be—good in practice, but not theoretically perfect.[39]

Madison's discussion of the "difficulties which the Convention must have experienced in the formation of a proper plan" in Federalist No. 37 contains the clearest indication of *The Federalist*'s reliance on the figure of the closet philosopher to set up a contrast between what might be good in theory but not so in practice. Feigning a measure of authorial distance from what had transpired, Madison explained that the convention had been "compelled to sacrifice theoretical propriety" for the sake of what the framers had set out to complete. Here Madison distinguished between plans for a government born of "an abstract view of the subject," of the sort "an ingenious theorist" could use "to bestow on a Constitution planned in his closet or in his imagination," and the framework the convention produced. He steered readers away from dwelling on theoretical perfection of things that might have been. Instead, he urged them to bear in mind how remarkable it was that in the process of creating a constitution outside the closet, "so many difficulties should have been surmounted, and surmounted with a unanimity almost as unprecedented as it must have been unexpected."[40]

The distinctions Madison had described between governments planned by a closet philosopher and a constitution born of rejecting theoretical perfection were readily available points of reference for Hamilton as he prepared Federalist No. 70 for publication in the *Independent Journal* in March 1788.[41] Indeed, the argumentative power of the relationship Hamilton emphasized between theory and practice is best understood against this backdrop of other contrast-negative arguments both in *The Federalist* and in the wider intellectual and political context of the time.

III.

When Americans of the founding era and the early republic referred to closet philosophy and closet philosophers, they had actual examples in mind. Chief among them was the seventeenth-century English philosopher John Locke. With his own failed constitutional project for the English colony of Carolina, Locke provided Americans of this time with the most vivid, immediate example of the perils of a closet philosopher creating a constitution.[42]

The Fundamental Constitutions of Carolina (1669)—which, as eighteenth-century Americans understood it, Locke had crafted on behalf of Lord Anthony Ashley Cooper, later the Earl of Shaftesbury, one of the lords proprietors of the colony of Carolina—consisted of 120 briefly stated declarations called "constitutions." It proposed an anti-democratic system of government that placed all authority in the hands of the lords proprietors.[43] Landownership was similarly aristocratic; it guaranteed a significant portion to the proprietors.[44] In short, the system of government *The Fundamental Constitutions* proposed was a feudal one, complete with titles of nobility such as landgrave. In the late seventeenth century, the plan was pushed through multiple revisions but was never fully implemented, due in large part to its complexity and incongruity with realities on the ground. By 1719, even the pretense of adhering to *The Fundamental Constitutions* was gone.[45]

By the end of the eighteenth century, observers knew *The Fundamental Constitutions* as the work of Locke.[46] It was printed under his name in 1720 and by 1751 had become part of his collected works.[47] They were also generally recognized as having been a complete and utter failure, known, in the words of one later critic, as "the crude and monstrous scheme of government, framed by Mr. *Locke*."[48]

Locke's role as archetype for the failures of closet philosophy was rich with irony. Americans knew Locke best for his arguments against innate ideas in his famous *Essay Concerning Human Understanding* (1690). And for a generation of revolutionary leaders, Locke's political writings, especially the second of his *Two Treatises of Government* (1690), had been a touchstone for thinking about the origins and purposes of civil government. For American observers, contrasts between Locke's philosophical—or theoretical—successes and the failure of his *Constitutions* made him a particularly good example of how even the best philosophers could fail when it came time to put their ideas into practice.

Indeed, when Publius contrasted theory and practice and spoke of closet philosophy in the late 1780s, Locke and his *Fundamental Constitutions* would have been among the first points of reference for readers of *The Federalist*. This was due in large part to the popularity of a recent work by John Adams, *A Defence of the Constitutions of Government of the United States of America* (1787).

Adams wrote his *Defence* while serving as foreign minister in London in late 1786 to rebut French statesman Anne Robert Jacques Turgot's assessment of the Americans' "slavish imitation of English forms" in their government.[49] Published in London in early 1787, the first volume of Adams's *Defence* arrived in Philadelphia in time for the Constitutional Convention. Many of those who participated in the summer's deliberations read it. Both Benjamin Franklin and James Madison, for example, specifically noted the extent and nature of the *Defence*'s influence at the time of the convention.[50] Letter LIV of Adams's *Defence* discussed "Locke, Milton, and Hume."[51] Its purpose, as Adams put it, was to explain that "chimerical systems of legislation are neither new nor uncommon, even among men of the most resplendent genius and extensive learning."[52]

With Locke specifically on his mind, Adams noted that "a philosopher may be [a] perfect master of Descartes and Leibnitz, may pursue his own enquiries into metaphysics to any length you please, may enter into the inmost recesses of the human mind, and make the noblest discoveries for the benefit of his species; nay, he may defend the principles of liberty and the rights of mankind, with great abilities and success; and, after all, when called upon to produce a plan of legislation, he may astonish the world with a signal absurdity." That theory fell short in political practice with sobering frequency was, for Adams, a reality supported by the example of "Mr. Locke." Adams noted that when Locke "was employed to trace out a plan of legislation for Carolina," the result was a "new oligarchical sovereignty."[53] Partially echoing Hume's assessment in his "Idea of a Perfect Commonwealth" that "all plans of government, which suppose great reformation in the manners of mankind, are plainly imaginary," Adams concluded, sardonically, that Locke "should have first created a new species of beings to govern, before he instituted such a government."[54]

Adams's ideas reached the American public through a variety of outlets. His *Defence* was published in Philadelphia and New York in 1787 and in Boston in 1788. On both sides of the Atlantic, magazines and newspapers were quick to reprint selections from the letter.[55] And in the 1790s, works of history and geography describing characteristics of the new United

States echoed Adams's discussion of Locke's "signal absurdity," although they did not always attribute the phrase to Adams.[56] Decades later, in his *Commentaries on American Law,* New York jurist James Kent quoted Adams on Locke's most "unwise" attempt to put theory into practice.[57]

Indeed, attention to Locke's shortcomings with respect to his "signal absurdity" grew more intense over the course of the nineteenth century. Time and again, both northern and southern commentators understood Locke's *Fundamental Constitutions* as "proving, if proof were necessary, how utterly incompetent are abstract politicians and speculative scholars, to construct a frame of government for man as he is."[58] In his 1828 work *A Political and Civil History of the United States of America,* lawyer and historian Timothy Pitkin, for example, noted that Locke's "theoretical and complex system of government, formed in the closet, was ill adapted to the circumstances and situation of a people settling in a wilderness; and was soon found, in some respects, impracticable, and in others, extremely inconvenient and oppressive."[59] Long after the figure of the closet philosopher proved so useful to Publius, it continued to help Americans think through the perils of a priori theorizing and to communicate their understanding that speculative political creations often failed, no matter how wise or good their progenitors were.

IV.

Contextualizing Hamilton's opposition between theory and practice helps explain why he thought it clinched his case for an energetic executive in Federalist No. 70. This particular distinction between theory and practice also played a role in other aspects of Publius's defense of Article II. The question of reeligibility—that is, whether the office holder should be allowed to serve more than a single term—provides a good case in point.

Writing several months before the Constitutional Convention, prominent Philadelphian and staunch supporter of a vigorous federal government, Benjamin Rush, articulated a version of what would become a customary argument in favor of reeligibility. In Article V, the Articles of Confederation had limited the number of years a delegate to Congress could serve to three out of every six years. (Constrained by this rule, James Madison had been forced to leave Congress in the fall of 1783.)[60] In early 1787, Rush observed that this "custom of turning men out of power or office, as soon as they are qualified for it, has been found to be as absurd in practice, as it is virtuous in speculation."[61] While Rush's reference here was to members of Congress, his argument—that however "virtuous" limiting an office holder's eligibility was in theory, it was decidedly otherwise in practice—transferred well to discussions of executive reeligibility.

At the Constitutional Convention that summer, reeligibility proved controversial, particularly as it related to the executive. A plan Virginia governor Edmund Randolph introduced envisioned an executive who would be appointed by the "National Legislature" for a term of an unspecified length who would be ineligible for election "a second time."[62] By contrast, South Carolina delegate Charles Pinckney proposed a plan that did not bar the executive from holding office again.[63] After the convention was over, the controversy over reeligibility continued. During the process of ratification, the issue of executive reeligibility featured prominently in discussions and debates. For example, it was the first of the "pretended defects" of the proposed government Hamilton mentioned, by way of conclusion, in Federalist No. 85, the final essay of *The Federalist*.[64]

In Federalist No. 72, Hamilton addressed the issue of executive reeligibility in detail, echoing the tenor of Rush's argument the year before: "That experience is the parent of wisdom is an adage the truth of which is recognized by the wisest as well as the simplest of mankind. What more desirable or more essential than this quality in the governors of nations? Where more desirable or more essential than in the first magistrate of a nation? Can it be wise to put this desirable and essential quality under the ban of the Constitution, and to declare that the moment it is acquired, its possessor shall be compelled to abandon the station in which it was acquired and to which it is adapted?"[65] Nowhere, as Hamilton makes clear, were the benefits of reeligibility more pronounced or more important than with the executive. The reasons for this were twofold. First, the election of the executive was not the endpoint; the president was supposed to gain experience on the job. Second, with reeligibility opening up the possibility of future terms, the executive would be more responsible to the people.[66]

As seen through Hamilton's eyes, the framers' answer to the problems born of uncertainty regarding the executive with which this chapter began was to create a position whereby the executive could learn from experience so the American people could continue to benefit from this growing practical wisdom. Hamilton emphasized that excluding the executive from holding office again would rob "the community of the advantage of the experience gained by the Chief Magistrate in the exercise of his office."[67] A reeligible executive, in short, promoted the public good.

Hamilton's arguments in Federalist No. 72 were echoed in the states' debates over ratification. During the North Carolina convention, for example, delegate William R. Davie explained the consequences of preventing an office holder from standing for reelection. When "an enlightened, upright man had discharged the duties of the office ably and faithfully" and was then prevented from holding office again, he argued, "it would be depriving the people of the benefit of his ability and experience."[68] Reeligibility was essential because the public stood to benefit from a chief magistrate's experience and not just his ability. And the importance of experience was not to be taken lightly. It was integral to the concept of political improvement and the idea that an executive could be an improving statesman.[69]

Indeed, celebrating improvements gained through political experience (of the sort proponents of executive reeligibility articulated) was what many observers were coming to regard as a constitutive element of a new—and distinctively American—science of politics. As Benjamin Rush had noted to his Philadelphia audience in early 1787, "government is a science; and can never be perfect in America, until we encourage men to devote . . . their whole lives to it."[70] In Rush's estimation, good government would derive from the improvements gained from the practical experience of governing, not just thinking, or theorizing, about politics. New York jurist James Kent, a keen observer of the new national government, put it this way when he concluded, several years after ratification, that "it is an excellent provision recently introduced into politics, to have government contain within itself the principle and means of its own improvement." He argued that "it can in this way without the slightest interruption to justice, accommodate itself from time to time, to the progress of manners and the lessons of experience."[71]

In the eyes of its defenders, the energetic, reeligible executive encapsulated this impulse for improvement in their country's new political order. And those who were confident that improvement through experience was essential to good government could feel vindicated by the words of Hume that Hamilton used to conclude *The Federalist*: "The judgments of many must unite in the work; EXPERIENCE must guide their labor; TIME must bring it to perfection, and the FEELING of inconveniences must correct the mistakes which they *inevitably* fall into in their first trials and experiments."[72] As Washington celebrated his inauguration in the spring of 1789, the project of forming a more perfect union linked to the meaning of an "energetic executive" was only just beginning. More than two centuries later, debates about the nature and purpose of such "energy" are still under way.[73]

Notes

1. [Alexander Hamilton], "Introduction," no. 1 in Alexander Hamilton, James Madison, and John Jay, *The Federalist Papers*, ed. Lawrence Goldman (Oxford: Oxford World's Classics, 2008), 11. Citations in this chapter to *The Federalist* are from this edition.

2. For a good overview of the process of ratification, see Pauline Maier, *Ratification: The People Debate the Constitution, 1787–1788* (New York: Simon & Schuster, 2010). The most important collection of sources related to ratification by the people in the states is *The Documentary History of the Ratification of the Constitution*, Digital Collections, University of Wisconsin Libraries, http://digital.library.wisc.edu/1711.dl/History.Constitution, hereafter abbreviated as DHRC.

3. The McLean edition of *The Federalist*, published in New York in two volumes on March 22 and May 28, 1788, contained eighty-five essays; only eighty-four were published in New York newspapers.

4. For the relative unimportance of *The Federalist* in states outside of New York at the time, see Maier, *Ratification*, 84. For *The Federalist* in twentieth-century American thought, see Douglass Adair, "The Federalist Papers," in *Fame and the Founding Fathers: Essays*, ed. Trevor Colbourn (New York: Norton, 1974), 251–58.

5. For the comparatively little attention Article II and the executive branch received from those who advocated for ratification in 1787 and 1788, see Jack N. Rakove, *Original Meanings: Politics and Ideas in the Making of the Constitution* (New York: A. A. Knopf, 1996), chapter 9, especially 279.

6. [Hamilton], "Concerning the constitution of the President: A gross attempt to misrepresent this part of the plan detected," no. 67 in Hamilton, Madison, and Jay, *The Federalist Papers*, 330.

7. A good overview of discussions about the executive inside the convention is Michael J. Klarman, *The Framers' Coup: The Making of the United States Constitution* (New York: Oxford University Press, 2016), 213–38. Chief among the framers' concerns regarding the executive was the matter of the relationship between the executive and legislative branches. On this point and others, see Thomas E. Cronin, "Presidential Term, Tenure and Reeligibility," in *Inventing the American Presidency*, ed. Thomas E. Cronin (Lawrence: University Press of Kansas, 1989), 61–88; and David J. Siemers, *The Myth of Coequal Branches: Restoring the Constitution's Separation of Functions* (Columbia: University of Missouri Press, 2018).

8. Rakove, *Original Meanings*, 245. For the importance of the states' experience, see also Rakove, *The Beginnings of National Politics: An Interpretive History of the Continental Congress* (1979; repr., Baltimore, MD: The Johns Hopkins University Press, 1982), 395–96.

9. For a discussion of how only Delaware, New York, and South Carolina had more than one-year terms for their governors, see Cronin, "Presidential Term, Tenure and

Reeligibility," 63. On the relationship between attitudes toward the British monarchy and attitudes toward the executive branch, see Eric Nelson, *The Royalist Revolution: Monarchy and the American Founding* (Cambridge, MA: The Belknap Press of Harvard University Press, 2014); and Nelson, "Publius on Monarchy," in Rakove and Sheehan, *Cambridge Companion to the Federalist*, ed. Jack N. Rakove and Colleen A. Sheehan (Cambridge: Cambridge University Press, 2020), 426–63.

10. The essays in this volume are important contributions to our understanding of the intellectual and theoretical sources of ideas about the American presidency. For additional context on the writings of John Locke; Henry St John, Viscount Bolingbroke; and others, see Nelson, *The Royalist Revolution*, 9–23 and Rakove, *Original Meanings*, 247–50. For a broader discussion of Blackstone's influence, in particular, see Nelson, *The Royalist Revolution*, 226–27; and John V. Jezierski, "Parliament or People: James Wilson and Blackstone on the Nature and Location of Sovereignty," *Journal of the History of Ideas* 32, no. 1 (1971): 95–106. On Montesquieu, see Paul A. Rahe, "Montesquieu, Hume, Adam Smith, and the Philosophical Perspective of *The Federalist*," in Rakove and Sheehan, *Cambridge Companion to the Federalist*, 228–62.

11. Rakove, *Original Meanings*, 245.

12. Jonathan Gienapp calls ensuring the proper energy in the executive a "virtual obsession" for some framers. See Jonathan Gienapp, *The Second Creation: Fixing the American Constitution in the Founding Era* (Cambridge, MA: The Belknap Press of Harvard University Press, 2018), 149.

13. Max Farrand, ed., *The Records of the Federal Convention of 1787*, 3 vols. (New Haven, CT: Yale University Press, 1911–37), 1:66. Hereafter cited as Farrand, *Records*.

14. James Madison to Thomas Jefferson, October 24, 1787, in Farrand, *Records*, 3:132. Compared to Hamilton, Madison was less interested in questions concerning executive power. See Nelson, *The Royalist Revolution*, 199; and Rakove and Sheehan, "Introduction," in Rakove and Sheehan, *Cambridge Companion to the Federalist*, 6.

15. On energy and the executive, see Harvey C. Mansfield Jr., *Taming the Prince: The Ambivalence of Modern Executive Power* (1989; repr., Baltimore, MD: The Johns Hopkins University Press, 1993), e.g., 250, 267.

16. [Hamilton], "The same view continued in relation to the unity of the executive, with an examination of the project of an executive council," no. 70 in Hamilton, Madison, and Jay, *The Federalist Papers*, 344.

17. Alexander Hamilton to James Duane, September 3, 1780, in *The Papers of Alexander Hamilton*, ed. Harold C. Syrett and Jacob Ernest Cooke, vol. 2, *1779–1781* (New York: Columbia University Press, 1961), 404. For more on Hamilton, the executive, and the Articles of Confederation, see Klarman, *The Framers' Coup*, 47–48.

18. James Madison's notes from Monday, June 18, 1787, in Farrand, *Records*, 1:292.

19. On Hamilton's ideas about the executive and the extent to which his own views matched what he articulated as Publius, see Forrest McDonald, *The American Presidency: An Intellectual History* (Lawrence: University Press of Kansas, 1994), 205, 208; Eric Nelson, "Publius on Monarchy," in Rakove and Sheehan, *Cambridge Companion to the Federalist*, 426–63; and Siemers, *The Myth of Coequal Branches*, 52–53.

20. On the critical context of international diplomacy and *The Federalist*, see David

M. Golove and Daniel J. Hulsebosch, "'The Known Opinion of the Impartial World': Foreign Relations and the Law of Nations in *The Federalist*," in Rakove and Sheehan, *Cambridge Companion to the Federalist*, 114–63.

21. [Hamilton], "The same view continued in relation to the unity of the executive, with an examination of the project of an executive council," no. 70 in Hamilton, Madison, and Jay, *The Federalist Papers*, 343–44, my italics.

22. When thinking about the relationship between theory and practice in the 1780s, it is important to keep in mind that such discussions predate Immanuel Kant's now-famous discussion of the matter in "On the Common Saying: That May Be True in Theory, but It Is of No Use in Practice" (1793).

23. The literature on the relationship between political theory and practice or the experience of practice is vast. In the second half of the twentieth century, there was an important shift in how historians, philosophers, and political scientists talked about the role that theorizing—or thinking abstractly—about politics played for Publius. Broadly speaking, scholars moved away from arguing for a sharp distinction between theory and practice (or practical experience) and toward understanding the ways in which the one influenced the other. On the one hand, by highlighting the important ways that experience, theory, and practice were intertwined, historians like Douglass Adair and Jack Rakove illuminated the impact that experience—in Adair's formulation as both the "political wisdom gained by participation in events and wisdom gained by studying past events"—had on both the political theory in *The Federalist* and the ideas of its authors. See Adair, "'Experience Must Be Our Only Guide': History, Democratic Theory, and the United States Constitution" in Colbourn, *Fame and the Founding Fathers*, 110. On the other hand, Adair and Rakove demonstrated the extent to which Publius—James Madison, in particular—applied theory (and theorizing or thinking abstractly) to practical political ends. As Rakove has shown, Madison was nothing short of "an activist who evidently realized that to accomplish what he sought to do required a significant measure of reasoning abstractly [or theorizing] about politics." See Jack N. Rakove, "Thinking Like a Constitution," *Journal of the Early Republic* 24, no. 1 (2004), 11. On Madison specifically, see also Rakove, *A Politician Thinking: The Creative Mind of James Madison* (Norman: University of Oklahoma Press, 2017). The broader literature on the topic of theory, practice, and experience as it relates to the present discussion includes Bernard Bailyn, "Political Experience and Enlightenment Ideas in Eighteenth-Century America," *American Historical Review* 67, no. 2 (1962): 339–51; Morton White, *Philosophy, The Federalist, and the Constitution* (New York: Oxford University Press, 1987); and Mansfield, *Taming the Prince*.

24. Morton White provided a careful investigation of David Hume's rendering and use of experience. See White, *Philosophy, The Federalist, and the Constitution*, 14–20. On the meanings of experience more broadly, see Adair, "'Experience Must Be Our Only Guide,'" 107–23.

25. James Madison's notes from Friday, June 1, 1787, in Farrand, *Records*, 1:68. For more on Wilson's role in creating the presidency as contained in Article II, see, for example, Daniel J. McCarthy, "James Wilson and the Creation of the Presidency," *Presidential Studies Quarterly* 17, no. 4 (1987): 689–96.

26. [Hamilton], "The same view continued in relation to the appointment of the officers of the government," no. 76 in Hamilton, Madison, and Jay, *The Federalist Papers*, 374.

27. Henry Knox, New York, September [?], DHRC, http://digicoll.library.wisc.edu/cgi-bin/History/History-idx?type=turn&id=History.DHRCv4&entity=History.DHRCv4.p0109&q1=deliberations%20on%20government, published in *Ratification of the Constitution by the States: Massachusetts (1)*, ed. John P. Kaminski, Gaspare J. Saladino, Richard Leffler, and Charles H. Schoenleber (Madison: State Historical Society of Wisconsin, 1997), 26.

28. [Hamilton], "Introduction," no. 1 in Hamilton, Madison, and Jay, *The Federalist Papers*, 11.

29. Because of uncertainty about the original text, the DHRC editors enclosed "closet" in square brackets with a question mark. Henry Knox, New York, September [?], DHRC, and in *Ratification of the Constitution by the States: Massachusetts (1)*, 26–27.

30. Henry Knox to Jean-Baptiste Gouvion, New York, February 19, 1788, DHRC, http://digicoll.library.wisc.edu/cgi-bin/History/History-idx?type=turn&id=History.DHRCv16&entity=History.DHRCv16.p0176&q1=might%20probably%20have%20been%20formed%20with%20greater%20consistency, published in *Commentaries on the Constitution, Public and Private*, vol. 4, *1 February to 31 March 1788*, ed. John P. Kaminski, Gaspare J. Saladino, and Richard Leffler (Madison: State Historical Society of Wisconsin, 1986), 142.

31. "Remarks on Manners, Government, Law and the Domestic Debt of America—Addressed to the Citizens of the United States," *Pennsylvania Packet*, February 19, 1787, DHRC, http://digicoll.library.wisc.edu/cgi-bin/History/History-idx?type=goto&id=History.DHRCSuppPA&isize=M&submit=Go+to+page&page=64, published in *Ratification of the Constitution by the States: Pennsylvania. Microform Supplement*, vol. 2 (Madison: State Historical Society of Wisconsin, 1976), 64.

32. Samuel Johnson, *A Dictionary of the English Language*, vol. 1 (London: Printed by W. Strahan, 1755), s.v. "closet." "Closet" as Johnson defined it was used frequently in a range of texts well known to Americans. See, for example, its use throughout John Trenchard and Thomas Gordon, *Cato's Letters, or Essays on Liberty, Civil and Religious, and Other Important Subjects*, 2 vols., ed. Ronald Hamowy (Indianapolis: Liberty Fund, 1995).

33. *Oxford English Dictionary*, s.v. "closet."

34. Johnson, *A Dictionary of the English Language*, vol. 2, s.vv. "theorick" and "theoretical."

35. David Hume, "Of the Study of History," in *Essays: Moral, Political, and Literary*, ed. Eugene F. Miller, rev. ed. (Indianapolis: Liberty Fund, 1987), 568. "Of the Study of History," first published in 1741, was not included in editions of *Essays and Treatises on Several Subjects* published after 1760. Hume's invocation of the closet philosopher has received little attention, although an exception is Michael B. Gill, "A Philosopher in His Closet: Reflexivity and Justification in Hume's Moral Theory," *Canadian Journal of Philosophy* 26, no. 2 (1996): 231–55.

36. David Hume, "Whether the British Government Inclines More to Absolute Monarchy, or to a Republic," in *Political Essays*, ed. Knud Haakonssen (Cambridge: Cambridge University Press, 1994), 31.

37. On Hume and *The Federalist*, see Douglass Adair, "The Tenth Federalist Revisited," *William and Mary Quarterly* 8, no. 1 (1951): 48–67; Adair, "'That Politics May Be Reduced to a Science': David Hume, James Madison, and the Tenth Federalist," *Huntington Library Quarterly* 20, no. 4 (1957): 343–60; Rahe, "Montesquieu, Hume, Adam Smith, and the Philosophical Perspective of *The Federalist*," in Rakove and Sheehan, *Cambridge Companion to the Federalist*, 247–52; and Nelson, "Publius on Monarchy," in Rakove and Sheehan, *Cambridge Companion to the Federalist*, 431–40. See also Mark G. Spencer, *David Hume and Eighteenth-Century America* (Rochester, NY: University of Rochester Press, 2005). For Hume's influence on Hamilton, see Darren Staloff, *Hamilton, Adams, Jefferson: The Politics of Enlightenment and the American Founding* (New York: Hill and Wang, 2005). Hume, Staloff observed, "exercised an influence on Hamilton's vision greater than that of any other author" (78).

38. [Hamilton], "A further view of the constitution of the Senate in relation to its capacity as a court for the trial of impeachments," no. 65 in Hamilton, Madison, and Jay, *The Federalist Papers*, 324–25.

39. [Madison], "The same subject continued," no. 10 in Hamilton, Madison, and Jay, *The Federalist Papers*, 52; [Madison], "The same subject continued in relation to the same point," no. 56 in Hamilton, Madison, and Jay, *The Federalist Papers*, 279.

40. [Madison], "Concerning the difficulties which the Convention must have experienced in the formation of a proper plan," no. 37 in Hamilton, Madison, and Jay, *The Federalist Papers*, 178–79.

41. For a discussion of the internal nature of the theoretical paradigm Hamilton relied on by drawing from Madison's earlier *Federalist* essays, see Rakove, *Original Meanings*, 280–83.

42. Other examples of plans of government devised by those whom Francis Bacon famously termed "legislatores" or "lawgivers" included Solon and Lycurgus in ancient Greece; see Francis Bacon, "Of Honor and Reputation," in Richard Whately, *Bacon's Essays with Annotations* (Boston: Lee and Shepard, 1868), 542. Other points of reference included various utopian designs of government such as those of Thomas More or James Harrington. For a discussion of Bacon's work and early American political thought, see Gerald Stourzh, *Alexander Hamilton and the Idea of Republican Government* (Stanford, CA: Stanford University Press, 1970), 174–75.

43. John Locke, *The Fundamental Constitutions of Carolina*, in *Political Writings*, ed. David Wootton (Indianapolis: Hackett, 2003), 211. See also David Armitage, "John Locke, Carolina, and the *Two Treatises of Government*," *Political Theory* 32, no. 5 (2004): 609. Eighteenth- and nineteenth-century assessments of Locke's role in drafting *The Fundamental Constitutions of Carolina* frequently do not reflect what we now know about it. The contrasts between Locke as wise philosopher and someone who failed to implement his own ideas largely muddle the relationship between *The Fundamental Constitutions* and Locke's other writings. Moreover, the nature of Locke's involvement is debated today. See, for example, Holly Brewer, "Slavery, Sovereignty, and 'Inheritable

Blood': Reconsidering John Locke and the Origins of American Slavery," *American Historical Review* 122, no. 4 (2017): 1038–78.

In drawing attention to the ways that Americans construed Locke, in some respects, as an archetype of closet philosophy, my aim is *not* to reinstitute an outdated separation between theory and practice of the sort Charles A. Beard made when he famously drew a distinction between closet philosophers, or "dust sifters," such as Locke and men of practical politics, such as Publius. See Charles A. Beard, *The Enduring Federalist* (Garden City, NY: Doubleday, 1948), 20.

44. For this division, see Locke, *The Fundamental Constitutions of Carolina*, 211.

45. Mark Goldie, "Locke and America," in *A Companion to Locke*, ed. Matthew Stuart (Malden, MA: Wiley Blackwell, 2016), 549. For how *The Fundamental Constitutions* did initially "formally provide the frame of government for the colony," see Armitage, "John Locke, Carolina, and the *Two Treatises of Government*," 607.

46. For example, Benjamin Franklin noted (positively) Locke's involvement in the Carolina constitutions in marginal comments on Allan Ramsay's *Thoughts on the Origin and Nature of Government* (1769); Benjamin Franklin, "Marginalia," in *The Papers of Benjamin Franklin*, ed. William B. Willcox et al. (New Haven, CT: Yale University Press, 1972), 16:319–20. And John Adams noted that Ralph Izard of South Carolina was descended from "one of Mr. Lockes Landgraves." John Adams, autobiographical entry for April 21, 1778, in the *Diary and Autobiography of John Adams*, ed. L. H. Butterfield (Cambridge, MA: The Belknap Press of Harvard University Press, 1961), 4:70.

47. *A Collection of Several Pieces of Mr. John Locke, Never before Printed, or Not Extant in His Works* (London: Printed by J. Bettenham for R. Francklin, 1720). For its inclusion in Locke's *Works*, see Jean S. Yolton, *John Locke: A Descriptive Bibliography* (Bristol, UK: Thoemmes Press, 1998), 399.

48. [William Barton], *Observations on the Trial by Jury: With Miscellaneous Remarks concerning Legislation & Jurisprudence, and the Professors of the Law; also, Shewing the Dangerous Consequences of Innovations, in the Fundamental Institutions of the Civil Polity of a State: Illustrated by Authorities and Manifested by Examples* (Strasburg, PA: Printed by Brown & Bowman, 1803), 33.

49. Joyce Appleby, "What Is Still American in the Political Philosophy of Thomas Jefferson?" *William and Mary Quarterly* 39, no. 2 (1982): 291.

50. For Franklin, this influence was forward looking when he wrote to Adams in May 1787 that the Philadelphia printing of the *Defence* had commenced. See Benjamin Franklin to John Adams, May 18, 1787, in *Papers of John Adams*, ed. Sara Georgini, Sara Martin et al., series III, vol. 19 (Cambridge, MA: The Belknap Press of Harvard University Press, 2018), 74. As Eric Nelson writes, "the myth that the *Defence* was received negatively in the United States derives almost entirely from a single snide remark offered by Madison" in a letter to Thomas Jefferson; Nelson, *The Royalist Revolution*, 335n125. But, as Nelson points out, Madison went on to note the extent of the influence of the *Defence* on the convention. For this letter, see James Madison to Thomas Jefferson, June 6, 1787, in *The Papers of James Madison*, vol. 10, *27 May 1787–3 March 1788*, ed. Robert A. Rutland, Charles F. Hobson, William M. E. Rachal, and Fredrika J. Teute (Chicago: University of Chicago Press, 1977), 29–30. For a detailed compilation of American reac-

tions to Adams's *Defence*, see Charles Warren, *The Making of the Constitution* (Boston: Little, Brown and Company, 1928), Appendix C, 815–18.

51. The numbering of the letters in early editions varied. For example, in the New York (1787) and Boston (1788) printings, Letter LIV became Letter LV.

52. John Adams, *A Defence of the Constitutions of Government of the United States of America*, vol. 1 (Philadelphia: Printed for Hall and Sellers, 1787), 365. On the details of Locke's plan, Adams got a few things wrong, including the date of *The Fundamental Constitutions*, which appeared in 1669, not 1663.

53. Adams, *A Defence of the Constitutions of Government of the United States of America*, 365.

54. Hume, "Idea of a Perfect Commonwealth," in *Political Essays*, 222; Adams, *A Defence of the Constitutions of Government of the United States of America*, 366. For a discussion of Adams's critique of Hume's "Idea of a Perfect Commonwealth," see Spencer, *David Hume and Eighteenth-Century America*, 236–39.

55. In November 1787, the *English Review* (London), for example, included excerpts of Adams's assessment of Locke's *Fundamental Constitutions of Carolina*. Three years later, the *Gazette of the United States* in New York reprinted the same selections. See "From the English Review, for November, 1787," *Gazette of the United States* (New York, NY), October 9, 1790.

56. For an account that did not cite Adams, see John Payne, *A New and Complete System of Universal Geography*, 4 vols. (New York: Printed for and Sold by John Low, 1799), 4:370. For an account that did, see William Winterbotham, *An Historical, Geographical, Commercial, and Philosophical View of the United States of America*, 4 vols. (New York: Printed by Tiebout and O'Brien, 1796), 3:22.

57. James Kent, *Commentaries on American Law*, 4 vols. (New York: O. Halsted, 1826), 1:264.

58. Review of Thomas Cooper, *The Statutes at Large of South Carolina; Edited under Authority of the Legislature* (Columbia, SC, 1836), in *American Jurist and Law Magazine* 19, no. 37 (1838): 238.

59. Timothy Pitkin, *A Political and Civil History of the United States of America from the Year 1763 to the Close of the Administration of President Washington, in March, 1797*, 2 vols. (New Haven, CT: Hezekiah Howe and Durrie & Peck, 1828), 1:59.

60. For further discussion of Article V and its implications for Madison, see Rakove, *The Beginnings of National Politics*, 368.

61. Benjamin Rush, "Address to the People of the United States," in *Friends of the Constitution: Writings of the 'Other' Federalists, 1787–1788*, ed. Colleen A. Sheehan and Gary L. McDowell (Indianapolis: Liberty Fund, 1998), 3.

62. Resolutions proposed by Mr. Randolph in Convention, May 29, 1787, in Farrand, *Records*, 1:21.

63. Cronin, "Presidential Term, Tenure and Reeligibility," 65.

64. [Hamilton], "Conclusion," no. 85 in Hamilton, Madison, and Jay, *The Federalist Papers*, 427.

65. [Hamilton], "The same view continued in regard to the re-eligibility of the President," no. 72 in Hamilton, Madison, and Jay, *The Federalist Papers*, 357.

66. On the importance of executive responsibility to advocates of an energetic executive, see Gienapp, *The Second Creation*, 149.

67. [Hamilton], "The same view continued in regard to the re-eligibility of the President," no. 72 in Hamilton, Madison, and Jay, *The Federalist Papers*, 357.

68. William R. Davie, remarks in the North Carolina Convention, July 26, 1788, in Farrand, *Records*, 3:347. For a discussion of speakers in state ratifying conventions who picked up on Hamilton's arguments, see Nelson, *The Royalist Revolution*, 224–25.

69. Readers will appreciate the parallel here with Edmund Burke's emphasis on the "ability to improve" as a quality of a good statesman. Edmund Burke, *Reflections on the Revolution in France*, ed. Frank M. Turner (New Haven, CT: Yale University Press, 2003), 133. For the absence of Burke's discussion on the U.S. Constitution and what unfolded in Philadelphia in 1787, see Jack N. Rakove, "Why American Constitutionalism Worked," in Burke, *Reflections on the Revolution in France*, 248–67.

70. Rush, "Address to the People of the United States," 3.

71. James Kent, *Dissertations: Being the Preliminary Part of a Course of Law Lectures* (New York: Printed by George Forman, 1795), 25.

72. [Hamilton], "Conclusion," no. 85 in Hamilton, Madison, and Jay, *The Federalist Papers*, 432, quoting David Hume, "Of the Rise and Progress of the Arts and Sciences," in *Essays: Moral, Political, and Literary*, 124.

73. A recent perspective on the energetic executive as the framers envisioned it in relation to the modern presidency can be found in Julian Davis Mortenson, "What Two Crucial Words in the Constitution Actually Mean," *The Atlantic*, June 2, 2019.

8

Is the Electoral College the Fundamental Problem?

New State Admissions and the U.S. Constitution

FRANÇOIS FURSTENBERG

> The prospect of many new States to the Westward was another consideration of importance . . . Let them have an equal vote, and a more objectionable minority than ever might give law to the whole.
>
> James Madison, June 19, 1787[1]

Americans have become well acquainted with the perils of running a twenty-first-century nation by the rules of an eighteenth-century Constitution. Two of this young century's three presidents have ascended to office in defiance of the popular vote, and commentators have focused particularly on the distortions produced by the Electoral College.[2] A vast literature, meanwhile, has drawn attention to the infamous three-fifths clause, which gave slave states greater clout in the election of presidents and helped ensure that twelve of the country's first fourteen presidents had owned slaves.[3]

Little analysis, however, has focused on what I will call here the problem of new states—that is to say, the effect of states created after the Constitution was written. In particular, few scholars have asked how those new states altered the delicate balance of power the constitutional system of 1787 crafted. A decade earlier, it was just thirteen "Free and Independent States" that had dissolved their political connection with the British Crown in 1776, insisting that they had the "full Power" to do all those things that "Independent States may of right do."[4] Those original thirteen states had sacrificed and suffered in a grueling war to bring their independence into reality. Those thirteen original states, all intensely jealous to maintain their sovereignty, came together in 1787 to forge a "peace pact," in David Hendrickson's formulation, in order to forestall future conflict among themselves.[5] And yet those thirteen states gave little thought to the rights that new states to the west would come to have.

Those new states, which now number thirty-five (Vermont and Maine were carved out of the original thirteen), obviously had no role in drafting the Constitution. The delegates at the Constitutional Convention had not represented their interests. The original thirteen states formed the Constitution to protect their interests; the Constitution subsequently enabled the formation of these new states. And yet these thirty-five states today entirely dominate the electoral politics of the United States. The original thirteen are completely outvoted; their interests are entirely dominated by the majority of new states. Without those new states, to take just one example, Al Gore would have won the presidency in 2000 and Hillary Clinton would have won in 2016, Electoral College or no. Notwithstanding the extensive literature that explores the defects of the Electoral College, I want to ask whether that is the primary structural cause of the country's current political impasse. Indeed, one might wonder whether the real constitutional flaw lies not with Article II, Section 1, which (as amended) establishes the Electoral College and the mechanism for electing the president, but whether it lies instead with Article IV, Section 3, which decrees simply: "New States may be admitted by the Congress into this Union."[6]

The irony, understood in these terms, is striking. The thirteen original states spent an entire summer hashing out a compromise by which all their interests would be represented. Big states, small states; slave states, free states; commercial states, agricultural states—could the divergent interests of all be reconciled? Several times during the course of that long, hot summer, delegates nearly walked out over one roadblock or another that threatened to make compromise impossible. Eventually, famously—heroically—they hammered out a complex and convoluted document that pieced those specific interests together in an exquisitely delicate balance. And then they opened a back door, as though without thought, that dramatically upended that fragile balance.

Two centuries on, it does not seem like an exaggeration to say that all thirteen of those original states have lost the political clout they fought so hard to maintain in 1787. What is more, they lost their power to states that had no voice in the creation of the Constitution, states that now subject them to—among many other indignities—the rule of a series of presidents they have not chosen.

This ironic result (if irony it is) raises an interesting historical puzzle. Given the extraordinary attention, discussion, and debate on so many less consequential issues, why did the Constitutional Convention spend so little time addressing the question of new state admissions? As we will see, the delegates were hardly blind to the potentially dangerous consequences. At several points, the subject came up for explicit debate. Yet in the end, the Constitution established no limits on the admission of new states. It created no minimal requirements for new states. It laid no restrictions on the number of new states. It did not even mandate a supermajority for the admission of new states (although it requires supermajorities on many other issues of far less significance). Why?

Alas, this essay will offer no definitive answers. It is the beginning of what I hope will be a longer set of reflections on this subject. Here, I will trace out some of the history, attempt to frame the problem with greater clarity, sketch out some of the broader puzzles it raises, and chart a few directions for further research.

Toward the Convention: The Postrevolutionary Context

Americans often imagine that their country was inevitably destined to expand across the continent. However, in the 1780s, few prospects seemed less likely. That the thirteen colonies could be conceived as a "rising Empire" in America, a British supporter of American independence wrote in 1781, was "one of the idlest, and most visionary Notions, that ever was conceived even by Writers of Romance."[7] Not only was such a future implausible; for many, it was also unwanted. "Westward expansion was a controversial project," Peter Onuf has observed of the postrevolutionary era. "Many easterners feared that it would lead to the depopulation and impoverishment of their states and to the weakening of the union."[8]

By the 1783 Treaty of Paris, which ended the American Revolution, Great Britain recognized the sovereignty of the United States over the territory stretching from the Atlantic Coast to the Mississippi River. Maps printed in Europe depicted these borders by shading in large parts of the continent as the United States (see figure 8.1). Such maps hardly reflected the reality on the ground, however; on the contrary, they were a speculative fantasy. Other than a few fingers of settlement jutting into western regions of Virginia and North Carolina, the new nation exerted no sovereignty in the

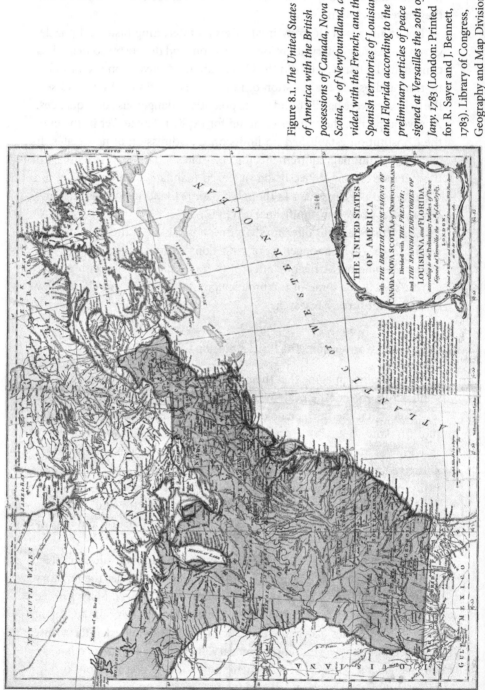

Figure 8.1. *The United States of America with the British possessions of Canada, Nova Scotia, & of Newfoundland, divided with the French; and the Spanish territories of Louisiana and Florida according to the preliminary articles of peace signed at Versailles the 20th of Jany. 1783* (London: Printed for R. Sayer and J. Bennett, 1783). Library of Congress, Geography and Map Division.

vast region between the Appalachian Mountains and the Mississippi River. Native American power dominated throughout. The few spaces of European control were limited to a handful of villages and trading posts controlled by French and *métis* settlers, who served as brokers for the lucrative trade along the major river arteries that connect the Great Lakes and the Mississippi River. British authorities maintained their hold on strategically situated military posts throughout the Northwest, often in alliance with Native American power, notwithstanding the commitments they made in the peace negotiations. The Spanish Empire had never acceded to the land cessions negotiated in the 1783 Treaty of Paris and continued to claim sovereignty over the Creek and Choctaw lands in the Southwest.[9]

Competing claims over the trans-Appalachian West were not limited to Native American and European powers, however. Individual states, invoking the original English charters, also claimed vast portions of the region. Indeed, these overlapping claims were so vexing that they delayed the ratification of the Articles of the Confederation until March 1781, just months before the Battle of Yorktown settled the outcome of the Revolution. Despite—or perhaps because of—the bitterly contested claims to the region, U.S. leaders almost immediately began to plan for its political integration into the Union. Many wondered if the United States could survive without that territory. Congress certainly needed the lands to raise the money to pay off the extraordinary debt it had accumulated in gaining its independence.

The Articles of Confederation anticipated the need for U.S. expansion. They included a provision, Article 11, for the nation's extension. Interestingly, that provision most immediately looked not west but north. According to Article 11, "Canada acceding to this confederation, and adjoining in the measures of the United States, shall be admitted into, and entitled to all the advantages of this Union." As for any other political entity, the terms for admission were more stringent. "No other colony shall be admitted into the same, unless such admission be agreed to by nine States."[10] That requirement was consistent with many others in the original compact among the states. The Articles required a two-thirds majority (nine states of thirteen) to engage in most major acts: declare war, make treaties, coin money, borrow money, and appoint a commander in chief of the army. It was hardly surprising that they required a two-thirds majority to admit new states into the Union.

If the Articles of Confederation specified the formal procedures for admission, they said nothing about the political nature of those new states.

Were their rights and powers—including voting rights in Congress—to equal those of the existing thirteen states? Perhaps because that question was so contentious, the articles ignored it entirely. Would their governments necessarily be republican in character? The Articles did not say, but the automatic admission of Canada as a state gave some indication that nonrepublican forms of government in the West might also be possible. No one would have forgotten the series of angry outbursts that followed the Quebec Act of 1774, which denounced the "Arbitrary government" in Canada, as the Declaration of Independence put it. Some commentators might have wondered how this province, which lacked any representative assemblies, would appoint its representatives to the Confederation Congress.[11]

Nevertheless, from their earliest discussions at the close of the Revolution, U.S. officials seem to have instinctively assumed that the trans-Appalachian would eventually, organically, develop into republican states with rights equal to those of the original thirteen. Julian Boyd follows Dumas Malon in arguing that the principle of admitting new states on an equal basis was "generally accepted" by 1784.[12] The first statement to articulate the principles that new states must be both republican and endowed with political rights equal to the original thirteen appears to have come in the Virginia deed of 1784 that ceded its western claims to the United States. That cession stipulated "that the States so formed shall be distinct Republican States and admitted members of the Fœderal Union, having the same rights of Sovereignty, Freedom and Independence as the other States."[13]

That mandate was written into the Ordinance of 1784, the first attempt by the U.S. government to clarify its western policy. Thomas Jefferson drafted most of it and Congress passed it in April of that year.

Whensoever any of the said states shall have of free inhabitants, as many as shall then be in any one the least numerous of the thirteen original states, such state shall be admitted by its delegates into the Congress of the United States, on an equal footing with the said original states; provided the consent of so many states in Congress is first obtained as may at the time be competent to such admission. And in order to adapt the said articles of confederation to the state of Congress when its numbers shall be thus increased, it shall be proposed to the legislatures of the states, originally parties thereto, to require the assent of two thirds of the United States in Congress assembled, in all those cases wherein by the said articles, the assent of nine states is now required, which being agreed to by them shall be binding on the new states.[14]

Three features of this policy stand out. First is the population requirement. Once a given territory (here referred to as a state) reached the equivalent of the smallest of the original thirteen, it gained admission to the Union. The second notable feature is the endowment of "equal footing": these new states would be granted all the powers of the original thirteen. That principle would come to play a central role in the future conception of statehood in the United States and even in the understanding of territories as it continues to the present. Peter Onuf has stressed this principle that was embedded in the early texts that articulated U.S. western policy. "Promises of statehood and eventual membership in the union remained fundamental" to the policy the 1784 and 1785 ordinances developed, he observes. "In both form and substance the 'charter of compact' between old and new states established the principle that the United States would be a union of equal states."[15] So far as I have been able to ascertain, the first use of the term *equal footing* in any legal document is found in the Ordinance of 1784. Finally, the third notable feature of this early congressional policy is the formulation of the two-thirds requirement. Unlike the Articles of Confederation, the Ordinance of 1784 specifies that two-thirds, rather than nine, would be the permanent threshold for admission of a new state. In other words, the threshold would rise to ten once the Union grew to fifteen states and would continue rising as the number of states grew.

Interestingly, the 1784 and 1785 plans encompassed the entire territory between the Atlantic states and the Mississippi—not just the Northwest. Consistent with the minimal population requirements for new states, Congress had initially envisioned sixteen future states in the trans-Appalachian West, ten of them north of the Ohio River. The famous Jefferson-Hartley map does not include all sixteen states, although it is the first cartographic representation of the West as Jefferson and the Confederation Congress imagined it in the mid-1780s.

One can say a great deal about this map but let me dwell for a moment on one aspect that the commentary too often overlooks. Consider the differences between this map and the layout of the western regions as Congress managed them in the ensuing years. This map, like all the early texts on western policy, does not distinguish between "state" and "territory." It would be many decades, after all, before these boxes, however they were eventually laid out, would attain statehood. Minnesota, at the far

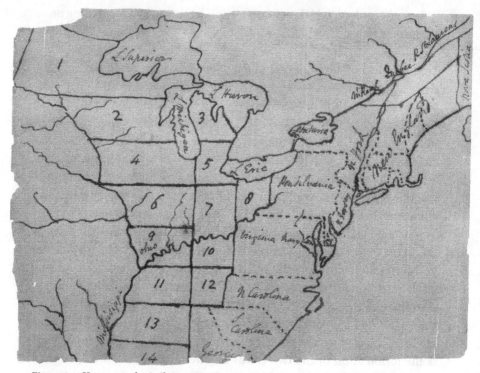

Figure 8.2. Known as the Jefferson-Hartley Map, this drawing was copied by David Hartley from an original drawn by Jefferson that no longer exists. Hartley was a member of the British parliament who signed the Treaty of Paris ending the American Revolution. *A map of the United States east of the Mississippi River in which the land ceded by the Treaty of Paris is divided by parallels of latitude and longitude into fourteen new states*, by David Hartley, 1784. William L. Clements Library, University of Michigan.

northwest of the region, would not become a state until 1858, some seventy-four years after Jefferson initially formulated his plans. In the meantime—and a very long meantime it was—these spaces would remain in the form of largely undifferentiated territories. The map thus highlights the ways that the earliest thinking about the U.S. West never formulated a territorial policy—indeed, did not recognize that a territorial policy would be necessary. At the risk of anachronism, one might say that they displayed an almost Turnerian faith in the teleology of western development: states that emerge organically from the movement of people into frontier regions.

If the documents that first explicated U.S. policy in the West all assumed that the region would instantaneously transform itself into states, the immediate reality of the 1780s proved to be very different. Native Americans continued to dominate the territory west of the Appalachians demographically and militarily. On the flanks of the United States, Iroquois, Cherokee, and Creek nations proved adept at advancing their own interests, often in alliance with British and Spanish officials. Centuries of imperial diplomacy and encounters with rapacious settlers had taught these powerful nations hard-won lessons; Native Americans were hardly going to welcome the creation of new states in their territory. In the Ohio Country and Great Lakes region, Shawnee, Miami, Ottawa, Illinois, and various Anishinaabe peoples, who had recently risen up under the banner of Ottawa leader Pontiac, were continuing the war to maintain sovereignty over their lands.

Meanwhile, uncontrolled and perhaps uncontrollable populations of squatters and speculators were making themselves particularly refractory to congressional control, grabbing land and provoking wars with Native American peoples. The need for the United States to project state power in the West in order to assert its sovereignty had become apparent by the mid-1780s. At the same time, dissent in Congress was emerging. In 1786, northern members of Congress, who were already displaying some ambivalence about western expansion, began to advocate for an increase of the population requirements for admissions to the Union to one-thirteenth the total population of the original thirteen states. Raising the threshold for admission to the Union to the average population of the United States, up from the population of the smallest state, would have dramatically raised the barrier for admission. Based on the 1790 census numbers, it would have quintupled the minimum population for new states—to 293,843, the average population of the original thirteen states, up from 59,094, the population of Delaware, then the smallest state. That change would have dramatically lengthened the time required for a territory or state to gain admission to the Union.

Altogether, the assumptions about western development embedded in these documents—that states would quickly appear in the West, full of settlers with an abiding desire to attach themselves to the United States—were proving wildly optimistic. As disenchantment with the Articles of Confederation grew during the mid-1780s, so did an awareness of that document's flawed western policy. As James Madison would later put it in Federalist No. 38:

> the Western territory is a mine of vast wealth to the United States.
> ... Congress have assumed the administration of this stock. ... They
> have proceeded to form new States, to erect temporary governments,

to appoint officers for them, and to prescribe the conditions on which such States shall be admitted into the Confederacy. All this has been done; and done without the least color of constitutional authority.

By the mid-1780s, the existing territorial policy seemed to have reached its limits. Policy makers began to confront the fact that government would have to precede settlement rather than the other way around. "By 1787," Onuf observes, "the distinction between a 'territory' governed by Congress and the 'state' that would eventually succeed it had become clear."[16] By the time the Constitutional Convention met that summer, leading Americans understood the need for a new colonial policy in the West, one that would project state power to foster development and might consequently drag on for an extended period of time. After all, with the possible exception of Kentucky, statehood in the West was nowhere in sight. The moment was thus ripe to consider alternatives to the failed policies of the previous five years, to rethink the nature of the polities that might emerge in the West, and indeed to question the teleology of western development itself.

The year 1787 thus set the stage for a dramatic turning point in U.S. western policy. What emerges so interestingly, however, is that the point both turned and didn't. As we shall see, delegates to the Constitutional Convention did in fact prove willing to abandon the previous national commitments and consider radical alternatives. But what emerges as such a puzzle is that faced with the failure of their previous western policy and searching for an entirely different kind of program to accompany the fundamentally new form of government for the nation, the delegates to the Constitutional Convention nonetheless and almost without thought embraced a return to previous ways of thinking about new states.

The Constitutional Convention Debates

Western policy during that summer of 1787 developed on two parallel tracks. In Philadelphia, when delegates to the Constitutional Convention addressed the topic of western expansion, they repeatedly proved themselves willing to consider dramatic alternatives to the policy of the previous years. Meanwhile, in New York, delegates to the Confederation Congress continued to build on previous policies. Let us begin with the debates in the Constitutional Convention, where if the subject of new states did not generate as much deliberation and argument as the more famous controversies dividing the delegates, it nonetheless appeared regularly.

Figure 8.3. *Gouverneur Morris.* The Miriam and Ira D. Wallach Division of Art, Prints and Photographs: Print Collection, The New York Public Library.

The question first emerged with some sharpness on July 5, the same day that a special committee on representation chaired by Elbridge Gerry of Massachusetts introduced what would become known as the Connecticut Compromise. By that point, the convention had nearly broken down several times. Even state delegations were deadlocked. Alexander Hamilton had given up, leaving Philadelphia for New York, soon to be followed by his fellow delegates from the state. Most members of the convention probably recognized, as Richard Beeman has observed, that the plan was "their best—and possibly last—hope for compromise."[17]

The day had been a long one and debates had grown heated. As the discussion turned to the question of representation in the House of Representatives, Gouverneur Morris of Pennsylvania rose to give a searing speech that concluded:

> He looked forward also to that range of New States which wd. soon be formed in the west. He thought the rule of representation ought to be fixed as to secure to the Atlantic States a prevalence in the National Councils. The new States will know less of the public interest than these, will have an interest in many respects different. . . . Provision ought therefore to be made to prevent the maritime States from being hereafter outvoted by them. He thought this might be easily done by irrevocably fixing the number of representatives which the Atlantic States should respectively have, and the number which each new State will have. This wd. not be unjust as the western settlers wd. previously know the conditions on which they were to possess their lands. It would be politic as it would recommend the plan to the present as well as future interests of the States which must decide the fate of it.[18]

If such a proposal seems far fetched today, it did not shock the delegates. On the contrary, John Rutledge, a delegate from South Carolina who would become an inaugural justice of the Supreme Court, concurred. "If numbers should be made the rule of representation," he observed, "the Atlantic States will be subjected to the Western."[19] It was left to George Mason of Virginia to object. "The case of new States was not unnoticed in the Committee," he commented. "But it was thought and he was himself decidedly of opinion that if they [were] made a part of the Union, they ought to be subject to no unfavorable discriminations. Obvious considerations required it."[20] With that, the Convention adjourned.

The issue returned the following day, as delegates continued to debate the allocation of representation in the lower branch of Congress. Rufus King of Massachusetts stood:

> With regard to New States, he observed that there was something peculiar in the business which had not been noticed. The U.S. were now admitted to be proprietors of the Country, N. West of the Ohio. Congs. by one of their ordinances have impoliticly laid it out into ten States, and have made it a fundamental article of compact with those who may become settlers, that as soon as the number in any one State shall equal that of the smallest of the 13 original States, it may claim admission into the Union. . . . It is possible then that if this

plan be persisted in by Congs. 10 new votes may be added, without a greater addition of inhabitants than are represented by the single vote of Pena.[21]

King's argument gained support from Pierce Butler of South Carolina, who "concurred with those who thought some balance was necessary between the old & New States."[22] Clearly, many delegates shared a concern that the original thirteen states then crafting a constitution might one day find themselves outvoted by new states. By this point in the debates, it seems fair to say that every delegate was sensitive to the danger.

On July 9, a committee chaired by Gouverneur Morris delivered a report on congressional apportionment. It proposed that "the Legislature

Figure 8.4. *Rufus King*, by Gilbert Stuart, 1819–1820. Oil on panel. National Portrait Gallery, Smithsonian Institution. This acquisition was made possible by a generous contribution from the James Smithson Society.

shall possess authority to regulate the number of representatives" accorded to new states.[23] Nathaniel Gorham of Massachusetts, who also served on the committee, defended its proposal as a response to fears that "Westn. States who may have a different interest, might if admitted on that principal by degrees, out-vote the Atlantic." His committee's proposal, he insisted, prevented such a fate. "The Atlantic States having ye. Govt. in their own hands, may take care of their own interest, by dealing out the right of Representation in safe proportions to the Western States."[24] Here, the convention seemed prepared to abandon the principle of equality among states and endow the U.S. Congress with the power to extend fewer political rights to new states. After all, as Hugh Williamson of North Carolina observed, "the Western States stood on different footing."[25]

This question about new states, however, emerged as a subset of the larger debate over apportionment among the existing states in the House of Representatives. Unable to come to agreement on this hotly contested issue, the convention spent several days debating fiercely and horse trading. Why did New Hampshire get three representatives instead of two? Why did North Carolina get five and not six? Should there be fifty representatives? Sixty-five? One hundred and thirty? How much should property count? And what about slaves? Throughout these days in the middle of July, the three-fifths ratio continually reared its ugly head. George Washington was despondent. "I almost despair of seeing a favorable issue to the proceedings of the Convention," he wrote on July 12, "and do therefore repent having had any agency in the business."[26]

During these animated discussions, questions about new states continued to reappear. Gouverneur Morris, an unrelenting opponent of the three-fifths rule, proved himself a consistent skeptic of new states as well. "He dwelt much on the danger of throwing such a preponderancy into the Western Scale, suggesting that in time the Western people wd. outnumber the Atlantic States. He wished therefore to put it in the power of the latter to keep a majority of votes in their own hands."[27] James Wilson of Pennsylvania disagreed. "Strong objection had been drawn from the danger to the Atlantic interests from new Western States," he responded on July 11. "If the Western States are to be admitted into the Union as they arise, they must," he repeated, "be treated as equals and subjected to no degrading discriminations." Indeed, Wilson insisted that they be "in all respects placed on an equal footing with their brethren."[28] Morris, however, was implacable. "If the Western people get the power into their hands," he warned, "they will ruin the Atlantic interests."[29] By this time, Madison had changed his mind about the danger new states posed. "Let them have an equal vote," he had warned his colleagues on June 19, "and a more objectionable minority than ever might give law to the whole." By July 11, he had reversed his position. "With regard to the Western States," Madison declared, he "was clear & firm in opinion that no unfavorable distinctions were admissible in either point of justice or policy."[30]

On July 14, the debate came to a head. Elbridge Gerry of Massachusetts unmasked himself as a skeptic of the wisdom of U.S. expansion. "He was for admitting them [new states] on liberal terms, but not for putting ourselves in their hands." He therefore "thought it necessary to limit the number of new States to be admitted into the Union, in such a manner that they should never be able to outnumber the Atlantic States."[31] Gerry introduced a motion:

> That to secure the liberties of the States already confederated, the number of representatives in the first branch from the States which shall hereafter be established, shall never exceed the representatives from such of the thirteen United States as shall accede to this Confederation.

Rufus King immediately seconded the motion. Roger Sherman of Connecticut, who had done so much to foster compromise among the feuding factions at the convention, thought the proposal silly. He "thought there was no probability that the number of future States would exceed that of the Existing States. If the event should ever happen," he added, "it was too remote to be taken into consideration at this time."[32] The convention proved itself divided on the motion, which was barely defeated, by a vote of 5–4. Massachusetts, Connecticut, Delaware, and Maryland all voted in favor of preserving an eternal constitutional advantage to the original thirteen states. New Jersey, Virginia, North Carolina, South Carolina, and Georgia all voted against the idea. Pennsylvania was divided and New York had lost its delegation. One wonders what might have happened had Alexander Hamilton been present to represent New York. If the division here was largely sectional, that rift was not a neat one: Maryland voted for the motion, New Jersey against, and Pennsylvania split.

Clearly, delegates had a hard time forging consensus on the political rights of new states. The July 14 vote decided—by a bare majority—that the original thirteen states would not get a permanent guarantee of political dominance over new states admitted to the Union. Left unresolved, however, were the precise terms by which new states would be admitted and whether they would have rights equal to those of the original thirteen.

The Committee of Detail

In light of the extensive debate and division over the potential dangers of new states, the Constitution's final text emerges as an extraordinary puzzle. The delegates had barely defeated a guarantee of permanent political supremacy for the original thirteen states. With this vote behind them, questions about the rights of new states dropped out of debate for the remainder of July, while the convention delegated the crafting of a first draft of the Constitution to the Committee of Detail.

The Committee of Detail's initial text imposed several restrictions on the admission of new states. In light of the final text, these proposals merit close attention. First, the committee's draft proclaimed that all future states could lie only within the 1787 limits of the United States, thus excluding the possibility of future states west of the Mississippi River. The provision was entirely consistent with previous western ordinances, which only addressed U.S. territory as far as the Mississippi River. Had that clause remained in the Constitution, the creation of states from the territory acquired in the Louisiana Purchase and all the territory seized from Mexico in 1848 would have required constitutional amendments—a high barrier indeed.

Second, the Committee of Detail's draft required the assent of two-thirds of both houses of Congress in order to admit new states. This minimum, which was consistent with the Articles of Confederation and the 1784 Ordinance, was also consistent with the text of the Constitution. Under the U.S. Constitution, most major actions—impeaching federal officials, expelling members of Congress, overriding presidential vetoes, ratifying treaties, or amending the Constitution—require two-thirds supermajorities to implement. Constitutional amendments have an even higher bar. So it made sense to require supermajorities for the admission of new states. After all, they have a major effect on the constitutional balance of power. Admission of new states changes the number of states, affecting federal-state relations, and increases the total number of congressional representatives and therefore the ratio of any individual state's representation. And of course, it reconfigures the Electoral College and thus the selection of the president. Indeed, no other provision in the Constitution so fundamentally alters the balance of power in the federal government. Given the ferociousness with which delegates had defended their state interests in the convention, it is little wonder that the Committee of Detail required that two-thirds of existing states assent to the admission of new states.

Finally—and also in continuity with the western policy under the Articles of Confederation—the committee's draft required that new states "shall be admitted on the same terms with the original states."[33] This provision would become a central constitutional principle in the centuries to come, known as the "Equal Footing Doctrine." It represented a dramatic extension of the mid-July debate over the rights of new states. Where that debate had successfully resisted enshrining the permanent political dominance of the original thirteen states, this provision went far in the other direction, permanently guaranteeing the constitutional equality of the new states relative to the original thirteen.

Altogether, these three principles of new states admissions were entirely consistent with western policy under the Articles of Confederation, with the internal logic of the Constitution, and with the tenor of the debates in the convention. That is why the final text—which abandoned every one of those principles—emerges as such a puzzle.

When it finally came time to debate these provisions in late August, Gouverneur Morris emerged to relitigate his case against admitting new states on an equal footing. Arguing that "He did not wish to bind down the Legislature to admit Western States on the terms [of equality] here stated," Morris moved to remove the equal footing requirement from the Constitution. James Madison, now a staunch defender of the interests of new states, resisted, "insisting that the Western States neither would nor ought to submit to a Union which degraded them from an equal rank with the other States." George Mason sided with Madison, but Morris would not budge: "He did not wish . . . to throw power into their hands." This time, Morris found more favor with the delegates than he had in July. John Langdon of New Hampshire speculated that "circumstances might arise which would render it inconvenient to admit new States on terms of equality." Hugh Williamson agreed: "The existing *small* States enjoy an equality now, and for *that* reason are admitted to it in the Senate." On the other hand, "This reason is not applicable to the new Western States." The vote was called and Morris's motion carried 9–2, with only Maryland and Virginia voting against.[34]

Let us dwell on that for a moment: the equal footing clause was explicitly and overwhelmingly removed from the Constitution. When compared with the split vote over the provision to permanently ensure a congressional majority for the original thirteen states, the original intent of the Founding Fathers and of the text seems abundantly clear. They did not mean (at least a bare majority of delegates did not mean) to permanently and unalterably deprive the new states of political power, but they very clearly (and overwhelmingly) gave future congresses the power to do so should they so choose.

Given later Supreme Court jurisprudence, that finding would be remarkable enough. But the constitutional puzzles continue. Having just carried his motion to allow Congress to deprive new states of equal rights if it should so choose, Morris then moved to substitute new language for the New States Clause. Pulling out the two-thirds requirement for the admission of new states, he offered, simply: "New States may be admitted by the Legislature into this Union." Delegates agreed to that clause unanimously. Thus, without any apparent debate, the supermajority requirement was removed from the Constitution.[35]

Here lie perhaps the greatest puzzles of all. Having agreed to strip the principle of equal footing from the Constitution, delegates suddenly changed course and agreed to make it easier, rather than harder, to admit new states to the Union. Why would the convention pass both an anti–new state provision (stripping equal footing) while almost simultaneously, and apparently without any debate, passing a pro–new state provision (abolishing the supermajority requirement for admission)? Were they imagining here a future in which Congress could exercise stringent requirements on the admission of new states? Were delegates imagining a future in which the original thirteen states might exercise imperial rule over the national domain?

What makes the question even more perplexing, moreover, is that none other than Gouverneur Morris stripped the supermajority requirement for the admission of new states. Having advocated over the course of the convention to grant the original thirteen states political dominance over the new states, Morris now opened the door to a future in which new states could come in more easily, thus making it more likely that the new states would soon outnumber the old. Why? Making matters even more ironic, not only did Morris make it easier for new states in general to be added, he also made it easier for new slave states to be added. And yet no delegate was more outspoken against slavery than Morris.

What is more, Morris's motion to reduce the admissions requirement was seconded by Luther Martin of Maryland—another small state. None of the small states opposed the measure. Only a month earlier, delegates from the small states had been willing to walk away from the convention to defend their voting rights under the new Constitution. In the great fight over representation, Gunning Bedford from Delaware had pointed out that "Delaware now stands 1/13th of the whole—when the system of equal representation obtains Delaware will be 1/90th."[36] That outcome was intolerable to him. And yet over time, thanks to the New States Clause, Delaware's political clout in Congress would get progressively diluted—an outcome the small states all helped bring with their support for Morris's language. Why?

And then there was the final change that Morris's motion enacted. The original proposal specified that new states could only be created in the existing territory of the United States, in other words as far as the Mississippi River. Morris's substitute language stripped that provision from the Constitution. Until August 29, 1787, every text regarding western expansion— the Ordinance of 1784, the Northwest Ordinance of 1787, and indeed the entire debate in the Constitutional Convention—had looked as far west as the Mississippi River but no farther. Suddenly, momentously, the nation opened up possible expansion beyond the Mississippi and potentially anywhere. Why? Perhaps the delegates assumed that the United States would naturally be limited by the Mississippi River. Sherman, for one, "thought there was no probability that the number of future States would exceed that of the Existing States."[37] Perhaps so, but then what could have been the harm in specifying the Mississippi as the western boundary for the nation?

It is fascinating to ponder the implications of these changes. Lowering the two-thirds requirement to a simple majority in order to admit new states was an extraordinarily momentous decision. Consider the later battles over new state admissions. Not a single one—not the admission of Missouri, of Texas, of California—passed Congress with anywhere near a two-thirds majority. Then again, these compromises never would have come to Congress in the first place had the Constitution maintained the language that new states could only be formed in the existing limits of the United States. The admission of Missouri, Texas, and California would all have required constitutional amendments. Is there any doubt about the odds of success on that one? All this is to say that Morris's change had a monumental effect on the politics of slavery in the nineteenth-century United States. It is perhaps more a subject for novelists than for historians, but it seems fair to assume that the United States could hardly have stumbled all the way to 1861 without Morris's substitute language. Would a civil war have broken out in 1820 to resolve the issue of slavery and western expansion? Perhaps, but a more likely scenario is the peaceful creation of two or more separate republics.

And finally, we come to the effect of new states on the presidency. As noted above, each new state admission affected the balance of power in the Electoral College. Consider the effects on presidential elections in the early nineteenth century. With the admissions of Kentucky and Tennessee, the Jeffersonian/Democratic Party gained hefty support in presidential contests. The election of Thomas Jefferson in 1800 was a nail-biter even with those admissions. Seven of his seventy-three electoral votes came from those two states. Jefferson and Burr might have squeezed past John Adams by one electoral vote in that election, but the already byzantine politics of that election would have only been more complicated and unpredictable in such a scenario.

Federalist politicians hoped that the admission of Ohio and other states in the Northwest would counterbalance the growing clout of the new states south of the Ohio. Later elections would prove them wrong, however: Ohio, Indiana, and Illinois would consistently vote Democratic. The first Federalist/Whig candidate to win a vote in any state west of the Appalachian Mountains was Henry Clay in 1824—himself, needless to say, a man from Kentucky. It was only thanks to Clay's electoral votes that a New Englander of Federalist stock ascended to the presidency, in what its opponents would call a "corrupt bargain." No Whig from the original thirteen states ever won the presidency thereafter. Until the Civil War, the Democratic Party dominated the presidential elections, in large part thanks to its centers of power in the new states. The only exceptions were William Harrison of Ohio, who won a single term in 1840, and Zachary Taylor of Louisiana, who won a term in 1848. And then, of course, Abraham Lincoln (of Kentucky and Illinois) won in 1860.

Not until the twentieth century did a Republican from one of the original thirteen states manage to win the presidency.[38] By then the western tilt to American politics was manifest. "As Ohio goes, so goes the nation" had long become a truism of American politics. If Republicans wanted to win the presidency, they needed a nominee from what the delegates to the Constitutional Convention, more than a century earlier, had called the new states.

To be sure, the Electoral College was necessarily complicit in this dynamic. Nevertheless, it seems clear that new states played a significant role in shaping the course of the American presidency.

Paths for Further Study: The Northwest Ordinance

By way of concluding observations, let us return to the eighteenth century to trace a few paths for further research into the question of new states. One path leads out of Philadelphia to New York City. For even as the document that emerged from the Constitutional Convention in Philadelphia proved inexplicably laconic about new state admissions, a different body was drafting a western policy with far more specificity. Ironically, that legislative body was the very Congress that the Constitutional Convention was just then in the process of toppling.

In early July 1787, as the delegates to the Constitutional Convention debated the merits of a proposal that would have ensured that the political weight of the new states would never exceed that of the original thirteen states, the Confederation Congress in New York was putting the final touches on the Northwest Ordinance. Reading the two documents alongside each other offers some insight even as it raises a set of further questions. In certain respects, the two documents present a stark contrast. Where the convention debates showed delegates willing to break from previous western policy, the delegates to the Confederation Congress were in the midst of extending and clarifying that policy. In other respects, however, the two documents may have been engaged in a collaborative enterprise.

The 1787 ordinance largely built on the principles of previous ordinances to clarify the terms of territorial development. It dramatically reduced the number of states planned for the territory above the Ohio River from ten to between three and five and fixed the minimum population requirements for statehood at 60,000. Even as it looked toward a future of republican governments in the West, it allowed for an appointed governor and judiciary to govern in the undefined period before statehood. Unlike the Ordinance of 1784, however, which applied to the entire trans-Appalachian region, the Northwest Ordinance applied only to territory north of the Ohio River. Despite its restrained geographical scope, the Northwest Ordinance—minus the controversial antislavery provisions—would come to dominate future territorial development in the United States.

The contrast between the convention in Philadelphia and the congress in New York is more than a little strange. In Philadelphia, the Constitutional Convention, then engaged in entirely redesigning the power balance among states, carefully avoided specifying criteria for the admission of new states. Meanwhile, "an enfeebled Congress looking forward to its own early demise," addressed them directly.[39] Peter Onuf has argued that the drafters of the Northwest Ordinance had a constitutional intent from the beginning. But even his analysis of the text, I believe, underplays the oddity of the situation: a rump Congress on the road to obsolescence drafting constitutional provisions even as a convention drafting a new constitution shied away from them. Why? Making the contrast even more curious is the gap in authority between the two documents. The Constitution is meant to be a foundational text, superior to simple statutes passed by Congress. And yet it was the Northwest Ordinance, a simple statute passed by a deposed Congress and then repassed, essentially word for word, by the first U.S. Congress, that somehow gained constitutional status. Particularly in our age of originalism, that seems like a bizarre outcome.

This strange duality between the documents raises a host of fascinating questions about the relationship between the Constitutional Convention and the Confederation Congress in the summer of 1787. Staughton Lynd has famously argued that the two documents "were clearly supplementary."[40] Lynd cites James Madison's recollection as relayed by his secretary Edward Coles: "Many individuals were members of both bodies, and thus were enabled to know what was passing in each—both sitting with closed doors and in secret session."[41] Lynd focuses on the three-fifths clause, which he argues was brokered as part of a "sectional compromise involving Congress and Convention, Ordinance and Constitution, essentially similar to those of 1820 and 1850."[42] Whatever one thinks of the overall merits of Lynd's argument about sectional compromise, he persuasively demonstrates the connection between the two bodies in ways that offer intriguing directions for future research on the subject of new states.[43]

As Lynd points out, several important figures served as delegates to both bodies, including Nathaniel Gorham and Rufus King of Massachusetts and James Madison of Virginia. He further notes that Gouverneur Morris—who was, as we have seen, the key figure in the debate over new states at the Constitutional Convention—spent a lengthy sojourn in New York before returning to Philadelphia on July 2, just a few days before the debate on new states began.[44] Lynd further highlights the intimate connection between the issue of new states and the issue of slavery. And finally, he emphasizes that the change in the ordinance from one that covered the entire trans-Appalachian West to one that only legislated for the territory north of the Ohio River was made very late, sometime between May and July of 1787.[45]

But what, precisely, was the relationship between the Constitution and the Northwest Ordinance on the question of new state admissions? Do we follow Lynd and see the two documents working in tandem as a sort of backroom compromise? By the time Gouverneur Morris proposed his substitute language in late August, all the provisions of the Northwest Ordinance would have been known to the delegates at the convention. But why would a hidden compromise have been necessary? After all, the question of new states was nowhere near as divisive as the slavery issue relentlessly tearing apart the convention. What is more, it is hard to know what would have been compromised. Rufus King, who was a member of both bodies, was the very person who had complained in the Constitutional Convention that Congress had "impoliticly" set the minimum population for statehood at the size of Delaware.[46] Why would he have agreed to a plan that potentially opened up the entire continent to new states, all of them requiring a population no greater than Delaware's for admission? Consider the stakes: had the proposal to alter the minimum state population requirement used the average state population rather than the smallest state, the process of new state formation would have been dramatically delayed. Wisconsin would not have become a state until 1900. Wyoming never would have become one.

In the end, the relationship between the two documents and the two bodies that produced them raises more questions than it answers.

Other Paths for Further Study

Perhaps fittingly, this analysis of the twists and turns of early U.S. western policy will end in an unsatisfying way. This chapter has raised several perplexing issues worthy of further study. I would like to close by raising a few more.

One issue worth dwelling on for a few moments was barely addressed by either the convention or the Confederation Congress, yet it serves as the essential subtext for all the discussion about new states: Native American power in the trans-Appalachian West. George Washington, for one, understood the essential relationship between the country's Native American policy and its western policy. When asked for his opinion on Indian Affairs in 1783, Washington provided an extensive and detailed response that even offered some preliminary outlines of new states in the Northwest. He added:

> At first view, it may seem a little extraneous, when I am called upon
> to give an opinion upon the terms of a Peace proper to be made with
> the Indians, that I should go into the formation of New States; but
> the Settlemt of the Western Country and making a Peace with the
> Indians are so analogous that there can be no definition of the one
> without involving considerations of the other.[47]

Further research will need to explore the connection between Native
American power in the West and the U.S. policy of state formation in the
region. If many Easterners had little interest in granting political power to
the settlers of the trans-Appalachian West—"a parcel of Banditti, who will
bid defiance to all Authority while they are skimming and disposing of the
Cream of the Country," as Washington put it in the same letter—neither
did they want to lose the territory to Indian power.[48] Further research on
U.S. western policy should look beyond legislative documents to the actions taken by the federal government under President Washington. Although we know a good deal about the Washington administration's focus
on the Northwest, an examination from the perspective of new state admissions might offer fresh insight.

Future research should also investigate the tortuous history of the equal
footing principle. The earliest use of that term that I have found so far
stems from Jefferson's 1784 ordinance. It was widely assumed to be a principle on which new states would be organized in the years leading up to
the Constitutional Convention. As we have seen, however, after debating
this issue, the delegates voted overwhelmingly to strip the requirement
from the final text. Nevertheless, over the course of the nineteenth and
twentieth centuries, the equal footing doctrine became constitutionalized
in violation of the text of the Constitution and the manifest intent of the
convention. Beginning in the 1830s, the Supreme Court began to ground
the principle of equal footing in the constitutional text. The principle was
central to Justice Roger Taney's holding in Dred Scott.[49] And it continued in future decisions. "Equality of constitutional right and power," the
Supreme Court declared in 1883, "is the condition of all the States of the
Union, old and new."[50]

Interestingly, the equal footing doctrine has recently reemerged as a
central issue in controversial jurisprudence. In its 2013 *Shelby County v.
Holder* decision, the Supreme Court struck down the enforcement provisions of the Voting Rights Act on these very grounds. The country, John
Roberts declared in his opinion, "was and is a union of States, equal in

power, dignity and authority."[51] In the beginning of *Shelby*, the court turned to the records of the Constitutional Convention to affirm that Congress has no right to veto state laws, demonstrating that a proposal to that effect was considered and then rejected by the delegates.[52] And yet in its ultimate holding, and particularly in its *Northwest Austin Municipal Utility District No. 1 v. Holder* decision, which the *Shelby* ruling relies on, the court ignored the records of the Constitutional Convention in favor of a centuries-long record of judicial activism on the question of equal footing.[53] Further research on the history of equal footing may help shed light on this complex and often sordid tale. Wherever the scholarship leads, however, the political implications of the Supreme Court's recent jurisprudence on the presidency seems clear. By mobilizing the equal footing provision to gut the Voting Rights Act, and given the slim margins by which the 2016 presidential election was decided in just a few key states, the Supreme Court's *Shelby County* decision may well have tilted the 2016 election by depressing the African American vote in Wisconsin and Florida. It very nearly did so again in 2020.

Finally, the historical record of new state admissions deserves further study. Given its broad latitude, how did Congress decide when and how to admit new states and what their borders would be? Questions of slavery and sectional parity of course governed the history of state admissions through the Civil War. But what about after? Did purely partisan considerations govern state admissions in much the same way they govern decennial redistricting in states? Why did the process stop with the admission of Alaska and Hawaii in 1959? It has now been sixty years since Congress admitted any new state into the Union, an unprecedented stretch in the history of the United States. And yet with a simple majority vote and no admissions criteria or territorial limitations imposed by the Constitution, nothing stops Congress from admitting Puerto Rico, Guam, the Virgin Islands, and more as new states.[54] Indeed, nothing would stop Congress from dividing Puerto Rico into four districts and admitting them each as a new state, sending eight Democratic senators to Washington and adding twelve Democratic votes in the Electoral College. Given the slim margins by which presidential elections are decided these days, such an event could easily prove decisive in the subsequent presidential elections.

Would Republicans complain? Perhaps. But then again, all four of those states would have a population greater than that of Wyoming.

Notes

1. In Max Farrand, ed., *The Records of the Federal Convention of 1787*, 3 vols. (New Haven, CT: Yale University Press, 1911), 1:322 (hereafter Farrand, *Records*).

2. See, for example, George C. Edwards, *Why the Electoral College Is Bad for America*, 2nd ed. (New Haven, CT: Yale University Press, 2011). A particularly helpful essay is Andrew Shankman, "What Were the Founders Thinking When They Created the Electoral College?" History News Network, accessed July 3, 2019, https://historynewsnetwork. org/article/164514.

3. The literature is too vast to cite here. Good introductions on various aspects include Don E. Fehrenbacher and Ward McAfee, *The Slaveholding Republic: An Account of the United States Government's Relations to Slavery* (New York: Oxford University Press, 2001); David Waldstreicher, *Slavery's Constitution: From Revolution to Ratification* (New York: Hill and Wang, 2009); Paul Finkelman, *Slavery and the Founders: Race and Liberty in the Age of Jefferson*, 3rd ed. (Hoboken, NJ: Taylor and Francis, 2014), esp. chapter 1; Matthew Karp, *This Vast Southern Empire: Slaveholders at the Helm of American Foreign Policy* (Cambridge, MA: Harvard University Press, 2016).

4. "The Declaration of Independence: A Transcription," America's Founding Documents, National Archives, accessed April 19, 2020, https://www.archives.gov/founding -docs/declaration-transcript.

5. David C. Hendrickson, *Peace Pact: The Lost World of the American Founding* (Lawrence: University Press of Kansas, 2003).

6. U.S. Constitution, art. IV, § 3, America's Founding Documents, National Archives, https://www.archives.gov/founding-docs/constitution-transcript. Henceforth, this essay will refer to this as the "New States Clause."

7. Quoted in Hendrickson, *Peace Pact*, 4.

8. Peter S. Onuf, *Statehood and Union: A History of the Northwest Ordinance* (Notre Dame, IN: University of Notre Dame Press, 2019), xv. This excellent book, first published in 1986, has recently been reissued, a happy development since it provides by far the best discussion of the history of the Northwest Ordinance and the most essential context for the issues raised in this essay.

9. I have elaborated on this context at greater length in François Furstenberg, "The Significance of the Trans-Appalachian Frontier in Atlantic History," *American Historical Review* 113, no. 3 (2008): 647–77. Andrew R. L. Cayton, "'Separate Interests' and the Nation-State: The Washington Administration and the Origins of Regionalism in the Trans-Appalachian West," *Journal of American History* 79, no. 1 (1992): 39–67, remains key reading on this issue. See also Jessica Choppin Roney, "1776, Viewed from the West," *Journal of the Early Republic* 37, no. 4 (2017): 655–700. On navigation of the Mississippi and the ratification controversy in Virginia, see Jeffrey Allen Zemler, *James Madison, the South, and the Trans-Appalachian West, 1783–1803* (Lanham, MD: Lexington Books, 2013), chapter 4.

10. "The Articles of Confederation: March 1, 1781," The Avalon Project: Documents in Law, History and Diplomacy, accessed September 15, 2019, https://avalon.law.yale. edu/18th_century/artconf.asp.

11. "Declaration of Independence."

12. "Editorial Note: Plan for Government of the Western Territory," Founders Online, National Archives, accessed April 11, 2019, https://founders.archives.gov/documents/Jefferson/01-06-02-0420-0001, published in *The Papers of Thomas Jefferson*, vol. 6, *21 May 1781–1 March 1784*, ed. Julian P. Boyd (Princeton, NJ: Princeton University Press, 1952), 581–600.

13. "II. Deed of Cession as Executed, 1 March 1784," Founders Online, National Archives, accessed April 11, 2019, https://founders.archives.gov/documents/Jefferson/01-06-02-0419-0003, published in *The Papers of Thomas Jefferson*, vol. 6, 577–80.

14. "V. The Ordinance of 1784, 23 April 1784," Founders Online, National Archives, accessed April 11, 2019, https://founders.archives.gov/documents/Jefferson/01-06-02-0420-0006, published in *The Papers of Thomas Jefferson*, vol. 6, 613–16.

15. Onuf, *Statehood and Union*, 49.

16. Onuf, *Statehood and Union*, 45. "The major contribution of the Northwest Ordinance was to reject the notion of territorial 'statehood' that was central to the 1784 ordinance" (55).

17. Richard Beeman, *Plain, Honest Men: The Making of the American Constitution* (New York: Random House, 2009), 204. See also John R. Vile, "The Critical Role of Committees at the U.S. Constitutional Convention of 1787," *American Journal of Legal History* 48, no. 2 (2006): 147–76.

18. Gouverneur Morris, July 5, 1787, in Farrand, *Records*, 1:533–34.

19. John Rutledge, July 5, 1787, in Farrand, *Records*, 1:534.

20. George Mason, July 5, 1787, in Farrand, *Records*, 1:534.

21. Rufus King, July 6, 1787, in Farrand, *Records*, 1:541.

22. Pierce Butler, July 6, 1787, in Farrand, *Records*, 1:542.

23. Journal, July 9, 1787, in Farrand, *Records*, 1:558.

24. Nathaniel Gorham, July 9, 1787, in Farrand, *Records*, 1:560.

25. Hugh Williamson, July 9, 1787, in Farrand, *Records*, 1:560.

26. George Washington to Alexander Hamilton, July 10, 1787, Founders Online, National Archives, accessed April 11, 2019, https://founders.archives.gov/documents/Washington/04-05-02-0236, published in *The Papers of George Washington*, Confederation Series, vol. 5, *1 February 1787–31 December 1787*, ed. W. W. Abbot (Charlottesville: University Press of Virginia, 1997), 257.

27. Gouverneur Morris, July 10, 1787, in Farrand, *Records*, 1:571.

28. James Wilson, July 11, 1787, in Farrand, *Records*, 1:578–79.

29. James Wilson, July 11, 1787, in Farrand, *Records*, 1:583.

30. James Madison, July 11, 1787, in Farrand, *Records*, 1:584.

31. Elbridge Gerry, July 14, 1787, in Farrand, *Records*, 2:2–3.

32. Roger Sherman, July 14, 1787, in Farrand, *Records*, 2:3.

33. Committee of Detail, in Farrand, *Records*, 2:147–48. See also Committee of Detail, in Farrand, *Records*, 2:173; and Report of the Committee of Convention, in Farrand, *Records*, August 6, 1787, 2:188.

34. Hugh Williamson, August 29, 1787, in Farrand, *Records*, 2:454.

35. Gouverneur Morris, August 29, 1787, in Farrand, *Records*, 2:455. Debate over the

New States Clause did continue but focused exclusively on the second part of the clause: the requirement that any existing state legislature needed to consent for any new state to be created out of an existing state.

36. Gunning Bedford, June 8, 1787, in Farrand, *Records*, 1:172

37. Roger Sherman, July 14, 1787, in Farrand, *Records*, 2:3.

38. That Republican was Theodore Roosevelt, who, in one of those funny quirks of history, wrote a biography of our man Gouverneur Morris. See Theodore Roosevelt, *Gouverneur Morris* (Boston: Houghton, Mifflin and Company, 1888).

39. Onuf, *Statehood and Union*, xxviii.

40. Staughton Lynd, "The Compromise of 1787," *Political Science Quarterly* 81, no. 2 (1966): 244.

41. Lynd, "The Compromise of 1787," 228.

42. Lynd, "The Compromise of 1787," 245. Lynd's argument has since been expanded in Robert Alexander, *The Northwest Ordinance: Constitutional Politics and the Theft of Native Land* (Jefferson, NC: McFarland & Company, 2017).

43. My own view is that the key role Lynd attributes to Manasseh Cutler is a bit far fetched. Is it possible that Cutler succeeded in brokering a compromise on the three-fifths issue where men like Benjamin Franklin had failed? Perhaps.

44. Lynd, "The Compromise of 1787," 227.

45. Lynd, "The Compromise of 1787," 231.

46. Does it bear noting that as of July 1, 2018, according to the Census Bureau, the ten smallest states in the Union together amount to just 68 percent of Pennsylvania's population? Together, they amount to just 22 percent of California's. Data from "2018 National and State Population Estimates," United States Bureau of the Census, December 19, 2018, accessed July 12, 2019, https://www.census.gov/newsroom/press-kits/2018/pop-estimates-national-state.html.

47. George Washington to James Duane, September 7, 1783, Founders Online, National Archives, accessed April 11, 2019, https://founders.archives.gov/documents/Washington/99-01-02-11798. This is an early access document; it has not yet been published in *The Papers of George Washington* and as such is an unofficial version.

48. On concerns about squatters and speculators and other uncontrollable elements in the West, see esp. Onuf, *Statehood and Union*, chapter 2.

49. *Dred Scott v. Sandford* 60 U.S. 393 (1857), 447ff.

50. *Escanaba Company v. Chicago*, 107 U.S. 678 (1883), 689.

51. *Shelby County, Alabama, v. Holder, Attorney General, et. al.* 679 F. 3d 848, reversed, Legal Information Institute, Cornell Law School, https://www.law.cornell.edu/supremecourt/text/12-96, citing *Coyle v. Smith*, 221 U. S. 559, 567 (1911).

52. *Shelby County v. Holder.*

53. *Northwest Austin Municipal Utility District No. 1 v. Holder,* 557 U.S. 193 (2009). On this issue, see esp. Zachary S. Price, "*NAMUDNO's* Non-Existent Principle of State Equality," *New York University Law Review* 88 (2013): 24–40.

54. The District of Columbia could be added to the list and is in many ways the most obvious candidate, although its status is distinct from that of a U.S. territory and it might be possible to argue that a constitutional amendment would be required rather than a simple majority vote of Congress.

PART III

Implementing an Ideal
Political Theory and Practice among the Early Presidents

9

The Political Practices
of the First Presidents
The Cabinet and the Executive Branch

LINDSAY M. CHERVINSKY

On November 6, 1801, President Thomas Jefferson sent a letter to his department secretaries and attorney general outlining how he planned to organize their communications and interactions while in office. He described how President George Washington had managed his administration during his first term. Jefferson recounted how the secretaries shared all correspondence and their proposed answers with the president. If a complicated issue arose, Washington reserved it for conference. Jefferson declared that through this method, "he was always in accurate possession of all facts & proceedings in every part of the Union, & to whatsoever department they related; he formed a central point for the different branches, preserved an unity of object and action among them, exercised that participation in the gestion of affairs which his office made incumbent on him, and met himself the due responsibility for whatever was done." Jefferson closed by suggesting that they "should adopt this course for the present."[1]

This document is remarkable because Jefferson called his election the previous fall the Revolution of 1800.[2] Voters had swept him into office on the promise that the Republican Party would abolish the monarchical practices of the Federalists and restore the government to its intended republican roots.[3] In some ways, Jefferson adopted drastic changes. He abolished the formal levees of the Washington and Adams administrations, he intentionally insulted diplomats by ignoring social protocol, and he showed up to greet guests in shabby clothes and house slippers.[4] And yet, as he considered how to structure his executive practices, arguably one of the most important parts of his presidency, he actively modeled himself after Washington, the first Federalist president.

Discussing the political theory and political practices of the presidents could fill thousands of pages, so for the sake of this volume, I have narrowed my focus in a few key ways. First, there is no scholarly consensus about which administrations constitute the "early presidents," so I have elected to include Washington, Adams, and Jefferson. This combination of administrations offers some interesting comparisons about personality, peaceful change of office, elections, and transfer of power between parties. Furthermore, after Jefferson retired, the overall structure of the presidency was established, and certain parameters of the institution remained the same for decades.

The policies and practices within these three presidencies are vast, so this chapter examines their cabinets and the presidents' relationships with their secretaries. Washington, Adams, and Jefferson's cabinets serve as an excellent window into their theories about leadership, executive power, their relationship with Congress, diplomacy, the Constitution, and so much more. Despite their many similarities, the first three presidents operated under very different approaches to their position. Washington exuded martial authority, Adams placed great faith in the power of the office, and Jefferson manipulated, cajoled, and cooperated to achieve his goals.

Washington: Martial Authority

Washington—as a man, as a leader, as a president—cannot be understood without fully considering his military experience and how it shaped his thinking and his personality. He did not seek to be a military president— he believed strongly in the separation of military and civilian authority. Rather, his military experience colored every aspect of his life. He sought efficiency, hierarchy, and powerful central authority in all his endeavors, qualities one associates with a lifetime of military training and experience. Washington's military experience shaped his approach to the presidency because of the complete lack of written guidelines for the position. Neither the Constitution nor subsequent legislation offered detailed governing instructions. As the first president, Washington also had no precedents or models to follow.

Washington's wartime experience convinced him of the need for a powerful federal government led by a strong executive. He encouraged the states to seek reform that included one "supreme power to regulate and govern the general concerns of the confederated Republic."[5] He witnessed firsthand the bumbling, inefficient nature of Congress during the war and quickly began to lobby for more executive power. Washington also voiced his frustrations in private communications to friends and acquaintances, including Benjamin Harrison, a former delegate to the Continental Congress, a signer of the Declaration of Independence, and the governor of Virginia. On March 21, 1781, Washington wrote, "If the States *will* not, or *cannot* provide me with the means; it is in vain for them to look to me for the end, and accomplishment of their wishes. Bricks are not to be made without straw."[6] Because he intentionally stayed out of the press, history has not remembered him as an advocate for executive power in the same way it has portrayed James Madison, Alexander Hamilton, Robert and Gouverneur Morris, John Jay, and others. Yet he wrote letters to Congress urging them to take action. At the end of the war, he wrote a very public circular to the states urging additional central authority. He also played a pivotal role at the Constitutional Convention.[7] He served as the president of the convention and his reputation lent the gathering critical legitimacy. He also voted with the Virginia delegation to increase presidential power and fully understood (along with everyone else there) that he would be the first president.[8]

Once in office, he appropriated military culture and applied it to the presidency. Article II, Section 2 of the Constitution states that the president has the authority to appoint foreign ministers and enter treaties with foreign nations with the advice and consent of the Senate.[9] Contrary to our twenty-first-century understanding of this clause, the delegates to the Constitutional Convention and the first officials in office expected the Senate to serve as a council on foreign affairs for the president. The relatively small size, only twenty-two senators in April 1789, seemed a decent size to offer guidance on issues of diplomacy.

Accordingly, in the summer of 1789, just a few months after taking office, Washington planned his first visit to the Senate. He planned to send commissioners to an upcoming peace summit between representatives of the federal government, the Carolina governments, and the Creek Nation. Washington had never authorized this type of summit before, so he wanted the Senate's advice on what his instructions to the commissioners should say before establishing precedent. To plan for his visit, he submitted all the previous treaties that the United States had signed with Native American nations and met with a committee to plan some of the details of the visit, including how he would enter, where he would sit, where John

Adams, the vice president and the president of the Senate, would sit, and so on.[10]

On August 22 11:00 a.m., Washington arrived at Federal Hall, on the corner of Wall Street in New York City, with Henry Knox, the acting secretary of war, at his side. Washington had brought Knox to answer any questions the senators might have about the previous treaties. He handed his address to Adams, who read the document out loud, including a list of questions at the end. Before Washington had arrived, the doorman had opened the window in search of a cooling breeze. Consistent with typical temperatures in August in New York, the room and the city were hot and muggy. As a result, all the noise from Wall Street outside—the horses dragging carts, the pedestrians walking by, the peddlers hawking their wares—flowed in through the window and drowned out Adams's voice.[11] It was not a very auspicious start to the working relationship between the president and the Senate.

Adams read the address again at the senators' request. This time, he was met with silence. Some senators shuffled their papers, others cleared their throat and avoided eye contact with Washington. After a few minutes of uncomfortable silence, Senator William Maclay from Pennsylvania stood up, suggested they refer the issue to a committee for further consideration, and asked Washington to return the following Monday. Outraged, Washington yelled, "This defeats every purpose of my coming here!"[12] After a moment, he regained his composure and agreed to return in a few days for their recommendation. But on his way out, Washington reportedly swore that he would never return for the Senate's advice, and he kept his word.

Why did Washington assume that the legislative branch would act with promptness and efficiency—qualities not usually associated with Congress? He expected the senators to debate and answer the questions he brought them. He called on them to operate like a council of war. During the Revolution, Washington had frequently convened councils that consisted of his officers and his aides-de-camp before entering winter quarters, adopting battle strategy, or starting a controversial retreat. He used councils to test out ideas, get advice, build consensus, and obtain political cover for tricky decisions. Prior to councils, he often sent the officers questions for them to consider or he brought questions to serve as the meeting's agenda. The officers then debated the issue at hand and offered their opinions. If they disagreed, Washington often requested written opinions so he could consider each position in more detail before deciding.[13] He expected the senators to act the same way. They were not his subordinate officers, however, and he was not their military commander ordering them to answer a question.

Washington's relationship with the cabinet reflected this approach to governing. Initially, Washington stuck to the guidelines offered in Article II, Section 2 of the Constitution and requested "written opinions" from the department secretaries. But he quickly discovered that the duties of office outpaced the slow and tedious process of passing handwritten letters with parchment and quill back and forth between his office and those of the secretaries. Washington frequently had follow-up questions or additional issues to discuss that were not covered in the original letter. In January 1790, he started inviting individual secretaries to meet with him after they sent written correspondence.[14] Only eight months into his presidency, Washington had essentially disregarded the two options provided to him for support in Article II, Section 2 of the Constitution.

Once Washington convened the first cabinet meeting on November 26, 1791, he adopted many of the same practices in his cabinet that he had used as commander in chief. He sent out questions ahead of meetings, requested written opinions if the secretaries disagreed, and used social events to build an esprit de corps among the secretaries. He also used cabinet meetings for many of the same purposes as councils: he sought advice; he tried to build consensus; and he secured political cover for controversial decisions.

The cabinet meetings served Washington's needs well. He was always slow to make decisions and he preferred to consider all options. Once he selected a plan of action, he implemented it with firmness and alacrity. Cabinet meetings reflected this preference. Washington asked the secretaries to share their opinions and debate with each other. While the secretaries may not have enjoyed the conflict, the president could hear all sides in detail, the secretaries could defend their opinions, and Washington could then consider the arguments before privately deciding at his own pace.

Washington also tried to replicate the social arrangement he had enjoyed in camp with his officers. During the war, he frequently invited his officers to dinner to meet with visiting dignitaries or discuss the day's events.[15] He also hosted dances and balls around the holidays to foster comradery among his aides and officers.[16] As president, Washington treated his secretaries as his official family. They frequently attended state dinners at the President's House, visited the theater as Washington's guest, or joined him for a ride on horseback outside Philadelphia. Washington also regularly invited his secretaries to a "family" dinner, especially if a cabinet meeting ran long. For example, in July 1793, Washington sent a note to Jefferson inviting him to one such dinner: "As the consideration of this business may require some time, I should be glad if you & the other Gentlemen would take a family dinner with me at 4 'Oclock. No other company is, or will be envited."[17] Perhaps he hoped that the dinner would erase the hurt feelings that arose in the course of cabinet debate or help the secretaries come to a consensus when debate resumed after the meal. Unfortunately, this strategy worked better with officers than it did with the secretaries, as no amount of social encounters would mollify the tempestuous relationship between Hamilton and Jefferson.[18]

Washington's relationship with Congress also reflected his militaristic approach to leadership and his deep conviction in the need for a strong, independent executive. At several key moments during his administration, Washington actively sidelined Congress and asserted executive authority.

First, in the spring of 1793, France declared war on Great Britain. Faced with the possibility of the warring European nations dragging the United States into the international conflict, Washington and the secretaries declared American neutrality. Washington issued a proclamation, the cabinet drafted a set of rules to enforce neutrality, and they insisted that foreign representatives abide by their policy. Citizen Edmond Charles Genêt, the French minister, flouted Washington's rules of neutrality by authorizing French privateers to seize British ships, drag them into American ports, and arm them as new French privateers. In the wake of this continued disobedience, the cabinet agreed to request his recall from the French government.[19] However, the Constitution did not explicitly state that Washington should follow these exact steps. Alternatively, he could have convened an emergency session of Congress to pass legislation declaring American neutrality, he could have asked Congress to design its own set of rules to govern neutrality, or he could have left prosecution of those policies up to Congress. Instead, Washington and the cabinet seized the initiative to craft foreign policy and bolster the power of the presidency.

Second, in the summer of 1794, the Whiskey Rebellion broke out in western Pennsylvania over an excise tax on whiskey. Again, the Constitution did not provide explicit guidance about how Washington should handle the domestic insurrection. He had four options: he could treat the uprising as a local matter and allow the states to deal with the rebels, he could wait until Congress returned in the fall and encourage it to take action, he could convene an early session of Congress to authorize the use of the army, or he could use a provision in a recent law that allowed the president to call up the state militias in the event of an insurrection.[20] Consistent with his actions during the neutrality crisis, Washington selected this final option. He refused to leave prosecution to Pennsylvania state officials and used the secretaries to force state compliance with federal action.[21] He also avoided any involvement by congressional officials—he did not convene Congress and did not send updates to members of Congress. Instead, Washington and the cabinet established executive authority during moments of domestic crisis.

Finally, in 1796, the House of Representatives sensed an opportunity to scuttle the Jay Treaty (signed in 1794), which resolved some of the lingering trade and territorial disputes left over from the Revolutionary War. While the treaty offered the United States the best chance of avoiding a costly war with Great Britain, many Americans felt that Jay had betrayed their interests during the treaty negotiations. Under the terms of the treaty, Americans agreed not to raise duties on British goods for twelve years but required Britain to make no such promise. Additionally, the treaty permitted Canadian merchants to cross American borders to sell their goods but prevented American traders from crossing Canadian borders. Finally, the treaty created a commission to adjudicate American debts to British merchants from before the war but required no similar commission for enslaved laborers that had run away from American plantations to safety among the British forces.[22] After the Senate had ratified the treaty and Washington had signed it, the treaty went to the House, as the committee to adjudicate prewar debts would require the House to authorize funds.[23] While debating the commission, the House requested all executive papers relating to the treaty negotiations.[24]

In April 1792, Washington and the cabinet had determined that the House had the constitutional right to request executive papers. They had also determined that the president had the right to assert executive privilege over his papers. At the time, Washington and the cabinet had elected to comply with the House's request and turned over all papers relating to the defeat of the American Army under the command of General Arthur St. Clair.[25] Four years later, it was a different story. Washington refused the House's request and asserted executive privilege for the first time. Washington also reminded the delegates that he had served as the president of the Constitutional Convention and that the delegates had decided that the Senate and the president would share treaty-making responsibilities.

Therefore, it was inappropriate for the House to try and acquire additional constitutional powers now; essentially, he challenged Congress to disagree with his interpretation.[26]

By asserting executive privilege, Washington also declared himself an arbiter of constitutional questions. In his letter to the House, he drew specific boundaries around executive privilege not delineated in the Constitution or legislation. Washington reiterated his "constant endeavor to harmonize with the other branches" of government, perhaps a nod to his previous helpful responses to congressional inquiries. He argued, however, that "the nature of foreign negociations requires caution; and their success must often depend on secrecy." If Washington had shared the documents, other countries might have been reluctant to engage in future negotiations. He also highlighted another specific exception—if the House had initiated an impeachment inquiry, he would have been happy to comply.[27] While the executive branch and the president's use of executive privilege have expanded significantly over the last 200 years, Washington's warning about impeachment inquiries remains relevant.

Washington approached all aspects of his presidency with a deep conviction that the executive branch needed to exercise power over many domestic issue, diplomacy, and constitutional questions. After decades of military service, he brought many army practices into the presidency and expected that his authority would receive the same respect as his command during the Revolutionary War from both his subordinates in the executive branch and officials in Congress.

Adams: Man Behind the Office

Like Washington, Adams's approach to the presidency was shaped by his previous experiences. He had spent much of his career at European courts, where a deeply ingrained respect for high office and the throne was an integral part of society. Obedience to those leaders was rarely challenged and any threats were usually met with bloody repression. Adams did not seek to replicate that sort of system, but he was keenly aware that the new U.S. government needed to foster respect for its offices and officials. The European atmosphere certainly invaded his thinking one way or another. He expected that the admiration and authority Washington commanded would transfer to the office of the president and he would be afforded the same dignity, respect, and obedience by his subordinates. He also hoped that voters, members of Congress, and his department secretaries would value his diplomatic and governing experience, and respect him accordingly.[28]

Operating under these expectations, Adams retained Washington's department secretaries. Adams wished to offer consistency and continuity, but he also believed that the secretaries would remain loyal to the office rather than to individuals and that they would serve the office dutifully. He even defended their actions in the 1796 election, assuring his friend Elbridge Gerry that they did not campaign for another candidate: "I believe there were no very dishonest Intrigues in this Business. The Zeal of some was not very ardent for me but I believe none opposed me."[29] For the same reason, he believed that they would faithfully pursue his wishes and goals, even when he left town to return home to Quincy for months at a time.

Adams also adopted many of Washington's cabinet practices: he drafted annual addresses to Congress with the secretaries' help, he sent out questions for the secretaries to consider before a cabinet meeting, he used those questions as an agenda for the meeting, and he requested follow-up opinions in writing if the secretaries disagreed.[30] Adams's continued use of Washington's secretaries and practices was not as ill advised as it may seem in retrospect. The peaceful transfer of power on the national stage was a tense moment. Other countries had succumbed to anarchy or military dictatorships when they faced similar challenges. Furthermore, Washington had established the only precedent for how a president governed and operated. Washington's example was the only model that the American public knew and had approved. Adams had good reason for following Washington's precedents.

While Adams's continuation of Washington's practices might be unsurprising in retrospect, his cabinet lent further weight to Washington's precedent. Had Adams pursued an alternative method of governing, history may have treated Washington's cabinet as an aberration. Instead, Adams ensured that the cabinet was a powerful custom that their successors would adopt. As a result, Adams's cabinet is just as important as Washington's, if not more so, for the development of the executive branch.

While Adams's relationship with the secretaries initially remained cordial, these relationships soured as their foreign policy goals diverged. After the United States signed the Jay Treaty, tensions with France escalated. France viewed the treaty as a revocation of the 1778 Franco-American alliance and began seizing American ships and crews in retaliation.

In early 1797, Charles Cotesworth Pinckney, the U.S. minister to France, was unceremoniously kicked out of the country. Adams nominated a new three-man peace commission that consisted of the humiliated Pinckney, John Marshall, and Elbridge Gerry. In early October 1797, the ministers met with the French foreign minister Charles Maurice de Talleyrand to exchange credentials. A few days later, they received the first of several visits from three unnamed agents employed by Talleyrand (known as the XYZ agents). Talleyrand selected these agents because of their ties to the United States and the American commissioners. The agents delivered messages and threats through unofficial channels. On October 18, Jean Conrad Hottinguer, Agent X, laid out the terms Talleyrand required to open negotiations. First, the United States had to take responsibility for recent American shipping losses French privateers had inflicted and the government must apologize for an "offensive" speech Adams had given on May 16, 1797. Next, the United States had to immediately offer a substantial loan, which France intended to use to fight its war with Great Britain. Finally, the United States had to give a sizable private gift, around £50,000, to Talleyrand and the other ministers to use at their discretion.[31] The first two conditions immediately contradicted the instructions Adams had issued to the commissioners—they were to seek reparations for ships seized by France and they were prohibited from offering a loan. The third condition, a bribe, while not mentioned in their instructions, deeply offended their republican sensibilities.[32]

Over the next several weeks, Hottinguer, Pierre Bellamy (Agent Y), and Lucien Hauteval (Agent Z) continued to visit the American commissioners. When their efforts to secure loans for the government through persuasion failed, they issued threats that the French nation would attack all neutral nations and blame the failed negotiations on the Federalist Party back in the United States.[33] Over the next few months, Talleyrand worked to divide and manipulate the commissioners.[34] On April 23, Marshall and Pinckney left Paris, and Gerry reluctantly followed on August 8, 1798.[35]

On March 5, 1798, Adams finally received the first dispatch from his envoys in Paris. Marshall's letters revealed their humiliating treatment from Talleyrand. Two weeks later, Adams informed Congress that the peace commission had failed. Republicans in Congress believed that the correspondence would reveal the administration's efforts to sabotage the peace process and they were eager to place the blame on the Federalists. They demanded access to the communications between Adams and the commissioners. On April 3, Adams gladly delivered the dispatches to Congress.

The contents outraged both Republicans and Federalists. Congress quickly adopted Adams's recommendations to form a provisional army, beef up the nation's defenses, and prepare for the possibility of war.[36]

In the summer of 1798, the cabinet challenged Adams's right as president to simultaneously seek peace and prepare for war—a situation Washington never experienced. Over the summer, Adams had received reports that the French ministry had changed its mind about negotiations. Letters from William Vans Murray in the Netherlands and John Quincy Adams in Prussia suggested a new French motive. Both Murray and John Quincy believed that the French ministry had attempted to intimidate the United States into a more favorable treaty during the XYZ Affair. The ministry altered course when Americans responded with strength and war appeared imminent. Talleyrand hinted in private letters that France now wished to enter sincere negotiations. John Quincy argued that even if France "was bluffing in its intimations of peaceful intent, better to call her bluff than run the risk of having the administration maneuvered into the position of not seeming sincerely anxious to repair the breach between the two countries."[37] Adams agreed that peace must be given an opportunity to succeed. Hamilton, a major general in the U.S. Army, Secretary of State Timothy Pickering, Secretary of the Treasury Oliver Wolcott Jr., and Secretary of War James McHenry refused to accept this final decision. They pressed him to continue preparing for war. On January 15, 1799, Pickering acknowledged that Talleyrand had recently seemed to favor peace, but the French minister had also written "Several pages . . . contrasting the evidences of [his] SINCERITY, *before* and *after* the publication of the Dispatches. . . . The *language* may perhaps be softened; but the *substance* seems to me very important to retain."[38]

While Jefferson had often disagreed with Washington's policies, once Washington made a final decision, he had mostly supported the administration. He often complained in private, but he never actively undermined Washington's administration from the inside. Adams did not command the same obedience from his secretaries. Recognizing the warmongering among the High Federalists in his cabinet and in Congress, he moved forward with his diplomatic plans in secret. On February 18, 1799, ignoring his party's wishes, Adams submitted Talleyrand's letter to the Senate and nominated Murray as minister plenipotentiary.[39] Adams caught everyone by surprise. He had acted without consulting party leaders, personal confidants, or cabinet secretaries. Even Jefferson—who read the statement in his capacity as vice president and president of the Senate—was shocked.

In August 1799, Talleyrand sent Adams assurances through diplomatic back channels that the French Directory would receive the new delegation. As the commissioners moved forward with their preparations for their mission, Adams vacationed in Quincy. Taking full advantage of the president's absence, Pickering and the other Hamiltonian Federalists worked to prevent the commissioners from departing. Such blatant disloyalty never occurred in Washington's administration. Jefferson may have naively trusted Genêt during the neutrality crisis in 1793, but he never intentionally undermined the president's final decision. Adams's inability to control his secretaries demonstrated the danger of relying on the trappings of the office to ensure cabinet cooperation.

Secretary of the Navy Benjamin Stoddert was one of the few secretaries who was fully loyal to Adams. He accurately sized up the other secretaries' intentions and wrote to the president begging him to end his vacation and rejoin the rest of the cabinet. In his letter, he alluded to the schemes taking place among the other cabinet secretaries to postpone the peace mission.[40] Adams initially demurred, reluctant to leave Quincy and his sickly wife, Abigail. A few days later, Pickering wrote to the president and encouraged him to stay at home. He also casually mentioned the need to delay the commissioners' departure. Adams decided such outright disobedience could not be overlooked.[41] On October 10, he arrived in Trenton, where the administration had set up shop to avoid a yellow fever outbreak in Philadelphia.[42] When Pickering, Wolcott, and McHenry failed to change Adams's mind about sending the commissioners, they called in reinforcements. Sometime in the period October 19–21, 1799, Hamilton arrived in Trenton and called on the president. He tried his best to persuade Adams to cancel his diplomatic efforts. He believed that the British war effort, led by Prime Minister William Pitt the Younger, would soon defeat Napoleon and reinstate the Bourbon monarchy in France. He argued that it would be a waste of time and resources to negotiate with the current French government when a monarchy would agree to much more favorable terms. Adams responded that he "differed with him in opinion on every point."[43]

Adams's steadfast commitment to pursuing peace caused Hamilton to lose his composure. He "repeated over and over again the unalterable resolution of Mr. Pitt and the two imperial courts . . . with such agitation and violent action."[44] The secretaries could not have selected a worse person to lobby the president, and Hamilton's presence had the opposite effect that was intended. Adams already hated Hamilton, but the visit only further cemented their broken relationship. Hamilton's presumption that he could lecture Adams on foreign policy raised his hackles and demonstrated the general lack of respect Hamilton and the secretaries had for Adams. Adams emerged from the meeting more determined than ever to pursue peace and convinced of Hamilton's "total ignorance . . . of every thing in Europe, in France, England, and elsewhere."[45] Overruling the secretaries' procrastination efforts, he sent orders to the commissioners to take passage to France and to set sail by the first of November at the latest.[46] That a similar situation could occur during Washington's presidency was unfathomable. Not only did Hamilton treat Washington with the utmost respect, but a private citizen would never have stormed into the president's study and challenged his authority. The cabinet divisions had taken their toll on Adams's administration and his stature as president.

On September 30, 1800, the commissioners signed the Treaty of Mortefontaine. While the peace mission failed to secure indemnities for past French depredations on American ships, the treaty established peace, dictated the terms of future interactions on the high seas, and protected neutral trade.[47] In the meantime, Pickering, Wolcott, and McHenry colluded with Hamilton to sabotage Adams's chances of reelection. News of the treaty arrived too late to influence the 1800 election and Adams came in a distant third to Thomas Jefferson and Aaron Burr. Yet the treaty also offered important long-term ramifications for the presidency. It vindicated Adams's stubborn efforts to pursue peace measures. The results also reinforced that the president controlled the diplomatic process, not the secretaries. Had the peace conference failed, Adams's contemporaries may have viewed his determined disavowal of the secretaries' advice in a different light. Instead, Adams asserted his own independence, even if belatedly, and continued Washington's important precedent of reserving the final decision for the president.[48]

In early 1800, Adams heard rumors that some of his secretaries were scheming to replace him on the Federalist ballot. Although Adams believed these reports, they were not offered by reputable sources and perhaps he thought it beneath him to confront the secretaries over this issue.[49] Whatever the reason, the frustrations boiled inside him until early May, when tensions spilled over while McHenry was visiting the White House to discuss nominees for an open position in the War Department. After handling the issues surrounding appointees, McHenry stood up to leave. Adams paused, then brought up a new topic. He shifted the conversation to the upcoming election and accused McHenry and the other department secretaries of scheming to thwart his reelection. He alleged, "with great warmth," that "Hamilton has been opposing me in New York. He has caused the loss of the election. No head of a Department shall be permitted to oppose me."[50] The conversation quickly escalated. Perhaps unintentionally, Adams took out years of his frustrations on McHenry. He hated being compared to Washington, he struggled with the impossibly high expectations for the second president, he was tired of his unruly cabinet, he loathed Hamilton, and he was fed up with the High Federalists. He unleashed all of these emotions in a tirade to McHenry: "Hamilton is an intriguant—the greatest intriguant in the World—a man devoid of every moral principle—a Bastard."[51] McHenry immediately offered his resignation, which Adams accepted.[52]

After his blowout with McHenry, Adams set out to establish discipline in the cabinet.[53] He never intended to undertake a systemic purge, for if he had, he surely would have requested the resignation of all Hamiltonians in the cabinet. He suspected that McHenry did not mastermind the schemes to undermine his administration—he was simply an inept secretary of war and a Hamilton lackey. Instead, Adams concluded that Pickering served as the ringleader. As secretary of state and a leading Federalist, Pickering was a formidable foe. On May 10, Adams requested his resignation to demonstrate that he harbored no fear of anyone in his cabinet. To maintain peace, Adams offered him the opportunity to resign as a way to exit the office with his honor intact. After so many years of political maneuvering, Pickering refused to exit quietly. On May 12, he offered his reply. Unlike his respectful interactions with Washington, he offered no apology or explanation for his damaged relationship with Adams. He insisted on staying in office, citing potential financial hardship.[54] However, once he decided on this course of action, Adams would not take no for an answer. He responded that afternoon by summarily dismissing Pickering from his office.[55] Many years after his removal from Adams's cabinet, Pickering wrote that he never believed that cabinet members were bound by a rule of "implicit obedience or resignation."[56] Adams clearly disagreed. As early as 1797, he defended the right of the executive to appoint and remove secretaries as integral to the power of the president:

As to having all his Executive officers Subject to his Nod—I suppose that means his Power of Removal. This Power I hold to be a Sacred Part of the Constitution without which the Government could not exist. If Executive officers, hold their offices independent of the head, and can intrigue with Members of Senate and the House, to assist them in opposing the Execution of the Laws, the Executive Authority would be a Nose of Wax.[57]

Adams had a similarly tempestuous relationship with Congress. He expected that members of Congress would respect his authority as president. After he nominated Murray, the High Federalists immediately attacked Adams in the press and sent a delegation of senators to meet with the President. A few days later, Senators Theodore Sedgwick (Massachusetts), Richard Stockton (New Jersey), Jacob Read (South Carolina), William Bingham (Pennsylvania), and James Ross (also Pennsylvania) arrived at the president's house without an invitation and demanded he withdraw the nomination. When Adams refused, the delegates threatened to veto Murray's nomination. Undeterred, Adams countered by threatening to resign and daring them to deal with Jefferson as president. The meeting finally ended when they reached a tense agreement. Adams would add two additional commissioners to accompany Murray in his negotiations with France. He also consented to hold back the commissioners until the French ministry provided further assurance the American ministers would be properly welcomed.[58] Only Adams and perhaps some members of his cabinet had been privy to the private communications with Talleyrand and the better likelihood for a peaceful resolution. All the same, he expected Congress to defer to him on issues of diplomacy, as it had often done with Washington.

Somewhat ironically, Adams's removal of Pickering from office helped create the type of relationships with his secretaries that he had expected to inherit. This step created the precedent that presidents were not obligated to follow their secretaries' advice and secretaries were not guaranteed the right to pursue their own agendas. By removing Pickering from office, he affirmed the constitutional right of removal for future presidents. When Congress did not challenge Pickering's dismissal, it effectively confirmed the president's complete authority over the secretaries. Adams had finally discovered the necessity of having full control over his cabinet and created a similar working environment to the one Washington had enjoyed.

Washington wielded significant authority because of his reputation and unparalleled status. While his secretaries bickered among themselves, they mostly followed his orders. Adams had to work much harder to achieve that level of obedience. Initially, he hoped that his secretaries would offer him the same loyalty and deference as they had given Washington out of respect for the office. He had similar expectations for Federalists in

Congress. Adams belatedly realized he needed to appoint his own loyal secretaries and cultivate the relationships necessary to ensure they did not derail his agenda.

Jefferson: Manipulate, Cajole, and Cooperate

Based on his experiences with the previous administrations, Jefferson shaped his cabinet to maximize the strengths of Washington's presidency while minimizing the weaknesses in Washington's second term and Adams's presidency. Jefferson was notoriously averse to conflict and went to great lengths to avoid it in his personal and professional life. He hated the contentious debates in Washington's cabinet meetings, once describing the process as a cockfight between Hamilton and himself.[59] He believed that the conflict undermined the executive branch and was convinced that the frequent cabinet meetings transferred too much authority to the secretaries. Jefferson concluded that regular cabinet meetings had offered Hamilton too much room to pursue his own agenda—especially when Washington instructed them to meet without him and report back their recommendations.

As vice president in the Adams administration, Jefferson did not participate in cabinet meetings and observed the presidency from his perch as president of the Senate. He concluded that Adams's absences allowed the secretaries to engage in nefarious activity and take over the reins of government: "During mr. Adams's administration, his long & habitual absences from the seat of government rendered [daily written correspondence and individual meetings] impracticable, removed him from any share in the transaction of affairs, & parceled out the government in fact among four independant heads, drawing sometimes in opposite directions."[60] Jefferson had observed Pickering, Wolcott, and McHenry conspiring with Hamilton to undermine Adams's peace mission and sabotage his reelection chances. This assessment tends to excuse the secretaries for their behavior and is a bit one sided. Yet Jefferson's observations shaped his own planning when he created his cabinet a few years later. He intended to keep a close eye on his secretaries; they would serve only one boss.

After his inauguration, Jefferson adopted several strategies for managing his cabinet: he kept meetings infrequent, ensured that all correspondence and information flowed through his office, and avoided conflict by convening the cabinet only when he felt the conversation would be productive.

In response to Jefferson's November 6, 1801, circular to the secretaries that offered an outline for their future communications, Secretary of the Treasury Albert Gallatin suggested that they plan a weekly meeting to touch base and discuss any issues of import that had occurred in the previous week.[61] He worried that infrequent cabinet meetings would get pushed off or rescheduled—something that had already happened several times, according to Gallatin's letter. Jefferson subtly rebuffed this suggestion, replying that there were not enough critical issues to warrant such meetings at this point but that they could amend their practices if necessary.[62]

Jefferson believed that regular cabinet meetings transferred too much institutional authority to the secretaries and allowed them to pursue their own agendas. In 1803 and 1807, Jefferson convened more cabinet meetings to discuss the Louisiana Purchase and conflict with Great Britain. But he avoided daily or even weekly meetings, even during periods of stress.

A quick comparison of the number of cabinet meetings Washington and Jefferson held is illuminating. On November 21, 1791, Washington convened his first meeting in his private office in the President's House in Philadelphia. During the remaining five and a half years of his presidency, he held ninety-eight additional cabinet meetings, usually to discuss diplomatic or constitutional issues. From November 1791 to December 31, 1793—the period between Washington's first cabinet meeting and Jefferson's resignation—Washington called fifty-nine meetings. The final meeting took place on January 12, 1797. However, the meetings tapered off significantly toward the end of Washington's administration. In the period 1791 to 1794, Washington summoned eighty-eight meetings. In the period 1795 to 1797, he held only eleven. Jefferson, in contrast, held sixty-seven meetings during the entirety of his presidency from 1801 to 1809. Jefferson's meetings were dispersed relatively evenly throughout his administration. He gathered eight meetings in 1801, two in 1802, seven in 1803, three in 1804, five in 1805, fourteen in 1806, fifteen in 1807, and thirteen in 1808. In other words, Jefferson hosted only eight more meetings during his entire eight-year tenure as president than he had attended in two years and two months as secretary of state.[63] Both presidents relied on the cabinet for advice and support during moments of crisis, but Washington was comfortable granting the cabinet more institutional authority through frequent meetings that took place even in his absence. Jefferson, however, wanted to prevent the transfer of any authority from the president to the secretaries.

Jefferson also made sure the meetings took place under his watchful gaze. Over the course of his presidency, Washington organized ninety-nine meetings but missed or instructed the secretaries to meet separately thirty-one of those times. Of the sixty-seven meetings Jefferson organized, only two took place in Madison's state department office and Jefferson attended both meetings. Furthermore, there is no record of Jefferson ever instructing the secretaries to meet without him.[64] While he never wrote down why he held his meetings in his study, he had witnessed Washington's secretaries debating without the president. Perhaps he saw the secretaries, especially Secretary of the Treasury Alexander Hamilton, pursue their own agendas in Washington's absence and wished to prevent similar conversations from occurring outside his supervision.

Finally, Jefferson avoided conflict in his cabinet meetings. He only convened a meeting when he believed it would prove productive; otherwise he spoke with the secretaries individually. For example, in 1807, Jefferson elected to consult with his secretaries one at a time instead of convening a cabinet meeting. William Short, the former American minister to Spain, recommended that Jefferson send a three-person diplomatic team to resolve lingering issues from the Louisiana Purchase. Jefferson replied that a third minister might resolve tensions: "The proposition in your letter of May 16 . . . struck me favorably on reading it, and reflection afterwards strengthened my first impressions." He elected to discuss Short's suggestion with the secretaries, but he did not reveal who was behind the idea. Jefferson admitted that "I adopted, in the present case, the mode of separate consultation, because it was that in which I could best be able to keep down any suspicion that the idea had come from you."[65] He did not want conflict to fracture his cabinet or one-upmanship among ambitious statesmen to be a guiding factor in nation policy making, as he had witnessed in the previous two presidencies.

Jefferson replicated many of the same approaches in his relationship with Congress. He worked to maintain the appearance of respecting congressional authority and avoiding any indication that he was dictating policies to sensitive members of Congress. For example, in July 1806, Jefferson encouraged Barnabas Bidwell to assume a leadership position in the House and postpone his retirement. Jefferson assured Bidwell that he would remain his own person:

> I d[id] not mean that any gentleman relinquishing his own judgment should implicitly support all the measures of the administration; but that, where he does not disapprove of them he should not suffer them to go off in sleep, but bring them to the attention of the house and

give them a fair chance. where he disapproves, he will of course leave them to be brought forward by those who concur in the sentiment.[66]

While Jefferson wanted a spokesperson for his administration in Congress, he took pains to assure Bidwell and other members of Congress that he was not trying to dictate their actions or policies. Jefferson meant every word. While he used every tool at his disposal to convince, cajole, and persuade his spokesmen to act on his behalf, sometimes they disagreed, and he found other ways to pursue his goals.

Rather than declaring a legislative agenda, Jefferson made the most of his secretaries' good relationships with individual members of Congress and slipped them legislation proposals, drafted suggested responses, and shared his opinion behind the scenes. For example, in October 1803, Gallatin sent Senator John Breckinridge a draft for a bill that authorized the president to occupy and temporarily govern the territory of Louisiana. At another moment, in February 1805, Senator William Giles wrote to Madison asking if he could recommend any amendments to an upcoming bill, which Madison was happy to provide. Gallatin and Madison's behind-the-scenes contributions of speeches, drafts of bills, and amendments helped smooth the way for the president's agenda. Significantly, all participants understood that these communications occurred with Jefferson's blessing. After being ousted from his leadership position in the House, John Randolph complained that the president had too much authority in Congress and denounced the "back-stairs influence—of men who bring messages to this House, which, although they do not appear on the Journals, govern its decisions."[67]

Jefferson also used strategies of subtle persuasion to build coalitions and goodwill. He held weekly dinner parties with carefully cultivated guest lists, menus, and wine selections. Jefferson also designed the space to encourage close conversations, prevent eavesdropping, and maintain control over the evening's proceedings. He carefully selected the guests to build alliances and kept meticulous records of how frequently members of Congress from both parties were guests at the White House.[68]

After participating in Washington's contentious cabinet debates and witnessing Adams's disloyal cabinet antics, Jefferson carved out his own strategy, which relied on much more subtle forms of governing and persuasion. He avoided the frequent cabinet meetings that he had seen transfer institutional authority to the secretaries during Washington's presidency. Jefferson also cultivated harmonious relationships with the secretaries to prevent the backbiting and conflict he had observed in Adams's cabinet. Finally, Jefferson used the same strategies to influence congressional debates in pursuit of his agenda instead of fighting with enemies in Congress. While Jefferson's presidency still faced its fair share of challenges, cabinet disunity was not one of them; his cabinet suffered the least turnover of any administration in American history.

Conclusion

By the end of Jefferson's administration, many of the fuzzy details surrounding the presidency had been filled in. Precedent existed to guide the president's relationship to Congress, his authority over diplomatic and military issues, and his interactions with the cabinet. And yet so many governing decisions remained open to the interpretation of the early presidents' successors. For better or worse, the precedents they set established that each president has a great deal of flexibility to carve their own path. This autonomy produced a near-treasonous cabinet in Adams's presidency and an incredibly productive tool that Jefferson used to promote his agenda. These dual realities—both the potential power of the presidency and the possibility for a new outcome with each administration—are some of the most permanent legacies of the early presidents.

Notes

1. "Circular to the Heads of the Department, 6 November 1801," Founders Online, National Archives, https://founders.archives.gov/documents/Madison/02-02-02-0346, published in *The Papers of Thomas Jefferson*, Original Series, vol. 35, *1 August–30 November 1801*, ed. Barbara B. Oberg (Princeton, NJ: Princeton University Press, 2008), 576–78.

2. Thomas Jefferson to Spencer Roane, September 6, 1819, Founders Online, National Archives, http://founders.archives.gov/documents/Jefferson/98-01-02-0734, early access document.

3. Francis D. Cogliano, *Emperor of Liberty: Thomas Jefferson's Foreign Power* (New Haven, CT: Yale University Press, 2014), 144–48.

4. Claude G. Bowers, *Jefferson in Power* (Boston: Houghton Mifflin Company, 1936); Robert M. S. McDonald, *Confounding Father: Thomas Jefferson's Image in His Own Time* (Charlottesville: University of Virginia Press, 2016); G. S. Wilson, *Jefferson on Display: Attire, Etiquette, and the Art of Presentation* (Charlottesville: University of Virginia Press, 2017).

5. George Washington to the States, June 8, 1783, Founders Online, National Archives, https://founders.archives.gov/?q=George%20Washington%20to%20The%20

States%20Author%3A%22Washington%2C%20George%22%20Dates-From%3A1783-06-01&s=1111311111&r=5&sr=, early access document.

6. George Washington to Benjamin Harrison Sr., March 21, 1781," Founders Online, National Archives, http://founders.archives.gov/documents/Washington/99-01-02 -05144, early access document.

7. George Washington to the States, June 8, 1783; "May 1787," in *The Diaries of George Washington*, ed. Donald Jackson and Dorothy Twohig (Charlottesville: University Press of Virginia, 1979), 4:147–64.

8. Washington's diaries during the summer of 1787 are full of entries that mention social engagements with the other delegates at the convention. They certainly discussed the day's events and their expectations about what would come next. "June 1787," in *The Diaries of George Washington*, ed. Donald Jackson and Dorothy Twohig (Charlottesville: University Press of Virginia, 1979), 5:164–72. See also Edward Larson, *The Return of George Washington* (New York: William Morrow, 2014), 137–40; and David O. Stewart, *The Summer of 1787* (New York: Simon & Schuster Paperbacks, 2007), 30–45.

9. U.S. Constitution, art. II, § 2, America's Founding Documents, National Archives, https://www.archives.gov/founding-docs/constitution-transcript.

10. George Washington to the United States Senate, May 25, 1789, Founders Online, National Archives, https://founders.archives.gov/documents/Washington/05-02-02 -0279, published in *The Papers of George Washington*, Presidential Series, vol. 2, *1 April 1789–15 June 1789*, ed. Dorothy Twohig (Charlottesville: University Press of Virginia, 1987), 391–92; George Washington to United States Senate, August 21, 1789, Founders Online, National Archives, https://founders.archives.gov/documents/Washington /05-03-02-0299, published in *The Papers of George Washington*, Presidential Series, vol. 3, *15 June 1789–5 September 1789*, ed. Dorothy Twohig (Charlottesville: University of Virginia Press, 1980), 515. See also Charlene Bangs Bickford, "'Public Attention Is Very Much Fixed on the Proceedings of the New Congress': The First Federal Congress Organizes Itself," in *Inventing Congress: Origins and Establishment of the First Federal Congress*, ed. Kenneth R. Bowling and Donald R. Kennon (Athens: Ohio University Press, 1999), 153–54.

11. Kenneth R. Bowling and Helen E. Veit, eds., *The Diary of William Maclay* (Baltimore, MD: Johns Hopkins University Press, 1988), 128.

12. Bowling and Veit, *The Diary of William Maclay*, 128.

13. For examples of the practices of councils of war, see "Council of War, 8 October 1775," in *The Papers of George Washington*, Revolutionary War Series, vol. 2, *September–December 1775*, ed. Philander D. Chase (Charlottesville: University Press of Virginia, 1987), 123–28; "Council of War, 18 October 1775," in *The Papers of George Washington*, Revolutionary War Series, 2:183–84; "Council of War, 2 November 1775," in *The Papers of George Washington*, Revolutionary War Series, 2:279–84; "Council of War, 29 August 1776," in *The Papers of George Washington*, Revolutionary War Series, vol. 6, *1 July 1790–30 November 1790*, ed. Mark A. Mastromarino (Charlottesville: University Press of Virginia, 1996), 153–55; Circular to the General Officers of the Continental Army, December 3, 1777, in *The Papers of George Washington*, Revolutionary War Series, vol.

12, *October–December 1777*, ed. Frank E. Grizzard Jr. and David R. Hoth (Charlottesville: University Press of Virginia, 2002), 506.

14. Henry Knox to George Washington, January 20, 1790, in *The Papers of George Washington*, Presidential Series, vol. 5, *January–June 1790*, ed. Dorothy Twohig, Mark A. Mastromarino, and Jack D. Warren (Charlottesville: University Press of Virginia, 1996), 24–25.

15. Arthur Lefkowitz, *George Washington's Indispensable Men* (New York: Stackpole Books, 2003), 74–75; David Humphreys to Alexander Scammell, June 28, 1781, Founders Online, National Archives, http://founders.archives.gov/documents/Washington /99-01-02-06209, early access document; John Ferling, *The Ascent of George Washington: The Hidden Political Genius of an American Icon* (New York: Bloomsbury Press, 2009), 156, 226.

16. "June 15, 1778," *New-York Journal*, quoted in Louise V. North, Landa M. Freeman, and Janet M. Wedge, [eds.,] *In the Words of Women: The Revolutionary War and the Birth of the Nation, 1765–1799* (Lanham, MD: Lexington Books, 2011), 121; Lefkowitz, *George Washington's Indispensable Men*, 198, 309; Robert Middlekauff, *Washington's Revolution: The Making of America's First Leader* (New York: Alfred A. Knopf, 2015), 178, 218.

17. George Washington to Thomas Jefferson, July 31, 1793, in *The Papers of George Washington*, Presidential Series, vol. 13, *June–August 1793*, ed. Christine S. Patrick (Charlottesville: University Press of Virginia, 2007), 309–10.

18. "Notes of Cabinet Meetings on Edmond Charles Genet and the President's Address to Congress, [18 November 1793]," in *The Papers of Thomas Jefferson*, Original Series, vol. 27, *1 September–31 December 1793*, ed. John Catanzariti (Princeton, NJ: Princeton University Press, 1997), 399–401.

19. "Cabinet Meeting. Opinion on a Proclamation of Neutrality and on Receiving the French Minister, [19 April 1793]," in *The Papers of Alexander Hamilton*, vol. 14, *February 1793–June 1793*, ed. Harold C. Syrett (New York: Columbia University Press, 1969), 328–29; "Notes of a Cabinet Meeting on Edmond Charles Genet, 23 July 1793," in *The Papers of Thomas Jefferson*, Original Series, vol. 26, *11 May–31 August 1793*, ed. John Catanzariti (Princeton, NJ: Princeton University Press, 1995), 553–56; "Cabinet Opinion on the Rules of Neutrality, 3 August 1793," in *The Papers of George Washington*, Presidential Series, 13:325–27.

20. Lindsay M. Chervinsky, *The Cabinet: George Washington and the Creation of an American Institution* (Cambridge, MA: Harvard University Press, 2020).

21. "Conference Concerning the Insurrection in Western Pennsylvania," [August 2, 1794,] in *The Papers of Alexander Hamilton*, vol. 17, *August 1794–December 1794*, ed. Harold C. Syrett (New York: Columbia University Press, 1972), 9–14; "Proclamation, 7 August 1794," in *The Papers of George Washington*, Presidential Series, vol. 16, *1 May–30 September 1794*, ed. David R. Hoth and Carol S. Ebel (Charlottesville: University Press of Virginia, 2011), 531–37; Edmund Randolph to James Ross, Jasper Yeates, and William Bradford, August 7, 1794, in *American State Papers: Documents, Legislative and Executive, of the Congress of the United States, from the First Session of the First to the Second Session of the Tenth, Inclusive*, ed. Walter Lowrie and Walter S. Franklin (Washington,

DC: Gales and Seaton, 1834), 87; Thomas Mifflin to George Washington, August 12, 1794, in *The Papers of George Washington*, Presidential Series, 16:553–59; Alexander Hamilton to George Washington, August 15, 1794, in *The Papers of Alexander Hamilton*, 17:96–97.

22. "Treaty of Amity, Commerce and Navigation," in *United States Statutes at Large* (Washington, DC: Little, Brown and Company, 1845), 116–31; Jerald A. Combs, *The Jay Treaty: Political Battleground of the Founding Fathers* (Berkeley: University of California Press, 1970), 150–57; Richard Buel Jr., *Securing the Revolution: Ideology in American Politics, 1789–1815* (Ithaca, NY: Cornell University Press, 1972), 56–68.

23. *Annals of Congress*, Senate, 4th Congress, Special Session, 863–64.

24. *Annals of Congress*, 4th Cong., 1st Sess., 400–401; *Annals of Congress*, 4th Cong., 1st Sess., 759.

25. "Introductory Note: To George Washington," [March 7, 1796,] in *The Papers of Alexander Hamilton*, vol. 20, *January 1796–March 1797*, ed. Harold C. Syrett (New York: Columbia University Press, 1974), 64–68; Alexander Hamilton to George Washington, March 7, 1796, in *The Papers of Alexander Hamilton*, 20:68–69.

26. George Washington to the United States House of Representatives, March 30, 1796, in *The Papers of George Washington*, Presidential Series, vol. 19, *1 October 1795–31 March 1796*, ed. David R. Hoth (Charlottesville: University Press of Virginia, 2016), 635–39.

27. Washington to the United States House of Representatives, March 30, 1796.

28. Nancy Isenberg and Andrew Burstein, *The Problem of Democracy: The Presidents Adams Confront the Cult of Personality* (New York: Viking Press, 2019).

29. John Adams to Elbridge Gerry, February 13, 1797, Founders Online, National Archives, http://founders.archives.gov/documents/Adams/99-02-02-1855, early access document.

30. For annual address, see John Adams to United States Congress, December 3, 1799, Founders Online, National Archives, http://founders.archives.gov/documents/Adams/99-02-02-4063, early access document; Oliver Wolcott Jr. to John Adams, November 18, 1799, Founders Online, National Archives, https://founders.archives.gov/documents/Adams/99-02-02-4050, early access document; Timothy Pickering to John Adams, November 20, 1799, Founders Online, National Archives, https://founders.archives.gov/documents/Adams/99-02-02-3991, early access document. For questions as agenda items, see John Adams to Timothy Pickering, March 14, 1797, Founders Online, National Archives, http://founders.archives.gov/documents/Adams/99-02-02-1893, early access document. For meetings and follow-up afterward, see Oliver Wolcott Jr. to John Adams, April 21, 1797, Founders Online, National Archives, http://founders.archives.gov/documents/Adams/99-02-02-1944, early access document; James McHenry to John Adams, April 29, 1797, Founders Online, National Archives, http://founders.archives.gov/documents/Adams/99-02-02-1950, early access document; Timothy Pickering to John Adams, May 1, 1797, Founders Online, National Archives, http://founders.archives.gov/documents/Adams/99-02-02-1954, early access document.

31. Paris Journal, entry for October 18–19, 1797, The Papers of John Marshall Digital Edition, University of Virginia Press, Rotunda, http://rotunda.upress.virginia.edu/founders/JNML-01-03-02-0107-0008. Published in *The Papers of John Marshall*, vol. 3,

Correspondence and Papers, January 1796–December 1798, ed. William C. Stinchcombe, Charles T. Cullen, and Leslie Tobias (Chapel Hill: University of North Carolina Press, 1979).

32. Carol Berkin, *A Sovereign People: The Crises of the 1790s and the Birth of American Nationalism* (New York: Basic Books, 2017), 172; Stanley Elkins and Eric M. McKitrick, *Age of Federalism: The Early American Republic, 1788–1800* (New York: Oxford University Press, 1993), 554–78; Gordon S. Wood, *Empire of Liberty: A History of the Early Republic, 1789–1815* (New York: Oxford University Press, 2009), 239–75.

33. Paris Journal, entry for October 20, 1797, The Papers of John Marshall Digital Edition, http://rotunda.upress.virginia.edu/founders/JNML-01-03-02-0107-0009, published in Stinchcombe, Cullen, and Tobias, *The Papers of John Marshall*, vol. 3; Berkin, *A Sovereign People*, 172–74; Paris Journal, entry for October 22, 1797, The Papers of John Marshall Digital Edition, http://rotunda.upress.virginia.edu/founders/JNML-01-03-02-0107-0011.

34. Paris Journal, entry for February 4, 1798, *The Papers of John Marshall Digital Edition*, http://rotunda.upress.virginia.edu/founders/JNML-01-03-02-0107-0045, published in Stinchcombe, Cullen, and Tobias, *The Papers of John Marshall*, vol. 3.

35. Elkins and McKitrick, *Age of Federalism*, 554–78, James Grant, *John Adams: Party of One* (New York: Farrar, Straus and Giroux, 2005), 385–97; Wood, *Empire of Liberty*, 239–75.

36. *Annals of Congress*, 5th Congress, 2nd Session, House of Representatives, April 3, 1798, 1374–75; Page Smith, *John Adams: Volume II, 1784–1826* (Garden City, NY: Doubleday & Company, 1962), 953–56; Berkin, *A Sovereign People*, 186–90.

37. Smith, *John Adams*, 995–96.

38. Timothy Pickering to John Adams, January 18, 1799, Founders Online, National Archives, http://founders.archives.gov/documents/Adams/99-02-02-3303, early access document; Elkins and McKitrick, *Age of Federalism*, 618–62; Grant, *John Adams*, 396–402; Wood, *Empire of Liberty*, 239–75.

39. John Adams to United States Senate, February 10, 1799, Founders Online, National Archives, http://founders.archives.gov/documents/Adams/99-02-02-3332, early access document.

40. Benjamin Stoddert to John Adams, August 29, 1799, Founders Online, National Archives, http://founders.archives.gov/documents/Adams/99-02-02-3928, early access document.

41. Timothy Pickering to John Adams, September 24, 1799, Founders Online, National Archives, http://founders.archives.gov/documents/Adams/99-02-02-4001, early access document.

42. John Adams to Abigail Smith Adams, October 12, 1799, Founders Online, National Archives, http://founders.archives.gov/documents/Adams/99-03-02-0471, early access document.

43. Alexander Hamilton to George Washington, October 21, 1799, in *The Papers of Alexander Hamilton*, vol. 23, *April 1799–October 1799*, ed. Harold C. Syrett (New York: Columbia University Press, 1976), 544–47, esp. 547n2.

44. Hamilton to Washington, October 21, 1799.

45. Hamilton to Washington, October 21, 1799.

46. John Adams to Timothy Pickering, October 16, 1799, Founders Online, National Archives, http://founders.archives.gov/documents/Adams/99-02-02-4014, early access document; John Adams, *Correspondence of the Late President Adams, Originally Published in the Boston Patriot, in a Series of Letters* (Boston: Published by Everett and Munroe, 1809), 29–30, first cited in Alexander Hamilton to George Washington, October 21, 1799, in *The Papers of Alexander Hamilton*, vol. 23, 544–47.

47. Alexander DeConde, *The Quasi-War* (New York: Charles Scribner's Sons, 1966), 252–55.

48. Elkins and McKitrick, *Age of Federalism*, 662–90; Wood, *Empire of Liberty*, 239–75.

49. Anonymous to John Adams, March 11, 1800, Founders Online, National Archives, http://founders.archives.gov/documents/Adams/99-02-02-4208, early access document.

50. "Enclosure: James McHenry to John Adams, 31 May 1800," in *The Papers of Alexander Hamilton*, vol. 24, *November 1799–June 1800*, ed. Harold C. Syrett (New York: Columbia University Press, 1976), 552–65.

51. "Enclosure: James McHenry to John Adams, 31 May 1800."

52. "Enclosure: James McHenry to John Adams, 31 May 1800"; Elkins and McKitrick, *Age of Federalism*, 736–37; Grant, *John Adams*, 424; Wood, *Empire of Liberty*, 272–75.

53. James McHenry to John Adams, May 31, 1800, Founders Online, National Archives, http://founders.archives.gov/documents/Adams/99-02-02-4387, early access document.

54. Timothy Pickering to John Adams, May 12, 1800, Founders Online, National Archives, http://founders.archives.gov/documents/Adams/99-02-02-4334.

55. Pickering to Adams, May 12, 1800.

56. T. Pickering to James McHenry, February 13, 1811, in Bernard Christian Steiner, *The Life and Correspondence of James McHenry: Secretary of War under Washington and Adams* (Cleveland, OH: Burrows Brothers Company, 1907), 568.

57. John Adams to Elbridge Gerry, May 3, 1797, Founders Online, National Archives, http://founders.archives.gov/documents/Adams/99-02-02-1958, early access document; Elkins and McKitrick, *Age of Federalism*, 736–37; Grant, *John Adams*, 424; Wood, *Empire of Liberty*, 272–75.

58. John Adams to United States Senate, February 25, 1799, Founders Online, National Archives, http://founders.archives.gov/documents/Adams/99-02-02-3355, early access document; Smith, *John Adams*, 1000–1003; Elkins and McKitrick, *Age of Federalism*, 632–62; Grant, *John Adams*, 396–402; Wood, *Empire of Liberty*, 239–75.

59. Thomas Jefferson to Walter Jones, March 5, 1810, in *The Papers of Thomas Jefferson*, Retirement Series, vol. 2, *16 November 1809 to 11 August 1810*, ed. J. Jefferson Looney (Princeton, NJ: Princeton University Press, 2005), 272–74.

60. Circular Letter from Thomas Jefferson, November 6, 1801, in *The Papers of James Madison, Secretary of State Series*, vol. 2, *1 August 1801–28 February 1802*, ed. Mary A. Hackett, J. C. A. Stagg, Jeanne Kerr Cross, and Susan Holbrook Perdue (Charlottesville: University Press of Virginia, 1993), 227–29; Dumas Malone, *Jefferson the President, First*

Term, 1801–1805 (Boston: Little, Brown and Company, 1970), 50–66; Noble E. Cunningham Jr., *The Process of Government under Jefferson* (Princeton, NJ: Princeton University Press, 1978), 60–71; Lindsay M. Chervinsky, "'Having been a member of the first administration under Genl. Washington': Thomas Jefferson, George Washington, and the Development of the President's Cabinet," *Journal of the Early Republic* (Winter 2020).

61. Albert Gallatin to Thomas Jefferson, November 9, 1801, *The Papers of Thomas Jefferson*, Original Series, 35:586–88.

62. Thomas Jefferson to Albert Gallatin, November 10, 1801, in *The Papers of Thomas Jefferson*, Original Series, 35:595–96.

63. George Washington to Thomas Jefferson, November 25, 1791, in *The Papers of George Washington*, Presidential Series, vol. 9, *23 September 1791–29 February 1792*, ed. Mark A. Mastromarino (Charlottesville: University Press of Virginia, 2000), 231–32; Chervinsky, "*The Historical Presidency*: George Washington and the First Presidential Cabinet," *Presidential Studies Quarterly* 48, no. 1 (2018): 139–52; Chervinsky, *The Cabinet*.

64. Washington to Jefferson, November 25, 1791; Chervinsky, "*The Historical Presidency*," 139–52; Chervinsky, *The Cabinet*.

65. Thomas Jefferson to William Short, June 12, 1807, Founders Online, National Archives, https://founders.archives.gov/documents/Jefferson/99-01-02-5747, early access document.

66. Thomas Jefferson to Barnabas Bidwell, July 5, 1806, Founders Online, National Archives, https://founders.archives.gov/documents/Jefferson/99-01-02-3958, early access document.

67. *Annals of Congress*, 9 Cong., 1 Sess., March 5, 1806, 561; "To James Madison from William B. Giles (Abstract), February 28, 1805, in *The Papers of James Madison, Secretary of State Series*, 9:77.

68. Scholars have written extensively on Jefferson's dinner parties. See Bowers, *Jefferson in Power*; Merry Ellen Scofield, "The Fatigues of His Table: The Politics of Presidential Dining during the Jefferson Administration," *Journal of the Early Republic* 26, no. 3 (2006): 449–69; Charles T. Cullen, "Jefferson's White House Dinner Guests," *White House History* 17 (Winter 2006): 30–36; McDonald, *Confounding Father*; and Wilson, *Jefferson on Display*.

10

Mirror for Presidents

George Washington and the Law of Nations

DANIEL J. HULSEBOSCH

[The French Minister] observed that the Government of this Country
had been of so fluctuating a nature no dependence could be placed on its
proceedings; which caused foreign Nations to be cautious of entering into
Treaties &ca. with the United States—But under the present Government
there is a head to look up to—and power being put into the hands of its
Officers stability will be derived from its doings.

George Washington, diary entry, October 9, 1789[1]

Introduction: The Missing Books

There are a lot of stories about George Washington's self-control, disci-
plined character, and practiced dignity. Some are true. Parson Weems gave
us perhaps the most famous, and fabulous, tale: a young George cut down
a prized cherry tree, owned up to the deed, and was declared a "hero" for
confessing. He could not tell a lie.[2] But that does not mean that Washington never committed what one of his few genuine peers, the very different
Benjamin Franklin, would have called errata.

One erratum was for a long time an open secret at the venerable New
York Society Library. On October 5, 1789, when New York City was still
the capital city, Washington visited the private lending library, which at the
time was housed inside Federal Hall alongside the new government, and
borrowed two books. They were due four weeks later. There is no record
that the volumes were ever returned. They were never again checked out,
and modern librarians could not find them in the stacks. Was Washington

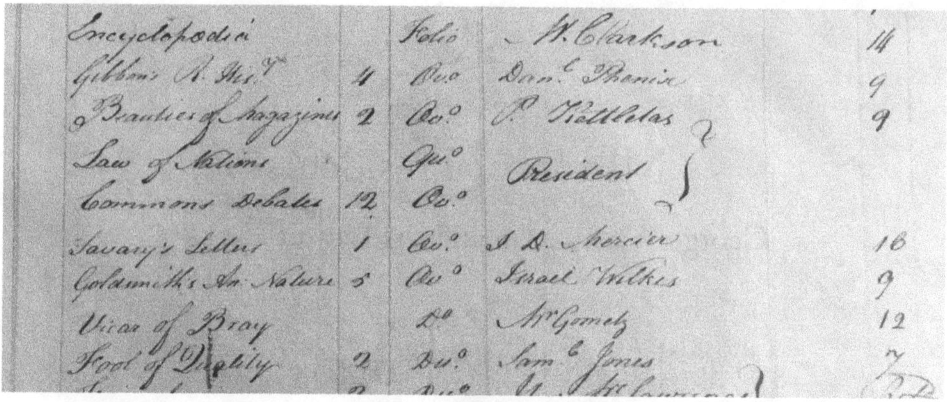

Encyclopaedia		Folio	W. Clarkson	14
Gibbon's R. His.y	4	Oc.o	Dan.l Phoenix	9
9 Beauties of Magazines	2	Oc.o	P. Ketteltas	9
Law of Nations		Qu.o	President	
Commons Debates	12	Oc.o		
Savary's Letters	1	Oc.o	J. A. Mercier	16
Goldsmith's An. Nature	5	Oc.o	Israel Wilkes	9
Vicar of Bray		D.o	McGomely	12
Fool of Quality	2	Du.o	Sam.l Jones	7

Figure 10.1. The New York Society Library Charging Ledger. The October 5, 1789, entry, lines four and five from the top, record that President Washington borrowed two books with no return date in the far right column. First Charging Ledger, the New York Library Society.

a book thief? Admitting the possibility, the Washington Library at Mount Vernon riffled through the first president's personal collection to try to locate the missing volumes. Not finding them, it purchased one of the volumes on the rare book market, delivering it to the New York Society Library in a ceremony of reconciliation. Two centuries of overdue fines were waived.[3]

This tale has a deeper point. It is not that Washington was obviously an intellectual and a closet thief, or the reverse. Instead, the important fact is what the first president sought to read six months into his first term. Where did he turn for guidance while transforming spare constitutional text into an office of power? The first book, and the one that Mount Vernon replaced, was Emer de Vattel's legal treatise on *The Law of Nations*, first published in French in 1758 and translated into English a year later.[4] The New York Society Library held an early London edition of the Swiss jurist's treatise, which was hailed in the Anglo-American world as a smart and elegant introduction to the laws of war and peaceful interaction between nations. No book on the law of nations circulated more widely in early America than Vattel's, and it was consistently invoked as authority, not just in the courts but also in Congress and in Washington's cabinet.[5] This was not Washington's first exposure to Vattel's treatise. On the eve of the Revolution, he had ordered a copy from a London bookseller for his stepson's education. During the war, aides on his general staff had invoked the international laws of war and its treatise literature when grappling with issues concerning, for example, the treatment of prisoners of war and when it was permissible to retaliate for British violations of American rights under the law of nations.[6] As Secretary of the Treasury Alexander Hamilton, Washington's former aide-de-camp, soon told him, Vattel was "perhaps the most accurate and approved of the writers on the laws of Nations."[7] Secretary of State Thomas Jefferson differed with Hamilton about much, but on Vattel's authority he agreed entirely.[8] Six months into his presidency, Washington wanted to read the book himself.

The second book that Washington borrowed was a volume of debates in the House of Commons during the spring and summer of 1779.[9] That included Parliament's investigation of Sir William Howe, the disgraced commander in chief of the British army in America. The House of Commons called several witnesses to explain how the empire's vaunted military, which a decade earlier had swept France from North America, could not quash a colonial rebellion, especially in the three years before it grew into a global war. Although the Commons eventually found Howe not culpable, the star of the proceedings was an antagonist in absentia: the commander in chief of the revolutionary army. "I am sorry to say," reported General Charles Grey (later Earl Grey), "that I think there can be no hopes of conquering America, or of being a match for General Washington's force of arms, with the present force we have there."[10] The debates traced Parliament's understanding of the colonial rebellion that Washington helped turn into an international war at the moment when the British public began to realize that the war might be unwinnable.

Washington was not just a man of action. He took reading and learning seriously even though he had never attended college, which was a source of personal embarrassment.[11] But like many self-taught and ambitious Americans, he knew what he lacked and where to get it, and throughout his life he turned to advice and etiquette books to help him make his way. Reading is usually solitary. Etiquette books, however, promote an unusually social form of reading: the reader is listening for advice from a didactic author and plans to use that advice when closing the book and returning to society. Throughout his life, Washington turned to such books as guides for conversing and acting in the company of others. That was the express purpose of the books he withdrew from the New York Society Library. Vattel's imagined reader, for example, was a national ruler; "prince" and "king" are how the author most often refers to the protagonists in his drama of governance. The president leaned on Vattel and other self-help books to learn how to govern—not just how to govern other people, but, more important, how to govern *with* other people, including advisors at home and other leaders abroad. The law of nations provided stage directions that showed an actor how to behave and what best to do. It also offered chunks of script to borrow. It did not, however, command a particular narrative. That was left to nations themselves. During his two-term presidency, Washington strove to thread the needle between adhering to the best practices of the law of nations and guiding the United States to become a new kind of nation, one that was deeply engaged in the Atlantic world of commerce and culture yet was also neutral and not beholden to any other nation. Here the personal became the political. Engaged detachment was the pose he had long assumed in Virginian society, and it was now how he positioned the presidency within the new three-branch, two-level federal government. In early October 1789, he sought advice.

One book he took from the library taught how to act like a nation. The other contained a morality tale about leadership, celebrating his own but also warning that leaders can disgrace themselves and forfeit loyalty. How Washington read these books is unknown. It requires little speculation, however, to understand why he wished to do so in October 1789. The first session of Congress had ended the previous week.[12] Drafting the customs statutes had devoured much of the summer. Vice President John Adams's curious fixation on titles of honor for the president also absorbed time. But the establishment of the three departments and their secretaries—State, War, and Treasury—incited the most constitutionally consequential debate of the first session. The Constitution specified that the president would appoint officers with the Senate's advice and consent. But it did not specify how (or even if) such officers would be removed, other than through impeachment by Congress. Could the president remove officers alone? Did he need to obtain the Senate's consent, as with the initial appointment? Or was impeachment the only way to replace officers? In the end, no single answer to the constitutional problem of removal gained the assent of a majority of federal legislators. The issue revealed that the boundaries of the president's office—and perhaps all federal power—could not be measured by text alone.[13] Inference would be necessary for interpretation, along with other kinds of extratextual analysis.

The same was true of the judiciary. Article III was even shorter than Article II. The last significant statute Congress passed was the Judiciary Act. There could be no revenue collection, almost everyone thought, without the backstop of an independent federal judiciary. The courts had jurisdiction, however, that reached beyond revenue cases, and the extent of that jurisdiction was a question that produced anxiety among those who feared the intrusion of federal power into the states. Washington spent the following two weeks nominating federal judges, district attorneys, and other court officers and then sent out their commissions. They and the treasury officials with whom they would work closely would personify the federal government on the ground. The last commissions were addressed to the justices of the Supreme Court. On October 5, the same day that he visited the library, the president sent John Jay his commission as chief justice.[14] Washington praised Jay for possessing "the talents, *knowledge and integrity* which are so necessary to be exercised at the head of that department which must be considered as the Key-Stone of our political fabric."[15] Courts would play a special role in the United States, he hoped, binding the nation in loyalty and obedience. But the underlying conception of the judicial office was common in the Atlantic World: Washington paraphrased Vattel's advice that the sovereign should appoint "judges, distinguished by their *integrity and knowledge.*"[16]

Two days later, the president received an intelligence briefing from Jay, who remained the secretary of foreign affairs, a position he had held for five years and retained until Jefferson took his oath as secretary of state six months later. They discussed Britain's effort to discover whether the new government was willing and able to uphold American obligations under the Treaty of Peace (1783). The treaty had recommended that the states compensate British loyalists for confiscated property, required them to remove all legal impediments blocking the repayment of debts owed to British creditors, and prohibited them from targeting any person after the war for behavior during it.[17] No one was more expert on these issues than Jay. Three years earlier he had prepared a long, scorching report for Congress documenting how every state had violated one or more of the treaty's provisions.[18] Breaches of international obligations then formed the premise of his influential *Address to the People of the State of New-York* (1788), a contribution to the ratification debate that condensed the major themes of *The Federalist.* As colonists, Jay argued, Americans had had little experience with foreign affairs, so it was understandable that the revolutionary legislatures neglected the law of nations and treaty obligations. "War, and peace, alliances, and treaties, and commerce, and navigation," he observed, "were conducted and regulated without our advice or controul," so the colonists had never realized "how exceedingly important they often were to the advancement and protection of our prosperity."[19] It was time, however, to learn how to act like a nation.

That, from the perspective of Federalists like Washington and Jay, was the main goal of constitutional reform. Vertically, the new Constitution divided power between the states and the federal government. Although the precise lines separating federal from state authority became famously unclear, the main division was crystalline from the outset: the federal government had a monopoly over foreign affairs. Horizontally, the drafters apportioned power across the three branches to buffer foreign relations from legislative decision making. The framers' declared goal was to remove diplomacy from the purview of populist legislatures and reintegrate the United States into the Atlantic world of commerce and culture. The burden of nationhood therefore fell heavily on Washington's executive branch and Jay's judiciary.[20] The two branches worked closely together during the 1790s to comply with the law of nations and engage the world commercially, a collaboration personified by John Jay's multiple roles as acting foreign secretary, chief justice, and diplomat.

Washington relied on Jay for legal advice throughout his presidency, a relationship that might explain why he borrowed Vattel the same day that he sent Jay his Supreme Court commission. The largest diplomatic problem facing the nation, they agreed, was Britain. The problem was *still* Britain. It had been the focus of Washington's ambitions for himself, his province, and now his nation, for decades.[21] That fixation did not end with victory in war. When Washington resigned his post as commander in chief of the army in 1783, he had warned that the United States was already at risk of losing the peace. In a circular to the state governments that was, effectively, his first farewell address, he observed that although the nation was blessed with peace, vast lands, and the wealth of Enlightenment learning to draw upon when writing constitutions, some Americans behaved in a way that revealed an incapacity act to like a nation. "This is the time of their political probation," he cautioned the state legislatures, "when the eyes of the whole World are turned upon them." It was a moment to discipline themselves and act with dignity, or to "ruin their National Character for ever" and become "the sport of European politics." So many questions remained unanswered, not least "whether the Revolution must ultimately be considered as a blessing or a curse: a blessing or a curse, not to the present Age alone, for with our fate will the destiny of unborn Millions be involved."[22] He proceeded to limn the outlines of his second, more famous Farewell Address of 1796: the United States had to behave respectably, under the law of nations, which would then empower it to remain neutral among the old political antagonisms of Europe. Americans could be in the Atlantic world and yet apart from it. If the United States could not achieve both integration and distance, its experiment in republican government would fail. In focusing on national character and the fear that hard-won gains could easily be lost, it was as if Washington were generalizing his personal ethic, matching unflappable integrity with ferocious ambition.[23] Life among nations was also a constant test of character.

After receiving Jay's latest update on British skepticism about the United States, Washington broached a new idea. He wanted to send an informal diplomatic agent to London to gauge whether the government was willing to negotiate directly about the grievances between the two nations. For years, the British ministry had scoffed at American invitations to settle old issues and negotiate a new commercial treaty.[24] Had the new Constitution changed their minds?

At that moment, Washington made the first diplomatic move in a long process that would culminate in the Jay Treaty of 1794, negotiated by the same John Jay and finally proclaimed in 1796, the last year of Washington's second term. It began as the president's idea. Notably, he issued the commission to his informal agent without any advice or consent of the Senate. He did not scour the text of Article II for clauses that might be interpreted in a way to permit him unilaterally to pursue new diplomatic relations with a foreign nation. Neither did the few advisors he consulted. Jay thought the mission was a good idea. So did Alexander Hamilton, who recommended Gouverneur Morris as the emissary because he was already in Europe on private business. The third advisor, James Madison, did suggest waiting until Jefferson returned from his post in Paris, where, closer to London, he might have good information about Britain's intentions.[25] His was not, however, a constitutional objection but instead a prudential scruple that probably reflected his concern about the only other advisors Washington consulted—Hamilton and Jay—who favored improved relations with Britain and opposed Madison's more combative strategy of commercial sanctions.[26] But all three shared the premise that the president had the power—even the prerogative—to conduct diplomacy, including through emissaries the Senate did not know of and had not approved, and without any financial appropriation from Congress. They implicitly distinguished this mission from formal treaty negotiations, for which Washington always sought prior consent, if not advice, from the Senate before commissioning treaty negotiators.[27] Likewise Washington usually sought an appropriation from Congress to fund those negotiations in advance.[28] With the Morris mission, the executive sought reimbursement after it was over.[29] The first president explored the boundaries of his own discretion with the help of

THE
LAW OF NATIONS;
OR
PRINCIPLES
OF THE
LAW OF NATURE:

APPLIED TO THE CONDUCT AND AFFAIRS

OF

NATIONS AND SOVEREIGNS.

By M. DE VATTEL.

A WORK tending to Diſplay the TRUE INTEREST of POWERS.

Nihil eſt enim illi principi Deo, qui omnem hunc mundum regit, quod quidem in terris fiat,
acceptius, quam concilia cœtuſque hominum jure ſociati, quæ civitates appellantur.

CICER. *Somn. Scipion.*

TRANSLATED from the FRENCH.

VOL. I.

LONDON:
Printed for J. NEWBERY, J. RICHARDSON, S. CROWDER, T. CASLON,
T. LONGMAN, B. LAW, J. FULLER, J. COOTE, and G. KEARSLY.
MDCCLX.

Figure 10.2. Title page of Vattel, *Law of Nations* (London, 1759/1760). Rare Book Room, the
New York Society Library.

three advisors and selected an emissary who had been a strong advocate of an independent executive at the Constitutional Convention.[30]

Six months after his inauguration, Washington was making his office the central institution by which the federal government would fulfill what he saw as the purpose of the Constitution: integrating the revolutionary United States into the so-called civilized world.[31] Everyone knew that the separate executive branch was a crucial reform in the new framework of government, but no one had a clear sense of exactly how it would operate. Even the drafters were uncertain. The final text of Article II came only in the last few weeks at the convention, and it provided little more than an outline.[32] Washington grasped the office's potential immediately. Once again, he was the commander in chief. He was also more; he was at the head of a new government and in an office with few direct precedents. He assumed that as head of state, he had the responsibility not just to nominate and receive ambassadors and the like but also to initiate and guide foreign policy.[33] As Washington imagined and performed the office, executive power entailed a lot of discretion. That discretion was bounded by the Constitution; he never claimed power to exceed it. But where was the limit? How did this old surveyor map the boundaries of his own discretion? Groping for wisdom and advice, he reached for Vattel.

The Law of Nations as a Mirror for Princes—and Presidents

Vattel's *Law of Nations* is remembered as an influential introduction to what is now called international law. It was that, but it was also much more. Early modern law-of-nations treatises were moralistic advice manuals written for statesmen and their advisors and were intended to be put to work. They descended from a Renaissance advice-book genre known as "mirror for princes." As Quentin Skinner explained, those books held up "a 'mirror' to princes, presenting them with an ideal image and asking them to seek their reflection in its depth."[34] These princely advice books influenced jurists in the law-of-nations tradition as they sought to abstract the nation from its ruler, providing him advice in the form of "reasons of state." One goal was to restrain the prince for the benefit of the state. What jurists saw in the older advice books was "a discourse less of prudence and expedience than of law and obligation."[35] They tried to persuade the prince that it was not only, or primarily, his honor and gain that was at stake in his decisions; the honor and the flourishing of the nation and its people were paramount.

In his treatise, Vattel detailed the many rights and duties of a sovereign, whom the author repeatedly referred to as "the prince." The Swiss jurist had republican sympathies, and he based his principles of government and international relations on a theory of popular sovereignty. But that sovereignty was embodied in the person of a ruler. In Vattel's version of the social contract, each person transferred "the natural right of conducting himself in every thing as he pleased according to the dictates of his own understanding" to a sovereign—a prince, a king, or possibly a collective body. In return, the sovereign was duty bound to govern in the interest of the people. Above all, the prince was supposed to provide protection and avoid war.[36] "The end or object of civil society," Vattel argued,

> is to procure for the citizens whatever they stand in need of, for the necessities, the conveniences, the accommodation of life, and, in general, whatever constitutes happiness,—with the peaceful possession of property, a method of obtaining justice with security, and, finally a mutual defence against all external violence.[37]

The sovereign owed the people the protection of life, liberty, and property.

More specifically, Vattel divided the rules or "maxims" of sovereign duties into four categories. Part I covered "Of Nations Considered in Themselves," or a nation's domestic constitution and policies. Part II analyzed "Of a Nation Considered in Her Relation to Other States," or international relations. Part III was "On War," or when peaceful relations with other nations failed. Part IV, "Of the Restoration of Peace; and of Embassies," covered treaties and the various categories of diplomatic emissaries. The first three parts were roughly the same length, while Part IV was about half the length of the others. Strikingly, the laws of war, which are often treated in modern scholarship as the centerpiece of the law of nations, accounted for less than a third of Vattel's treatise. The maxims for good government analyzed in Part I ("Of Nations Considered in Themselves") accounted for about the same. Consequently, Vattel's book provided as much advice about the best policies within a nation as it did about peaceful international relations. The two were inextricable: good government at home would promote productive international relations, while good diplomacy furthered the interests of each nation.[38] Washington did not need to learn all of these ideas from Vattel. But what he read confirmed his Federalist view of purpose of the new national government.

In Book II, for example, Vattel emphasized the twin principles of territorial sovereignty and self-preservation, on the one hand, and the duty to engage in commerce with other nations, on the other.[39] That was a major premise of the treatise: interstate connections were inescapable and good, although determining how best to forge them was an ongoing project. Vattel believed that if each sovereign ruler strove to foster the flourishing of their own people, all nations would benefit from the plural experiments and together they would enjoy progress. This notion of "virtuous competition" was displacing the old ideal of a united "great republic of nations" while avoiding the pessimistic fear of anarchy among nations.[40]

The early modern law of nations, therefore, embraced more than the law between states, or what now is called international law. It also included transnational law. This was a legacy of the oldest connotation of the law of nations: the *jus gentium*, or the law that the Romans claimed was, or should be, common to all peoples. The concept is echoed in modern notions of *jus cogens*, "best practices," and other aspects of modern transnational law. Law of nations treatises therefore retained a connection to Renaissance instructional guides for princes and kings, the most famous (and unrepresentative) of which was Niccolò Machiavelli's *The Prince* (1532). Indeed, Vattel criticized Machiavelli for celebrating Caesar Borgia's "mischievous" policies.[41] Less famous examples in the genre functioned like etiquette and instructional manuals that tried to persuade the ruler how to govern at home for the good of himself and his subjects. They were guides for sovereigns who were learning what might be expected of them and what they could expect from other rulers. Accordingly, Vattel instructed the sovereign to promote commerce, immigration, and education. It was the sovereign's duty to help his subjects reach their potential as individuals and, especially, together as a nation. He also argued that there were preferred means to obtain these ends: liberal trade and immigration policies, for example, and publicly supported infrastructure to facilitate the transportation of people and goods.

Some of these policy principles had been goals of the American Revolution. Washington and his advisors propounded them repeatedly during his presidency. Vattel's treatise reinforced those commitments. Education, for example, figured large in Washington's plans for the nation. He called on Congress to establish "a National University" in the new capital for "education of our Youth in the Science of *Government*," and to harmonize "our customs, measures, and laws; in a word, to become one people."[42] That effort failed, but he more successfully promoted the related causes of immigration and commerce by supporting liberal naturalization and intellectual property laws, both of which were designed to entice talent and ideas from

Europe.[43] Vattel also counseled that a good prince should tolerate religious diversity, give asylum to refugees, and prevent his own subjects from inflicting damage on people from other nations or on foreign nations directly. Again, Washington's policies were consistent: he disfavored religious establishments, he used something like an executive order to divert federal funds to support refugees from foreign revolution (albeit white slaveholding refugees from San Domingue), and he repeatedly enjoined American citizens to avoid violating the rights of foreign nations and backed those warnings with criminal prosecutions.[44]

In sum, Vattel argued that the sovereign prince should promote the development of his own nation and pursue peaceful relations with others. Vattel knew that skeptics, or what he called "cabinet politicians," might "ridicule" his belief that nations owed "common duties . . . toward others" and that there were "offices of humanity between nations."[45] Let them scoff. Statesmen would not, of course, "strictly conform" to the laws of nature. However, "to renounce all hope of making impression on at least some of them, would be to give up mankind as lost."[46] His American readers would have agreed that men were not angels.[47] They would also have agreed that society was doomed if all men were devils. The task was to build a state that would accept human fallibility, try to counterbalance it, and avoid cynicism. "Every nation," Vattel counseled, "is obliged to cultivate the friendship of other nations, and carefully to avoid whatever might kindle their enmity against her."[48] As Washington construed the new Constitution, the president, like Vattel's prince, should take the lead by reaching out with friendly gestures and avoiding enmity.

From Sovereign Prince to Constitutional Executive: Rules Applied with Collective Judgment

Unlike the sovereign prince who was Vattel's imagined reader, and despite the structurally unitary form of the president's office under the new Constitution, Washington never made decisions alone. The mirror-for-princes books were directed at princely advisors too. Many of Washington's advisors cited Vattel repeatedly, along with other similar treatises. One reason was because these books were part of a transatlantic legal culture of diplomacy, a common resource across nations. Another was because of the unusual dependence of early American statesmen, many of whom were lawyers, on texts to guide their actions. As Jay observed, they lacked much experience with European diplomacy. But they had European books, and in the absence of a stock of precedents, they relied on that legal literature more heavily than their counterparts in other nations.[49] Books provided some guidance when grappling with difficult questions about national rights under treaties and the law of nations. It was not that Vattel's book was simply a how-to manual, providing precise solutions. Only rarely does a law book deliver a simple answer to a complex problem. Vattel instead offered "maxims," or principles, and examples of how those principles had operated in the past. Maxims were focal points statesmen could turn to for an orientation toward foreign relations and for guidance in moments of crisis.[50]

If early federal administrators leaned hard on books, ideology also flowed into the void of diplomatic experience. Beyond a shared premise of Enlightenment-inflected republicanism, the president's advisors offered multiple interpretive approaches. Washington's own understanding of the law of nations resembled his conception of individual character and duty. That was also the premise of Vattel's conception of the law of nations, and anthropomorphizing nations was common in the founding generation. What set Washington apart was the heroic effort he devoted to his own moral performance. Everyone noticed this aspect of his character. His burnished self-presentation was obviously studied and yet manifestly superior and elegant. It was better than natural. His self-control had made him a national institution, an "indispensable" part of the revolutionary project of self-government.[51] Character could be *constituted*.

Washington had been concerned with his own moral performance for decades. Years earlier, in his commonplace book, he had penned 110 "Rules of Civility and Decent Behaviour in Company and Conversation." Remembered, sometimes mocked, by historians for displaying Washington's concern for the etiquette surrounding drinking, eating, and even spitting, the rules had deeper meaning for their author. Civility was not instinctive; it was learned. All public life was a performance in front of a judgmental audience. Young George most likely found the rules in a popular seventeenth-century English etiquette manual, which in turn was derived from maxims first penned by French Jesuits in the late sixteenth century to train missionaries to North America.[52] As if closing a circle, the president of North America's first recognized independent nation took the rules to heart and performed them for citizens very much in need, he thought, of leadership and civilizing. Although it was not representative of the rules—many of which did cover table manners—perhaps the last rule in his transcribed list of 110 captured his sense of the political stakes as the new nation attempted to act and converse in the company of other nations: "Labour to keep alive in your Breast that Little Spark of Ce[les]tial fire Called Conscience."[53] The mechanism of conscience, for Washington's generation, was the impartial spectator: the imaginary of a well-meaning but severe external judge of morality.[54] What do others expect from us, they asked, and we from them?

Washington continued to read advice manuals as an adult. Toward the end of September 1787, as the Constitutional Convention finalized the text of the Constitution, he purchased Lord Chesterfield's *Letters to His Son*, a recent and popular eighteenth-century manual that purported to teach "the Art of Becoming a Man of the World and a Gentleman."[55] When it came to nations, Washington also turned to rulebooks and observation. That meant law and precedent. The latter he gleaned from the battlefield and from history, or, in other words, the practice of nations. The former explains why he planned a crash course on the law of nations in October 1789 and why he kept asking the lawyers around him for guidance throughout his presidency.

Washington worked collectively in two ways, one social and the other abstract. He preferred to make decisions through collective deliberation in a close circle of advisors. He had developed this method of discussion-based decision making during the Revolution with his general staff and now transposed it onto the new federal executive, relying on some of the same individuals, such as Secretaries Alexander Hamilton and Henry Knox.[56] The goal was consensus. Second, he and his advisors gauged their decisions against the barometer of self-respect. This again meant behaving in a way that would command the respect of others. For personal morality, the goal was to earn the respect of other people in one's moral community, represented by Adam Smith's fictive impartial spectator. For national morality, the audience was the judgment of other respectable nations in the Atlantic World. Washington and his advisors repeatedly attempted to forecast that judgment by measuring their decision making against the maxims of the law of nations and what James Madison called "the known opinion of the impartial world."[57] The first circle included his close advisors, then it widened out to include the network of so-called civilized nations. For Washington and the early American law-making elite, state building under the Constitution was a civilizing process.

The Morris Mission: Washington's First Survey of Executive Power

Along with Washington's instructions to Gouverneur Morris to take Britain's diplomatic temperature, he included a letter of introduction to "give you the Credence necessary to enable you to do the Business which it commits to your management."[58] Washington might have learned about "letters of credence" from Vattel's treatise, which in Book IV, chapter VI laid out "the several Orders of public Ministers."[59] There were various kinds and levels of emissaries, but Vattel emphasized that each was like an attorney whose power was defined in a commission of appointment. Although Vattel did not refer to any of the types as "a private Agent," that was what Washington called Morris in his letter of credence. Vattel suggested that the term "agent" lacked technical meaning and was falling into desuetude, except as a title for "persons simply appointed by princes to transact their private affairs." However, "agent," like all diplomatic titles, should be interpreted functionally. The question was what power was invested in the agent. "If this prince," Vattel continued, "sends an agent with credentials and for publick affairs, the agent from that time forward becomes a publick minister: the title makes no alteration."[60] By qualifying Morris as a "private" agent, Washington meant that Morris's mission was relatively secret. Few beyond his inner circle knew about it. Even Vice President Adams, who had been the first and only American minister to Britain just four years earlier, did not learn about the mission for over eight months.[61] But the letter of credence made Morris a public minister: he carried a limited but official commission, to ascertain the intentions of British ministry without the capacity to negotiate.

The main reason Washington gave the mission a low public profile was that he was concerned about sacrificing national respect. He was worried about what today would be called "the optics." Here was the second meaning of "informal."[62] He did not want to send another full minister to Britain, as in 1785, and again risk that Britain would not reciprocate. As Adams remarked after Washington informed him of the new mission, "to send a Minister again to St. James's till that Court explicitly promises to send one to America is an humiliation to which the United States ought never to submit."[63] They feared, in a word, disgrace. As Washington explained when publicizing the British mission to Congress sixteen months later, he sought only an "informal conference with their ministers" so that should the talks prove fruitless, "we should stand less committed" by commissioning only a "private" American citizen "on the spot," instead of sending "a public person."[64] What he meant was that a rebuff to an informal emissary would allow him to save face—personally and nationally. Yet at the same time he could convey good faith to Britain, which he like many Federalists believed was a critical commercial partner.

In sum, Washington began to map the boundaries of executive discretion immediately and targeted what he considered to be the major problem of American foreign policy: the legacies of the Revolution that imperiled peace. These included the British military's occupation of forts in American territory, which violated contemporary understandings of territorial sovereignty and, according to Americans, the Treaty of Peace. The British also continued to trade with Native American nations in the Northwest and held out the possibility of assisting them militarily against the United States, which Americans like Jefferson claimed violated the "Jus gentium for America" that forbade one empire from aiding or trading with indigenous people residing within another's borders.[65] Additional problems included anemic transatlantic trade, which was still dominated by British shipping, and clogged lines of credit caused by public and private defaults in America that violated treaty commitments. Put more positively, the president's goal was to open the spigots of national development by expanding international trade and parceling out the western territory to raise federal revenue and lure settlers, not least European immigrants. All of this he could see in Vattel's mirror.

Neutrality in a Dangerous World of Opportunity: Nootka Sound and the French Wars

While Gouverneur Morris was sounding out Britain's intentions toward the United States, that empire's attention shifted to the west coast of North America. In the fall of 1789, Spanish colonial officials detained a few British ships and their crews anchored in the Nootka Sound, on the west coast of present-day Vancouver Island, on charges of violating Spain's territorial and navigational rights on the continent's western shore. Britain prepared for war. One point of contention between the two empires had not changed for centuries: Spain claimed the entire Pacific as its sphere of colonial influence, based on papal grants and the law-of-nations Doctrine of Discovery. Britain, by contrast, argued that all colonial claims must rest on actual possession, and Spain had no dense settlements on the Pacific coast.[66] Morris quickly reported these events back home, where Washington's administration began to consider the consequences of war for the United States. The president's advisors all assumed that if war ensued, Britain would try to capture New Orleans to gain the right to navigate the Mississippi River. The cabinet feared that Britain would march troops from Canada to the Mississippi, across the Ohio Valley. If Britain asked permission to do so, how should Washington respond? And if Britain crossed American territory without permission, what should he do? Once again, no part of the Constitution specified that the president should monitor geopolitical developments, anticipate threats to American territorial sovereignty, and develop contingency plans—and do all this while consulting the law of nations. But that is what Washington and every member of his cabinet thought he should do. Washington requested written opinions from his three departments and from Vice President Adams and Chief Justice Jay.[67] Article II granted the president the power to "require the Opinion, in writing, of the principal Officer in each of the executive Departments."[68] That did not technically include the chief justice, who was the head of the independent judicial branch and not an executive department, or the vice president.[69] Nonetheless, everyone responded at length, with citations.

The practical advice varied, but the starting point was the same for each: the law of nations concerning the rights and duties of a neutral nation caught between two neighboring nations at war. Jefferson, Jay, and Hamilton combed through Vattel's *Law of Nations* and other early modern treatises, such as those by Hugo Grotius (1583–1645), Samuel von Pufendorf (1632–94), and Jean Barbeyrac (1674–1744), to discover the rights and responsibilities of neutral nations, while Adams and Knox referred, without citation, to what the former termed "an honest neutrality" under law of nations.[70] They all arrived at the same conclusion: a sovereign nation had the right to refuse another nation's request to march troops through its territory for hostile purposes. On the other hand, Spain could construe granting permission to Britain to march its troops through American soil as a violation of American neutrality, which could justify its own attack on the United States. In short, giving permission would likely result in war. Similarly clear was the legal position of a neutral nation that refused permission and suffered an invasion. It was justifiable, possibly required as a matter of honor, for it to respond with force. That would mean war with Britain. The choice, then, was whether to risk war with Spain or Britain, with the possibility that the United States could end up losing territory to either or both.

It is instructive to see how Washington proceeded as his advisors spun out potentially disastrous scenarios. All his advisors began with the law of neutrality, which provided consensual baselines in the international field. The strategies for playing within that field differed, however. Each one cautioned the president to avoid war, at least as long as possible, yet they also tried to gauge which course of action would lead to the best outcome for the United States. Some of those outcomes were dim—being surrounded by a single empire rather than two, for example. Some were bright, like gaining access to the Mississippi River and New Orleans. The consensus was that the United States should seek "perfect" neutrality and avoid partiality to either side. However, the geopolitical calculations differed in characteristic ways. Jefferson, for example, suggested that the United States approach France and Spain with the proposal of coordinating against Britain. Hamilton, on the other hand, argued that the United States owed no "gratitude" to Spain for its indirect support during the Revolution and that it was in the American interest to seek cooperative commercial relations with Britain. The treasury secretary's practical advice might have reminded Washington of the inquisition of William Howe in 1779: war was to be avoided at all costs except to preserve national honor, because the people would not bear the expense for anything less. "The support of public opinion (perhaps more essential to our government than to any other)," Hamilton warned, "could only be looked for in a war evidently resulting from necessity."[71]

If forced to make a decision, Washington probably would have polled his advisers and followed the majority view, as he had usually done with his general staff during the Revolution. But in this instance, he never had to call the vote. The Revolutionary French Assembly gave only halting approval to renewing the Family Compact with Spain, after which Britain and Spain compromised, with Britain getting the far better half of the bargain—the right to fish and trade on the Pacific Coast, at least outside territories Spain actually possessed. For Washington, it was nonetheless a useful drill for the more dramatic conflict three years later, after the outbreak of the Wars of the French Revolution.

The overthrow (and later execution) of King Louis XVI set in motion a skein of defensive alliances that soon engulfed Europe in war, with naval action extending across the Atlantic to the Caribbean. The Girondin government of France expected to supply their privateers in American seaports, to recruit American ships and sailors to aid their assaults on Britain's transatlantic shipping, and to stage an invasion of New Spain from America's western territory. Washington's closest advisors all agreed that consenting to these gambits would require the federal government to violate "perfect neutrality" between France and her enemies, particularly Britain.[72] Using American territory as a base of actions on sea and land would also go well beyond any obligation under the Franco-American Treaty of Alliance (1778), which only required the United States to assist in the defense of French colonies in the Caribbean if France requested that it do so. All of Washington's advisors hoped that request would never come. France much preferred some version of American neutrality to shield American shipping and ports from direct British assault. Indeed, the only major dispute in Washington's cabinet was whether the United States would have to uphold the defensive agreement if the French revolutionary government asked it to or whether, as Hamilton argued, a response should be held in abeyance until the political identity of that government became settled. Jefferson disputed Hamilton's interpretation of Vattel's counsel about when a nation could avoid a treaty obligation owed to another. Attorney General Edmund Randolph withheld his vote until he could read Vattel on this point. The cabinet adjourned, each member submitted a written opinion, and after having read Vattel, Randolph agreed with Jefferson's interpretation. Washington accepted the judgment of two of the three lawyers in his cabinet that the defensive treaty was binding.[73] France never did ask for that assistance. Nonetheless, the president believed it was his constitutional—and international—duty to prepare for the possibility. He and his advisors did so, with Vattel at hand.

Aside from the interpretation of the French treaty, Washington's advisors all agreed about the basic principles of neutrality and how to carry them out. Critically, they agreed that the president could issue a proclamation warning American citizens not to participate in the war effort on either side and that violations would be prosecuted as crimes. Again, the law-of-nations principle beneath this decision was clear. "If you let loose the reins to your subjects against foreign nations," Vattel explained, "these will behave in the same manner to you; and, instead of that friendly intercourse which nature has established between all men, we shall see nothing but one vast and dreadful scene of plunder between nation and nation."[74] The knotty interpretive point instead involved domestic constitutionalism. What gave the president the constitutional authority to declare neutrality? Was it based on Hamilton's interpretation that the French treaty could not oblige the United States to join the war? Or did the president only have the power to declare the status quo—peace—until Congress weighed in with its own interpretation of whether the United States was obligated to declare war? All agreed nonetheless that the president had the power to declare his sense of the United States' international obligations when surrounded by war, despite the absence of any clause granting that power in the Constitution. The law of nations filled the gap. Vattel's prince was required to restrain people in his territory from offending other nations. The consensus in the executive branch, and then the judiciary, was that the president should do the same.

Many hands helped pen the public proclamation, but the resulting text captured Washington's stern sense of self-discipline. Because the nation should "with sincerity and good faith adopt and pursue a conduct friendly and impartial toward the belligerent powers," the president warned citizens "to avoid all acts and proceedings whatsoever, which may in any manner tend to contravene such disposition."[75] Washington followed this public notice with instructions to federal district attorneys to prosecute all those who violated the nation's duties as a neutral country. Federal judges instructed grand juries to indict violators of national neutrality and prosecutions followed.[76] Congress had not yet passed any statute defining crimes against neutral duties, observed the attorney for one defendant, so whence came these nonstatutory offenses? "The answer is," Supreme Court Justice James Wilson concluded for a unanimous federal circuit court, "against many and binding laws. As a citizen of the United States, [the defendant] was bound to act no part which could injure the nation; he was bound to keep the peace in regard to all nations with whom we are at peace. This is the law of nations; not an ex post facto law, but a law that was in existence long before [he] existed."[77]

Soon after, when the outraged minister from France ignored the president's command not to commission a privateer in the capital of Philadelphia, every member of the president's inner circle agreed that he should request the minister's dismissal. The early executive was unitary in the sense that key decisions rested with the president. But it was collective in the way that Washington made his decisions, by consensus among his advisors, guided by standards articulated in the law of nations.

The Farewell Address

Rapprochement with Britain was a major, though controversial, goal of Washington's presidency, and it took both terms to accomplish it.[78] The Morris mission started a process that culminated in the Jay Treaty (1794), which removed British troops from U.S. soil, resolved other conflicts between the two nations that stemmed from the Revolution, and indirectly catalyzed treaties with the Northwest Indian nations, on the one hand, and Spain, on the other, that allowed the federal government to begin to govern the land and people of the American West for the first time. Jeffersonian Republicans in Congress, however, criticized the treaty in the winter of 1796 because of its failure to open trade within the British Empire to American ships, its capitulation to British definitions of neutral shipping, its prohibition of economic sanctions to leverage changes in British policy, and its tacit renunciation of southern claims for compensation for expropriated property during the Revolution—meaning enslaved property. Washington took the criticisms personally but never directly responded to them. His Farewell Address in the fall of 1796, however, can be read as a justification for both his rapprochement with Britain and his policy of neutrality.

Washington defended both policies as the most effective means of obtaining the goals of the Revolution as he understood them, goals that Vattel advised a sovereign to pursue: political autonomy and commercial integration. In this final address to Congress and the American people, he famously counseled the nation to "steer clear of permanent Alliances, with any portion of the foreign World," which implicitly included a veiled criticism of the treaty commitment to aid France's defense of its Caribbean colonies. By contrast, he recommended "liberal intercourse with all Nations" in order to "diffus[e] and diversif[y] by gentle means the streams of Commerce, but forcing nothing," which was a veiled criticism of the Jeffersonian strategy of "peaceable coercion," or trade sanctions, as leverage to enter new markets.[79] Like all of Washington's public addresses, this one had plural authors—Hamilton, Madison, and the president. Each of them could have been following the advice of Vattel, who maintained that "nations, as well as individuals, are obliged to trade together for the common benefit of the human race, because mankind stand in need of each other's assistance."[80] Although each nation retained the power to deny trade to another to preserve its own welfare, the baseline duty was to engage rather than threaten, and to enter treaties of amity rather than of defense. It was not a policy of Anglophilia or monarchy, as the nascent Republican Party called it. It was, Washington believed, the premise of the Enlightenment law of nations, and it was the advice he relayed to the American public. But that law was changing, and new books, along with new presidents, would elevate collective self-expression above self-discipline.

Conclusion

Article II's outline of the executive's powers is spare. What, for example, were the bounds of the "executive power" vested in the president, and which laws was the president supposed to put into effect in the clause enjoining him to "take care that the laws be faithfully executed"?[81] Strikingly, the first president and his advisors rarely framed the question of executive power in these clause-bound and textual terms. Instead, Washington turned to many sources of understanding and of law, and he repeatedly canvassed the opinions of the prominent lawyers who served in his cabinet and on the Supreme Court. One source that they all drew upon during his eight years in office was the law of nations, the international and transnational law that was supposed to define the duties and rights of nations and guide Europe's rulers. Vattel's *Law of Nations* and similar treatises were written as advice manuals for the enlightened prince. Like any area of law, the law of nations was complex, forbidding to novices, and frustrating even to jurists. Few Americans entered the Revolution as experts. Some Americans then dove deeply into the law of nations, learning quickly how to claim nationhood, how to fight to earn it, and then how to govern themselves in order to keep it. For two decades, Washington presided over that effort, in every sense. Electing a war hero as the first president symbolized the belief that the Revolution was incomplete without establishing an orderly peacetime government that could earn the respect of other "civilized nations." Without that respect, the United States would remain, as Washington had put it in his 1783 farewell to the states, "the sport of European Politicks."[82]

To avoid control by others, the nation had to control itself. Here is where the first president left his most personal mark on the executive branch. Few Americans had devoted more effort to self-mastery than George Washington. It was a point of pride and a defining feature of his character. Self-discipline is also what he sought for the nation. That Washington turned to the law of nations to understand the boundaries of his own discretion reveals much not only about the original understanding of the executive but also about early American understandings of what it meant to be a "civilized nation."

Notes

1. George Washington, diary entry for October 9, 1789, Founders Online, National Archives, https://founders.archives.gov/documents/Washington/01-05-02-0005-0002-0009, published in *The Diaries of George Washington*, vol. 5, *1 July 1786–31 December 1789*, ed. Donald Jackson and Dorothy Twohig (Charlottesville: University Press of Virginia, 1979), 457–58.

2. Mason Locke Weems, *The Life of George Washington* (Philadelphia: J.B. Lippincott & Co., 1858), 16.

3. Rich Shapiro, "President Washington Racks up $300,000 Late Fee for Two Manhattan Library Books," *New York Daily News*, April 16, 2010; Christina Boyle, "Book that George Washington Borrowed from New York Library Is Returned—221 Years Later," *New York Daily News*, May 19, 2010. See also Sara Holliday and Melissa Wood, "Historic Mount Vernon Returns Copy of Rare Book Borrowed by George Washington in 1789 to The New York Society Library," May 19, 2010, press release, The New York Society Library, https://www.nysoclib.org/about/historic-mount-vernon-returns-copy-rare-book-borrowed-george-washington-1789-new-york-society. Theodore Christov uses this anecdote to introduce an essay on the revolutionaries' use of Vattel's conception of sovereignty to justify independence at the outset of the Revolution. Theodore Christov, "Emer de Vattel's *Law of Nations* in America's Independence," in *Justifying Revolution: Law, Virtue, and Violence in the American War of Independence*, ed. Glenn A. Moots and Phillip Hamilton (Tulsa: University of Oklahoma Press, 2018), 64–82.

4. Emer de Vattel, *The Law of Nations: Or, the Principles of the Law of Nature Applied to the Conduct and Affairs of Nations and Sovereigns*, ed. Béla Kapossy and Richard Whitmore (Indianapolis, IN: Liberty Fund, 2008).

5. Christov, "Emer de Vattel's *Law of Nations* in America's Independence"; Charles G. Fenwick, "The Authority of Vattel," *American Political Science Review* 7, no. 3 (1913): 395–410; Edwin D. Dickinson, "Changing Concepts and the Doctrine of Incorporation," *American Journal of International Law* 26, no. 2 (1952): 259n132; Donald S. Lutz, "The Relative Influence of European Writers on Late Eighteenth-Century American Political Thought," *American Political Science Review* 78, no. 1 (1984): 193. Cf. Brian Richardson, "The use of Vattel in the American Law of Nations," *American Journal of International Law*, 54 (2012): 547–71 (warning against relying solely on Vattel to gauge early American understandings of the law of nations).

6. George Washington to Robert Cary & Company, October 6, 1773, Founders Online, National Archives, https://founders.archives.gov/documents/Washington/02-07-02-0252-0001, published in *The Papers of George Washington*, Colonial Series, vol. 9, *8 January 1772–18 March 1774*, ed. W. W. Abbot and Dorothy Twohig (Charlottesville: University Press of Virginia, 1994), 343–45 (ordering books by Vattel, Grotius, Bynkershoek, Adam Smith, and others for John Parke Custis). The first preserved memorandum from Alexander Hamilton to Washington, for example, analyzed the appropriate conditions for prisoners of war under "the laws of war and nations." Alexander Hamilton, "Notes on a Proposed Cartel for the Exchange of Prisoners of War," [April 10–11, 1778], Founders Online, National Archives, https://founders.archives.gov/documents/

Hamilton/01-01-02-0427, published in *The Papers of Alexander Hamilton*, vol. 1, ed. Harold C. Syrett (New York: Columbia University Press, 1961), 462–65 ("prisoners not to be thrown into dungeons or other unnecessarily rigorous confinement; but for a flagrant breach of the laws of war and nations"). For American encounters with the laws of war during the Revolution, see John Fabian Witt, *Lincoln's Code: The Laws of War in American History* (New York: Free Press, 2012), 13–48.

7. Hamilton to Washington, September 15, 1790, Enclosure: Answers to Questions Proposed by the President of the United States to the Secretary of the Treasury, Founders Online, National Archives, https://founders.archives.gov/?q=Ancestor%3AGEWN-05-06-02-0212&s=1511311111&r=2, published in *The Papers of George Washington*, Presidential Series, vol. 6, *1 July 1790–30 November 1790*, ed. Mark A. Mastromarino (Charlottesville: University Press of Virginia, 1996), 443.

8. Jefferson recommended Vattel to a young law student in 1773; lent a copy to the Continental Congress, which he later sold to James Monroe; recommended that another law student read it in 1790; and cited it repeatedly in cabinet discussions. Thomas Jefferson to John Minor, August 30, 1814, including Thomas Jefferson to Bernard Moore, [ca. 1773?]: List of Books Sold to James Monroe, [10 May 1784], in *The Papers of Thomas Jefferson*, Retirement Series, vol. 7, *November 1813 to September 1814*, ed. J. Jefferson Looney (Charlottesville: University of Virginia Press, Rotunda, 2010), 625–31; Thomas Jefferson to John Garland Jefferson, June 11, 1790, Founders Online, National Archives, https://founders.archives.gov/documents/Jefferson/01-16-02-0278, published in *The Papers of Thomas Jefferson*, Original Series, vol. 16, *30 November 1789–4 July 1790*, ed. Julian P. Boyd (Princeton, NJ: Princeton University Press, 1961), 480–82; Opinion on the Treaties with France, April 28, 1793, Founders Online, National Archives, https://founders.archives.gov/documents/Jefferson/01-25-02-0562-0005, published in *The Papers of Thomas Jefferson*, Original Series, vol. 25, *1 January–10 May 1793*, ed. John Catanzariti (Princeton, NJ: Princeton University Press, 1992), 608–19.

9. The volume must have been *The Parliamentary Register; or, The History of the Proceedings and Debates of the House of Commons . . . During the Fifth Session of the Fourteenth Parliament of Great Britain*, vol. XII (1779; repr., London, 1802).

10. *Parliamentary Register*, 23–25. For a narrative account of the investigation, see David Smith, *Whispers across the Atlantick: General William Howe and the American Revolution* (London: Osprey Publishing, 2017).

11. Kevin J. Hayes, *George Washington: A Life in Books* (New York: Oxford University Press, 2017); Paul K. Longmore, *The Invention of George Washington* (Berkeley: University of California Press, 1988); Adrienne M. Harrison, *A Powerful Mind: The Self-Education of George Washington* (Lincoln, NE: Potomac Books, 2015).

12. Congress adjourned on September 29, 1789; United States House of Representatives, "1st to 9th Congresses (1789–1807)," History, Art & Archives, https://history.house.gov/Institution/Session-Dates/1-9/.

13. For a classic interpretation of the removal debate, see Charles C. Thach Jr., *The Creation of the Presidency, 1775–1789: A Study in Constitutional History* (Baltimore, MD: Johns Hopkins University Press, 1922), 140–68. For a recent account, see Jonathan Gienapp, *The Second Creation: Fixing the American Constitution in the Founding Era* (Cam-

bridge, MA: The Belknap Press of Harvard University, 2018), 126–63. Some scholars of the founding-era presidency argue that the office was almost monarchical in its discretionary powers. See Saikrishna B. Prakash, *Imperial from the Beginning: The Constitution of the Original Executive* (New Haven, CT: Yale University Press, 2015); and Eric Nelson, *The Royalist Revolution: Monarchy and the American Founding* (Cambridge, MA: Harvard University Press, 2014).

14. George Washington, diary entry for October 5, 1789, Founders Online, National Archives, https://founders.archives.gov/documents/Washington/01-05-02-0005 -0002-0005, published in *The Diaries of George Washington*, vol. 5, *1 July 1786–31 December 1789*, ed. Donald Jackson and Dorothy Twohig (Charlottesville: University Press of Virginia, 1979), 452–53; Charging Ledger, 1789–1792, p. 21, City Readers: Digital Collections at the New York Society Library, https://cityreaders.nysoclib.org/Detail/objects/10.

15. Washington to John Jay, October 5, 1789, Founders Online, National Archives, https://founders.archives.gov/documents/Washington/05-04-02-0094, published in *Papers of George Washington*, Presidential Series, vol. 4, *8 September 1789–15 January 1790*, ed. Dorothy Twohig (Charlottesville: University Press of Virginia, 1993), 137–38, my italics.

16. Vattel, *The Law of Nations*, bk. I, chap. XIII, s. 163, p. 187, my italics.

17. "Definitive Treaty of Peace between the United States and Great Britain, 3 September 1783," articles IV, V, and VI, Founders Online, National Archives, https://founders. archives.gov/documents/Franklin/01-40-02-0356, published in *The Papers of Benjamin Franklin*, vol. 40, *May 16 through September 15, 1783*, ed. Ellen R. Cohn (New Haven, CT: Yale University Press, 2011), 566–75.

18. Daniel J. Hulsebosch, "Being Seen Like a State: How Americans (and Britons) Built the Constitutional Infrastructure of a Developing Nation," *William & Mary Law Review* 59 (2018): 1239–1319.

19. John Jay, *Address to the People of New-York, on the Subject of the Constitution, Agreed upon at Philadelphia, the 17th of September, 1787* (New York: Printed by S. and J. Loudon, 1788), 6.

20. David M. Golove and Daniel J. Hulsebosch, "A Civilized Nation: The Early American Constitution, the Law of Nations, and the Pursuit of International Recognition," *New York University Law Review* 85, no. 4 (2010): 932–1066; David M. Golove and Daniel J. Hulsebosch, "'The Known Opinion of the Impartial World': Foreign Relations and the Law of Nations in the Federalist," in *The Cambridge Companion to the Federalist*, ed. Jack N. Rakove and Colleen Sheehan (Cambridge: Cambridge University Press, 2020), 114–63. This interstate anxiety was a secular version of the earlier "fear of godly punishment and the desire to have a reputation suitable to a Christian and civilized prince." Pärtel Pirramäe, "The Westphalian Myth of Sovereignty and the Idea of External Sovereignty," in *Sovereignty in Fragments: The Past, Present and Future of a Contested Concept*, ed. Hent Kalmo and Quentin Skinner (New York: Cambridge University Press, 2010), 80.

21. That had been the case since Washington was in his early 20s. His 1754 account of his military adventures in the Ohio Valley, intended to earn him a military commission,

became a transatlantic sensation. Joseph Ellis, *His Excellency: George Washington* (New York: Alfred A. Knopf, 2004), 3–6.

22. George Washington, "Circular to the States," June 8–21, 1783, in *The Writings of George Washington from the Original Manuscript Sources 1745–1799*, vol. 26, *January 1, 1783–June 10, 1783*, ed. John C. Fitzpatrick (Washington, DC: United States Government Printing Office, 1938), 486.

23. In the substantial literature on Washington's character, particularly helpful studies are Longmore, *The Invention of George Washington*; Hayes, *George Washington*; Ellis, *His Excellency*; Harrison, *A Powerful Mind*.

24. From the perspective of the irredentists in the British ministry, who dominated foreign policy at the time, it looked like the states wished to recover all the benefits of empire without paying the cost, not least political subjection, and without fulfilling their obligations under the treaty.

25. George Washington, diary entry for October 8, 1789, Founders Online, National Archives, https://founders.archives.gov/documents/Washington/01-05-02-0005-0002, published in *The Diaries of George Washington*, vol. 5, *1 July 1786–31 December 1789*, ed. Donald Jackson and Dorothy Twohig (Charlottesville: University Press of Virginia, 1979), 456.

26. If these were Madison's scruples, they went unrecorded and they might have been answered by Jay's unofficial carryover status.

27. Washington famously entered the Senate in August 1789 to seek advice about a proposed treaty negotiation with the southern Native American nations but found the exercise frustrating and did not repeat it. However, he routinely sought advice by written instrument and provided updates on progress. See Ralston Hayden, *The Senate and Treaties, 1789–1817: The Development of the Treaty-Making Functions of the United States during Their Formative Period* (1920; repr., New York: Da Capo Press, 1970), 18–27.

28. At least he always sought prior appropriations for Native American treaty conferences, which typically entailed substantial gift giving as compensation. Washington did not seek appropriations from the House of Representatives before sending Jay to London in 1794.

29. Although Washington did not seek an appropriation for the mission beforehand, a year later he allotted $1,000 to Morris, taken from Congress's annual appropriation to the president for the diplomatic establishment. George Washington to Gouverneur Morris, December 17, 1790, in *The Papers of George Washington*, Presidential Series, vol. 7, *1 December 1790–21 March 1791*, ed. Jack D. Warren Jr. (Charlottesville: University Press of Virginia, 1998), 92–94; Thomas Jefferson to Gouverneur Morris, December 17, 1790, in *The Papers of George Washington*, Presidential Series, 7:94n1; Thomas Jefferson to George Washington, December 15, 1790, in *The Papers of George Washington*, Presidential Series, 7:84–86.

30. Morris was a defender of an independent executive, especially in foreign affairs; he called the president "the general Guardian of the national interests." Max Farrand, ed., *The Records of the Federal Convention of 1787* (New Haven, CT: Yale University Press), 2:540–41.

31. Golove and Hulsebosch, "A Civilized Nation," 1065.

32. The president did not receive the powers to make treaties and appoint officers until September. He shared both with the Senate, but in early August both had been solely in the Senate, which was originally envisioned as a kind of executive council. Instead, both powers soon became sources of substantial executive power, more power perhaps than anyone in Philadelphia could have imagined. Jack N. Rakove, "Solving a Constitutional Puzzle: The Treatymaking Clause as a Case Study," *Perspectives in American History*, n.s., 1 (1984): 233–81.

33. U.S. Constitution, art. II, §§ 2 and 3, National Archives, America's Founding Documents, https://www.archives.gov/founding-docs/constitution-transcript.

34. Quentin Skinner, *Foundations of Modern Political Thought*, vol. 1, *The Renaissance* (Cambridge: Cambridge University Press, 1978), 118.

35. Christopher A. Ford, "Preaching Propriety to Princes: Grotius, Lipsius, and Neo-Stoic International Law," *Case Western Reserve Journal of International Law* 28, no. 2 (1996): 313–66; Richard Devatak, "Law of Nations as Reason of State: Diplomacy and the Balance of Power in Vattel's *Law of Nations*," *Parergon* 28, no. 2 (2011): 105–28.

36. Vattel, *The Law of Nations*, bk. I, chap. IV, s. 38, pp. 96–97 (defining sovereignty).

37. Vattel, *The Law of Nations*, bk. I, chap. II, s. 15, p. 86.

38. Notably, Vattel focused on policies rather than constitutional structure and he did not recommend particular forms of national government.

39. See, e.g., Vattel, *The Law of Nations*, bk. II, chap. II, s. 21, pp. 273–74 ("Men are therefore under an obligation to carry on that commerce with each other, if they wish not to deviate from the views of nature; and this obligation extends also to whole nations or states"); and 288 ("Every nation, as well as every man, has therefore a right to prevent nations from obstructing her preservation, her perfection, and happiness,—that is to preserve herself from all injuries").

40. Béla Kapossy and Richard Whatmore, "Introduction," in Vattel, *The Law of Nations*, xvii. Outside Europe, however, Vattel was skeptical about the political and economic capacity of non-Christian indigenous polities and treated them as wards of the state when they were located on land claimed by a European power. Vattel, *The Law of Nations*, bk. I, s. 209, pp. 216–17. See also Kapossy and Whatmore, "Introduction," xv.

41. Vattel, *The Law of Nations*, bk. II, chap. IV, s. 53, p. 289.

42. George Washington to United States Congress, December 7, 1796, Founders Online, National Archives, https://founders.archives.gov/documents/Washington/99-01-02-00063, early access document. See also George Thomas, *The Founders and the Idea of a National University: Constituting the American Mind* (New York: Cambridge University Press, 2015), 3, 31, Washington's emphasis.

43. See Doron Ben-Atar, *Trade Secrets: Intellectual Piracy and the Origins of American Industrial Power* (New Haven, CT: Yale University Press, 2004).

44. See, e.g., Golove and Hulsebosch, "A Civilized Nation," 1032–37.

45. Vattel, *The Law of Nations*, bk. II, chap. 1, s. 1, p. 259.

46. Vattel, *The Law of Nations*, bk. II, chap. 1, s. 1, p. 261.

47. [James Madison,] "The Federalist No. 51," in *The Federalist*, ed. Jacob E. Cooke (1961; repr. Middletown, CT: Wesleyan University Press, 1982), 349.

48. Vattel, *The Law of Nations*, bk. II, chap. I, s. 12, p. 267.

49. On the importation of law books after the Revolution, see Daniel J. Hulsebosch, "An Empire of Law: Chancellor Kent and the Revolution in Books in the Early Republic," *Alabama Law Review* 60, no. 2 (2009): 377–24. See also Benjamin C. Lyons, "The Law of Nations in the Diplomacy of the American Revolution" (PhD diss., Columbia University, 2016).

50. For focal points as permitting tacit coordination in political interactions, see Thomas C. Schelling, *The Strategy of Conflict* (Cambridge, MA: Harvard University Press, 1960), 57–58.

51. James T. Flexner, *Washington: The Indispensable Man* (Boston: Little, Brown, 1974). See also Glenn A. Phelps, "The President as a Moral Leader: George Washington in Contemporary Perspective," in *George Washington: Foundation of Presidential Leadership and Character*, ed. Ethan M. Fishman, William D. Pederson, and Mark J. Rozell (Westport, CT: Praeger Publishers, 2001), 3–4 ("Washington believed that his demeanor as President would be his greatest political asset and, in turn, the greatest asset of the new government. . . . Virtue, disinterested self-denying service for the good of the commonweal, was the means by which one laid claim to fame."), and 8 (he "carefully crafted his public persona so as to deny his very real passions" and with the possibly staged exception of his senate outburst, "he never revealed anything outside his small circle of advisers but the stolid, even-tempered demeanor of his public persona"); John Ferling, *The Ascent of George Washington: The Hidden Political Genius of an American Icon* (New York: Bloomsbury Press, 2009), 5 ("His self-control permitted his other virtues to flourish, for naturally dangerous inclinations were always 'obedient to his stronger mind.'"); and Richard Brookhiser, *George Washington on Leadership* (New York: Basic Books, 2008), 203 ("Self-possession was a lifelong value of his.").

52. Charles Moore, "Origin of the Rules of Civility," in *George Washington's Rules of Civility and Decent Behaviour in Company and Conversation* (Boston: Houghton Mifflin, 1926), x–xii, xiv. See also Hayes, *George Washington*, 20–22; and generally, Norbert Elias, *The Civilizing Process* (Oxford: Basil Blackwell, 1994).

53. Moore, *George Washington's Rules of Civility and Decent Behaviour in Company and Conversation*, 21.

54. See, e.g., George Washington to Benjamin Harrison, March 9, 1789, in *The Papers of George Washington*, Presidential Series, vol. 1, *24 September 1788–31 March 1789*, ed. Dorothy Twohig (Charlottesville: University Press of Virginia, 1987), 375–77; David Humphreys to George Washington, Lisbon, March 24, 1793, Founders Online, National Archives, https://founders.archives.gov/documents/Washington/05-12-02-0292, published in *The Papers of George Washington*, Presidential Series, vol. 12, *16 January 1793–31 May 1793*, ed. Christine Sternberg Patrick and John C. Pinheiro (Charlottesville: University of Virginia Press, 2005), 367–71; and William Livingston to George Washington, November 27, 1776, Founders Online, National Archives, https://founders.archives.gov/documents/Washington/03-07-02-0089, published in *The Papers of George Washington*, Revolutionary War Series, vol. 7, *21 October 1776–5 January 1777*, ed. Philander D. Chase (Charlottesville: University Press of Virginia, 1997), 225–26.

55. George Washington, Philadelphia Cash Accounts, May 9–September 22, 1787, Founders Online, National Archives, https://founders.archives.gov/documents/Wash

ington/04-05-02-0162, published in *The Papers of George Washington*, Confederation Series, vol. 5, *1 February 1787–31 December 1787*, ed. W. W. Abbot (Charlottesville: University Press of Virginia, 1997), 173–81. An edition of Chesterfield published in New York in 1775 was in Washington's library at his death (181n46).

56. Ellis, *His Excellency*, 197–98; Lindsay Chervinsky's essay in this volume.

57. [James Madison,] "The Federalist No. 68," in *The Federalist*, ed. Jacob Cooke (Middletown, CT, 1983), 463.

58. George Washington to Gouverneur Morris, October 13, 1789, Founders Online, National Archives, published in *The Papers of George Washington*, Presidential Series, vol. 4, 179–80.

59. Vattel, *The Law of Nations*, bk. IV, chap. VI, p. 690.

60. Vattel, *The Law of Nations*, bk. IV, chap. VI, s. 75, p. 693.

61. George Washington, diary entry for July 1, 1790, Founders Online, National Archives, https://founders.archives.gov/documents/Washington/01-06-02-0001-0007, published in *The Papers of George Washington*, Diaries, vol. 6, *1 January 1790–13 December 1799*, ed. Donald Jackson and Dorothy Twohig (Charlottesville: University Press of Virginia, 1979), 79–95 (noting that, once informed, Adams approved of the mission).

62. This connotation is implied in a note to Jefferson six months after the mission ended. There Washington suggested that calling it "informal" in a letter to Congress was redundant; everyone knew that "we have no person in a public character at the Ct of London." George Washington to Thomas Jefferson, February 9, 1791, Founders Online, National Archives, https://founders.archives.gov/documents/Washington/05-07-02-0193, published in *The Papers of George Washington*, Presidential Series, vol. 7, 325. The implication was that any emissary who was not at the level of a full minister or empowered to negotiate a treaty was "informal."

63. John Adams to George Washington, August 29, 1790, Founders Online, National Archives, https://founders.archives.gov/documents/Adams/99-02-02-1065, published in *The Papers of George Washington*, Presidential Series, vol. 6, *1 July 1790–30 November 1790*, ed. Mark A. Mastromarino (Charlottesville: University Press of Virginia, 1996), 359.

64. George Washington to the United States Senate and the House of Representatives, February 14, 1791, Founders Online, National Archives, https://founders.archives.gov/documents/Washington/05-07-02-0205, published in *The Papers of George Washington*, Presidential Series, vol. 7, 346.

65. Jefferson coined the phrase "Jus gentium for America" in 1784 to describe the property doctrine of preemption of Native American lands and then expanded that doctrine to rebut claims of the British that they were entitled to trade with Native American polities in the Ohio Valley. Thomas Jefferson, Notes of a Conversation with George Hammond, June 3, 1792, Founders Online, National Archives, https://founders.archives.gov/documents/Jefferson/01-24-02-0023, published in *The Papers of Thomas Jefferson*, Original Series, vol. 24, *1 June–31 December 1792*, ed. John Catanzariti (Princeton, NJ: Princeton University Press, 1990), 26–33.

66. On these competing modes of claims making, see Anthony Pagden, *Lords of All*

the World: Ideologies of Empire in Spain, Britain and France c. 1500–c. 1800 (New Haven, CT: Yale University Press, 1995).

67. George Washington to Alexander Hamilton, August 27, 1790, Founders Online, National Archives, https://founders.archives.gov/documents/Hamilton/01-06-02-0478, published in *The Papers of Alexander Hamilton*, vol. 6, *December 1789–August 1790*, ed. Harold C. Syrett (New York: Columbia University Press, 1962), 572–73. The substance of this letter was copied and sent to the four other advisors.

68. U.S. Constitution, art. II, § 2, National Archives, America's Founding Documents, https://www.archives.gov/founding-docs/constitution-transcript.

69. Although Jay's Supreme Court refused to issue "advisory opinions" collectively as an institution, Jay repeatedly provided his own advice directly to the president. For the development of the prohibition on official advisory opinions, see Stewart Jay, *Most Humble Servants: The Advisory Role of Early Judges* (New Haven, CT: Yale University Press, 1997).

70. The various opinions can be found in Washington's papers. See John Jay to George Washington, August 28, 1790 (citing Vattel), Founders Online, National Archives, https://founders.archives.gov/documents/Washington/05-06-02-0170, published in *The Papers of George Washington*, Presidential Series, vol. 6, *1 July 1790–30 November 1790*, ed. Mark A. Mastromarino (Charlottesville: University Press of Virginia, 1996), 353–56; Thomas Jefferson to George Washington, August 28, 1790, Founders Online, https://founders.archives.gov/documents/Washington/05-06-02-0171, published in *The Papers of George Washington*, Presidential Series, vol. 6, 356–58. Adams to Washington, August 29, 1790; Henry Knox to George Washington, August 29, 1790, Founders Online, National Archives, https://founders.archives.gov/documents/Washington/05-06-02-0175, published in *The Papers of George Washington*, Presidential Series, vol. 6, 365–67 and Alexander Hamilton to George Washington, September 15, 1790 (citing Barbeyrac, Grotius, Pufendorf, and Vattel), Founders Online, National Archives, https://founders.archives.gov/documents/Washington/05-06-02-0212-0001, published in *The Papers of George Washington*, Presidential Series, vol. 6, 439–40.

71. Hamilton, Enclosure in Hamilton to Washington, September 15, 1790, Founders Online, National Archives, https://founders.archives.gov/documents/Washington/05-06-02-0212-0002, published in *The Papers of George Washington*, Presidential Series, vol. 6, 452.

72. For an overview of the neutrality controversy, see Stanley Elkins and Eric McKitrick, *Age of Federalism: The Early American Republic, 1788–1800* (Oxford: Oxford University Press, 1993), 303–73. For an analysis of the legal positions Washington's cabinet and the Supreme Court staked out, see Golove and Hulsebosch, "A Civilized Nation," 1019–39. For a "realist" interpretation of the Neutrality Crisis, see Charles S. Hyneman, *The First American Neutrality* (Urbana: University of Illinois Press, 1934).

73. For an account of this interpretive dispute in Washington's cabinet, see Robert J. Reinstein, "Executive Power and the Law of Nations in the Washington Administration," *University of Richmond Law Review* 46 (2012): 373, 410–17 (documenting debates over the meaning of Vattel in Washington's cabinet early in the neutrality controversy in 1793).

74. Vattel, *The Law of Nations*, bk. II, chap. VI, s. 72, p. 299.

75. George Washington, Neutrality Proclamation, April 22, 1793, Founders Online, National Archives, https://founders.archives.gov/documents/Washington/05-12 -02-0371, published in *The Papers of George Washington*, Presidential Series, vol. 12, 472–74.

76. On the legal issues surrounding enforcement, see Golove and Hulsebosch, "A Civilized Nation," 1028–35.

77. Henfield's Case, 11 F. Cas. 1099, 1119–1120 (C.C.D. Pa., 1793).

78. See Jerald A. Combs, *The Jay Treaty: Political Battleground of the Founding Fathers* (Berkeley: University of California Press, 1970); Todd Estes, *The Jay Treaty, Public Opinion, and the Evolution of American Political Culture* (Amherst: University of Massachusetts Press, 2006). See generally Bradford Perkins, *The First Rapprochement: England and the United States, 1795–1805* (Philadelphia: University of Pennsylvania Press, 1955).

79. George Washington, Farewell Address, September 19, 1796, Founders Online, National Archives, https://founders.archives.gov/documents/Washington/99-01-02-00963, early access document.

80. Vattel, *The Law of Nations*, bk. I, chap. 8, s. 94, p. 132.

81. U.S. Constitution, art. II, § 3, America's Founding Documents, National Archives, https://www.archives.gov/founding-docs/constitution-transcript.

82. George Washington, "Circular to the States," June 8–21, 1783.

11

Liberty and Power

The Classical Republicanism of George Washington and Mercy Otis Warren

ROSEMARIE ZAGARRI

For many years, Mercy Otis Warren and George Washington enjoyed a mutual admiration society. Before the American Revolution, Warren had emerged as one of the very few women in the North American British colonies to publish works dealing with war, politics, and political ideas—realms that were considered exclusively male preserves. Especially in her native Massachusetts, Warren's poems, plays, and satirical writings stoked the fires of resistance to British tyranny and incited American colonists toward war and independence. Washington and Warren met in person once, during the early days of the war, and occasionally corresponded with one another in subsequent years. Warren felt the highest admiration for Washington, who, she said, "united all hearts in the field of Conquest." Washington, in turn, generously expressed his enthusiasm for Warren's great poetical skills and acknowledged her impressive literary reputation.[1]

Warren and Washington shared another bond. Like many other Americans of the time, both individuals interpreted their experience of the American Revolution through a commitment to the ideology of classical republicanism. Based on a belief in the intellectual linkages between the ancient and modern worlds, Washington and Warren used classical republican discourse to make sense of the political transformations occurring around them. During the Revolution, both modeled their public personas on classical republican figures and invoked classical allusions to explain the new republican order. Both saw the potential for their newly independent nation to become a modern-day Rome. After the Revolution, both feared that their own country, like the Roman republic, might fall into a cycle of decay and decline, leading it to an untimely end. Seeking to prevent this fate, Warren and Washington depicted the American Revolution as part of a grand historical narrative, a morality play that stretched from ancient times to the present and offered new hope for the future.[2]

Despite these unifying beliefs, Washington and Warren expressed their classical republicanism in distinctly gendered forms. Washington's republicanism stressed the importance of masculine characteristics, especially the kinds of manly actions and martial bravery associated with the Latin concept of *virtus*.[3] Warren, on the other hand, expressed her republican sentiments through one of the very few venues open to her as a woman: the medium of the printed word. By the time Washington became president, Warren had become one of his fiercest critics. Although Washington believed that he had simply accommodated his republicanism to the realities of governing a new nation, Warren interpreted Washington's actions as a falling away from the path of republican rectitude and a rejection of the republican commitment to the common good. In her view, Washington, who had once seemed to be the embodiment of a classical republican hero, appeared to have betrayed his principles in the pursuit of power and fame. Ironically, despite Warren's and Washington's shared republican discourse, their distinctly gendered means of expression ultimately undermined their common bond.

At the time of the American Revolution, both Washington and Warren found themselves to be the heirs of a number of intellectual traditions that shaped their revolutionary ideals and experience. One essential tradition was based in the Anglo-American belief in the primacy of the British constitution. Drawing on the power of custom, precedent, and parliamentary statute, this tradition asserted that the rule of law was essential and that customary legal rights and privileges were critically important in shaping colonial political thought. During the decades prior to the Revolution, colonists invoked the British constitution to justify resistance against Britain. They portrayed their rebellion as defensive in nature—a protection of customary rights inherited from time immemorial rather than an assertion of new privileges and prerogatives. Another tradition was Lockean liberalism. Inherited from the philosopher John Locke, this discourse declared the primacy of natural rights—rights that had been given by God, inscribed in nature, and were irrefutable and inalienable. These beliefs helped justify the right to rebel and underlay the creation of a new government based on the people's consent.[4]

During the Revolutionary era, colonists blended these intellectual traditions with a third discourse, known as classical republicanism. Based on a study of ancient Athenian democracy and the Roman Republic, classical republicanism was passed down from ancient times to the revolutionary generation. It flourished among the civic humanists in medieval Florence, was transmitted to the rebels of the English Civil War, and was adopted by opposition writers and politicians in early eighteenth-century Britain. Disseminated to the colonies through pamphlets, political treatises, and newspapers, classical republicanism became widely diffused throughout British North America. Overlapping with yet distinct from constitutionalism and Lockean liberalism, classical republicanism provided a critical intellectual vehicle that both guided and framed the colonists' understanding of their revolutionary experiences.[5]

Both Warren and Washington believed that certain key tenets of classical republicanism had persisted throughout the ages. Tyranny constantly threatened liberty, virtue vied with corruption, and freedom was liable to devolve into oppression. While self-governing republics were one of the highest forms of government, this kind of polity was an especially fragile entity, constantly subject to the threat of decay, decline, and corruption. Only the people's continual vigilance and virtue could preserve freedom. Only an unceasing willingness to sacrifice for the common good could maintain liberty. A failure to defend liberty could be catastrophic, resulting in what classical authors called "slavery"—a condition in which individuals would be subject to the will of another person, unable to exercise their own choices. Ironically, classical republican thought paid far more attention to the political status of subjugated white people than to the actual condition of enslaved Black people.[6]

Neither Warren nor Washington learned their ideas about classical republicanism in the typical way. In the colonial era, the most common route to a knowledge of antiquity was by studying the classics of ancient Greece and Rome in college. Washington, however, never attended college. For a different reason, Warren, too, never went to college. As a female, institutions of higher learning were not open to those of her sex. Yet through self-education, both Warren and Washington came to embrace the principles of classical republicanism and drew on them to understand and interpret the tumultuous times they lived in.[7]

Washington absorbed the tenets of classical republicanism through sustained effort. At this time, knowledge of the classics was considered to be the hallmark of masculine gentility and elite rank. As a youth, Washington

Figure 11.1. *George Washington* (Lansdowne Portrait), by Gilbert Stuart, 1796. Oil on canvas. National Portrait Gallery, acquired as a gift to the nation through the generosity of the Donald W. Reynolds Foundation.

had received his education from a private tutor, who trained him in practical subjects such as geography, history, and mathematics. After Washington's father died when he was eleven years old, it was clear that the family would not be able to afford to send him to college. As a result, Washington never learned to read Greek and Latin. Instead, as a young man, Washington set out to establish himself professionally as a surveyor, marking out property lines, devising territorial boundaries, and describing topographical features for land-hungry white colonists. He then served as an officer in the French and Indian War. Tales of his strong leadership abilities and bravery in battle began to foster the beginnings of his reputation as a hero in the classical republican mold.[8]

After the French and Indian War, Washington, eager to assume his place as a gentleman of the first rank, sought to rectify his educational deficiencies and to secure a knowledge of the ancient world. After marrying Martha Custis, a wealthy widow, in 1759, Washington moved her former husband's extensive library, which included a number of classical works, to Mount Vernon, where he began his self-education. Over the years, Washington systematically acquired other classics, including Plato's *Republic*, Livy's *History of Rome*, and Suetonius's *History of the Twelve Caesars*. Because he was not schooled in Greek or Latin, he read these works in translation. As he immersed himself in these tomes, he found that he gravitated toward the Stoic philosophers, especially Seneca, whose emphasis on moderation, frugality, temperance, and honor seemed most compatible with his own evolving political philosophy. When Edward Gibbon published his classic six-volume *History of the Decline and Fall of the Roman Empire* in the period 1776 to 1783, Washington made sure that he purchased a copy, perhaps as a continuing reminder of the fate that could befall republican governments.[9]

One early expression of Washington's affinity for classical ideas appears in his enthusiasm for the play *Cato*. Written by the radical Whig author Joseph Addison, the play was first staged in London in 1713, where it became an immediate sensation. In subsequent decades, the work was performed many times on both sides of the Atlantic and was published in multiple print editions. Based on historical events in ancient Rome, the play dramatized the story of Cato the Younger's resistance in the first century BCE to the Roman dictator Julius Caesar. Bent on imperial conquest and glory, Caesar sets out from Rome to conquer territory throughout Europe and North Africa. In the process, he overthrows the Roman Republic, abolishes the citizens' right to self-government, and installs himself as dictator. The play focuses on Cato's stalwart resistance to the impending threat of tyranny. As Caesar's forces approach Utica in North Africa, Cato calls on the city's inhabitants to rise up to defend their rights and liberties. Laying out the threat to their future, Cato urges them to fight until their last breath. Dying as a free man, he insists, would be preferable to living as a slave. In fact, when Caesar's victory seems inevitable, Cato chooses to take his own life rather than submit to tyranny. Dramatic and inspiring, the play highlights the centrality of honor, bravery, and manly valor in pursuit of liberty.[10]

Cato was one of Washington's favorite plays. He saw it performed several times in the theater and cited it numerous times in his private letters and public speeches. On May 11, 1778, Washington instructed his soldiers at Valley Forge to perform the play for the assembled troops. His men had just endured a terrible winter, and Washington believed the play would inspire and motivate them. He wanted the soldiers to see themselves as part of a long tradition of valorous fighters who were willing to risk their lives for liberty and the sake of the larger good.[11]

Washington also seems to have identified with the play's hero. Speaking as Caesar's troops approached the city, Cato proclaims:

Remember, O my friends, the laws, the rights,
The generous plan of power delivered down,
From age to age, by your renowned forefathers,
(so dearly bought, the price of so much blood.)
Oh let it never perish in your hands.[12]

As leader of the Continental Army, Washington found himself engaged in the fight to defend ageless freedoms from tyranny, even at "the price of so much blood." He was determined to never let liberty "perish" in his hands. This was his promise to the American people in general and to his troops in particular. Thus, despite Cato's suicide in the play, audiences in the era of the Revolution might take away an optimistic and inspirational message. The play also portrayed a version of classical republicanism that was especially appealing to Washington: an action-oriented form of civic virtue that was associated with men and masculinity. In fact, the Latin word *virtus* is based on the Latin root *vir*, meaning "man." From early in his career, then, Washington gravitated toward a particular form of classical republicanism that emphasized the performance of manly virtue through actions such as patriotism, bravery, and heroism.[13]

If the play revealed Cato to be a positive classical role model for

Washington, the tyrant Caesar offered a starkly negative referent. As a young man, Washington had admired Caesar and Alexander the Great for their tremendous military prowess, leadership abilities, and world conquest. In 1759, he had ordered busts of several great men, including Caesar, to display in his home at Mount Vernon. Yet with the coming of the American Revolution, Washington's attitude toward Caesar changed. Aware of his own lust for power, Washington knew he must subordinate his ambitions in order to ensure the triumph of the greater good. Otherwise, the very principles of the Revolution might be lost. *Cato* reflected Washington's new perception of Caesar. Despite his military prowess, Caesar destroyed the people's liberties for the sake of his ambition. Washington was determined to be the anti-Caesar.[14]

Washington's rejection of Caesar corresponded with his embrace of another classical republican figure, Lucius Quinctius Cincinnatus. Like Cato, Cincinnatus put the good of the country above his self-interest. According to Livy's *History of Rome* (a book that Washington owned), Cincinnatus was a Roman statesman and military leader who lived in the fifth century BCE. Legend had it that he was at work in his fields when word came that the republic was in danger. Dropping his plow, he took up his sword and sped to the field of battle, where he soon led his army to victory. After his success, he set aside his weapons and returned home to his farm. Later, when asked to serve as a temporary leader of the Roman Republic, he again abandoned his private station and served for a time in office. When the job was finished, he left his public role behind and retired to private life. As a myth and a symbol, Cincinnatus, according to historian Eran Shalev, appealed to the public more for his personal character than for his military abilities, "epitomiz [ing] the integrity that could sustain a republic."[15]

Washington's identification with Cincinnatus intensified after the American Revolution. In 1783, Henry Knox spearheaded the creation of the Society of the Cincinnati. Transatlantic in scope, the organization was intended to preserve and foster the bonds of friendship between French and American officers who had fought together during the American Revolution. Besides being a fraternal society, the group offered charity and other kinds of financial assistance to its members and their widows and children. From the beginning, however, the organization proved to be a lightning rod for controversy. Fearful of the society's quasi-military nature and aristocratic character, some Americans believed that its members would form a secret cabal that would undermine the civilian government or plot to overthrow the country's elected leaders. Even in republican Rome, it was said, the threat of a military coup had been a constant threat.[16]

The organization's membership requirements added fuel to the fire. In both the United States and France, participation was open only to officers, not to enlisted men. Membership was hereditary, passed down to the eldest son after the original member's death. These strictures offended many Americans who opposed all forms of hereditary privilege. Seeking to level the playing field, they desired to create an open society in which all people (or at least all white males) could advance without the constraints of inherited status limiting their opportunities. The Society of the Cincinnati struck at the very heart of those ideals. As Mercy Otis Warren, a harsh critic, put it in her *History of the American Revolution*, "[Many feared] that this self-created peerage of military origin, would throw an undue weight into the scale of the army; while sincere votaries to freedom, and the natural equality of man, apprehended that this institution would give a fatal wound to the liberties of America." Equality, not aristocracy, should be cultivated in the new nation.[17]

Although he was initially enthusiastic about the organization, Washington, who was elected its first president, soon had second thoughts. As popular opposition grew, he demanded that the group undertake certain reforms that would make it more compatible with republican principles. He asked that the society abolish the requirement of hereditary membership, eliminate any discussion of present-day politics, and prohibit foreign donations. At one point, he even threatened to resign if his demands were not met. Yet his entreaties had only a limited effect. While certain local groups agreed to the changes, many others resisted. Disenchanted, Washington began to distance himself from the organization. By the mid-1780s, he decided that he would no longer wear his membership badge, (which featured a shiny golden eagle) in public. Much like the ancient Cincinnatus, Washington had too much integrity to give his unqualified support to an organization whose purposes he had come to mistrust.[18]

Throughout his adult life, Washington chose to identify with Cincinnatus over Caesar. Just as important, many Americans viewed Washington as the modern-day embodiment of Cincinnatus. Like the original figure, Washington self-consciously styled himself, according to the historian Garry Wills, as "a virtuoso of exits." During the French and Indian War, for example, after displaying his leadership in many arduous battles, Washington resigned his commission. Much to the sorrow of his troops, Washington decided that he needed to attend to his private life, whereupon he set off to marry Martha Custis. The pattern recurred throughout his career. At the end of the American Revolution, in a dramatic public ceremony in Annapolis, Washington handed in his resignation as commander in chief to the members of the Confederation Congress. Although his immense stature might have made it possible for him to seize power as a dictator, he chose not to do so. Instead, he acknowledged the subordination of military officials to civilian authorities and returned to private life at Mount Vernon. Having heard rumors of Washington's intended resignation, King George of England purportedly exclaimed, "If he does that, he will be the greatest man in the world." Yet he did so, happily. As a Georgia commentator at the time noted, Washington returned "to his farm perfectly contented with being a plain citizen after enjoying the highest honor of the Confederacy." The pattern continued throughout his life. In 1796, after serving two terms as president, Washington notably declined to stand for a third term, setting a precedent that lasted for almost 150 years. As much as power appealed to Washington's vanity and ambition, he always understood that the ultimate goal of the Revolution was to create a self-governing republic, not a monarchy or dictatorship. As Washington saw it, he responded to the call of his country when necessary, but voluntarily relinquished power when the job was done. For this, his countrymen were eternally grateful.[19]

Before he resigned in 1783, Washington issued a circular letter to the states that expressed his vision for the country's future. Echoing classical republican themes, he warned Americans that they must constantly pursue the republican ideal, avoiding "the extreme of anarchy" on the one hand and the "extreme of Tyranny" on the other. This stance required a delicate balancing act. "Arbitrary power," he declaimed, "is most easily established on the ruins of Liberty abused to licentiousness."

Washington's fears were quickly realized. As early as the mid-1780s, Washington concluded that the county for which he had sacrificed so much was already in danger of failing. Internal conflicts and social unrest threatened the union from within while foreign influences and the possibility of invasion threatened from without. The public virtue that had sustained Americans throughout the American Revolution seemed to be on the wane. Citizens chose selfishness, greed, and personal ambition over commitment to the common good. States, too, refused to do their part, refusing to pay the taxes needed to sustain the central government. In 1786, during Shays' Rebellion, Washington lamented the decline in classical republicanism among the people. "We have probably had too good an opinion of human nature in forming our confederation," he told John Jay. "Experience has taught us, that men will not adopt & carry into execution, measures the best calculated for their own good without the intervention of a coercive power." A stronger form of government seemed necessary.[20]

This crisis of the confederation meant that Washington had to decide what kind of republican hero he would be. When he had resigned as commander in chief of the Continental Army in 1783, he believed that he had left public life for good. He had fulfilled his youthful ambitions for military glory and had no desire to seek power for its own sake. However, circumstances conspired to drive him back into the public life. In 1787, he was asked to attend a meeting in Philadelphia for the purpose of revising the Articles of Confederation. Although he initially refused, friends and colleagues pressured him to go, claiming that his presence would give the proceedings a weight and legitimacy that they would otherwise lack. He ultimately agreed to attend, and was immediately elected to be the presiding officer. During the convention, delegates assumed—without consulting Washington—that the former commander in chief would also agree to serve as the nation's highest elected official in any new government they proposed. In fact, they actually wrote the provisions for the presidency into the Constitution with Washington in mind. Washington's commitment to classical republican principles made him ideal for the job. Among the country's leaders, only he had the honor, integrity, moderation, and restraint that commanded the entire country's trust and respect.[21]

Washington nonetheless resisted the idea of serving as president. During the debate over the ratification of the Constitution, he feared that if he participated in the public debate he would be seen as campaigning for the presidency. As a result, he neither published essays nor openly campaigned for the cause. Yet Washington's support for the proposed government was widely known. He spoke privately to many people who visited Mount Vernon and wrote numerous letters to individuals throughout the country expressing his enthusiasm for the plan. To his great embarrassment and irritation, some of his personal letters were leaked to the press and printed. As his views became more widely known, his support boosted the momentum in favor of ratification.[22]

Once the Constitution was ratified, Washington agonized over whether he should accept the presidency. Having vowed to retire from public life, he feared that he would be criticized for violating his promise. In addition, he had spent many years away from Mount Vernon, sacrificing his own peace and prosperity for the sake of the country. He wished to spend his remaining years tending to his farm and family. His friends and colleagues, however, refused to take no for an answer. Appealing to his classical republican principles, they implored him to deny his own wishes for the sake of the common good. He alone, they said, could unite the country during this time of unsurpassed peril, a period of transition that would transform the country from a loose confederation of thirteen fractious states into a single, more highly centralized republic. When he finally agreed to accept the job, he was under no illusions about how difficult the task would be. As he told his good friend David Humphreys, "If my appointment & acceptance be inevitable, I fear I must bid adieu to happiness, for I see nothing, but clouds & darkness before me: and I call God to witness that day which shall carry me again into public life, will be a more distressing one than any I have ever yet known—."[23]

Washington's commitment to classical republicanism was deep and abiding. It was also a particularly masculine form of republicanism that depended on the performance of heroic actions and the practice of martial bravery. Leading by example, Washington supported liberty against tyranny, civic virtue over self-interestedness, and the collective good over personal ambition. He abhorred the wanton abuse of power and loathed those who used their public positions to advance their own interests. He hoped his example of self-sacrifice, honor, and discipline, in imitation of the ancients, would inspire his troops and, later, his fellow Americans to follow his example. After the American Revolution, when he sensed a rapid decline in civic virtue, he opted to support a movement to create a stronger central government. Under the Constitution, the government would be able to preserve the people's liberties even if the people were not virtuous. When events forced him out of retirement, he agonized over his public role, hoping to avoid even the appearance of impropriety or the pursuit of self-interest. Many Americans saw him as a republican hero, the embodiment of a modern-day Cincinnatus. This was an identity that he embraced.

In contrast to Washington, who led primarily by example, Mercy Otis Warren's gender forced her to express her classical republicanism in a different manner. Her republican ideals appeared in her writings, especially in her poems, plays, and monumental *History of the American Revolution*. Even though she lived in an age of patriarchy, Warren had many advantages. She received a much more extensive formal education than Washington had had. In fact, she received more education than most men or most women at the time. In her native New England, although many

Figure 11.2. *Mrs. James Warren (Mercy Otis)*, by John Singleton Copley, about 1763. Oil on canvas. Photograph © 2021 Museum of Fine Arts, Boston.

women achieved a basic level of literacy, it was thought that females had no need to read anything more advanced than Bibles or cookbooks. Warren was different. With her father's permission, a private tutor educated her alongside her brother, James Otis Jr. Under his guidance, she learned history, philosophy, and literature and composed poetry and essays. She read the great works of English literature, including Shakespeare, Milton, and Sir Walter Raleigh, and absorbed the classics of Greek and Roman history and literature. Unlike her brother, however, who would be attending college, Warren was not taught to read the ancient languages, Greek and Latin. Instead, she, like Washington, read the classics in translation.[24]

As a woman, Warren faced a more constrained set of choices for her future than her brother or George Washington. She could neither attend college nor head off to military glory. Women had only one basic path: to become wives and mothers. Thus, in 1754, when she was 26 years old, Mercy Otis wed James Warren, the son of a well-off farmer and merchant from nearby Plymouth. They were married for fifty-four event-filled years and had five sons whom Mercy nurtured and adored. In her young adulthood, in between carrying out her maternal responsibilities, she often turned to writing for both solace and as an emotional outlet. Although at that point she did not seek to publish her work, she shared her writings with a close-knit circle of family and friends. Erudite and eloquent, she was known to have a gift with the pen.[25]

As political conflict with Britain intensified during the 1770s, Warren drew upon her knowledge of the classics to make sense of the tumultuous political world around her. In private correspondence with her friend Abigail Adams, she signed herself "Marcia," a reference to the woman who had been the wife of the Republican orator Hortensius, a defender of the Roman Republic. Similarly, Adams called herself "Portia," after the daughter of Cato the Younger who was the wife of the republican martyr Brutus. By assuming the personae of Roman matrons, the friends reminded each other that women in the ancient past had made enormous sacrifices to preserve their freedom. Now it was their turn.[26]

Warren acknowledged that she struggled to be true to her classical republican ideals. Although she knew that war might be necessary to defend the people's liberties, she dreaded the prospect. A military conflict would bring widespread suffering and devastation to the country and would cost many lives. She feared that her husband or her sons might be required to leave home, take up arms, or risk their lives for the cause. "I tremble for the event of the present commotions," she told her friend Hannah Winthrop in 1774. "There must be a noble struggle to recover the expiring liberties of our injured country [and] we must re-purchase them at the expence of blood."[27] If such a conflict be inevitable, "we must tamely acquiesce, and embrace the hand that holds out the chain to us and our children." Steeling herself for whatever might come, she admitted, "While I feel greatly concerned for the welfare of my country, my soul is not so far Romanized but that the apprehensions of the wife and the mother are continually awake."

Committed though she was to the American cause, she did not feel herself to be as brave as the Roman matrons of long ago. Nonetheless, she aspired to follow their lead.[28]

The growing controversy with Britain unexpectedly opened up new opportunities for Warren to push against the typical gender boundaries that limited women's sphere of activity. Beginning with the Stamp Act of 1765, Britain enacted a series of laws that undermined the colonists' most fundamental rights and liberties, including the rights to self-government, trial by jury, a free press, and taxation by their own legislature. Her husband James Warren, her brother, James Otis Jr., and family friend John Adams were all early supporters of the colonial opposition in Massachusetts. During the 1760s, they often met at her house in Plymouth to discuss the latest set of British depredations against the colonists. Over time, these men became leaders of the resistance movement: speaking out in public, organizing protests and demonstrations, and writing political tracts against British oppression. By the early 1770s, as hostilities with Great Britain intensified, they realized that Mercy Warren might be of assistance. Her flair with the pen could be put in the service of the patriot cause.[29]

Warren entered the political arena reluctantly. In the eighteenth century, politics was regarded strictly as a male affair. A woman who dared to speak or write about politics often encountered public hostility and private derision. She might even be regarded as a dangerous deviant or taunted as a "manly woman" who transgressed into male territory. Fully aware of these prejudices, Warren told John Adams that she was wary of writing about politics, fearful of crossing "beyond the Line of my sex." Calming her fears, her husband told her, "God has given you great abilities. They are all now to be called into action for the good of Mankind, for the good of your friends, and for the promotion of Virtue and Patriotism." Mercy decided to act. Beginning in 1772, she turned out a series of poems and satirical plays that attacked British policies, satirized the Crown's representatives in Massachusetts, and encouraged popular participation in politics. Published in newspapers or as pamphlets, her literary works helped galvanize public opinion against Great Britain.[30]

Through her political writings, Warren began to flesh out her understanding of classical republicanism. In her early poems and plays, she made direct comparisons between the fall of the Roman Republic and the colonists' struggle. Britain was a degenerate Rome, a threat to the people's rights and liberties. To avoid the fate of Rome, the colonists needed to reaffirm the virtues of the ancients, including vigilance, simplicity, and a willingness to sacrifice for the common good. Abjuring luxury and frivolity, they would be called upon to exercise self-restraint and valor in their own daily lives.[31]

Warren also wrote works in a classical vein that were designed to appeal specifically to women. Drawing on ancient history, she pointed to figures such as Cornelia, Portia, and Arria as models for American women to emulate. She urged women to become politically active in ways appropriate for their sex. When the Continental Congress called for a boycott on British goods to protest the Coercive Acts, she called on American women to support the movement. In solidarity with other colonists, they should refuse to buy imported goods such as fancy cloth, china, ribbons, feathers, and tea. In recognition of the threat to their liberties, they should simplify their lives and test their wills. "By quitting the useless vanities of life," she proclaimed, women would make it possible "at once to end the great politic[al] strife." Such sacrifices would prepare Americans to defend their rights, through the force of arms, if necessary. "They'll fight for freedom," she announced in another poem, "And for virtue bleed." For Warren, women as well as men could practice the kind of civic virtue that would enable Americans to defend their liberty against British tyranny. "These are the sentiments," she declared, "which make us men."[32]

Warren's plays expressed her classical republicanism in even more explicit terms. The Adulateur (1772), The Defeat (1773), and The Group (1775) expose the full range of Britain's assaults on American rights and liberties. Written in bitingly satirical blank verse, the works portray Britain as a declining Roman republic that threatened to corrupt the colonists' virtue and undermine their liberty. The classical virtues of vigilance, virtuousness, and valor would deflect the assault.[33]

In The Adulateur, for example, the action occurs in a mythical kingdom called Servia, a not-so-subtle allusion to colonial Massachusetts. The main character, Rapatio, is a thinly veiled reference to Thomas Hutchinson, the colony's notorious lieutenant governor. Like his real-life counterpart, Rapatio and his "'fawning courtiers" pursue their selfish ambitions at the colonists' expense, willing to accede to Britain's demands even if they betray the colonists' freedom in the process. A band of brave citizens rise up to defend the kingdom. Although they bear names of ancient Roman heroes, they clearly represent local Massachusetts patriots: "Brutus" (James Otis Jr.), "Hortensius" (John Adams), and "Rusticus" (James Warren). Other characters also have Roman names, such as Junius and Portius.[34]

In The Adulateur, a rebellion against tyranny was imminent. Cassius (who in ancient times was a loyal defender of the ancient republic against Caesar's tyranny) warns his fellow citizens about the dangers they face in a land where an oppressive government "tread[s] down our choicest rights." He recalls how their ancestors had "grasp'd at freedom and they nobly won it . . . [at] the price of so much labor, cost and blood." Brutus, a stern republican, responds by acknowledging their debt to forebears, expressing a "hope" that "a manly sense of injur'd freedom" will "wake" his fellow citizens from their slumber, alerting them to the dangers to their liberty. In a stirring call to arms, he declares:

Come patriots, let the bright example fire you.
By all that's sacred! By our father's shades!

Moved to action, the citizens reply:

We'll pour our choicest blood. . . .
Carnage, blood and death, shall be familiar,
Though Servia weep her desolated realms.

Encouraged by their response, Brutus concludes, "While from our fate shall future ages know / Virtue and freedom are thy care below." The lesson for American colonists was clear, they needed to be prepared to defend their rights against British tyranny, using force if necessary.[35]

As in her other prerevolutionary plays, Warren's *The Adulateur* adapted the themes of classical republicanism to an American setting and disseminated these ideas to a wide audience. Instead of providing a dry recitation of political theory, her plays were meant to entertain the masses as they instructed them. Although Massachusetts prohibited public theater performances, the pieces were intended to be read aloud. Sitting in private parlors or in public taverns and coffeehouses, citizens of both sexes could learn about the colony's latest political controversies and do so in a way that touched their hearts as well as their minds. References to ancient Rome provided an additional layer of meaning, pitting "republican virtue against sinister, despotic, and Caesarian forces." According to Eran Shalev, Warren's work encouraged Americans to see their conflict with Britain in larger terms: not simply as the product of petty, local grievances but rather as a part of "a cosmic millennia-old struggle between the forces of tyranny and freedom that began centuries before on the Italian peninsula."[36]

Warren also deployed classical republican themes in the poems and plays she wrote during and immediately after the American Revolution. Her 1785 play *The Sack of Rome* provided a cautionary tale. Clearly influenced by Gibbon's *Decline and Fall of the Roman Empire*, the play depicts the collapse of the Roman empire as a consequence of corruption both inside and outside the polity. Barbarian hordes are gathered at the city's gates, waiting to invade, but Rome is already primed for collapse. The despotic emperor Valentinian has systematically stripped the people of their liberties, leaving them servile and complacent, unable to rise up to defend their freedom. Despite heroic action on the part of the emperor's wife, Edoxia, the invaders succeed in breaching the gates, overwhelming the city, and destroying the ruling family. The empire falls along with the people's liberty. Permeated with a sense of ominous foreboding, the play was meant to warn Americans that threats to their liberty were constant and ongoing. The end of the War for Independence did not free Americans from the need to practice classical republican virtues. "Empire decays," Edoxia warns, "when virtue's not the base / And doom'd to perish when the parts [are] corrupt."[37]

Warren was the colonists' secret weapon, a literary powerhouse who assisted them in doing battle against British oppression. Like most political writers of the time, Warren published her works anonymously or under a pseudonym. Yet many local inhabitants realized who the elusive author really was. Massachusetts political leaders, including John Adams and Samuel Adams, actively supported her authorship and celebrated her contributions to the patriot cause. Ironically, however, even as they used her talents for their own political purposes, the men in Mercy's life measured her gifts by a male standard. Mercy, according to her husband, possessed "a Masculine genius."[38]

At the same time, the experience of living through the American Revolution altered Mercy's understanding of herself as a woman. After the Revolution, Warren was bolder, less apologetic, and more willing to venture into the male realm of politics. Rejecting the assertion "that all political attentions lay out of the road of female life," she insisted that "a concern for the welfare of society ought equally to glow in every human breast." She expressed this newfound confidence in 1790, when she decided to publish a book of her selected poems and plays. One of her first decisions was to publish the volume using her own name, Mrs. Mercy Warren.[39]

As she prepared her manuscript, Warren boldly decided to ask the country's new president whether she might dedicate her forthcoming work to him. In a letter to Washington, she celebrated his honor and heroism during the Revolution. "The approbation of one who has united all hearts in the field of Conquest, in the Lap of peace, and at the head of the

Government of the United States must for a time give countenance to a Writer who[,] claiming the honour of private friendship[,] hopes for this indulgence." She then modestly added that "it must be a bold adventurer in the paths of Literature who dreams of fame in any degree commensurate with the duration of Laurels reaped by an Hero who led the armies of America to glory, victory and independence." Although Washington was often reluctant to draw unnecessary attention to himself, he agreed to her request. After publication, she sent him a copy. Immediately responding, he thanked her for the volume and noted, "From the reputation of the Author and from the parts I have read. . . . I am persuaded of the book's gracious and distinguished reception by the friends of virtue & science."[40]

Yet even at this high point in their relationship, Warren's esteem for Washington had begun to falter. One red flag first emerged during the debate over the ratification of the Constitution. Washington and Warren took opposing positions. While Washington had been reluctant to enter the public debate, Warren did not hesitate to make her opinion known. In 1788, she published a pamphlet titled *Observations on the New Constitution, and on the Federal and State Conventions* under the pseudonym "A Columbian Patriot." The pseudonym perfectly encapsulated Warren's position. "Columbia," with whom Warren identified, was a classical-era figure who was frequently used on maps and other documents at the time to depict the American continent. And in calling herself a "Patriot," Warren announced that opposition to the Constitution was consistent with the patriotic sentiments of the American Revolution. Not incidentally, Warren was the only woman known to have participated in the public debate over ratification.[41]

Drawing on classical republican principles, Warren's tract presented a withering assault on the proposed Constitution. She believed that the new form of government might accelerate the country's decline into decay and collapse. In addition to offering a general critique, Warren's pamphlet listed eighteen specific objections to the document. The country, she said, was too extensive and too heterogeneous to support a single republican government. The new government would be too powerful, too aristocratic, and too removed from the people to be effective. Authority would be consolidated in the hands of a small number of elites who were not necessarily to be trusted. Freedom would be put at risk. "Let the best informed historian produce an instance," she declared, "when bodies of men were intrusted with power, and the proper checks relinquished, if they were ever found destitute of ingenuity sufficient to furnish pretences to abuse it." Most of all, she objected to the fact that the document lacked a bill of rights. Without explicit protections for individual rights and liberties, the people's freedom was in jeopardy. "The virtues of a Cato," she warned, "could not save Rome. . . . Every age has its Bruti and its Decci, as well as its Caesars and Sejani." In later years, the addition of a Bill of Rights in 1792 somewhat placated Warren, but she never truly felt comfortable with the strong, centralized form of government that the Constitution had created or with the office of the presidency, which reminded Warren far too much of the detested British monarchy that the Americans had so recently overthrown.[42]

Although personally sympathetic to Washington, Warren's disillusionment with his administration deepened with each year of his presidency. Her objections surfaced in her magisterial three-volume study of the Revolution, *History of the Rise, Progress and Termination of the American Revolution, Interspersed with Biographical, Political and Moral Observations.* Published in 1805, the study was one of the earliest and most comprehensive accounts of the Revolution. It was also the first full-length account written by a woman. Initially Warren began composing the work during the Revolution itself, using letters, documents, eyewitness accounts, and official documents obtained through her famous friends. John Adams encouraged her efforts, insisting that she should produce an accurate rendering of events, and then "let Censure fall where it will." She did not, however, complete the work in a timely fashion. A series of personal tragedies that included the deaths of three of her five sons and her alienation from Federalist policies during the 1790s (by which time she had become a staunch Jeffersonian), distracted her. Over the years, she continued to add new sections to the work. By the time she was ready to publish her tome, the *History* covered events from before American independence through the presidencies of Washington and John Adams.[43]

Throughout the *History*, Warren deployed the language of classical republicanism to explain the Revolution. As she had done in her prerevolutionary poems and plays, she initially portrayed Britain as the source of evil, avarice, and corruption, all of which aimed to undermine the people's rights and liberties. Yet Warren had come to see that independence from Britain did not solve all of the country's problems. Like Washington, Warren chronicled a "relaxation in manners" after the Revolution that led to a decline in Americans' commitment to classical republican ideals. Instead of strengthening "the independent feelings of ancient republics, whose prime object was the welfare and happiness of their country," Americans of the postrevolutionary era engaged in an orgy of consumption and self-indulgence, pursuing wealth and power at the expense of the public good. Party spirit thrived, creating divisions and undermining a sense of common purpose. Reminding her readers about the fate of ancient Athens, Warren remarked, "never let it be said about [Americans that] 'the inconstancy of the people was the most striking characteristic of its history.'" The *History's* message was consistent and unrelenting: the republic's success depended on a reaffirmation of the principles of classical republicanism, principles that were currently under assault.[44]

In the later sections of the *History*, Warren tracked a similar decline in the country's greatest leader, George Washington. Her attitude toward Washington shifted radically over the course of her narrative. In the history's first volume, written in the 1770s and 1780s, she praised Washington's bravery and heroism and lavished accolades on him for his performance of masculine virtue. Drawing on classical allusions, she remarked that as commander in chief Washington had demonstrated "the caution of Fabius, the energy of Caesar, and the happy facility . . . of the illustrious Frederick [the Great]." She celebrated his stupendous victory at Yorktown, noting that "the manoeuvres of the American commander [were] so judicious, that the British themselves acknowledged, their own was fairly *outgeneralled.*" Describing the end of the Revolution, she lauded Washington's decision to voluntarily resign his commission. "After acting so conspicuous a part on the theatre of war, [Washington] retired from public scenes and public men, with a philosophic dignity honorary to himself and to human nature." Such self-abnegation was unprecedented. "Without arrogating any undue power to himself, which success and popularity offered, and which might have swayed many more designing and interested men, to have gratified their own ambition at the expense of the liberties of America, [Washington] finished his career of military glory, with decided magnanimity, unimpeached integrity, and the most judicious steps to promote the tranquillity of his country." With this act, he sealed his image as a classical republican hero. He had "raised his reputation," Warren said, "to the zenith of glory."[45]

If Warren's study had ended with the War of Independence and been published immediately thereafter, as she had originally intended, Washington would have emerged as a paragon of virtue, a living embodiment of classical republican ideals. As it was, however, the delay in publication led Warren to extend her story into the Confederation era and through the 1790s. A different Washington emerged in this part of the story.

Warren traced the beginning of Washington's decline to his involvement with the Society of the Cincinnati. She loathed the organization. Instead of imitating "the humble and disinterested virtues of the ancient Roman" after whom they were named, "members ostentatiously assum[ed] hereditary distinctions, and the insignia of nobility." She chastised Washington for supporting and encouraging the group. It was a "blot" on his character, she said, "a blameable deviation in him from the principles of the revolution, which he had defended by his sword, and appeared now ready to relinquish by his example." Unfortunately, according to Warren, Washington's "deviation" from republican virtue persisted. His decision to come out of retirement and assume the presidency was an enormous mistake. "Had [Washington] persevered in his resolution, never again to engage in the thorny path of public life, his repose might have been forever insured, in the delightful walks of rural occupation." Though Warren did not use the word *hypocritical* to describe Washington's decision, her meaning was unmistakable. Returning to public life "appeared to be in counteraction of his former determinations."[46]

In later sections of the *History*, Warren mercilessly critiqued Washington's two terms as president. Although she admitted that "no man in the union" except Washington "had it so much in his power to assimilate the parties, conciliate the affections, and obtain a general sanction to the new constitution," she did not believe that he had accomplished these goals. Soon after taking office, she argued, he fell under the spell of a "young officer of foreign extraction," Alexander Hamilton, who promoted a pro-British, crypto-monarchical financial scheme for funding the national debt. Under Hamilton's influence, Washington turned against France, the country's first and best ally, and began to favor Great Britain, the hated former mother country. Continuing his missteps, Washington engaged in a disastrous and ill-planned Indian war in the Ohio territory. (Not incidentally, Warren's favorite son, Winslow, died in that war, along with more than 600 other American troops.) She also believed Washington had betrayed American interests abroad. In 1795, a fierce partisan conflict erupted over the Jay treaty negotiated with Great Britain. Opponents claimed that the agreement was deeply flawed, that it sacrificed the country's diplomatic leverage for ridiculously few tangible commercial benefits or political gains. Washington put his prestige on the line to win the treaty's approval. Warren denounced the agreement as "degrading to the United States." She also claimed that Washington had bungled domestic affairs. In 1794, political unrest roiled the Pennsylvania frontier. In response, Washington,

with Hamilton at his side, gathered over 15,000 soldiers to quell the uprising. On arriving, they encountered absolutely no resistance and saw no
signs of upheaval. What the Federalists had labeled "the Whiskey Rebellion," Warren dismissed as a "trivial insurrection," She insisted, moreover,
that a more devious purpose lay behind such an excessive show of force.
The march, Warren said, was "not so much [to] promote the honor of the
national character, as to establish the basis of a standing army, and other
projects approaching to despotic sway." Once a vanquisher of "despotic
sway," Washington was now edging closer to becoming a despot himself, at
least as Warren saw it.[47]

Chronicling the end of Washington's presidency, Warren portrayed a
man who had kept the form but abandoned the substance of his classical republican principles. Near the end of his second term as president,
Washington circulated a document—the so-called farewell address—that
expressed his hopes and fears about the country's future. Deploying the
language of classical republicanism, Washington reaffirmed the nation's
traditional values and asserted the importance of sobriety, temperance,
and industry as the basis for republican government. He emphasized the
importance of sacrifice for the common good and the need for national
unity. He warned against the dangers of partisanship at home and the perils of foreign entanglements abroad. Warren would have none of it. As far
as she was concerned, Washington's actions as president had undermined
the nation's ability to act with the honor, virtue, and integrity required of
republican polities. Washington's parting remarks were too little, too late.
"This was indeed," Warren wrote, "after [the people] were split into factions; after an exotic taste had been introduced into America which had
a tendency to enhance their public [debts] and to accumulate their private debts; and after the poison of foreign influence had crept into their
councils, and created a passion to assimilate the politics and government
of the United States nearer to the model of European monarchies." While
Washington could still deploy the language of classical republicanism, his
presidency had stoked internal divisions, intensified partisanship, and promoted self-interest over the common good. In fact, Washington's own "deviation" from classical republican principles had contributed to the country's decline.[48]

Washington did not live long enough to read about himself in Warren's
History of the American Revolution; he died five years before it was published. But Washington's vice-president, John Adams, did read the work
and was outraged. Although he particularly objected to the way he himself

was portrayed, he claimed to see other problems as well. In a series of angry letters, he accused Warren of omitting certain key facts, misrepresenting others, and skewing the whole presentation to serve her personal agenda. Dismissing the entire project, he privately told Elbridge Gerry that "History is not the Province of the Ladies. . . . Little Passions and Prejudices, want of Information, false Information, want of Experience, erroneous Judgment, and Frequent Partiality are among [the *History*'s] faults." Had he lived, Washington may well have agreed with Adams. Although he was not nearly as irascible as his former vice-president, he too may have felt misunderstood, mischaracterized, and betrayed.[49]

As a writer, Warren had successfully breached a barrier that assumed women could not write about politics. Her gender, however, prevented her from ever taking a next step: engaging in electoral politics herself or serving in public office. Her exclusion from government and politics had profound consequences in shaping her views toward politics in general and Washington in particular.

Throughout her career, Warren analyzed and evaluated politics from two unique positions, as a woman and as a classical republican. These vantage points were both her strength and her weakness. On the one hand, she had a unique and unmistakable voice that rendered firm and incisive political judgments. These insights emerged from her distance from politics as a woman and her unwavering belief in the critical importance of classical republican ideals in the maintenance of liberty. When Americans veered from the path of classical republicanism, she called them out, insisting that they needed to remain true to their foundational principles. When the country's greatest leader faltered, she did not hesitate to take him to task. Warren even criticized herself when she felt that she had not fully lived up to her classical republican ideals. She was a consistent classical republican to the end.

While Warren's gender preserved her republican principles intact, it also made her less understanding about the pragmatic realities of governing a new nation. Unlike Washington, Warren was never told that the republic's very existence depended on her return to public life. Unlike Washington, Warren did not have to reconcile competing interests or accommodate warring factions in order to prevent the union from being torn apart. Unlike Washington, Warren did not have to face hostile foreign powers on the frontier whose main intent was to destroy the new nation's fragile unity. While Washington was willing to moderate his classical republicanism for the sake of political pragmatism, Warren would brook no compromise.

For her, compromise was capitulation, tantamount to a complete abandonment of the classical republican principles that she believed were at the heart of the American experiment.

In their own distinctive ways, however, both Warren and Washington continued throughout their careers to remind Americans of the centrality of classical republican principles in the ongoing struggle for freedom. Both insisted that ideas of liberty and civic virtue were part of a longstanding tradition that extended beyond Great Britain and reached back to the classical past of ancient Greece and Rome. Both figures also reminded Americans that the winning of the American Revolution did not mean an end to threats to American liberty. The need for republican virtue persisted. History taught that tyranny constantly threatened liberty and liberty could easily degenerate into slavery. Only constant virtue and vigilance could combat the forces of corruption and decline. Forging ahead meant navigating between the "licentiousness of liberty," on the one hand, and the "daring encroachments of arbitrary power," on the other. The challenge was great and required, as Warren said, "all the wisdom and firmness of the most sagacious heads, united with the most upright hearts" that American women and men could muster.[50] For both Washington and Warren, failure was not an option.

Notes

1. Mercy Otis Warren to George Washington, May 18, 1790, note 1, Founders Online, National Archives, https://founders.archives.gov/documents/Washington/05-05-02-0256, published in *The Papers of George Washington*, Presidential Series, vol. 5, *16 January 1790–30 June 1790*, ed. Dorothy Twohig, Mark A. Mastromarino, and Jack D. Warren (Charlottesville: University Press of Virginia, 1996), 402–4.

2. Carl J. Richard, *The Founders and the Classics* (Cambridge, MA: Harvard University Press, 1994); Caroline Winterer, *The Culture of Classicism: Ancient Greece and Rome in American Intellectual Life, 1790–1910* (Baltimore, MD: Johns Hopkins University Press, 2001); Eran Shalev, *Rome Reborn on Western Shores: Classical Imagination and the Creation of the American Republic* (Charlottesville: University of Virginia Press, 2009).

3. Ruth H. Bloch, "The Gendered Meanings of Virtue in Revolutionary America," *Signs* 13, no. 1 (1987): 37–58.

4. Jerome Huyler, *Locke in America: The Moral Philosophy of the Founding Era* (Lawrence: University Press of Kansas, 1994); T. H. Breen, "Subjecthood and Citizenship: The Context of James Otis's Radical Critique of John Locke," *New England Quarterly* 71, no. 3 (1998): 378–403; John Phillip Reid, *Constitutional History of the American Revolution*, abridged ed. (Madison: University of Wisconsin Press, 1994).

5. Bernard Bailyn, *The Ideological Origins of the American Revolution* (Cambridge,

MA: Harvard University Press, 1967); J. G. A. Pocock, *The Machiavellian Moment: Florentine Political Thought and the Atlantic Republican Tradition* (Princeton, NJ: Princeton University Press, 1975); Gordon S. Wood, *The Creation of the American Republic, 1776–1787* (New York: W. W. Norton & Co., 1969); Robert Shalhope, "Toward a Republican Synthesis: The Emergence of an Understanding of Republicanism in American Historiography," *William & Mary Quarterly* 29, no. 1 (1972): 49–80; Robert Shalhope, "Republicanism and Early American History, *William & Mary Quarterly* 39, no. 2 (1982): 334–56.

6. Wood, *The Creation of the American Republic*, 46–124; Pocock, *The Machiavellian Moment*, 506–52; Pauline Schloesser, *The Fair Sex: White Women and Racial Patriarchy in the Early American Republic* (New York: New York University Press, 2002), 83–113; Mary V. Thompson, *"The Only Unavoidable Subject of Regret": George Washington, Slavery, and the Enslaved Community at Mount Vernon* (Charlottesville: University of Virginia Press, 2019), 61–78. Significantly, neither Warren nor Washington interpreted "slavery" in the classical republican tradition as a reference to the condition of enslaved African Americans in their midst.

7. Douglas Southall Freeman, *Washington* (New York: Collier Books, 1968), 10–12; Paul K. Longmore, *The Invention of George Washington* (Berkeley: University of California Press, 1988), 1–16; Rosemarie Zagarri, *A Woman's Dilemma: Mercy Otis Warren and the American Revolution* (Wheeling, IL: Harlan Davidson, Inc., 1995), 1–21.

8. Freeman, *Washington*, 16–20; Rosemarie Zagarri, "Introduction," in *David Humphreys' "Life of General Washington," with George Washington's "Remarks,"* ed. Rosemarie Zagarri (Athens: University of Georgia Press, 1991), 6–7.

9. Kevin J. Hayes, *George Washington: A Life in Books* (New York: Oxford University Press, 2017) 14, 66–67, 96, 114–15, 176; Longmore, *The Invention of George Washington*, 213–26; *"History of the Decline and Fall of the Roman Empire*, vol. 1," "Label," George Washington's Mount Vernon, https://www.mountvernon.org/preservation/collections-holdings/browse-the-museum-collections/object/w-401a/.

10. Joseph Addison, *Cato: A Tragedy, and Selected Essays*, ed. Christine Dunn Henderson and Mark Yellin (Indianapolis: Liberty Fund, 2004).

11. Garry Wills, *Cincinnatus: George Washington & the Enlightenment* (Garden City, NY: Doubleday & Co., 1984), 133–37; Shalev, *Rome Reborn on Western Shores*, 99–101; Hayes, *Washington: A Life in Books*, 114–15, 208–9; Longmore, *The Invention of George Washington*, 173–74; Richard, *The Founders and the Classics*, 58–60.

12. Addison, *Cato*, act 3, scene V, lines 71–76.

13. Jason Shaffer, *Performing Patriotism: National Identity in Colonial and Revolutionary American Theater* (Philadelphia: University of Pennsylvania Press, 2007), 59–62; Bloch, "The Gendered Meanings of Virtue in Revolutionary America," 41–43.

14. Hayes, *Washington: A Life in Books*, 66–67; Wills, *Cincinnatus*, 133–37.

15. Shalev, *Rome Reborn on Western Shores*, 219–22, quote on 220; Hayes, *Washington: A Life in Books*, 129, 212.

16. Minor Myers Jr., *Liberty without Anarchy: A History of the Society of the Cincinnati* (Charlottesville: University of Virginia Press, 2004); Ellis, *His Excellency: George Washington* (New York: Alfred A. Knopf, 2004), 158–60.

17. Mercy Otis Warren, *History of the Rise, Progress and Termination of the American*

Revolution Interspersed with Biographical, Political and Moral Observations, ed. Lester H. Cohen (1805; repr., Indianapolis, IN: Liberty Fund, 1988), 2:616–20, quote on 619–20.

18. Wills, *Cincinnatus*, 140–48; Hayes, *Washington: A Life in Books*, 212–14. Richard, *The Founders and the Classics*, 55.

19. Wills, *Cincinnatus*, 1–6, quotes on 1, 13; Ellis, *His Excellency*, 39, 145–46, 230–40; Shalev, *Rome Reborn on Western Shores*, 219–22, quote on 221.

20. Wood, *The Creation of the American Republic*, 393–467; Nicolas P. Cole, "George Washington and Republican Government: The Political Thought of George Washington," in *A Companion to George Washington*, ed. Edward G. Lengel (Malden, MA: Wiley Blackwell, 2012), 430–46; George Washington to the States, June 8, 1783, Founders Online, National Archives, https://founders.archives.gov/?q=is%20most%20easily%20established%20on%20the%20ruins%20of%20Liberty%20abused%20to%20licentious ness&s=1111311111&sa=&r=4&sr=, early access document; George Washington to John Jay, August 15, 1786, Founders Online, National Archives, https://founders.archives.gov/documents/Washington/04-04-02-0199, published in *The Papers of George Washington*, Confederation Series, vol. 4, *2 April 1786–31 January 1787*, ed. W. W. Abbot (Charlottesville: University Press of Virginia, 1995), 212–13.

21. Glen A. Phelps, *George Washington and American Constitutionalism* (Lawrence: University Press of Kansas, 1993), 91–120; Whit Ridgway, "George Washington and the Constitution," in *A Companion to George Washington*, ed. Edward G. Lengel (Malden, MA: Wiley Blackwell, 2012), 413–29.

22. Phelps, *George Washington and American Constitutionalism*, 91–120; Ridgway, "George Washington and the Constitution," 413–29.

23. Zagarri, *David Humphreys' "Life of General Washington*," 51.

24. Joel Perlman and Dennis Shirley, "When Did New England Women Acquire Literacy?" *William & Mary Quarterly* 48, no. 1 (1991): 567–82; E. Jennifer Monaghan, "Literacy Instruction and Gender in Colonial New England," in *Reading in America: Literature and Social History*, ed. Cathy N. Davidson (Baltimore, MD: Johns Hopkins University Press, 1989), 53–80.

25. Zagarri, *A Woman's Dilemma*, 1–47.

26. Caroline Winterer, *The Mirror of Antiquity: American Women and the Classical Tradition, 1750–1900* (Ithaca, NY: Cornell University Press, 2007), 44–52; Zagarri, *A Woman's Dilemma*, 86–87.

27. Mercy Otis Warren to Hannah Winthrop, 1774, in *Mercy Otis Warren: Selected Letters*, ed. Jeffrey H. Richards and Sharon M. Harris (Athens: University of Georgia Press, 2009), 10.

28. Mercy Otis Warren to Hannah Winthrop, August 1774, "Correspondence of Mercy Otis Warren and Hannah Winthrop," Massachusetts Historical Society, https://www.masshist.org/database/viewer.php?item_id=3368&img_step=1&noalt=1&br=1&mode=dual#page1. See also Zagarri, *A Woman's Dilemma*, 84–87, 104–8.

29. Zagarri, *A Woman's Dilemma*, 48–77.

30. Zagarri, *A Woman's Dilemma*, 71–77; *Warren-Adams Letters, Being Chiefly a Correspondence among John Adams, Samuel Adams, and James Warren* (Boston: Massachu-

setts Historical Society, 1917): Mercy Warren to John Adams, September 4, 1775, 1:106–7, and James Warren to Mercy Otis Warren, April 6, 1775, 1:46.

31. Zagarri, *A Woman's Dilemma*, 48–77.

32. Mercy Otis Warren, *The Plays and Poems of Mercy Otis Warren*, ed. Benjamin Franklin V (Delmar, NY: Scholars' Facsimiles and Reprints, 1980): *The Adulateur*, 19; "A Political Reverie," 191; "To the Hon. J. Winthrop, Esq.," 208, 212.

33. Warren, *The Adulateur*, *The Defeat*, and *The Group*, in Warren, *Plays and Poems of Mercy Otis Warren*.

34. Warren, *The Adulateur*, 26.

35. Warren, *The Adulateur*, 5, 6, 7, 8.

36. Eran Shalev, "Mercy Otis Warren, the American Revolution, and the Classical Imagination," *Transatlantica: American Studies Journal* 2 (2015): 28, https://journals.openedition.org/transatlantica/7713?lang=en.

37. *The Sack of Rome*, in Warren, *Plays and Poems of Mercy Otis Warren*, 80; Kate Davies, *Catharine Macaulay & Mercy Otis Warren: The Revolutionary Atlantic and the Politics of Gender* (Oxford: Oxford University Press, 2005), 278–80; Zagarri, *A Woman's Dilemma*, 100, 135–36; Winterer, *Mirror of Antiquity*, 51–52.

38. Zagarri, *A Woman's Dilemma*, 69–77; James Warren to Mercy Warren, June 6, 1779, in *Warren-Adams Letters*, 2:101.

39. Zagarri, *A Woman's Dilemma*, 132–39; Warren, *History of the Rise, Progress and Termination of the American Revolution*, 1:xli–xlii.

40. Mercy Otis Warren to George Washington, May 18, 1790, note 1.

41. Zagarri, *A Woman's Dilemma*, 121–23; Mercy Otis Warren, *A Columbian Patriot*, in *Observations on the New Constitution, and the Federal and State Conventions* (Boston, 1788).

42. Warren, *Observations on the New Constitution*, 13, 18.

43. Warren, *History of the American Revolution*; John Adams to Mercy Warren, March 15, 1775, in *Warren-Adams Letters*, 1:42–44.

44. Warren, *History of the American Revolution*, 2:641, 644, 648, 686; Lester H. Cohen, "Explaining the Revolution: Ideology and Ethics in Mercy Otis Warren's Historical Theory," *William & Mary Quarterly* 37:2 (1980), 200–218; Shalev, "Mercy Otis Warren," 29–41.

45. Warren, *History of the American Revolution*, 1:129, 2:476, 636, 662, 673.

46. Warren, *History of the American Revolution*, 2:618, 619, 662, 663.

47. Warren, *History of the American Revolution*, 2:663, 668, 672.

48. "Washington's Farewell Address 1796," Avalon Project, Yale Law School, https://avalon.law.yale.edu/18th_century/washing.asp; Warren, *History of the American Revolution*, 2:673.

49. Zagarri, *A Woman's Dilemma*, 149–55; John Adams to Elbridge Gerry, April 17, 1813, in *Warren-Adams Letters*, 2:380.

50. Warren, *History of the American Revolution*, 2:625.

CONTRIBUTORS

Claire Rydell Arcenas is assistant professor of history at the University of Montana. She is currently writing a book about John Locke in America.

Lindsay M. Chervinsky is White House Historian at the White House Historical Association. She is the author of *The Cabinet: George Washington and the Creation of an American Institution.*

François Furstenberg is professor of history at the Johns Hopkins University. He is the author of *When the United States Spoke French: Five Refugees Who Shaped a Nation* and *In the Name of the Father: Washington's Legacy, Slavery, and the Making of a Nation.*

Jonathan Gienapp is assistant professor of history at Stanford University. He is the author of *The Second Creation: Fixing the American Constitution in the Founding Era.*

Daniel J. Hulsebosch is the Charles Seligson Professor of Law and associate professor of history at the New York University School of Law. He is the author of *Constituting Empire: New York and the Transformation of Constitutionalism in the Atlantic World, 1664–1830.*

Ben Lowe is chair and professor of history at Florida Atlantic University. He is author of *Commonwealth and the English Reformation: Protestantism and the Politics of Religious Change in the Gloucester Vale, 1483–1560* and *Imagining Peace: A History of Early English Pacifist Ideas.*

Max Skjönsberg is postdoctoral research associate in history at the University of Liverpool. He is the author of *The Persistence of Party: Ideas of Harmonious Discord in Eighteenth-Century Britain.*

Eric Slauter is deputy dean of humanities and associate professor of English at the University of Chicago. He is the author of *The State as a Work of Art: The Cultural Origins of the Constitution*.

Caroline Winterer is William Robertson Coe Professor in the Department of History at Stanford University. Her books include *American Enlightenments: Pursuing Happiness in the Age of Reason*, *The Mirror of Antiquity: American Women and the Classical Tradition, 1750–1900*, and *The Culture of Classicism: Ancient Greece and Rome in American Intellectual Life, 1780–1910*.

Blair Worden is emeritus fellow of St. Edmund Hall at the University of Oxford. His recent publications include *God's Instruments: Political Conduct in the England of Oliver Cromwell*, *The English Civil Wars 1640–1660*, and *Literature and Politics in Cromwellian England: John Milton, Andrew Marvell, Marchamont Nedham*.

Rosemarie Zagarri is university professor and professor of history at George Mason University. She is the author of *A Woman's Dilemma: Mercy Otis Warren and the American Revolution*, *Revolutionary Backlash: Women and Politics in the Early American Republic*, and *The Politics of Size: Representation in the United States, 1776–1850*.

INDEX

Page references in italics refer to illustrations.